Accounting Classics Series

Publication of this Classic was made possible by a grant from Arthur Andersen & Co.

Suggestions of titles to be included
in the Series are solicited and should
be addressed to the Editor.

Accounting, Evaluation and Economic Behavior

RAYMOND J. CHAMBERS
Professor of Accounting
The University of Sydney

Scholars Book Co.
4431 Mt. Vernon
Houston, Texas 77006

Standard Book Number: 0-914348-15-9
Library of Congress Card Catalog Number: 66-13944
Printed in the United States of America

The Development of the Theory of Continuously Contemporary Accounting

The method of accounting proposed in this book differs only in some, but important, respects from the traditional mode of accounting. It makes use of initial prices for all inputs. All buying and selling, stock and bond issues, loan repayments and lending, are accounted for in the same way as in traditional accounting. The system differs only in respect of the subsequent valuation of non-monetary assets and the calculation of income. It takes into the accounts the effects of changes in particular asset prices and changes in the general purchasing power of money. The statements that the system yields would give a continuous and complete historical account of the financial affairs of a firm, since at each balancing date the amounts of assets and equities are expressed in up-to-date terms at that date.

It is just 10 years since the manuscript of the book was completed. The early 1960s was a high time for debate about accounting principles, postulates, concepts and theorizing—debate mostly in the abstract. Coming so soon afterwards, the book seems to have been considered by many as just another example of the same abstract theorizing. But its origins were otherwise and its intent was otherwise.

Early indications. In 1943–45, while working in the Australian Prices Commission, I was engaged in the analysis of the financial statements and cost calculations of firms. Prices were controlled by reference both to costs and profits. Ideally the figures supplied by firms should have been derived by the same rules, so that comparisons of firms and industries could be readily made. I had previously worked in two large manufacturing companies and had some idea of the rather crude ways in which cost calculations and asset valuations were made. Now, confronted by the accounts of many firms in many industries, all using their own combinations of accounting rules, the impression of disorder was intensified. The task of administering a public policy, of making decisions which would be just and fair alike to companies and consumers of their products, in the face of idiosyncratic accounting was very much a hit-or-miss affair. I faced the same difficulties on the other side of the fence, as a consultant for a trade association petitioning the Prices Commission, for some years in the late 1940s. This work on comparative analysis was similar to the work of security analysts, though for different purposes. It left a firm impression that the securities market was also hampered by individual differences in the accounting methods of companies.

Management studies. For nine years, from 1945, I was engaged in teaching aspects of management. I taught in all sections of the program, introducing a course in financial management in 1946 and courses in economics, statistics, organization theory and administrative theory from 1949 onwards. All this prevented me from taking too narrow a view of my own specialism. And, when dealing with financial planning and control, I was forced, as in 1943–45, to consider accounting from the user's point of view—both internal and external users. The traditional accounting textbook literature hinted at the use of accounts in financial analysis and budgeting. But it asked no pointed questions about the adequacy of the figures for these purposes. That such questions should be asked, and answered, was strongly suggested by the coexistence of different accounting rules yielding figures of greatly varying quality. How discriminating managers, investors and creditors could use such figures was at least puzzling.

On the management process itself, there was little good work at the time. We regarded Barnard's *The Functions of the Executive* and Simon's *Administrative Behavior* as the best. But they said relatively little about the economic objectives and constraints of managers. A theory of management, it seemed to me, should be based on a few key ideas—economic, legal, psychological and social—from which management rules and procedures might be deduced. The ubiquity of potential conflict suggested that one of the prime tasks of management was to maintain a workable equilibrium between the interests of "participants" in organizations. The ways in which interests were interlocked suggested that business behavior was necessarily adaptive in all respects—technical, economic, financial, social and political. For the viability of firms, Cannon's *The Wisdom of the Body,* and for the processes of management, Wiener's *Cybernetics,* were strongly suggestive. Cybernetics, or steersmanship, was what managing is about. And that depended on continuously up-to-date information. The track led back to accounting.

Early work in accounting. In 1947 I had published *Financial Management,* an attempt to link the financing of business with internal financial administration, and to link both with accounting. A number of other slight articles followed. An occasion for greater concentration arose in 1949 when I was invited to give three lectures in Australian universities under the general title "Accounting and Financial Policy." The first of these [3]* argued that accounting rules and processes cannot properly be accepted unless their products aid directly the financial administration of business. Accounting is fact-finding; there could be no place in accounting for conservatism. The second lecture [5] dealt with the interest of external parties in financial information. It criticized traditional notions of the accounting entity, stewardship and the going concern. Contrary to widely expressed views, I held that the balance sheet and the income account were of equal importance to outsiders, and that the balance sheet should be equally serviceable for analysis of the past and consideration of the future.

The third lecture [11] dealt with the relation of accounting information to financial policy. The post-war inflation had for some years concerned businessmen. Under conventional accounting rules, reported profits were high. So were taxes and the prices of industrial goods. But the purchasing power of money was falling, and widespread fears were expressed about the erosion of capital and the maintenance of industrial capacity, with particular reference to the severity of taxes. Such complaints are an accepted part of the process of trying to influence governmental action and public opinion. But the defects of accounting gave businessmen cause of complaint, in my opinion. I had been collecting expressions of the views of company directors and examples of the devices they had adopted to cope with inflationary conditions— from Australia, the United Kingdom and the United States. I cited them in support of the conclusion that accounting information must be relevant to decision making and that "contemporary values, costs or prices are the relevant magnitudes."

These lectures and others of the same period [4,6,7] were the

*References at end of this essay, p. xxiii.

beginnings of much of what I have done since. In 1953 I had been appointed in the University of Sydney and was free to concentrate on accounting.

Accounting as Communication. The notion of financial statements as messages to many interdependent parties, treated at some length in 1952 [5] was further developed at book length in 1955 [10], based on a study of the reports of 150 Australian, U.K. and U.S.A. companies. Many of the observed deviations in practice from avowed principle could have little justification otherwise than as yielding better messages; but the conflict of practice with principle seemed to justify the description of the state of accounting in Orwell's terms, "doublethink" and "double-talk" [15]. Even when addressing colleagues and students—through articles and textbooks—accountants failed to convey clear messages [20,24]. It was not surprising therefore that whereas the laws relating to accounts expected the truth to be reported, practice did not yield true and significant statements [13,16,19]. Of course, faulty communication and difficulties in communication are almost universal. I benefited and took some comfort later from Ogden and Richards' *The Meaning of Meaning,* Cherry's *On Human Communication,* Morris' *Foundations of the Theory of Signs* and other works on language and linguistics. My interest was not merely academic. I was concerned with the concrete or practical setting of accounting. I wished to know the conditions of effective communication, the information which was pertinent to recipients of messages, and the number and variety of the causes of failure of financial statements to inform users [22,25,26].

Observation of practice and of its consequences. The textbooks and much of the periodical literature of the fifties gave the impression that most writers were too fond of prescribing to spend time or energy in observing what was going on about them. The literature was dogmatic. Many of the things being done in practice were either disregarded or dismissed as improper. Some of the literature purported to be theoretical. But is was short on analysis, loose in argument and ambivalent in conclusion. I proceeded with two kinds of work in parallel; observing accounting practices and their consequences, and trying to put into some coherent order the general ideas which were held to constitute the theory of accounting.

The history of science and scientific ideas and the biographies of scientists of every type have long been of interest to me. They demonstrate that, although new ideas spring from the imagination, they are prompted by observables and are subsequently confirmed or rejected by reference to observables. It is impossible to experiment with the accounting of on-going firms in such a way that one or another method of accounting can be shown to be superior. But it is possible by observation to reach some conclusions about what is inferior or unserviceable. A study of inventory valuation methods in 1949 suggested the hazards of inter-company comparisons [2]. A later study of a larger sample, with some international comparisons, indicated the persistence of variety, and the difficulties of serious analysts [22]. An examination of asset revaluations and stock dividends of Australian companies over a ten-year period cast considerable doubt on the validity of some widely held accounting ideas [15]. A study of the general reporting practices of 150 companies in three countries has been mentioned above [10]. The inadequacies of the information available to investors was suggested by an examination of the antecedents of some mergers and defences against takeovers [15,22], and by reference to litigation and reports of official investigations into company failures [13,26]. I also drew on the histories of companies and on journalistic accounts of the activities of promoters, brokers and financiers of the recent and more distant past. Many of the then current practices are recurrent, and many of the practices of the day were understandable only by reference to events of the past.

One of the alternatives to experimentation is the observation of international differences. In all modern industrial countires, accounting serves substantially the same functions. As the study of other technologies has no national boundaries—basic physics, chemistry, engineering, mathematics, medicine and so on, are international—there was no good reason why there should be "national varieties" of accounting. But there were such differences. They must, it seemed, have arisen from particular local events, or the particular local development of laws and institutions, and were not necessary parts of a generally serviceable style of accounting. Beside the doctrines, laws and practices of Australia, the United Kingdom and the United States—which I could study intensively—I made more modest examination of some of the theory, laws and practices of a number of European countries. I found analogous but not identical reactions to the stress of inflation, and taxation, both where their effects were mild and where they were severe. And I found similar but not identical looseness in practice notwithstanding that the guiding principles were generally acceptable in themselves.

Much of what these local and international inquiries yielded was unusual; the whole corpus of practices was not explicable in terms of any consistent set of rules. Much also was anomalous, not to be expected in the light of the doctrines or principles avowed among accountants. But, so many of the variants and anomalies could be considered as responses to the same defects in conventional practice, that some general remedy seemed to be necessary and possible.

Accounting concepts. Concurrently with these explorations and inquiries, I was concerned with what purported to be accounting theory. Textbooks and articles are the common source of teaching material. But I found them very difficult to use. So often important ideas were undefined. Categorical statements were made without apparent reason. Links between the propositions of what was called accounting theory and the prescribed rules of the textbooks were obscure or missing altogether. There had been critics before. Paton (1922) had suggested the flimsiness of some of the "postulates" of accounting as it then was. Canning (1929) and Gilman (1939) had pointed out in graphic passages the inadequacy and inconsistency of some of the key ideas of traditional doctrine and practice. Sweeney (1936) had given critical attention to elementary but pervasive flaws in the basic arithmetic of conventional accounting. But, to judge from the textbook literature, a generation of teachers and researchers had eliminated none of the defects.

In a number of the articles already referred to, I dealt critically with all the main general ideas—the accounting entity, the accounting period, the going concern, stewardship, conservatism, consistency, the constant money-value assumption. Two summary articles in the early sixties [20,24] were prompted by the fact that, although for about 15 years I had indicated faults in the conventional expositions of those ideas, they were still treated in the text books in the same inadequate way.

Criticism as such was not my object. I thought it should be possible to teach accounting in a logical and principled way, each idea being clear itself and clearly linked to other ideas, and the whole giving a coherent prescription for practice. I formulated new connotations for some of the customary terms—new notions of the accounting entity, stewardship, the going concern, consistency. At an early stage I thought I was merely improving them singly, giving them some specific connection with business affairs. But if many such separate changes are made, the whole set of ideas becomes a different whole. New ideas, new terms must be introduced and explained; old terms which were undefined must be defined; and what survived of the old and what was new must be consistent and coherent, if teaching was to be by reason rather than by rote. I thought the reasoning should be explicit, in the nature of the theorems of geometry, for instance; and I developed theorems on periodical accounting [12] and neutrality [21] after that style.

Theory Construction. By 1954 I believed it necessary, at least for myself, to set down the way in which a theory of accounting should be developed. In none of the important works on accounting was there a treatment of methodology. There was no pattern to follow except that of the well-developed sciences. And writers on accounting were following no pattern. My principal formal guides were Cohen and Nagel's *An Introduction to Logic and Scientific Method,* Larrabee's *Reliable Knowledge* and Robbins' *The Nature and Significance of Economic Science.* If the exercise was foolhardy and the result trifling, perhaps I would soon be told. I wrote "Blueprint for a Theory of Accounting" [8] in 1955 and two other pieces [9,12] shortly afterwards in response to some criticism. I returned to the matter in the early sixties [17,21] because no material change had occurred in the way in which accountants dealt with the construction and validation of their ideas.

The "Blueprint" paper was not simply a paper on method. It set out four substantive propositions which seemed to be necessary premises of an accounting theory. They were (i) organizations depend on the participation of many parties, (ii) organizations are managed rationally with the object of meeting the demands of those parties, (iii) financial statements facilitate rational management, (iv) accounting, the deriving of relevant financial information, is a service function. These ideas emerged from my work in the teaching of management. They seemed to some to have little to do with accounting. But they were the basis of all of my later work. They were developed and augmented in class notes and lectures over the next five years by ideas drawn from economics and other social sciences. Weber's *The Theory of Social and Economic Organization* and von Mises' *Human Action* were helpful—and interesting, since, among other things, they both had some interesting observations on monetary calculation and accounting.

In 1954, too, I developed a short accounting course for students of economics. Many students of economics would not undertake accounting courses. But they would encounter discussions of wealth, income, capital, profits, costs and benefits. They should know how these were calculated. The course dealt with accounting for households, small firms, large and complex firms, banks and other financial institutions, non-commercial institutions, governments, international dealings and national aggregate accounts. In each case the kinds of decision to be made were indicated. These decisions determined the kind of information which accounting should produce. The material developed for this purpose was published in book form in 1957 [14]. That it might be possible to construct a general theory of accounting emerged from this exercise. The relative scarcity of money and goods, the necessity of choosing, and the necessity of information for knowledgeable choice, are universals. Investors, managers, creditors, analysts, governmental regulators, all needed to know the past and present financial facts relating to domestic and commercial affairs. The differences between them were differences in detail, not differences in principle.

Visiting Britain, Europe and the United States in 1959 I hoped to encounter others who were working in a similar direction. The hope was disappointed. But I had for years talked and written enough about what accounting and accounting theory should be. It was time to attempt a comprehensive essay. The result was "Towards a General Theory of Accounting" [18 (1961)].

Towards a general theory. The paper dealt with accounting (1) under perfectly static conditions and (2) when changes occur in prices and in the general purchasing power of money between balance dates. The historical cost method was deemed to be satisfactory under perfectly static conditons. But if prices changed, non-monetary assets should be valued at balance date at replacement prices, in principle; if replacement prices were not available, they could be approximated by using an index of changes in the general level of prices. The amount of the net adjustment in asset values would be credited or charged to a residual equity adjustment account. It is not in the nature of income and its amount would not be available for dividends.

A substantial part of the paper was devoted to building up a set of foundations, assumptions or postulates. This seemed necessary if a firm case were to be made for any set of accounting principles or rules. The lack of it seemed to be the cause of the chaotic state of traditional accounting. Much of this part of the paper developed into the earlier chapters of *Accounting, Evaluation and Economic Behavior.* The "General Theory" paper also introduced the device of a highly simplified, transactionless, firm to work out the effects of changes in the level of prices. This simplification, an exercise in "comparative statics," was similar to those commonly used in scientific work and problem solving. I also rejected the old balance sheet notation, Assets = Liabilities + Proprietorship, for a notation which distinguished monetary and nonmonetary assets. The adoption of these two devices— since used by many others—was an important step in my work; they enabled me to experiment (on paper) with a wide variety of combinations of the variables. But the conclusions of the paper on a method of accounting I subsequently found to be far from satisfactory—in respects presently to be mentioned.

Measurement in accounting. For about 15 years I had been concerned with clarifying and arranging in an orderly fashion some of the principal accounting ideas. For some years in the late fifties I had been urged by Ernest Weinwurn (then of De Paul University) to give attention to measurement aspects of accounting; but it seemed wise first to be sure what accounting was about. I turned to the literature of measurement in 1962. Campbell's *Foundations of Science,* Churchman's *Prediction and Optimal Decision,* Hempel's *Fundamentals of Concept Formation in*

Empirical Science, Margenau's *The Nature of Physical Reality* and Stevens' paper "On the Theory of Scales of Measurement" were my main guides. This literature related principally to the physical sciences. But the parallels with financial matters were plentiful. The foot (or the meter), the pound (or the gram), the hour, the degree (of angle or temperature)—were neither more nor less "conventional" than the dollar or the pound. Measurements made with reference to these units were combined to yield derived measurements, such as density and velocity; there are analogous measurements in financial matters, such as rate of return and gearing. All measurements of change entailed observations of initial and terminal states; and if the conditions differed under which the two measurements were taken, adjustments were made of one or both measurements to measurements under a set of "standardized" conditions. On these last two points the practice of accounting differed from physical measurement; terminal states were obtained by calculation, not by observation; and no adjustment was made for the change in the conditions of measuring, changes in the significance of the unit and changes in the relativities of the measures (prices) of particular goods. Failure at these two points seemed to be the reason for the variety of "accounting results" possible for the same set of events, and for the irrelevance of the figures to action at the terminal date. What should be done?

(1) The only observable financial magnitude of an asset at a given date is its price, and market prices are one of the key elements of choice. Dated financial positions should therefore be derived from market prices at stated dates. (All invented values, such as L.I.F.O. valuations, calculated depreciation figures, amounts of "deferred" charges and credits, were not measures of anything). (2) But which market prices—buying or selling? As accounts describe the accumulation of money-measurable wealth, market resale prices should be used for nonmonetary assets, for they alone represent the money equivalents of assets at any date. (3) Finally, as the increment in wealth (owners' equity) in a specific period was to be reported as part of the wealth of a firm at the end of the period, the opening amount of net wealth had to be adjusted for the change in the general significance of the monetary unit. The firm is not better off by the amount of this adjustment, since its effect is merely to secure the maintenance of the general purchasing power of the opening net wealth. I sketched the conclusions in "Measurement in Accounting" (1963) a redraft of which was published in 1965 [27].

These conclusions differed materially from some ideas I had earlier supported. In 1952 [5] I had suggested "superimposing on existing accounting technique machinery for taking into account by an index number correction the effects of changes in the purchasing power of money." In 1961 [18] I had supported the use of replacement prices in principle, but the use of an index of changes in the general level of prices as an approximation where replacement prices were not available. By 1963 I had concluded that this was wrong on at least three counts. The use of replacement prices has been justified as a means of calculating income, the surplus after providing for the maintenance of capital, "capital" meaning, variously, physical goods or physical capacity or earning capacity. But these connotations are either irrelevant or vague to the point of uselessness. In the context of financial arrangements, capital means a stock of purchasing power, in whatever form it is held. In the second place, the use of a general index was no proper substitute for actual prices, since no firm bought or held just those assets upon which a price index was constructed. In the third place, replacement prices are strictly prices of goods that a firm does not hold and may never hold; this seems a far cry from a dated financial position based on the assets a company does hold.

The book. I commenced writing *Accounting, Evaluation and Economic Behavior* early in 1963 and finished the manuscript in December 1964. It was published in February 1966. It is one thing to see a desired end or conclusion; it is another to mount a coherent argument from elementary premises to that conclusion. I have seldom gone back over previous writing when setting out to write a new piece. I have tried to think about the matter before me as if it were new to me, without wondering whether my conclusions were consistent with what I had written before. Previous errors, in premise or argument, might thus be avoided. I have had no compunction about rejecting an idea I once espoused, if there were better argument or evidence for an alternative. In the late forties I had expounded traditional historical cost accounting in the absence of any systematic alternative. But by the early fifties it seemed to have so many flaws that some kind of price-level-adjusted historical cost accounting seemed preferable. By the early sixties the arguments for replacement price accounting seemed convincing, price-level-adjusted historical cost serving as an approximation—until it was discarded, as explained in the previous paragraph. I had in fact spent some years working over, successively, each of the main types of actual and proposed accounting system, on the way to the system proposed in this book.

It seemed that, in the general context of the book's title, some elements of every system must survive. Historical cost would be the first entry in any asset account; but it would not remain the basis of subsequent accounting for any asset. Replacement (or purchase) prices are necessary information whenever a replacement (or purchase) was under consideration; but only then. Present (discounted) values are necessary when choosing between alternative prospective projects or operations; but only then. It is necessary to use an index of the general level of prices whenever we wish to convert a quantity of money at one date into a quantity having equivalent purchasing power at another date; and that is necessary only for income calculation purposes. Market selling prices of non-monetary assets are necessary for the derivation of any dated statement of financial position. Each class of information thus had its proper place and function, if the whole course of ex ante analysis, accounting, and ex post judgment was considered.

To organize this account of the background of the book has not been easy. Over the whole period, many kinds of reading, searching and writing interacted—and interacted with educational and commercial experiences, for I was engaged as a consultant from time to time by firms large and small, in a variety of industries and by some governmental authorities. I was concerned persistently with the utility of financial information to those it served; technique had to be subordinate to this. The typical stance of others was just the reverse. Technique came first, the utility of the product being virtually an article of faith, and as such unanalyzed.

The work described was done over many years. This was important. It enabled me to observe many financial and commercial events—inflation and recession, increases and decreases in the severity of taxation, changes in company laws and regulations—and the influence they had on the accounting of many companies. It enabled me to study the successes and failures of many companies; reorganizations, reconstructions, mergers and litigation; and the connections between these things and accounting practices. And it gave me time to work intensively over the views of the proponents and critics of conventional and other forms of accounting, time to benefit from the stimulus of writers, in a wide variety of other related fields.

x x x x

The sequel. Towards the end of the book I wrote: "We have not come to the end of the road." This remark, intended to be merely descriptive, was unwittingly prophetic.

First, there were objections to the valuation of assets at resale prices. The idea had no respectable antecedent in the literature. MacNeal's *Truth in Accounting* came closest to it; but he proposed a mixed set of valuations, market prices, replacement prices and original prices. I had wished to avoid this mixture, on the ground that the sum of such prices could have no substantive meaning. But I also wished that my proposal should be workable, and palatable. Without abandoning resale prices in principle, I allowed that replacement prices and indexed calculations might be used as approximations or as "a matter of expedience, or of necessity, in the face of ignorance of the more pertinent price data" (*A.E.E.B.*, p 248). Reviewers and critics saw this as inconsistency. But is seemed to me to be no different from the ways in which practising engineers, physicians and agronomists cope with practical difficulties. The theories which lie at the core of their technologies are idealizations; they guide, they do not dictate willy-nilly. Nevertheless, in the interest of logical rectitude, I have abandoned the use of replacement prices and indexed calculations "as approximations," in favor of their use "in deriving approximations" to the resale prices of assets—but only where there is a resale market. No statement of financial position is made the better by putting some figure other than an approximate resale price beside the asset. Some critics have expressed dismay at the rapid rate at which an asset value may fall, particularly in the initial years of its use. But they confuse user-value with exchange value, whereas only the latter has reference to financial position. These objections have been dealt with at length from time to time [53,58,59,60].

Competing systems. One is apt to be over-enthusiastic and credulous about his own work. But if it is to survive, either as a personal commitment or against the competition of other ideas, it must stand comparison, to its advantage, with all other actual or possible schemes. The first test of survival is frontal assault by others. Direct critical appraisals have provided occasion for working out in greater detail one facet or another of the theory [35,39,75]. Examination in depth of other proposals has generally confirmed the comparative advantage of continuously contemporary accounting; price-level-adjusted historical cost [31,34,74], present (discounted) value [39,58,59], and replacement price [29,49,60], theories have been so examined. And, of course, the accumulation of evidence and argument to the disadvantage of traditional accounting has continued [32,46,48,56,71].

Piecemeal comparisons or judgments tend, however, to convey little impression of the comparative advantages of one proposal against the rest. I have argued that the goal of inquiry is the discovery of what is best [41]. Simultaneous analysis of the main types of system, using the same tests across the board, is a common way of ranking possibilities. Two exercises of this kind have been carried out [32,50]. It has been alleged that these have demonstrated the superiority of continuously contemporary accounting—only to *my* satisfaction [67]; but there has been no attempt to demonstrate in a similar way the superiority of any other system.

It is still widely contended, of course, that it is not possible to judge what is best, most serviceable, as a style of periodical reporting. This professed inability to choose seems curious, coming from a class of persons who claim that the products of accounting assist in choosing or decision-making. The case for uniformity (*A.E.E.B.*, pp. 152 ff), restated at length [36], and the case against diversity of accounting as between firms [22,30,36] have never been rebutted. Unable or unwilling to choose what is best, some have supported supplementary financial statements, or multicolumn accounting on a variety of bases in parallel. The case against these suggestions, based on overloading users with contradictory "information" [32,34,66,67,75] has not been answered.

The persistence of the debate about the merits of alternatives can be laid squarely on the failure to specify clearly the function of continuously generated information on the financial progress of a firm. That financial statements should be equally serviceable in making judgments about the past and decisions about the future was argued as far back as 1952 [5]. In the light of continuing confusion about the "objectives" or function of accounting, the argument has been restated [66,75,78].

An improved notation. It was perhaps inevitable that the symbolic demonstration of the early part of Chapter 10 of the book would be used by others, who would assign different significances to its elements and conclusions. As I have pointed out already, I had myself misconstrued the result when I had first developed it [18]. Later debate suggested that the notation was inadequate. Though the change in the purchasing power of the dollar ("the dimension of the monetary unit") was noted in the accompanying text, it could be overlooked in the absence of appropriate symbols in the equations [33]. Attempts to deal with changes over a number of years [40] also were complicated by the lack of differentiating symbols. A dollar sign with identifying subscripts was introduced. The following outline of the argument, first developed in 1969 for [54], is taken from [50f].

Let $\$_0$ and $\$_1$ represent dollars of the purchasing power of the dollar at the dates t_0 and t_1 respectively, the opening and closing dates of an accounting period.

Let $\$_0 M_0$ and $\$_1 M_1$ represent the amounts of the net monetary assets of the firm at the two dates. Net monetary assets are cash balances and accounts receivable, net of accounts payable. M_0 and M_1 are two different numbers in the usual case.

Let $\$_0 N_0$ and $\$_1 N_1$ represent the amounts of the non-monetary assets at the two dates. They are the sums of the resale prices of all assets other than monetary assets.

Let $\$_0 R_0$ and $\$_1 R_1$ be the amounts of the owners' or shareholders' equity in the net assets of the firm at the two dates.

Now, the balance sheets of the firm at the two dates may be shown thus:

$$\text{at } t_0, \quad \$_0 M_0 + \$_0 N_0 = \$_0 R_0$$
$$\text{at } t_1, \quad \$_1 M_1 + \$_1 N_1 = \$_1 R_1$$

The amounts on the left-hand sides of these equations are derived by actually checking the quantities of assets and liabilities, and using the resale prices of non-monetary assets. They are factual statements at the dates to which they relate. We want to find what the profit of the year is.

Let p be the proportionate change in the general level of prices during the year, expressed as a decimal fraction (such as .10, where the price index has risen by 10 per cent).

We may then write $\$_0 1 = \$_1 (1 + p)$.

At the end of the year the only dollars in circulation and the only dollars in which prices are then expressed are $\$_1$. We can write the balance sheet at t_0 in terms of $\$_1$ by using the relationship $\$_0 1 = \$_1 (1 + p)$, thus:

$$\text{at } t_0, \quad \$_1 M_0 (1 + p) + \$_1 N_0 (1 + p) = \$_1 R_0 (1 + p)$$

and as we have said above

$$\text{at } t_1, \quad \$_1 M_1 + \$_1 N_1 = \$_1 R_1$$

These two equations are all in terms of $\$_1$. We can therefore subtract the right-hand sides, at t_0 from t_1, to obtain the net profit, thus:

$$\begin{aligned}
\text{Net profit } &= \$_1 R_1 - \$_1 R_0 (1 + p) \\
&= \$_1 (R_1 - R_0 - R_0 p)
\end{aligned}$$

And we can represent the owners' equity at t_1 thus:

Opening balance	R_0 $\left.\right\rbrace$ i.e.,
Capital maintenance adjustment	$R_0 p$ $\;$ $\$_1 R_0 (1 + p)$
Profit of the year	$\$_1 (R_1 - R_0 - R_0 p)$
Total closing owners' equity	$\underline{\underline{\$_1 R_1}}$

Now what should happen if we accumulate entries of transactions in the books of account during a year, if we incorporate price variations in the accounts as they occur, and if changes in the purchasing power of the \$ are occurring slowly during the year? We cannot keep track of $s with a whole series of different purchasing powers. We keep the daily records only in terms of numbers of $s regardless of their purchasing power. We could keep the whole year's records in the same way as they are now kept, if we wished, provided only that the opening and closing balances were correct in terms both of quantities and the unit prices then prevailing. But in this case the account balances would not be continuously consistent with current prices during the year. We mention the possibility, however, simply to show that if we know the kinds of figures we need at the year's end, and if we obtain them from observations independently of the book balances (correcting the book balances where necessary), no major change need be made in day-to-day bookkeeping. The critical differences between this system and traditional accounting are the unit selling prices used at balance dates and the simple calculation of the capital maintenance adjustment.

Extensions. Group accounts were treated only briefly in the book. The notion of a group, for which consolidated accounts could be prepared, was accepted. But the whole drift of the book was away from invented fictions—and the "group" is a fiction. Legally it owes nothing, owns nothing, has no stockholders, cannot sue or be sued. Financially, therefore, group accounts are meaningless. The function which consolidated accounts serve can be served far better by aggregative information on subsidiaries in parallel with the financial statements of the parent company [38]. The same arguments stand against the so-called "equity method" of reporting by investor companies on associated companies [79].

Firms which have branches or subsidiaries in foreign countires are subject to several different influences which purely domestic firms escape. The specific prices of similar assets may differ between countries, the general levels of prices may vary at different rates, and the rates of exchange of domestic for foreign currencies may change from time to time. Continuously contemporary accounting is the only form of accounting by which account can readily be taken of these shifts, in such a way that the relative performances of sectors of multinational firms—as sectors in their own countries and as parts of the whole enterprise—may be assessed [65].

Other particular issues considered have included tax allocation [43] and the capitalization of mining exploration and development costs, and of research and development costs [72]. In financial terms, both have been argued to be examples of misleading fictions; that continuously contemporary accounting finds no place for them is thus a point in its favor.

Economics and the law. It seems to be widely believed that economists have long supported forms of accounting which entail the use of replacement prices or present (discounted) values for assets. In particular "Hicks' definition" of income (*Value and Capital,* Ch. XIV) has been cited frequently. One wonders, indeed, how many of those who cite Hicks have read the chapter; for Hicks gives six possible definitions, three *ex ante* and three *ex post.* As periodical accounting is an *ex post* form of calculation, it is of interest that the definition of income *ex post* which Hicks favors coincides with the notion of income under continuously contemporary accounting. Some arguments for replacement price accounting and present value accounting seem to be based on inadequate discrimination between what economists have asserted in different contexts [28,62]. It seems also that some critics of continuously contemporary accounting are unaware that its ideas of money, financial position, economic calculation and related matters are consistent with those of eminent economists and basic economics [37,45,67,71 (pp 120–1)]. Sterling's *Theory of the Measurement of Enterprise Income* (published in 1970, but written apparently some ten years before) remains the only work similar to my own. Its derivation from substantially the same sources—economics and measurement theory—is some assurance of the consistency between those sources and our common conclusions.

Some supporters of alternative systems of accounting seem to consider that the law requires accounts to be kept in ways inconsistent with commercial reality. The basic laws on company accounting, under both the U.S. and the English systems, make no such demand. Contemporary information which corresponds with the substantive results and positions of companies seems to be exactly what the laws prescribe [48,71,73].

Method. In empirical science, method is the handmaid of substance— and important on that account. Imagination is all that invention requires, but whether an invention is viable or serviceable is demonstrable only by recourse to the setting in which it is to serve. That accounting should be a signalling system of some sensitivity, the signals of which correspond with commercial and financial reality, seems incontestable. It is one of the key elements of continuously contemporary accounting. Yet the notion of correspondence continues to be ignored even by those who write of accounting as communication. Its neglect has prompted restatement in different settings on a number of occasions [47,52,55,56].

That a signal shall correspond with some empirical fact, event or circumstance requires that the fact, event or circumstance be carefully observed. That a theory or a system of accounting shall correspond with the setting in which it is to be serviceable requires, in turn, that

that setting shall be carefully observed. Imagination and invention are otherwise undisciplined. This has seemed to be characteristic of a great deal of accounting invention, on the part of professional associations and teachers alike. It has been counter-productive [63,68,70]. The statistical analysis of stock market price behavior, to which some have resorted, and lines of argument which purport to link accounting information with the outcomes of selected courses of action, are unproductive of solutions to the problem of choosing between alternative accounting rules; for financial information is only one of the determinants of choice and, therefore, an even more remote determinant of the pay-off of a decision [77,80].

The necessity of linking the observable with the theoretical I have tried repeatedly to stress [17,42,57,64,69,76]. It has been one of the two main desiderata of my work. Observation of real world events cannot prove what it is right or best or most useful to do; but it can be suggestive. On the other hand, observation may reveal flaws and faults in what is currently done, and their particular forms. The imagination may thus proceed from both directions to a conclusion which is free (or freer) of the observed faults and which serves best (or better) those who expect to be well-served. The earlier part of this essay indicated that the method had long been followed. But the published pieces were spread over about 15 years and the examples used were only a small fraction of what had come under my notice. That I had not shown, adequately and in one place, its influence on the development of the theory was perhaps an impediment to wider sympathy with the theory. An outline of the "evidence for" the theory [56] was later developed into Securities and Obscurities [71]. That book makes reference to some of the accounting practices of over 250 named companies American, English and Australian—and of many hundreds of others. Incidents in the lives of successful and failed companies; takeovers, litigated cases, official investigations; professional, official, judicial and scholarly dicta—from all these directions was drawn evidence of the inadequate and misleading nature of published financial information, or indications to the effect that financial calculations and statements based on market prices best serve managers, investors, creditors and others.

The second main desideratum of my work has been the pursuit of logical rigor. (I say "pursuit" advisedly. I have found myself in error too often to speak of the "attainment" of logical rigor). The most obvious example of this is the attempt to link all the main propositions (premises, assumptions, definitions and influences) in Accounting, Evaluation and Economic Behavior, so that they are a progressive and coherent whole. Their numbering and their identification as premises of conclusions in the "Argument" section of each chapter is indicative of their association. The pursuit of rigor has prompted close examination of the arguments and conclusions of others, in respect of both substance and method [e.g. 20,23,29,30,74,77]; examination of the conditions of valid aggregation, relation and comparison [e.g. 35,40,46,51]; examination of the quality of actual and potential accounting information as raw material for the inferences and judgments of users [46,51,55,56,61,75].

The interplay of the observable, the logical and the imaginative is, as it seems to me, after the "circular" pattern of empirical science generally. To paraphrase Cohen and Nagel (1934, p 396), evidence for principles has been obtained by appealing to empirical material, to what is alleged to be "fact"; empirical material has been selected, analyzed and interpreted on the basis of principles. In virtue of this give and take between facts and principles, many things that were dubitable have fallen under careful scrutiny at one time or another. Observations and events since writing the book have only served to strengthen my confidence in the validity of its main conclusions and in the superiority of the method of accounting that they entail.

x x x x

I am grateful indeed that the book will continue in circulation—to Professor Sterling for his initiative, and to the sponsors of the reprint for their generosity.

August 1974.   R. J. CHAMBERS

References

This is not a full bibliography. Items starred * are reproduced in [44], *Accounting, Finance and Management.*

1   *Financial Management,* Sydney, The Law Book Co., 1947, 442 pp. Revised 1953, 432 pp. Revised 1966, 433 pp.

2 * "The Spice of Accounting," *The Australian Accountant,* XIX (November 1949), 398–401.

3 * "The Relationship between Accounting and Financial Management," *The Australian Accountant,* XX (September 1950), 333–55.

4 * "Accounting and Inflation," *The Australian Accountant,* XXII (January 1952), 14–23.

5 * "Accounting and Business Finance," *The Australian Accountant,* XXII (July and August 1952), 213–30, 262–6.

6 * "Effects of Inflation on Financial Strategy," *The Australian Accountant,* XXII (September 1952), 304–11.

7 * "Financial Practice and Fiscal Policy," *The Australian Accountant,* XXII (November 1952), 391–8.

8 * "Blueprint for a Theory of Accounting," *Accounting Research,* 6 (January 1955), 17–25.

9 * "A Scientific Pattern for Accounting Theory," *The Australian Accountant,* 25 (October 1955), 428–34.

10   *The Function and Design of Company Annual Reports,* Sydney, The Law
        Book Co., 1955, 322 pp.

11 * "The Formal Basis of Business Decisions," *The Australian Accountant,* 26
        (April 1956), 155–74.

12 * "Detail for a Blueprint," *The Accounting Review,* XXXII (April 1957),
        206–15.

13 * "The Function of the Balance Sheet," *The Chartered Accountant in Australia,*
        XXVII (April 1957), 565–70.

14   *Accounting and Action,* Sydney, The Law Book Co., 1957, 248 pp. Revised
        1965, 287 pp.

15 * "The Implications of Asset Revaluations and Bonus Share Issues," *The
        Australian Accountant,* 27 (November 1957), 507–31.

16 * "Measurement and Misrepresentation," *Management Science,* 6 (January
        1960), 141–8.

17 * "The Conditions of Research in Accounting," *Journal of Accountancy,* 110
        (December 1960), 33–9.

18 * *Towards a General Theory of Accounting,* Australian Society of Accountants,
        1962, booklet, 48 pp.

19 * "Non-Comments on Non-Accounting," Meeting of the North Eastern
        Division of the American Accounting Association, Boston, October
        1962, mimeo., 11 pp.

20 * *The Resolution of Some Paradoxes in Accounting,* Faculty of Commerce and
        Business Administration, University of British Columbia, Occasional
        paper No. 2, 1963, booklet, 33 pp.

21 * "Why Bother with Postulates?", *Journal of Accounting Research,* 1 (Spring
        1963), 3–15.

22 * "Financial Information and the Securities Market," mimeographed 1963,
        44 pp. *Abacus,* 1 (September 1965), 3–30.

23 * "The Moonitz and Sprouse Studies on Postulates and Principles," *Proceed-
        ings* of Conference of the Australasian Association of University
        Teachers of Accounting, January 1964, 34–54.

24 * "Conventions, Doctrines and Common Sense," *The Accountants' Journal*
        (N.Z.) 43 (February 1964), 182–7.

25 * "The Role of Information Systems in Decision-Making," *Management
        Technology,* 4 (June 1964), 15–25.

26 * "Company Losses—Safeguarding the Investor," *Current Affairs Bulletin,*
        34 (October 1964), 162–76.

27 * "Measurement in Accounting," *Journal of Accounting Research,* 3 (Spring
        1965), 32–62.

28 * "The Complementarity of Accounting and Economics," *Calculator Annual,*
        Singapore Polytechnic Society of Commerce, 1964–65, 78–86.

29 * "Edwards and Bell on Business Income," *The Accounting Review,* XL
        (October 1965), 731–41.

30 * "A Matter of Principle," *The Accounting Review,* XLI (July 1966), 443–57.

31 * "A Study of a Price Level Study," *Abacus,* 2 (December 1966), 97–118.

32 * "The Foundations of Financial Accounting," *Berkeley Symposium on the
        Foundations of Financial Accounting,* University of California, Berkeley,

January 1967, 26–44.

33   "Price Variation Accounting—An Improved Representation," *Journal of Accounting Research,* 5 (Autumn 1967), 215–20.

34   "A Study of a Study of a Price Level Study," *Abacus,* 3 (August 1967), 62–73.

35 * "Continuously Contemporary Accounting Additivity and Action," *The Accounting Review,* XLII (October 1967), 751–7.

36 * "Uniformity in Accounting," *The New York Certified Public Accountant,* XXXVII (October 1967), 747–54.

37 * "Reality and Illusion in Accounting, Finance and Economics," *Michigan Business Review,* XX (January 1968), 1–9.

38 * "Consolidated Statements are not really Necessary," *The Australian Accountant,* 38 (February 1968), 89–92.

39 * "Measures and Values—A Reply to Professor Staubus," *The Accounting Review,* XLIII (April 1968), 239–47.

40 * "New Pathways in Accounting Thought and Action," *The Accountants' Journal* (N.Z.), 46 (July 1968), 434–41.

41 * "Accepted, Better or Best?—The Goal of Inquiry in Accounting," *The Singapore Accountant,* 3 (1968), 27–33.

42 * "The Linked Logics of Pedagogy and Practice," *Proceedings* of Conference of the Australasian Association of University Teachers of Accounting, August 1968.

43   "Tax Allocation and Financial Reporting," *Abacus,* 4 (December 1968), 99–123.

44   *Accounting, Finance and Management,* Arthur Andersen & Co., and Butterworth & Co (Australia), Sydney, 762 pp. Collection of 50 articles, 1948–68.

45   "Money and the Monetary Unit," *The Singapore Accountant,* 4 (1969), 79–85.

46   "What's Wrong with Financial Statements?", August 1969; *The Australian Accountant,* 40 (February 1970), 19–28.

47   "Financial Information Systems," *The Australian Accountant,* 39 (August 1969), 364–8.

48   "The Missing Link in Supervision of the Securities Market," *Abacus,* 5 (September 1969), 16–36.

49   "Accounting and the Public Interest," in *Abram Mey Tachtig Jaar, Liber Amicorum,* Bussum, Netherlands, 1970, 44–53.

50   Methods of Accounting—a series, *The Accountant,* 1970
       a. "The Elements of Price Variation Accounting," 26 February, 299–303
       b. "Historical Cost Accounting and its Variants," 5 March, 341–45
       c. "Price Level Adjusted Accounting," 19 March, 408–13
       d. "Replacement Price Accounting," 2 April, 483–86
       e. "Present Value Accounting," 16 April, 551–55
       f. "Continuously Contemporary Accounting," 30 April, 643–47.

51   "Accounting—From a Logical Point of View," *The Singapore Accountant,* 5 (1970), 13–18.

52   "Financial Reporting and Administrative Accounting: Harmony or Conflict?", *Canadian Chartered Accountant,* 97 (August 1970), 114–20.

53   "Second Thoughts on Continuously Contemporary Accounting," *Abacus,* 6 (September 1970), 39–55.

54   "Towards a Theory of Business Accounting," in Roy Sidebotham, *Introduction to the Theory and Context of Accounting,* Second ed., 1970, 132–44.

55   "The Commercial Foundations of Accounting Theory" in Williard E. Stone (ed.), *Foundations of Accounting Theory,* University of Florida Press, Gainesville, 1971, 59–77.

56   "Evidence for a Market Selling Price Accounting System," in Robert R. Sterling (ed.), *Asset Valuation and Income Determination,* Scholars Book Co., Lawrence, Kansas, 1971, 74–96.

57   "Investigacion contable y tecnologica" ("Accounting Research and Technology"), *Revista Temas de Negocios,* Monterrey Institute of Technology, Second series, 1 (Spring 1971), 49–56 (Spanish language).

58   "Asset Measurement and Valuation," *Cost and Management,* 45 (March–April 1971), 30–35.

59   "Measurement and Valuation Again," *Cost and Management,* 45 (July–August 1971), 12–17.

60   "Value to the Owner," *Abacus,* 7 (June 1971), 62–72.

61   "Kaikeiriron Kesei no Hoho" ("Accounting Theory Construction"), *Kigyo Kaikei (Accounting),* 23 (August 1971, 16–21; September 1971, 21–26) (Japanese language); *Proceedings.* Third International Conference on Accounting Education, Sydney, 1972. 138–51.

62   "Income and Capital: Fisher's Legacy" (Irving Fisher, *The Nature of Capital and Income,* 1906), *Journal of Accounting Research,* 9 (Spring 1971), 137–49.

63   "The Anguish of Accountants," *Proceedings* of Annual Conference of Australasian Association of University Teachers of Accounting, Christchurch, August 1971; *Journal of Accountancy,* 133 (March 1972), 68–74; *The Australian Accountant,* 42 (May 1972), 154–61.

64   "The Validation of an Accounting Theory," *Waseda Business and Economic Studies,* 7 (1971), 1–21.

65   "Accounting in an International Economic Community," *Journal U.E.C.* (Dusseldorf), January 1972, 52–69 (English, French and reduced version in German); *Rivista dei Dottori Commercialisti,* XXII (1971), 1771–87.

66   "Multiple Column Accounting—Cui Bono?", *The Chartered Accountant in Australia,* 42 (March 1972), 4–8.

67   "Quo Vado?", *The Chartered Accountant in Australia,* 43 (August 1972), 13–15.

68   "Accounting Theory, Practice and Policy," *The Singapore Accountant,* 7 (1972), 39–43.

69   "Variedades de Investigacion Contable" ("Varieties of Accounting Research"), *Revista Temas de Negocios,* Monterrey Institute of Technology, Second series, 2 (Spring 1972), 353–60 (Spanish language).

70   "Accounting Principles or Accounting Policies?", *Journal of Accountancy,*
        May 1973, 48–53.
71   *Securities and Obscurities,* Gower Press Australia, 243 pp., May 1973.
72   "Mining, Taxing and Accounting," Australian Society of Accountants,
        State Convention, Mt. Isa, June 1973, 10 pp. Unpublished.
73   "Accounting Principles and the Law," *Australian Business Law Review,*
        1 (June 1973), 112–29.
74   "General Purchasing Power Accounting—ED8 is not the Answer," *The
        Accountant,* 5 July 1973, 15–18.
75   "Misurazioni, Stime e Valutazioni nelle Decisioni Finanziarie" ("Measure-
        ment, Estimation and Valuation in Financial Decision Making"), *Revista
        dei Dottori Commercialisti,* XXIV (1973), 1001–22.
76   "Observation as a Method of Inquiry—the Background of *Securities and
        Obscurities,*" *Abacus,* 9 (December 1973), 156–75.
77   "Stock Market Prices and Accounting Research," *Abacus,* 10 (June 1974).
78   "The Objectives of Accounting," *The Singapore Accountant,* 9 (1974).
79   "The Use of the Equity Method in Accounting for Investments in
        Subsidiaries and Associated Companies," *The Australian Accountant,*
        44 (February 1974), 40–44; *The Chartered Accountant in Australia,*
        44 (February 1974), 18–22.
80   "The Possibility of a Normative Accounting Standard," *The Accounting
        Review* (forthcoming).

Table of Contents

Preface

Evaluating and acting are every man's business. Each has his preferences, makes his guesses, and lays out his strategies for solving his problems. Within the social framework, his preferences and modes of acting are moderated by those of others. Knowledge of the physical and social environment is the foundation upon which he builds his expectations and chooses his behavior. No man, however, is his own sole source of knowledge. He depends on others to supply special kinds of knowledge which he requires from time to time. The knowledge yielded by accounting and accountants is one such special kind of knowledge, a kind which is individually and socially significant in societies where interpersonal dealings of great variety are effected by the use of money. In such societies the language of monetary signs is a social language, the most commonly used of all technical languages and only less universal than the vernacular. The object of this book is to consider the conditions under which, by means of this language, complex messages are generated which provide the basis for informed economic action.

Economists, social psychologists, political scientists, and organization theorists, in their several ways, are concerned with such a language system. But in spite of its universality, relatively little attention has been paid to accounting as a critical means of discovery and communication. Businessmen, financiers, investors, and public officials employ its products, but often with little concern for their own implication in its processes. A synthesis has been attempted therefore which recognizes a common element in the interests of all these groups and a singular orientation for the processes of accounting and the endeavors of accountants. Whether one is concerned with business behavior, the securities market, organizational communication, or public accountability, an adequate system of financial measurement and communication is either assumed or required. We have sought to make explicit the features of such a system under the basic conditions of human uncertainty and interdependence.

Inevitably, evaluations of future courses of action turn on conjectures about the future. But the choices we make also turn on our beliefs about the environmental setting of our actions. These beliefs are likewise conjectures, hypotheses, or theories. Their conjectural character is often not recognized, for when the expected consequence of an action does not materialize the vagaries of circumstance are taken as the cause rather than the imperfection of our set of beliefs about the environment. Disappointment is assuaged by remedial action. In these circumstances our beliefs about the system in which we act may be flimsy, transient, and unstable; and our expectations of the future can be no more reliable than those beliefs. Into this complex, of beliefs about the system in which action is taken and beliefs about the future, is fed the facts of our present situation. But what we deem to be the facts of a situation are also determined by our beliefs about the system; what we deem to be facts are therefore also no more reliable, as premises of action, than our beliefs about the system.

Where the actions of men are recognized as members of a class of a recurrent series of actions having a particular common orientation, men have sought to obtain more reliable beliefs about the systems within which they act, and consequentially more reliable methods of getting at the facts which are uniquely pertinent to particular categories of action. This is the business of science. Its methods are exploratory, experimental, and self-critical. Its conclusions are general and are valued for their explanatory and predictive powers. On the ground that accounting is a process of discovery, of getting at the facts which are pertinent to economic categories of action, in this book we expound the view that it differs in no respect from other empirical sciences.

Accordingly, we have attempted to discipline ourselves by the same principles as have proved to be so fruitful in other fields. The view we take of the environment we believe to be based firmly on observable realities. Nevertheless, our conclusions, though stated positively are not held dogmatically. We do offer general solutions to present problems, but we do not deny the possibility that changes in the cultural environment in which any particular solution is offered may lead to its supersession. For example, although many of the ideas incorporated in this book have been long and widely accepted, the particular setting they have been given would have been impossible but for the developments in the theories of organization, communication, and regulatory systems which have occurred in the quite recent past. We venture to suggest at the end, perhaps with unbecoming immodesty, that the consequence may be a Copernican revolution in accounting.

The system presented is a lineal descendant of work begun some twenty years ago. The first published indication of direction was "Blueprint for a Theory of Accounting" (*Accounting Research*, 1955). A more comprehensive development was offered in *Towards a General Theory of Accounting* (1962). These and other exercises in the interval and, indeed, the present volume, are to be considered as stages in the growth of an idea (whether to maturity or senility the reader must decide). Some views once held with confidence have been modified, some rejected; others have been given new forms of expression which do not match forms previously used. These changes have been dictated by the search for a self-consistent vocabulary, and a self-consistent framework of ideas which is at the same time consistent with reality.

We would like to thank Professor William Cooper of the Carnegie Institute of Technology, Associate Professor Yuji Ijiri of Stanford University, and Professor Maurice Moonitz of the University of California, Berkeley, who read the manuscript and on whose recommendations and judgments our publishers have depended.

We also acknowledge the help of all who have moulded our views. To pay specific tribute however is neither fair nor possible. Those who have agreed with us have given encouragement; those who have disagreed have stimulated us. Friends in business, in government and in academia, at home and abroad, have given the benefit of their experience and knowledge. Students of diverse ages and maturities have forced us to clarify and restate our position. Authors many of whose names now elude us have shed light and shade, both necessary, on our problems. The work is a tribute to all but we lay it on the shoulders of none.

R. J. CHAMBERS

Introduction

THE STUDY OF ACCOUNTING

The study of accounting properly begins with a study of why it should be studied and how it may be studied.

Why study accounting? We are not concerned here with the reasons why people may study to be proficient in performing the tasks which go by the general name, accounting. We are concerned with the reasons why those tasks exist and why the specific operations which are or may be carried out are what they are, and why they should or should not be supplanted by others. Why should accounting be studied in this way? The reasons are no different from those which may be given for the study of any part of the environment or the behavior of men.

The general purpose of inquiry is to add to the existing stock of ideas and knowledge, so that men may more readily adapt themselves to or seek to mitigate the effects of their environment. There is voluminous evidence in the history of the physical, medical and social sciences to support this view. It is of no consequence that some men may be said to have pursued their inquiries without regard for the practical outcome. It is neither possible nor necessary to examine the motives of individual researchers. But it is observable that the conclusions of inquiries, of practical and theoretical kinds alike, have all been turned to the protection of men from the effects of the hostile elements of their environments.[1]

No other reason need be offered for the study of accounting. Is the stock of ideas or the state of knowledge of accounting inadequate? There is no dearth of specific prescriptions, descriptions, and distinctions (all of them implying or expressing "ideas") in the practice and literature of accounting. But the distinctive feature of a body of knowledge is its orderliness. There may be many ideas, too many ideas, conflicting ideas—a disorderly array. The distinctive feature of the pursuit of knowledge is the attempt to reduce the diversity of experience to an orderly array of statements *about* the content of experience.

What is generally understood by the study of accounting is the study of accounting methods and rules. That a knowledge of methods and rules is useful is obvious. But statements of methods and rules are not statements about accounting. They are part of accounting as it is practised or as it is recommended to be practised. As such, they give no understanding of the nature and function of accounting. We may acquire skills by learning the rules, but skills without understanding are potentially dangerous. Unless we understand the nature and function of accounting, we have no basis on which to decide whether any rule or rules will be consistent with its capacities and its function. In these circumstances the only warrant for the continued acceptance of a rule is the fact that it has been used before, that its use has become hallowed by time or by popular acceptance. The survival of methods and rules may predispose people to persist in applying them. Their survival, however, is no reason for believing them to be useful or relevant. The methods of medieval scholasticism were accepted for centuries; but they were only a hindrance to the advancement of knowledge. Their vestiges held back the development of natural science and medical practice, and even today, we are not entirely free of them. Again, the adoption of methods and rules as habits has frequently stood in the

---

1 "... a scientific law is a rule by which we guide our conduct and try to ensure that it shall lead to a known future." J. Bronowski, *The Common Sense of Science* (Penguin Books, 1960), p. 110. "In modern science, a theory is regarded as an instrument that serves towards some definite purpose. It has to be helpful in predicting future observable facts on the basis of facts that have been observed in the past and present. It should also be helpful in the construction of machines and devices that can save us time and labor." Phillip G. Frank, "The Variety of Reasons for the Acceptance of Scientific Theories", *The Validation of Scientific Theories*, Phillip G. Frank, ed. (New York: The Crowell-Collier Publishing Co., 1961), p. 22.

way of advances. In medical practice, septic conditions were allowed to persist long after the advantages of antisepsis were demonstrated. Anaesthesia and vaccination had to await the abatement of old habits of thinking, of prejudices and beliefs having mystical rather than reasoned bases, before they were adopted as general practices.

The reasons why some rules are preferable to others can only be discovered by thinking about the circumstances in which they are applied, the conditions under which they may be applied, and the consequences of their application.

Thinking about circumstances, conditions, and consequences entails something more than examining the rules of behavior themselves. It entails careful observation of the world in which the rules are, or are to be, used. It entails the search for similarities and differences, and discrimination between significant and insignificant similarities and differences. It is expected to yield generalizations of great power and usefulness, generalizations which collectively reflect the systematic interrelationships between objects or persons which constitute some phase of the world of experience.

The study of accounting may proceed from either of two bases.[2]

The Method of Criticism

We may, on the one hand, survey the methods of accounting and the rules which are actually applied. This survey may be as wide or as narrow as we choose. It may extend to all rules employed in a given time and place to a given type of circumstance; or it may extend to all rules employed at any time and in any place to every type of circumstance. But simply to list these rules will present a picture of enormous diversity. The diversity may be reduced to some semblance of order by classifying the rules so discovered according to the objects to which they are applied, according to the types of entity by which they are applied, or according to some temporal, regional, or social classification.

We may seek to understand these rules, however classified, by asking, "What are the assumptions on which each rule may be justified?" or, "What does each rule presuppose?" The purpose of laying bare these assumptions or presuppositions is to discover whether they are consistent with our understanding of the circumstances in which the rules are applied. If we have correctly stated the assumptions which underlie a rule (that is to say, if we have isolated the statements which entail the rule) and if we find these statements to be inconsistent with one another or with statements which we find on other grounds to be acceptable, we are entitled to conclude that

[2] See also R. J. Chambers, "Why Bother with Postulates?" *Journal of Accounting Research* (Spring 1963), Vol. I, No. 1, 3–15.

the rule is of doubtful value. If, on the other hand, the assumptions or presuppositions are found to be consistent with one another and with statements which are acceptable on other grounds, we are entitled to have some confidence in the usefulness of the rule.

At the risk of anticipating the main argument, we may take as an example the rule that the basis of accounting shall be the sums of money paid for the purchase of goods or services. Given that the function of accounting is to provide detailed and aggregate financial information as a guide to future action, this rule entails the assumptions (a) that sums of money paid for past purchases of goods and services are relevant, as a guide, to future actions, and (b) that sums of money paid at different past dates for the purchase of goods and services may be added to obtain aggregates which are relevant as a guide to future actions.

The first of these is inconsistent with our understanding of the nature of market prices and of human action. We know that past prices are not necessarily a guide (and, therefore, not generally a guide at all) to future prices of the same goods. We also know that the sum of money paid in the past is not necessarily the amount we could now get from the sale of the same goods to pursue any immediately future course of action. On these grounds, the rule cannot but fail to serve the stipulated function. The second assumption is equally questionable. We know that a sum of money at one point of time is not considered to be the same as the same sum of money at another point of time; the evidence lies in the practices of charging interest and of discounting. We also know that the purchasing power of a sum of money at one point of time differs from the purchasing power of the same sum of money at another point of time. We know, further, that it is pointless to add unlike things unless they are convertible, and have been converted, to "likeness." Now the stated function requires either or both of the present values of sums of money or the present purchasing powers of sums of money; whereas the rule precludes the conversion of sums of money paid out to "likeness." Hence the second assumption is inconsistent with the stipulated function. Being deficient in respect of both assumptions, the rule is of very doubtful utility.

This demonstration is to be taken as illustrative only. It is possible to set up alternative statements of the function of accounting; it may be possible to set up a statement of the function of accounting such that the assumptions underlying the stated rule are not inconsistent with the stated function. But whatever the function we stipulate, we may proceed, in the manner indicated, to examine all the rules of accounting, discovering which are consistent and which are inconsistent with our understanding of the function of accounting and the world about us.

This method of inquiry may be expected to provide a greater degree of confidence or distrust of the rules examined than will be provided by a simple authoritative statement or unsupported recommendation of those rules. But to follow it one must be predisposed to doubt. One must hold in mind the possibility that there is at least one other rule on any matter than the rule authoritatively promulgated. To say the least, this predisposition to doubt is not widely held. It is much easier to believe than to doubt. And those who are predisposed to believe, hold to their beliefs much more tenaciously than those who are predisposed to doubt. Any person who chooses to examine existing rules in the manner illustrated, is likely to meet the entrenched and cherished beliefs of his contemporaries head-on. He may believe his observations to be extensive and his conclusions to be valid, but the mere fact that they conflict with the prevailing state of opinion will interfere with their acceptance. Galileo tasted bitterly the consequences of his belief in the plurality of worlds and his advocacy of the Copernican heliocentric theory in opposition to the prevalent geocentric theory of the universe.

The method has other serious deficiencies. Any given inquirer can proceed to examine only those actual rules and practices which fall under his notice. This purely empirical basis will necessarily limit his conclusions to such rules and practices as are then known. Every new rule or practice which comes to his notice, or which is newly tried after such inquiry, will require fresh examination. It does not matter how carefully he analyzes the existing rules, his findings cannot be conclusive for all possible rules on a given matter. The existing rules are the product of a particular environment—a specific place, a specific time or time interval, a specific type of entity, a specific state of knowledge, a specific context of beliefs. Even if one were to know all the rules employed for all places, times, entities, and states of knowledge in the past, no judgment in respect of them could be considered conclusive for the future. For if the rules of one entity, in one place, at one time are the product of traditional, habitual, legal, or accidental factors, so also is the sum of all rules of all entities for all past intervals. Tomorrow may produce new rules. Rule making is a human propensity, an effort-saving propensity. But it is habit-forming. The economic environment is much more fluid than the rules men use to meet it. Because it is fluid and complex, it is easier to retain our conception of an earlier or idealized environment and our habitual rules than to discover rules pertinent in the contemporary environment. Our implicit theories of the environment outlive their usefulness.[3] Even when confronted with new problems, requiring new rules, we commonly attempt to resolve them as for an environment which no longer exists. The existent rules at any time and place are, therefore, partly reasoned and partly fortuitous.

In the interest of economy of inquiry and for the purpose of deriving conclusions which may be acceptable both in observable (past) situations

---

[3] See the treatment of the concept of conventional wisdom in J. K. Galbraith, *The Affluent Society* (London: Hamish Hamilton, 1958), Chap. 2.

and probable (future) situations, inquiry should be less restrictive than is permissible by the method of criticism. One should be free to imagine rules which have not been tried. This is the kind of inquiry which has yielded every invention of men from the first wheel to the latest space vehicle. Just as men invent artifacts, so they invent ideas and rules. Just as the invention of artifacts depends on knowledge of the qualities of their components in relation to the conditions in which they are expected to work, so the invention of rules depends on knowledge of their qualities in relation to the conditions in which they are expected to work.

The Method of Construction

This leads to the second method by which accounting may be studied. Its basis is not the overt features of existing rules, but the features of the environment in which possible rules are to apply. In its dependence on empirical facts, it is substantially the same as the former method. But, in the power and scope of its conclusions, it is vastly superior. Whereas the former method is an analysis of the observable rules to discover whether their presuppositions are verifiable or worthy of belief, this method proceeds from propositions which are more fundamental inasmuch as they relate to the conditions which a set of rule must satisfy.

This method begins with the observation that there is a class of objects, events, or operations, possessing some similarities and distributed in some way through the universe of experience. Each of these notions may be more or less vague at the outset; each comes to be more clearly defined as inquiry proceeds. We may, for example, observe a wide variety of monetary calculations; as we proceed to examine them closely, we find a subclass which we choose to call accounting or accounting operations. With these initially vague notions, we try to discover in what parts of the universe of experience they occur and under what conditions. We observe, to continue the example, that forms of accounting are found in an extensive range of situations, but not in others. The observation demands explanation. It gives rise to the conjecture that accounting is part of a particular type of system. What type of system may be discovered by recourse to the universe of experience. There are countless statements which may be given as partial descriptions of the universe of experience; from these we select those sufficient to define the type of system in which accounting appears to have a place.

We conjecture further that, as accounting is a human contrivance, it has a discoverable function within the specified system. We wish to discover what function, in relation to the behavior of men, accounting performs. Again, the answer will be sought in the universe of experience. We select, from the statements which specify the system in which accounting is found, a number of statements which when arranged systematically will represent the manner in which accounting is systematically linked with human behavior within the specified system. This limited set of statements will specify, or will enable us to specify, the kind of accounting which will perform the functions required of it in the specified system within the universe of experience. It may transpire that the general system in which accounting occurs requires varieties of accounting; but variants will require to be justified by the character of the general system and its components.

The set of statements which define accounting or a kind of accounting, it will be noted, is to be a systematic set. It may not include contradictory or inconsistent statements. It should include all statements necessary to define the processes which serve the required function, and no other statements. This set of statements, all derived from the universe of experience, will constitute a theoretical construction. It is the result of a series of conjectures or hypotheses. But it is no mere figment of the imagination, for all the statements it includes will be, ideally statements which are individually capable of being tested by other persons than the propounder of the theory.

But conjecture is not good enough support for a process which has wide application. The theory must be tested. It must be demonstrated to be workable and to serve the functions for which it was designed. One such test is by comparison of its entailed processes with existing processes, which were shown in the previous section to be the expression of a theory, even though it is not an explicit theory. If the two sets of processes differ, then, clearly, the theory derived in the above manner is inadequate to explain existing processes. The theory may require to be reconstructed, augmented, or abandoned. But the explanation of existing processes may well be a less important matter in practical affairs than the derivation of the most satisfactory method of performing specified functions. An alternative form of testing may be used.

The first stage in this testing process is deduction of all the possible consequences of the theory. The objective of deduction is to develop fully the meaning of the theory and to provide logical consequences which would be matters of experience if the theory represented the most satisfactory method of performing the specified functions. The extent to which the logical consequences of the theory conform with the required functions will then determine whether it is to be accepted as a basis for future beliefs and actions, or whether it is to be modified or rejected.

This procedure is in a large measure identifiable with the way in which thinking men ordinarily resolve their problems.[4] All prototype model-

4 "The method of scientific investigation is nothing but the expression of the necessary working of the human mind." Thomas H. Huxley, *Darwiniana* (London: Macmillan and Co., 1894), p. 363. "Everybody uses the scientific method about a great many things, and only ceases to use it when he does not know how to apply it." Charles S. Peirce, *Values in a Universe of Chance*, Philip P. Wiener, ed. (New York: Doubleday & Company, Inc., 1958), p. 108.

building is an expression of it. Practical men in professional affairs adopt it. If, for example, the rate of net income on funds employed in a business has fallen to a level of 2 per cent from some higher rate, this will create a state of uneasiness or dissatisfaction with the beliefs held immediately prior to the discovery of this fact. The manager or consultant or expert assistant will direct inquiry to the many elements which contribute to the discovered rate. He will analyze the external factors and the accounting process which yielded the rate; he will spell them out in as much detail as time permits. From his analysis, he will form some conjecture which he supposes will explain the fall in the rate. He will test his conjecture by working out its consequences in the light of the experience through which the business has just passed. If it turns out that the 2 per cent yield is a logical consequence of his conjecture, he will come to believe that some policy other than that which is the content of his conjecture must be followed if a greater yield than 2 per cent is to be expected in future. There is nothing particularly unusual about this procedure and we presume to believe that an inquiry carried out in this manner will not be challenged on the ground that its method of procedure is not understandable.

DOUBT AS TO THE GENERALITY
OF RULES AND PRACTICES

Now if, as we have said, inquiry stems from observation of things which are unusual or things which are not understandable, the reader is entitled to ask, "What are these unusual things in the present case?" There are many. A few will be given as illustration but without any suggestion of their priority in importance.

(a)   It is observable that in many countries there are business accounting rules which permit a wide range of individual choice to the compilers of accounts. Diverse rules yield results of diverse qualities. Yet these results are used, or are supposed to be used, by investors and prospective investors in choosing security investments. It is difficult, even impossible, to understand how results of diverse qualities can be used in making such choices. This difficulty gives rise to doubts about the efficacy of a system which permits diverse optional rules.

(b)   It is observable that the accounting rules permitted in different countries are different, although the underlying economic institutions appear to be substantially the same. These differences give rise to doubts about the generality of the specific rules which differ, and give rise to some uneasiness even about the rules which are common.

(c)   It is observable that there have been extensive controversies among accountants themselves on the aims and principles of their art, and that these controversies have been revived from time to time as economic conditions have changed. The persistence of such disputes raises doubts as to whether the generalizations or the rules of accounting are adequate to meet the varied conditions through which business enterprises pass.

(d)   It is observable that whereas economists and accountants are both concerned with features of the operations of business firms, their systems of ideas about business behavior are often, in significant respects, quite different. This gives rise to doubts as to whether the conceptions of economists or of accountants or of both are adequate, on the one hand, to describe and, on the other hand, to inform business behavior.

(e)   It is observable that the accounting methods of unincorporated business firms differ in some respects from those of corporate businesses, and both differ in some respects from the accounting methods of nonbusiness organizations. These differences give rise to doubt regarding the general applicability of statements made about accounting which contain no provisos as to the conditions under which those statements purport to be valid or appropriate.

The list could be extended. Any one or two of such occasions for doubt could provide sufficient stimulus to undertake a closer examination of the character of accounting, its principles, and its methods. Taken together their effect is even more provoking. It is such facts as those given above which have prompted the attempt to formulate a theory of accounting along lines similar to theories which have been formulated in other disciplines.

Doubts and uneasinesses may arise, and do arise, even in relation to rules and practices which are not in obvious conflict. Most writers who have attempted to set down the presuppositions and procedures of accounting have given only modest lists of principles, but have countenanced an enormous variety of rules. As to the principles, it might be expected that they would be adequate to explain all the rules. But, almost universally, the statements of principles have taken much for granted. The double-entry principle provides a pertinent example. This principle is deemed to be fundamental by most expositors and practitioners; but familiarity seems to have bred contempt, for, generally, it is taken as self-evident and is put forward as a dogmatic rule. Likewise the process of aggregating and relating sums of money is taken as a self-evident operation yielding a significant and readily interpretable result; but, as we shall show, this presumption is not well founded. The significances of the process of periodical summation and the derived summaries are taken for granted, whereas an adequate theory would demonstrate these significances.

The theory to be presented attempts to cover these commonplace things as well as the more difficult and controversial matters. It does not jettison the widely accepted principles and procedures which are consistent with its assumptions; there will be much that is familiar. But most of the familiar things are treated or derived in an unfamiliar, though we believe a valid and realistic way. And, familiar or not, the propositions to be derived will be admitted only because their premises are believed to be acceptable or demonstrable and because they comprise a consistent system. It is in this direction that any claim to novelty lies; and it is the attempt to work within these constraints which justifies the whole exercise.

"FIELDS" OF STUDY

It is conventional to divide knowledge or the pursuit of it into fields. Physical science is distinguished from social science; the sciences are distinguished from the humane arts; within any such field, as knowledge is advanced, new subdivisions are made which rapidly assume the appearance of fields in their own right. We distinguish history and archaeology, nuclear physics and astro-physics, organic chemistry and inorganic chemistry.

But in the pursuit of knowledge, there are no limited fields.[5] There is simply the totality of things observed and experienced. This does not mean that the conventional divisions are futile, or that to subdivide knowledge into fields is muddleheaded. The subdivision of all knowledge is a form of classification and as such it serves a useful purpose. No classification, however, is an end in itself. The possibility must be kept open that the statements which represent the totality of things observed and experienced may

5 " . . . . although the division of scientific knowledge into 'subjects' is a convenience . . . the 'subjects' themselves do not strictly speaking exist." Magnus Pyke, *The Boundaries of Science* (Penguin Books, Inc., 1963), p. 14. Pyke deals extensively with the way in which physics, chemistry and biological sciences have become interlocked. " . . . we may look at all sciences as dove-tailed . . . as parts of one science . . . because we cannot know anticipatively when it may be useful, and when not, to take into account all the statements together in analyzing certain correlations in a certain field." Otto Neurath, "Foundations of the Social Sciences," *International Encyclopedia of Unified Science* (Chicago: University of Chicago Press, 1944), p. 9.

be classified in many ways. There is widespread opinion in favor of inter-disciplinary studies. But all that this can mean is that students of a given conventional field should extend their studies by taking account of some of the objects of observation and experience which they have, by tradition or convention, disregarded. As knowledge is advanced, it becomes increasingly difficult to draw sharp lines of demarcation between mathematics and logic, chemistry and physics, biology and psychology, and many other pairs of separately designated fields. There will be disputes over border lines and limitations only if we suppose that some parts of all knowledge may be isolated from other parts. Conventional classification into fields is no more than a considerable convenience. It contributes to specialization in inquiry and thus to greater specific knowledge. But no such classification may be supposed to represent inherent or intrinsic differences. Distinctive designations are given to "fields" so that inquiry in each of them will be understood to have a specific orientation, not so that all propositions which constitute human knowledge may be unequivocally and exhaustively classified into fixed "subjects."[6]

It has seemed to be necessary to state this view clearly for two reasons.

Accounting Related to Other Fields

We shall, in what follows, find it necessary to use statements which may seem to belong to the fields of law, political science, psychology, economics, languages, and so on. This necessity arises from the concern of accounting with some aspects of the behavior of men, individually or as members of groups; of men as active, or passive, or unwitting collaborators with others. We will not therefore want to be constrained by such observations as, "that is not accounting, it is economics," or by such assertions as, "accountants are not concerned with psychology."

There can be no understanding of any aspect of human behavior, or of human behavior in any specific context, if we are forbidden to consider other aspects or contexts of human behavior. This does not entail substantial or special knowledge of subjects other than accounting; it is proper to rely on the substantiated statements of other experts in their fields. But it does require a readiness to look about in other fields for such propositions or conclusions as may be necessary to add to one's understanding of the functions, effects, and determinants of accounting methods and results.

It is indeed both useful and salutary to link the propositions dealing with one field of knowledge to those of other fields. The attempt to apply a proposition from one field to another provides a new occasion for testing

6 Neurath, "Foundations of the Social Sciences," p. 8.

it. If it satisfies the test, its dimension will have been extended; it will have become a more powerful generalization than it was before. If it fails the test, doubts may be raised about its propriety in its original field. Either way such an attempt recognizes the interdependence of human knowledge in all its fields. The development of any field is enhanced by the richness of its explicit associations with cognate fields. Again, the mere fact that a given proposition is widely accepted in another field or other fields provides a severe test of the propositions which are linked with it if it is introduced into the accounting field. The procedure has its dangers, one of which is the possibility that the adoption of any proposition may be considered to entail adoption of the whole theory of which it is a part. But the risk may be run provided the propriety of applying any specific proposition from another field is demonstrated independently in its new context. At the worst, if they are not probative, propositions from other fields may be strongly suggestive.[7]

Natural and Social Science

The second reason for suggesting the artificiality of fields lies in the frequency with which assertions are made to the effect that the methods and conclusions of the natural sciences and the social sciences are different in kind. There are differences; but there are more significant similarities. The assertions in question are made on several different grounds, but the general intention is to question the legitimacy of the use in studies relating to human behavior of methods found to be useful in the natural sciences.[8]

One ground for this belief is that the objects of natural science are inanimate, incapable of reacting to observations; it is therefore a relatively easy matter for different observers studying those objects independently to reach similar conclusions, or for a single observer to reach similar conclusions on successive trials. By contrast, it is alleged, the objects of social science are people who are capable of reacting to observation; it is therefore impossible to expect that different observers may reach similar conclusions, or that the same observer at different times may reach similar conclusions.

The observations of physical scientists do affect the objects of study, with the possible exception of objects studied at a distance. Analysis of a

7 On the role of analogy see Pierre Duhem, *The Aim and Structure of Physical Theory,* trans. Phillip P. Wiener (Princeton: Princeton University Press, 1954), pp. 95–97; Ernest Nagel, *The Structure of Science* (London: Routledge & Kegan Paul, Ltd., 1961), pp. 107–17.

8 For an extended discussion see Nagel, *The Structure of Science,* Chap. 13.

sample of a natural substance may be made by chemical and physical tests which inevitably change *its* character and make it unfit for any other observer to apply the same analysis for the purpose of confirming or rejecting the conclusions of the first. Other observers must use other samples; but scientists take care to see that samples used in independent tests are similar. It is possible in exactly the same way to observe persons, their responses and actions. Only if the behavior of persons is modified by the experience of being observed may they be considered unfit for subsequent observation for the same purpose.

The inferences drawn by physical scientists from studies of natural objects depend on their willingness to accept samples as indicative of all instances of those objects. If sufficiently fine and comprehensive examination were made of any number of instances, there would undoubtedly be grounds for differentiating them all.[9] Only if one is prepared to disregard some differences in instances is it possible to make general statements. The same is true of persons. All are different. But this does not mean that we may not make at least some general statements about them and their behavior.

Further the substance of natural sciences subsists in statements about objects, not in objects themselves. Men may make statements about animate objects just as easily as they may make statements about inanimate objects, and just as easily about human objects as about nonhuman objects. It is true that statements may not be made about human objects which are reliable for all times, for example, under different historical or social circumstances, or for all times in the life of any person. But no one need be misled if the conditions under which a general statement is said to hold are made explicit. The general statement need be no less useful on that account. In any case the statements which comprise the substance of the natural sciences are statements held only in the context of the existing state of knowledge. The geocentric view of the universe satisfied the canons of pre-Copernican science. It is only necessary to recognize the limitations of natural science in order to perceive that there is no difference between natural and social science on this score.

Another ground for the belief in question is said to be the fact that statements in the social sciences are much less reliable than statements in the natural sciences; that is to say, they are much less useful as predictors. Now if all this means is that the social sciences have not achieved the level of sophistication, the depth and breadth of knowledge, attributed to the

9 A physical law stated in mathematical form "is always relative; not because it is true for one physicist and false for another, but because the approximation it involves suffices for the use the first physicist wishes to make of it and does not suffice for the use the second wishes to make of it." Duhem, *The Aim and Structure of Physical Theory,* p. 172.

natural sciences, it says nothing about material differences between the two since there was a time when the natural sciences were far less sophisticated. If, on the other hand, the statement is concerned with reliability as a basis for prediction then, again, it rests on a misapprehension. The statements of the natural sciences are of the form: if x, then y. For example, the statement that light travels in straight lines is ordinarily accepted. But the scientific form of the statement is: if the medium through which light passes is of uniform density, light travels in straight lines. The statement enables us to predict the path of light only if the medium is of uniform density, or if we further develop our knowledge to the point where we can say what happens to light if the medium is not of uniform density. The statements of the social sciences are no different. The statement that men are creatures of habit is ordinarily accepted. But the scientific form of the statement would be something like this: if no experience induces men to change their beliefs, they will act according to habit.

The social sciences have fallen under the criticism that their general statements are always qualified by *ceteris paribus* or other forms of limitation. But that other things shall be considered to remain equal is just as much a condition of any brief statement in the natural sciences. We understand that water boils at 212° Fahrenheit; but the statement only holds for unadulterated water under ordinary atmospheric pressure at sea level. In the natural sciences as well as in the social sciences, all generalizations have the same restricted or provisional form. But it is precisely because there are conditions under which a scientific generalization holds true and those conditions are made explicit, that it is such a powerful device for the solution of problems.[10]

ACCOUNTING AS A FIELD OF STUDY

We have said above that accounting is concerned with the behavior of men as individuals and as members of groups. It is of considerable importance to be clear on the extent of this concern. Economics is concerned with the distribution of scarce goods among men; politics with the distribution of power among men; sociology with the behavior of men as members of groups; and so on. It seems as though almost every aspect of behavior is covered by some specialism, and that there is no aspect left with which accounting may be concerned.

Strictly, accounting is not concerned with any type of behavior as such. It is concerned with some of the antecedents of economic behavior. There

10 "A law of physics possesses a certainty much less immediate and much more difficult to estimate than a law of common sense, but it surpasses the latter by the minute and detailed precision of its predictions." Duhem, *The Aim and Structure of Physical Theory*, p. 178.

are no maxims in accounting to the effect that careless behavior on the part of acting men is bad; or that efficiency is worth pursuing; or that profit-making is reprehensible; or that the love of money is the root of all evil. Each of these statements is a judgment which expresses an evaluation of the whole or some part of human behavior. Similarly, accounting is not concerned with any specific method of distributing scarce goods among men, any specific economic system having any specific set of ends. Rather it is concerned with statements of the kind: *if* an actor wished to live within his means, this or that procedure will inform him whether he did in fact do so; or, *if* an actor wishes to dispose of the whole or part of his means, this or that procedure will inform him of the extent of his means; or *if* an actor wants to draw on his past experience to guide his future actions, this or that procedure will provide information which is pertinent because it represents his past experience. In short, accounting is concerned with the provision of some of the facts on the basis of which one may act knowledgeably given one's ends or purposes.

The theory we present here is a theory of accounting in the present context of institutions. This context has its antecedents and causal conditions, and in those conditions, the art and practice of accounting, as it is now, was developed. But the very belief in causal conditions of the present institutional context implies that what may have been a valid practice in the past is no longer necessarily a valid practice. There is no sense in which a theory may be developed which will be applicable to all environmental contexts through time. In particular the kind of accounting in an economy with no system of credit may well differ from that appropriate to an economy with a well-developed credit system. The kind of accounting appropriate to business entities where there is no corporate business and no widespread investment in corporate business may well differ from the kind of accounting appropriate in a highly industrialized economy where such devices and institutions exist. It is highly probable that the kind of accounting appropriate in a society which pays scant respect to the accumulation of wealth and economic power would have few similarities with the kind of accounting appropriate in a society which permits and esteems thrift and accumulation.

Our purpose is not to seek principles of universal validity in all institutional settings. It is to examine the features of the institutional setting of the present insofar as they provide the conditions for an accounting which is appropriate to that setting. There may emerge some principles which we may deem to be valid in a much wider setting and over a range of different historical contexts. But this is incidental. We shall not be able to free ourselves of the habitual elements of practice if we cling to the notion of historical necessity, to the belief that "what is" is necessarily best because it is a product of deliberate choice in the past.

We repeat that what follows is not claimed to be entirely novel nor to be opposed to or different from points of view expressed, conclusions reached and practices implied, in the extant literature of accounting. It will become apparent that there are divergences in many respects; but in the course of extending our knowledge we are continually humbled by the discovery that others have anticipated what seemed to be a novel or original idea. Though we seem to develop views on the basis of independent thought and observation, it is impossible to say how great is our debt for stimulation, suggestion, and provocation, to others both directly and through the prevailing knowledge and modes of thought of the time.

The development of the argument depends a great deal on the methods employed in, and on the assumptions and conclusions of, other fields of inquiry. It has seemed desirable to give some indication of the views of workers in other fields in their own words. The basic objective is to suggest strongly that the disciplined methods and the findings of other arts and sciences are applicable to the study of accounting and that the result is of a piece with the whole fabric of scientific knowledge. We make no pretense of an intimate knowledge of the literature of other fields, though we have taken care to ensure that the views of the particular authors cited are supported by the work of others. References to the literature of other fields are, therefore, eclectic and, to some extent, simplifications. We have endeavored to secure that the conclusions of others have not been misconstrued, though we must admit that the possibility exists.

References to the literature of accounting are given on a less liberal scale. As is the case in any field where there is an extensive literature, the terms used by different writers and the ideas they are intended to convey can scarcely be described satisfactorily by brief references, particularly where there are significantly different shades of meaning and where they may have been used to derive conclusions different from our own. We have chosen, therefore, to limit references to those which seem important for the system of ideas here developed. In many respects the terms used have connotations different from those of the same terms used elsewhere in the literature; definitions are, therefore, given, rather than argument about the merits of extant conflicting definitions.

At the end of each chapter a detailed summary is given. The object of the summary is to identify the propositions which are significant for the development of the argument. There are three classes of propositions: assumptions or postulates necessary for the subsequent argument; definitions, which are also postulates; and inferences based directly or indirectly on the postulates. The postulates and definitions are set in *italics*. All propositions are numbered, so that any subsequent inference may be connected with the postulates or conclusions on which it depends. This dependence is indicated by the proposition reference numbers shown in brackets after each. The object of this is to indicate that the system of ideas is a logical system; though the method of establishing conclusions is not always given, even in the text of each chapter, the dependence of each inference on the identified premises should be apparent. The basic premises or postulates themselves, it is hoped, will command general assent.

It is not claimed that the manner of reaching our conclusions is the most economical of assumptions or the most direct, or even that all the assumptions have been laid bare. The tasks of reduction and amplification lie in the future. However, they can only begin when a broad range of pertinent questions have been raised and their interrelationships have been probed. This is our present task.

Individual Thought and Action

1 We have observed that accounting is concerned with some of the antecedents of the behavior of persons. In the course of the inquiry it will be necessary to consider persons as actors directly affecting and being affected by their environments, and persons as "assistants to actors" by virtue of their interposition between actors and their environments. We need, therefore, to have some understanding of the capacities and limitations of sentient persons generally.

PERSONS AS HOMEOSTATIC SYSTEMS

The human individual is a complex organism, having the power to sense its own condition and the impact on it of its environment, the power to change its own condition and to modify the impact of its environment, and the power to discriminate, to learn, and to reason, and consciously to direct its sensory and motor apparatus in the light of discrimination, learning, and reasoning. But all these powers are limited even in the case of persons who are unimpaired by unusual physiological or psychological deficiencies.

There are no immediate indicative sensations of some bodily conditions. Men do not readily become aware of the "conditions" arising from dietary deficiencies or organic deterioration. Similarly, the impact of some elements of the environment is not directly or immediately sensed; some impacts may be camouflaged by or confused with others, as is the case with all sugar-coated pills, actual and figurative. But, to deficiencies, deterioration, and environmental influences the organism does react. It seeks to relieve itself of strains which past actions and experiences or present influences induce. We may, therefore, suppose that there is a preferred condition of no strain, a strain being any state of bodily or mental uneasiness.

Some changes in bodily condition occur involuntarily. We are not ordinarily conscious of, nor have we any power to direct, the ordinary bodily processes of the digestive, circulatory, and respiratory systems; but they may all react involuntarily to the environment at any time. Some involuntary changes, such as the dilation and contraction of the iris of the eye, in a more obvious fashion, enable the body to tolerate the impact of external conditions. All such involuntary systems are adaptive mechanisms. Within certain limits they serve to procure a more satisfactory relationship between the organism and its environment than would exist in their absence. But they are not independent systems; rather they are subsystems of the larger system which is the organism.

Bodily conditions and external stimuli may be or become such that involuntary adjustment is insufficient to procure a satisfactory relationship with the environment. A state of uneasiness or strain is experienced, the reaction to which is a desire for its relief.[1] Beyond the limits of involuntary adjustment, the human organism reacts through the mediation of thinking; action is taken more or less deliberately. Just as involuntary adjustments have the effect, within limits, of removing or alleviating the impact of the environment, so also we suppose deliberate action to be directed towards the removal or alleviation of the impact of the environment. The organism as a whole, therefore, is regarded as a homeostatic system, constantly adapting itself to its environment so that its capacity for functioning, its

---

[1] "... desires arise only when 'there is something the matter', when there is some 'trouble' in an existing situation. When analyzed, this 'something the matter' is found to spring from the fact that there is something lacking, wanting, in the existing situation as it stands, an absence which produces conflict in the elements that do exist." John Dewey, "Theory of Valuation," *International Encyclopedia of Unified Science* (Chicago: University of Chicago Press, 1939), Vol. II, No. 4, 33. "The incentive that impels a man to act is always some uneasiness." Ludwig von Mises, *Human Action* (London: William Hodge and Company, Limited, 1949), p. 13.

survival, is assured.[2] Even the combination of involuntary and voluntary adaptive mechanisms will not always secure survival, of course: sufficiently severe disturbances, as well as the process of degeneration, will cause the breakdown of these mechanisms themselves.[3] The state of adaptation may be considered as a state of no strain.[4] The object of action may thus be said to be the substitution of a less strained or less uneasy condition for a more strained or more uneasy condition. It is necessary to consider the manner in which such actions are selected, but it is not necessary for present purposes to consider the physiological aspects or bases of involuntary or voluntary actions.

SENSATION AND OBSERVATION

Sensations indicative of the conditions of the human organism and its relationships with the environment are apprehended through the many sensory organs. A number of features of the organism and its environment may, therefore, be sensed simultaneously. Each point of sensation may be a point at which uneasiness is felt, so that at any moment of time there may be a number of points of uneasiness. One may feel hungry, thirsty, weary, and cold at the same time. And there may be uneasinesses which have their origins in mental as well as in bodily states; doubt, insecurity and fear are uneasy conditions.

But though there are many possible points of simultaneous uneasiness, there is only one means of deliberation. Only a limited number of sensations may become the objects of attention. These are determined by the relative intensities of sensation. This presupposes a capacity for sensory discrimination between intensities of the same type of sensation, and hence of the same type of strain. Intensity of strain is the apprehended difference

2 The term "homeostatis," designating the steady states secured by "co-ordinated physiological processes" was proposed by Walter B. Cannon, *The Wisdom of the Body* (New York: W. W. Norton & Company, Inc., 1939), p. 24. Extension of the idea to the organism as a whole seems justifiable insofar as deliberate adaptation has the same survival value as unconscious bodily processes. As to the steady state, the organism "is stable and yet it cannot be rigid. It cannot be stable in the sense that a rock is stable. Its stability is an activity and not a static state of affairs. It is a dynamic state; an open system as opposed to a closed system." Anatol Rapoport, "Homeostasis Reconsidered," *Toward a Unified Theory of Human Behavior*, Roy R. Grinker, ed. (New York: Basic Books, Inc., 1956), pp. 225–26. See also Norman L. Munn, *Psychology*, 4th ed. (Boston: Houghton Mifflin Company, 1961), p. 262; Norbert Wiener, *The Human Use of Human Beings* (Garden City, N.Y.: Doubleday & Company, Inc., 1954), pp. 95–96.

3 Cannon, *The Wisdom of the Body*, Ch. XIII.

4 The state of no strain may not exist during hours of consciousness. As a concept it serves as a reference point, as does "equilibrium" in economics, or "absolute zero temperature" in physics.

between an actual strain and the preferred state of no strain. There is also, necessarily, a capacity for discriminating, as for the whole person, between the intensities of strain for all strains felt at any time. If this were not so, any response to a state of strain would be an equally effective response: one would perhaps sleep or warm himself if he were thirsty.

Giving attention is a mental, and on some occasions a physical, preparation for clearer apprehension. One wishes to discover the stimulus and condition of a particular state of uneasiness. Paying attention thus entails excluding from attention, or consciously limiting the span of attention for a time. Attention is focused on the most intense sensation, the sensation in respect of which the apprehended difference between an existing state and the state of no strain is greatest; for the relief of that strain represents the greatest possible relief of the organism as a whole at that time. To discriminate and to choose in this manner is deemed to be a characteristic of reasonable behavior.[5]

One of the objects of paying attention is to observe the impact of a stimulus and its effects more clearly. A stimulus is any object, event, or condition which gives rise to strain. The environment offers an unlimited variety of potential stimuli. Some are more or less continual, some are recurrent, and some are occasional. To some of these, the organism may become habituated; they cease to attract attention. Some are deliberately disregarded, at least for a time, while attention is devoted to others. What becomes an actual stimulus thus depends both on the state of the environment and the state of the person. The incidence and time of at least some stimuli is unpredictable, insofar as neither of these states is predictable. This, in itself, is a source of uneasiness. Any individual has, therefore, the choice between relieving immediate strains and making provision against the incidence of future strains. In this capacity to choose, to defer responses to stimuli, lies the difference between reflective human behavior and the behavior of nonhuman organisms.

Given adequate time, one may observe many things about a stimulus and its impact. What one observes depends, in part, on inquisitiveness and, in part, on the extent of one's recollection of past experiences. As inquisitiveness may be developed and may decline, and as one is constantly having new experiences, the capacity for observation is always changing. Experience and learning may predispose us to observe some things and to disregard others in any specific situation. The unaided senses may be inadequate for the observation of some properties of the objects observed, so that the comprehensiveness of observation may depend on the availability of special

5 " . . . discrimination is the simplest and most basic operation performable . . . When we attempt to reduce complex operations to simpler and simpler ones, we find in the end that discrimination, or differential response is the fundamental operation." S. S. Stevens, "Psychology and the Science of Science," *Psychological Bulletin*, April, 1939, Vol. 36, No. 4, 246, 248.

instruments or of the time for constructing them. New strains may supervene, limiting the opportunity for observation. Generally, therefore, the
capacity for observation of any person is limited at any time.

Notwithstanding the limitation of one's capacity for observation, the sum
of all the properties of any stimulus is the stimulus to which responses are
made. To the extent, therefore, that observation is incomplete or inaccurate,
there is a possibility that responses will be unproductive of the effects they
are desired to bring about. There is the further possibility that, insofar as
the recollection of the consequence of any such response affects one's
responses to future stimuli of a similar kind, future responses will likewise
be disappointing. Observation of the environment is the primary source of
the knowledge necessary to enable one to make intelligent adaptations to it.
But observation of itself is nothing more than the apprehension of certain
sense-data. These require to be interpreted.

PERCEPTION AS INTERPRETATION

Perception is the process by which sensations acquire
significance, or by which sensations are interpreted. It is the process by
which a stimulus is recognized to be a stimulus; by which an object is
recognized as being related to a felt strain; by which objects, where only
some properties are sensed, are recognized as having properties other than
those sensed; by which objects are recognized as having similarities to and
differences from other objects, previously or presently observed.

The interpretation of objects and events depends on past experiences
and what has been learned from them. The mind deals with the objects to
which it attends in terms of ideas which are signs of those objects. In the
early stages of conscious experience one learns to distinguish separate
objects and to associate with each object a name or sign. Subsequently,
ideas are formed in respect of distinguishable properties of objects. The
idea of any property is a sign of that property. The idea of an object then
consists in the aggregate of the simple ideas or single signs which are
associated with it. The signs of objects and properties may be mental images
which the mind has constructed out of past experiences; they may be words
which the user has learned to associate with objects and properties; or they
may be numbers or other abstract symbols which have been learned or
invented by the user.[6]

6 "... all thought is in signs." Peirce, *Values in a Universe of Chance*, p. 34.
"Throughout almost all our life we are treating things as signs.... In all thinking
we are interpreting signs." C. K. Ogden and I. A. Richards, *The Meaning of Meaning*
(London: Routledge & Kegan Paul, Ltd., Tenth Ed., 1960). pp. 50, 244. "... the
human mind is inseparable from the functioning of signs—if indeed mentality is not
to be identified with such functioning." Charles W. Morris, "Foundations of the
Theory of Signs," *International Encyclopedia of Unified Science* (Chicago: University
of Chicago Press, 1955), Vol. 1, 79.

In the interpretation of sensations or observations, something is added to what is directly apprehended. We sense heat; but we perceive that the coffee is hot or that the room is hot, as the case may be. What is added is some part or the whole of past experiences and learning. A penny on a table at a short distance is, to the senses, a brown elliptical shape. An observer who has had experience of pennies will perceive that it is a penny, that from a different angle it would appear to be circular, that it is a small unit of currency, that it bears certain marks on both sides, and so on. An observer who has had no experiences of pennies would perceive it to be something else.

The interpretation of objects and events also depends on the context of observation. The context includes the immediate environment of an object itself. There is scarcely any object or sign the interpretation of which does not vary according to the frame of reference in which it is observed. The immediate environment and the events leading up to an observation influence the psychological set or state of expectancy of an observer. Responses to what one is induced to accept as an illusion differ from the responses which a similar but "real" event would evoke. In a less direct but no less important way, the whole of the past experiences and present needs of an observer determine his state of expectancy in every situation.[7] What one perceives is thus influenced by what one wishes to perceive and what others may induce one to perceive as well as by the objects observed themselves. Perceptions are interpretations; clearly they may be mistaken interpretations.

The simplest interpretations are of signs as objects or properties; we see a shape, we perceive that the shape is a tree; we see a color of part of the tree, we perceive it to be green. We learn also to perceive relationships between objects. Some are perceived to be similar to others; some to be separated from others in space or time; some objects are perceived to be identical with other objects at another place or time; some objects are perceived to be larger or smaller than others, to have different shapes, forms, textures, to have more or less of specific properties than other objects. We speak of the things we perceive about objects as our knowledge of those objects. Knowledge of the properties of objects and of the relationships referred to is the product of observation and comparison. One's knowledge of objects enables one to decide what can be done to them or with them in any situation in which action is contemplated.

7 "Perception is functionally selective," as also is memory. David Krech and Richard S. Crutchfield, *Theory and Problems of Social Psychology* (New York: McGraw-Hill Book Company. 1948), pp. 87, 132. George H. Mead. *Mind, Self and Society* (Chicago: The University of Chicago Press, 1934), pp. 129 ff.

The relationship of cause and effect is an additional relationship which permits the formation of expectations of the outcome of actions. If two objects a and b have occurred in experience in such a way that a preceded b in time, that a was always followed by b, that b did not occur without a, the relationship between a and b is judged to be that of cause and effect. Knowledge of the relationship of cause and effect is, at the same time, more useful and less easy to establish than other knowledge. It is more useful, for, if we know that a is the cause of b, we have grounds for believing that if we can procure a we can procure b. This knowledge provides the basis of the choice of actions in terms of their expected consequences. But it is less easy to establish. For, in the first place, any two objects which may be related as cause and effect may occur in clusters of other objects, so that the causal connection may not be readily inferred and mistaken inferences may be drawn. In the second place, the mere fact that experiences, up to any point of time in respect of a and b, have been such as to suggest a causal relationship does not necessarily give grounds for believing that a and b will always occur in the same relationship in the future. Repeated observation of a and b in the same relationship will increase the strength of the belief that b may be expected in the future whenever a occurs. For practical purposes, many such beliefs are held with the utmost confidence, as if they were certainties. But the frequency with which beliefs held to be reliable in the past have been shown to be mistaken, and the limitations of human experience and reasoning, enjoin the view that knowledge of causal relationships is always probabilistic.

Numerous allusions have been made already to points of time, intervals of time, and the succession of events in time; and the importance of the sequence of things in time will become increasingly apparent. All events occur at particular points of time. Sensations are felt at particular times and in particular sequences. The sequences of such occurrences determine the reactions of men to them; different sequences produce different responses, different inferences as to cause and effect, for example. Time is irreversible, not only in terms of our experience of its passing (we grow old, we do not grow young) but also in respect of its significance in relation to the interpretation of past events and experiences and in relation to action (we can know much about the past and present; but we can only speculate about the future).

Further, to each person, there is only a limited amount of time—his lifetime. For all his purposes, time is limited. There being many actual or potential strains, the time he has to devote to the relief of any one of them is limited, and the time he may devote to deliberation on the relief of any one of them is limited.

LEARNING, HABITS AND BELIEFS

Reference has been made to the part learning plays in observation and perception. It is characteristic of living things, and particularly of the human organism, that experiences through the passing of time lead to modifications which improve their capacity for adaptation to the environment. Human learning involves modification of the organism in such a way that its responses to stimuli occur more rapidly and with less conscious effort. Learning may range from the development of simple conditioned responses, through simple motor and mental skills to complex technical skills. The effects of the modifications called learning lie in the fixation of beliefs or habits and in the removal of doubts.

Although the discussion has proceeded in terms of an individual person, most of the beliefs and much of the knowledge of an individual is acquired from others.[8] The interpretation of most of the objects of experience and many of our responses are learned by vicarious experience. What is learned in this way is accepted very largely on the strength of reliance on the authority and experience of our mentors. But as the experience of all persons is limited, what may have been effective interpretations of or responses to objects on their part, or in the circumstances under which they themselves learned, may not necessarily be equally effective for their successors or in different circumstances. Many transmitted statements of relationship are accepted uncritically and many transmitted responses are accepted as habits without question.[9] In many respects what we receive from our antecedents is the accumulated knowledge and wisdom of the past, and the habits we adopt become habits because they are believed to be serviceable. Neither the acceptance of transmitted knowledge nor the adoption of habits may be regarded as nonrational, however. Both serve to relieve us of the strain of examining things afresh or of the strain of doubt. What has been said of bodily homeostatic devices may be said also of habits; they free us from the deliberate management "of the details of bare existence ... and ... release the highest activities of the nervous system for adventure and achievement."[10] But, habits and received beliefs may and do outlive their usefulness.[11] The

---

8 " ... mind ... is essentially a social phenomenon." Mead, *Mind, Self and Society*, p. 133.

9 "Man is primarily a creature of habit." Munn, *Psychology*, p. 286. " ... belief ... is something that we are aware of ... it appeases the irritation of doubt ... it involves the establishment in our nature of a rule of action, or say for short, a *habit*." Peirce, *Values in a Universe of Chance,* p. 121.

10 Cannon, *The Wisdom of the Body*, p. 297.

11 " ... there are three ways by which human thought grows, by the formation of habits, by the violent breaking up of habits, and by the innumerable fortuitous variations of ideas combined with differences in the fecundity of different variations." Peirce, *Values in a Universe of Chance*, p. 257.

probabilistic character of knowledge obliges men continually to submit their old beliefs to the test of direct experience.

Direct experience is the second method by which habits and beliefs are acquired. There is no question as to the value of experience as a source of knowledge, provided experience is understood as active and critical examination of the events in which one participates and self-conscious participation on one's own part. Habitual responses constitute passive participation; they serve to reinforce habits rather than to add to knowledge. Novel situations in which one is unable to rely on existing habits and beliefs are therefore more likely to be productive of new knowledge than situations which have frequently been encountered in the past.

But what is learned from direct experience may also have limited serviceability as a basis of adaptive behavior. We have noted that in any situation the focus of attention is limited with the object of clearer apprehension. If the time available for responding is short and one seeks relief both from the provoking strain and the strain of giving attention, little may be learned as to the relationships between stimulus, action, and consequence which will serve as a useful belief in the future. Again, there are many circumstances in which we are unable to perceive directly the extent to which any response of itself results in the removal of strain. Nevertheless, in the absence of more reliable knowledge, experiences even though they are fragmentary, and often even though they are passive, give rise to, or reinforce, beliefs which form the basis of future actions. Beliefs arise from the organization of one's past experiences, direct and vicarious, and are thus limited in quality and extent by the carefulness of observation and the extent of past experiences.[12]

When, through experience, it is discovered that beliefs and habits are inadequate, new responses and new beliefs must be learned. The process of learning thus includes relearning, learning to respond in a new way rather than in the previously established way. The difficulties of acquiring new beliefs in place of old ones are twofold. There is the notorious difficulty of breaking with one's old beliefs. It is not uncommon to find that when an experience seems to conflict with established beliefs, men prefer to regard the experience as anomalous rather than to regard old beliefs as dubitable. To believe is easier than to doubt. And there is the difficulty of embracing new beliefs of the effects of which one has had little or no experience. These difficulties account for the general persistence of established beliefs long beyond the time of the discovery of more efficacious ways of thinking and acting.

All learning depends on memory, the capacity for storing and recalling

---

[12] Boulding refers to ideas held about the elements of experience as "images"; the notion corresponds, in relation to action, with our use of "beliefs." Kenneth E. Boulding, *The Image* (Ann Arbor Paperbacks, The University of Michigan Press, 1961).

beliefs relating to objects, events, and relationships. The greater the effort made in learning, the greater will be the probability of retention; and the greater the opportunity for the exercise of learned responses, the more readily and easily will they be made. Rapidity and ease in responding to any sign depends on the organization of experiences or beliefs into patterns or the association of ideas. But the more diverse one's experiences, the more diffuse will be the association of ideas and the greater will be the hesitancy to resort to purely habitual responses. Increased learning is accompanied by increased powers of discrimination. Consequently each situation in which a response is required is seen to be in some respects unique, and, therefore, beyond remedy by an habitual response.

REASONING

The most deliberate procedure for selecting ameliorative actions where strain exists or is to be avoided is reasoning. It is resorted to when involuntary and habitual modes of adaptation fail. Reasoning requires sustained attention, time, and deferring the time of relief from a strain— all of them sacrifices which the human organism prefers to avoid. But they are sacrifices deemed to be necessary for the relief of a greater strain, the irritation of doubt.[13] Reasoning in this connection is the combining of beliefs with the object of deriving (by relation, comparison, development, inference, and similar processes) additional beliefs, in a situation where doubt exists. We may, of course, apply the thought processes we describe as reasoning to sets of statements which have no foundation in beliefs, as, for example, when logical operations are performed on abstract symbols or hypothetical statements. Even this kind of exploratory reasoning, however, is related to the solution of problems and the removal of doubts.

Reasoning, then, proceeds from statements (beliefs) about the objects of experience. But it has to do with more than one object, or with more than one property of an object or objects. We wish to know whether an object a will be serviceable in producing a situation b; or whether believing a statement c entitles us also to believe a statement d; or whether an object having a property e also has a property f; or whether, if x is a g, y is also a g. Obtaining the answers to any such questions involves organizing or ordering our primary beliefs; and this entails using the signs which express those beliefs in an orderly or consistent manner. We seek to use signs in a consistent manner by stating the interpretation we intend to give them, by definition.

The most common signs used by men are units of language. No unit of

---

13 "Reasoning does not occur unless there is a difficulty, or unless a question has arisen for which there is no ready answer." Munn, *Psychology*, p. 485. See also Peirce, *Values in a Universe of Chance*, p. 121.

language, and generally no sign of any kind, stands alone. Each sign has meaning, or is interpreted, only in the system of signs of which it is a part; its meaning may be developed only by reference to such a system. The system of signs within which a given sign is interpreted by any person includes his sensations and his memories at the time. Our common understandings of "table," "stone," "water," consist in the properties, such as flatness, hardness, and wetness, which we associate with those terms and with the objects of which they are signs. But in the context of physical or chemical inquiry a quite different set of properties would be predicated. Further, there is no single sign which is a unique sign of any object or property; a house-cat may be a "cat," a "pet," or a "nuisance." But if our *pet* cat is hungry and we go to buy *pet* food, we do not return with birdseed. Intelligent behavior depends on reasoning with signs having specific interpretations for the purpose in mind, or in the context of behavior.

The ordering of ideas is not only a phase of the reasoning process. It is an adaptive response to the heterogeneity of experience and of the objects of experience. The elements of the environment are so diverse and numerous that they cannot all be comprehended as individual elements at any time. Nor can they be given attention simultaneously, as individuals, for the purpose of making comparisons of them or judgments about them. Yet any one of them or any combination of them may become a stimulus and an object of reasoning. They are reduced to order by reduction to classes of objects which have some common property or form. Forming conceptions entails perceiving similarities (as, for example, between the particulars apple tree, peach tree, and oak tree) and differences (as between trees and things other than trees). One's conceptions of "tree," "book," "man," embrace the ideas representing the common properties of things experienced, but they are not identical with one's perception or recollection of any particular tree, book, or man. As conceptions have reference to the common properties or forms of objects, they are abstractions from the totality of properties which every particular object of any class possesses. In respect of a common property or properties, conceptions are generalizations about the classes of objects to which they refer. The formation of conceptions enables men to reason about and respond to the elements of experience more economically than if each element were considered to be unique. But the very generality and abstractness of words or signs for conceptions makes definition the more important if the full powers of those signs are to be exploited without error. And this importance increases as, by further abstraction, more general conceptions are formed.

Recognition of the elements of experience (including objects, events, statements) as instances of a class of objects having common properties is induction. Induction provides us with beliefs about all instances of defined classes of objects. We would like to believe that if a response of a certain kind (involving the properties denoted by the conception of a class) is appropriate to some instances it is appropriate to all. A belief of such universality can only be held with certainty if we are able exhaustively to enumerate all the instances of a class; and as experiences are limited, this is not possible. Clearly, it is not possible in respect of any future experience; yet it is for the purpose of meeting future events that universal statements are valued.

The step from beliefs about objects to beliefs about classes of objects, relationships between classes and causal relationships is a non-logical step.[14] Whenever a general or universal statement exceeds in scope the things which have been experienced, the possibility of being deceived by it may only be avoided by holding it always as a statement capable of being falsified.[15] As the result of experience we may judge that under specified conditions a is the cause of b. But for the purpose of acting, we suppose that all actions of the class of which a is a member (including future actions) will procure effects of the class of which b is a member. We then deduce from the latter general statement, together with certain specific statements about present or expected conditions, that an action a' will procure an effect b'. If b' is a desired effect, action a' will be taken.

The general supposition linking a's and b's is a universal statement of the nature of an hypothesis. All general beliefs are of the same nature, and indeed so are all interpretations of objects and all conceptions. Insofar as actions in the world at large are only likely to procure the effects desired if general beliefs correspond to the relationships which do exist (irrespective of beliefs), it is a matter of importance that general beliefs be submitted to the most rigorous tests, with the object of discovering whether they are false.

One method of attempting to improve the strength of belief in a general statement is to increase the number of instances which are capable of description in terms of the belief. This increases the weight of evidence, but never to the point of establishing the certainty of a belief; for experience being limited, time being short, and the future being unavail-

14 "No rules can be offered for obtaining fruitful hypotheses." Morris R. Cohen and Ernest Nagel, *An Introduction to Logic and Scientific Method* (London: Routledge & Kegan Paul, Ltd.. 1957), p. 392. " ... there is no such thing as a logical method of having new ideas. ... " Karl R. Popper, *The Logic of Scientific Discovery* (New York: Science Editions, Inc., 1961), p. 32. See also W. I. B. Beveridge, *The Art of Scientific Investigation* (New York: Random House, 1957), Chaps. 4–7, and A. J. Ayer, *The Problem of Knowledge* (Penguin Books, Inc., 1956), pp. 71 ff.

15 Taking the view that induction is not a logical method, Popper, *The Logic of Scientific Discovery*, p. 61, proposes in lieu of the "Principle of causality" a methodological rule, "we are not to abandon the search for universal laws and for a coherent theoretical system, nor ever give up our attempts to explain causally any kind of event we can describe."

able, all instances cannot be enumerated. Nevertheless men act upon the weight of evidence; and insofar as additional experiences are regarded as corroboration or as noncorroboration of beliefs, it is reasonable to do so. But there are methods which offer a more positive program for the testing of beliefs.

These methods of testing general or universal statements involve deductive processes. We begin with an idea, supposition, hypothesis, or theory which, it is felt, will serve as an explanation of certain events. The hypothesis will be expressed in the clearest possible manner; its terms and statements will be developed in such a way that they are distinguishable from other similar terms and statements. From the hypothesis and one or more other statements which are accepted at the time, we deduce specific consequences which, if the hypothesis is serviceable, may be found to conform with experience or with the results of an experiment. The specific consequences will be expressed in a form which is capable of being tested against experience or by experiment, and they will be so tested. If the expected logical consequences do occur, we accept the hypothesis as corroborated and as a serviceable basis for future actions. If the expected consequences do not occur, we consider the hypothesis to be uncorroborated; we may modify it (formulate a new hypothesis) and try again; we may question the other statements used in conjunction with the hypothesis in deriving specific consequences; or we may question the experience or the experiment by which those consequences were tested.

Some uneasiness may be felt about the use in conjunction with the hypothesis of "other statements which are accepted at the time." But these in turn may be subjected to the same process of testing; and the process may be carried backwards as far as it is deemed to be necessary, so that at last some statement is accepted because it has withstood the tests made of it.

If it is sought to establish a theory, to have it accepted, it will be submitted to the most rigorous possible tests. Where possible, one may devise a crucial experiment, submitting the theory to the test of extreme conditions. But even crucial experiments are not conclusive; for they depend on the acceptance of all the theories upon which the individual experimental operations are based, and these may be open to question just as much as the specific theory being tested. Repeated corroboration and crucial experiments serve well the testing of theories which are relatively isolated from other theories. Where a theory may be linked with many other theories in other fields of inquiry, its corroboration may be effected by tests designed to discover its compatability with theories accepted in diverse fields, particularly in fields where a substantial body of accepted generalizations already exists.

HYPOTHESES, THEORIES
AND THEIR TESTING

As, when acting, we wish to procure some effects and not others, we seek beliefs which will enable us to choose actions which will exclude undesired effects. A theory of the form, "if *a*, then *b* or *c*" or of the form "if *a* or *b*, then *c*," is of little use in this respect. For such a proposition as "if *a*, then *b* or *c*," may be expressed in the form of two propositions: "if *a*, then *b*" and "if *a*, then not *b*." Such statements assert too much to be useful; they are self-contradictory, incompatible, or inconsistent. In general, one of the tests of the usefulness of a hypothesis or theory is that its statements and any logical inferences from those statements shall be consistent.

Again, when acting, we wish to be assured that our beliefs or inter-pretations of the world in which we act are not simply figments of our own imaginations. We seek beliefs which are not likely to be falsified because our perceptions or our reasoning may be mistaken. The usefulness of a belief does not consist in the strength of the conviction with which an individual holds it, but in its capacity for informing him about the world of experience. Our convictions, evaluations, or opinions we acknowl-edge to be personal, not necessarily shared by others and beyond testing; they may be described as subjective. They are distinguished from objective statements which "are capable of test by reference to evidence which is public, that is, which can be secured by different observers and does not depend essentially on the observer."[16] That a general statement has been corroborated by the tests of others adds to the confidence with which it is regarded as a useful basis of action.

The kind of acceptance implied is not mere acceptance as by a democratic process, but acceptance after independent observation and testing. Acceptance by a democratic process closes the examination of a statement. All evidence which falsifies the statement is explained in terms of additional *ad hoc* hypotheses; and given the opportunity for introducing *ad hoc* hypotheses, any general statement may be confirmed. But all *ad hoc* hypotheses themselves require to be tested. It is, thus, much more difficult to corroborate a system of statements comprising a large range of *ad hoc* statements than to confirm a single general statement. For this reason many such systems remain untested. And for this reason we prefer the theory which requires the fewer separate hypotheses, that is, the smaller number of statements about which doubt may be entertained. We prefer the simpler theory.

16 Carl G. Hempel, "Fundamentals of Concept Formation in Empirical Science," *International Encyclopedia of Unified Science* (Chicago: The University of Chicago Press, 1952) Vol. II, No. 7, 22. Popper, among others, describes the requirement as "inter-subjective testability." Popper, *The Logic of Scientific Discovery*, p. 44.

This preference may be stated in another way. As between any two general statements, we prefer that which is the most fruitful of predictions, or inferences which meet the tests to which they are subjected. A general statement which requires supporting *ad hoc* statements as additional premises for the deduction of any conclusion has very limited generality of itself. It provides ground for few predictions, and, therefore, a basis for very few actions. For every specific action there must be selected that collection of *ad hoc* hypotheses which taken in conjunction with the general hypothesis permits the deduction of the consequence we seek. As in any situation, except the purely experimental situation, the time available for examining the whole class of *ad hoc* hypotheses and their combinations is limited, the possibility of erroneous selections is ever present.

The preferences we have indicated in the preceding paragraphs—for objective (testable) propositions, which are self-consistent, which are simpler than others, and more fruitful of predictions than others—are all implicit in the general proposition that men seek to be relieved of strain.[17] They are not requirements of taste or opinion or aesthetics. They are necessary conditions for the economical selection, from all possible ways of acting, of those ways of acting which are the more likely, in the existing state of knowledge, to procure selected ends.

The above account, it will be noticed, is concerned with reasoning as a process of testing statements postulated on any basis. It does not concern itself with the manner in which such statements come to be formulated, except to the extent of suggesting that the wider one's familiarity with other knowledge and the more intensively one examines experiences, the more likely are possible general statements to arise—as hypotheses. It does not concern itself with beliefs which are not testable. The general beliefs held at any time with reference to matters that are testable constitutes the state of knowledge at that time. Note that we do not say "beliefs which have been tested." The state of knowledge consists in what has not been falsified. It may, thus, include many statements which have neither been corroborated nor falsified, but which at some future time may come to be confirmed or rejected. Corroboration or falsification up to a point of time is all that can be expected of any general statement or theory.

The persistence of beliefs is due in part to inertia or habit, in part to the inability to put them under test because their terms provide no indication of the manner in which they may be tested, and in part to the extent to which they have been corroborated. But the adoption of new beliefs

---

17 " ... the criterion of simplicity, which enables us to select one coordination (of experimental facts) rather than another ... appears to be linked with our valuing of the expenditure of effort." A. d'Abro, *The Evolution of Scientific Thought* (New York: Dover Publications, Inc., 1950), pp. 359–60. See also Duhem, *The Aim and Structure of Physical Theory,* pp. 21, 39.

depends on their accepted superiority over old beliefs, and this depends entirely on corroboration. The reason for the durability of old beliefs as against new ones, already mentioned when discussing learning, is suggested by this difference.

The objective of the processes of observation and reasoning which we have described is to obtain the most reliable knowledge or understanding of the matter examined. This knowledge consists of propositions of two kinds, empirical statements and formal statements. Empirical statements are descriptive of what is given by experience; the terms or signs used are those commonly used to describe sensations or observations or observable things. Formal statements are descriptive of our ways of regarding things, as members of classes or as having properties or relationships not directly observable, for example. These two kinds of statements represent two ways of knowing or two kinds of knowing. We may seek to make our knowledge of what we observe more reliable by resorting to reason, or to make the products of our reasoning more reliable by reference to what is observable. The gap must be bridged between the empirical and the formal; between the terms or signs by which we describe experiences ("concepts by inspection"), and the abstract or invented terms or signs upon which we perform logical operations ("concepts by postulation" or "constructs").[18][19] The bridging is done by rules of correspondence, by understandings which enable us to move freely between the realm of observation and the realm of reasoning. As constructs are inventions, it is clear that there may be many more ways of looking at things than there are observable properties. It is not necessary that all of our constructs shall be referable to empirical statements about observable things and qualities. It is sufficient that the constructs shall be logically related and that an adequate proportion of them shall be linked with observable things by rules of correspondence.

If, in respect of a given range of observable phenomena, laws or theories or principles are obtained which serve to account for the occurrence of the phenomena, or to enable the future occurrence of similar phenomena to be predicted, the body of facts and laws, theories, or principles is described as a science. It is not necessary that the laws, theories, and principles shall account for all known phenomena or that they shall enable the prediction of every future occurrence. This is the ideal towards which inquiry is directed; but in terms of economy of thought and action less embracing propositions are no less useful. And indeed, at any stage in the development of a science, its laws, theories, and principles may be regarded

18 F. S. C. Northrop, *The Logic of the Sciences and the Humanities* (New York: The Macmillan Company, 1947), Chap. 8.

19 Henry Margenau, *The Nature of Physical Reality* (New York: Copyright © 1950 by, and used by permission of, McGraw-Hill Book Company), pp. 84 ff.

as only provisional, pending the development of more satisfactory and more comprehensive notions.

If the process of inquiry and the nature of knowledge are thus regarded, the processes of induction and deduction will be seen as joint contributors to knowledge. They are not different methods of proceeding but parts of the same method. Induction is nothing more than the postulation of general hypotheses or theories; deduction is nothing more than drawing out the implications of those theories so that their conclusions may be tested by reference to the classes of facts which gave rise to the initial inductions. When, however, one wishes to establish in the minds of others the reasonableness of a conclusion, the process is, so to speak, reversed. The assumptions or postulates, formal statements linked to empirical statements by rules of correspondence, are set up, and the conclusion is derived by logical (deductive) processes from the assumptions. The process appears to be entirely deductive; but it is the choice from among possible hypotheses which provides the tentative conclusion to which the deductive demonstration is directed.[20] The reliability of the conclusion thus depends on the validity of the argument and the consistency of the conclusion with the environment of experience.

Argument

> Note: The propositions which are set in *italics* in this and succeeding summaries are assumptions or postulates or definitions. All other propositions are inferences or conclusions.)

1.11   *We are concerned with sentient, discriminating persons. Every such person has*

1.12   *—limited capacity for sensation and observation.*

1.13   *—limited experiences.*

1.14   *—limited capacity for recollection.*

1.15   —limited knowledge.   (*1.12, 1.13, 1.14*)

1.16   *—limited capacity for perception.*

[20] "... among all scientific inferences there is only one of an overreaching type: that is the inductive inference. All other inferences are empty, tautological; they do not add anything new to the experiences from which they start. The inductive inference does; that is why it is the elementary form of the method of scientific discovery." Hans Reichenbach, *Experience and Prediction* (Chicago: The University of Chicago Press, 1961. Copyright 1938 by The University of Chicago Press), p. 365.

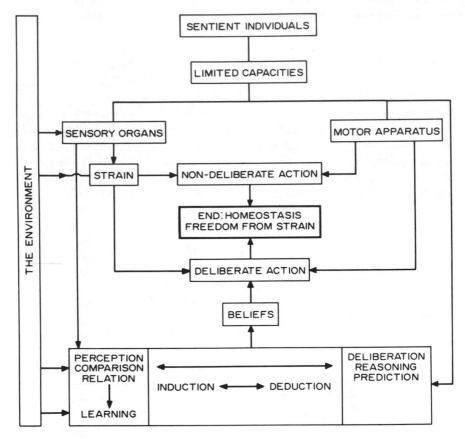

Figure 1
OUTLINE OF CHAPTER 1: INDIVIDUAL THOUGHT AND ACTION.

1.17   —*limited capacities for action (physical and mental).*

1.18   —*limited time for action.*

1.21   *Every person is sensitive to strains, or sensations of uneasiness (including doubt), of many kinds.*

1.22   *There is a preferred condition of no strain; less strain is preferred to more strain.*

1.23   *Action (physical or mental) is a condition of strain.*

1.24   *Persons are homeostatic systems; the object of action is the relief of strain, that is, the attainment of the preferred condition of no strain.* (1.17, 1.21, 1.22)

1.31   *A stimulus is any object, event, or condition giving rise to strain.*

1.32   *The incidence of stimuli, in time and in severity, is unpredictable.*

1.33   *For any kind of strain, intensity of strain is the apprehended difference between an actual state and the preferred state of no strain.*

1.34   Any kind of strain may be felt with different intensities. (1.11, 1.21, 1.33)

1.35   *There is a capacity for discriminating, as for the whole person, between the intensities of strain for all strains at any time.*

1.36   The number of sensations which may be perceived and considered at any time is limited; the span of attention is limited. (1.16, 1.17, 1.21)

1.37   Those sensations will be considered, for relief by action, in respect of which the intensity of strain is relatively the greater. (1.22, 1.24, 1.35, 1.36)

1.41   *Perception is the interpretation of observations and sensations as signs of objects or events, or of properties of objects or events. Perception includes apprehension of similarities, differences, temporalities, and causal relationships.*

1.42   *Interpretation is the process of comparing or relating present observations or sensations, in the context of observation and of recollected ideas or signs of past experiences.*

1.43   *Direct comparison and relation, and the process of aggregation are possible only in respect of properties possessed in common by the objects observed.*

1.44   Any particular interpretation may be mistaken. (1.12, 1.13, 1.14, 1.18, 1.42)

1.45   A primary object of perception is the identification of objects (as stimuli or as means of removing stimuli) with strains. (1.22, 1.31, 1.41)

1.51   *All mental operations are operations with signs.*

    1.511   *A sign is anything which refers to some thing for some person (an interpreter).*

1.512   *Objects, properties of objects, and relationships between objects are themselves signs.*

1.513   *There are verbal and other signs for objects, properties of objects, and relationships between objects.*

1.52   *A conception is a sign denoting a common property or form of a collection of objects in abstraction from the totality of properties of those objects individually.*

1.53   *Classification is the grouping and ordering of objects according to conceptions.*

1.54   The strain of mental operations is reduced by the use of conceptions and classifications.

(*1.23*, 1.36, *1.52*, *1.53*)

1.61   *Learning is modification of the capacity for action by the fixation of beliefs or habits, and thus by the removal of doubts. The fixation of beliefs and habits is a response to the strain of doubt.*

(*1.21*)

1.62   *Beliefs are complex signs representing, to a person, interpretations of objects, properties, and relationships.*

1.63   Beliefs arise from the organization in a person of his experiences (direct and vicarious) and are, thus, limited in extent and in quality by the capacity for observation and the extent of past experiences.

(*1.12*, *1.13*, *1.62*)

1.64   *Beliefs include subjective statements, which the maker alone can affirm, and objective statements, which others can independently affirm or deny.*

1.65   Beliefs as to present objects limit the range of possible future actions.

(*1.24*, 1.45, *1.62*)

1.66   Beliefs as to relationships influence the choice of future actions from the range of possible actions.

(*1.24*, 1.45, *1.62*, 1.65)

1.67   As the capacity for observation and the extent of past experiences are limited and the future is unknown, all beliefs as to specific future events are in part subjective; no such belief may be held with certainty.

(*1.12*, *1.13*, 1.15, *1.64*)

1.68   The greater the correspondence between objects and beliefs in respect of them, the greater is the probability that actions taken on those beliefs will procure the effects they imply.

(*1.24*, 1.44, 1.45, 1.63)

1.71   *Reasoning is the combining of beliefs with the object of deriving (by relation, comparison, inference, and so on) new, additional, or alternative beliefs.*

1.72   *Reasoning includes the formation of conceptions and generaliza-*

tions in the nature of hypotheses (induction) and the discovery of the implications of conceptions and hypotheses (deduction).

1.73   *Discovery of the implications of beliefs enables them to be tested (and corroborated or rejected) by reference to experiential objects or events.*

(1.63, *1.72*)

1.74   The greater the corroboration of a belief, the greater is the confidence with which it is acted upon.

(1.68, *1.73*)

1.75   The greater the number of particular beliefs as to relationships of the objects linked in any experiential situation, the greater is the difficulty of testing any such particular belief.

(*1.23*, 1.36, *1.73*)

1.76   That theory, or ordered set of beliefs, is preferred which involves the fewer hypotheses and which has the greater predictive capacity.

(*1.23*, 1.54, 1.68, 1.75)

Ends and Means

2

ENDS AND PREFERENCES

We speak of preferred situations or preferred effects as ends. Ends are the objects of actions. As a sentient person may experience at the same time a number of strains, he will at that time have a number of ends. When the means of attaining ends are scarce, ends are ranked in the order in which they are preferred. It is unnecessary to suppose all ends to be so ranked; for, the capacity of the mind to comprehend and compare diverse things is limited, and as ends are constantly changing, the effort involved in a complete ranking would be disproportionate to the benefit, in terms of improved choice, to be expected. The occasion of preferring is the existence of a limited number of strains which are felt more intensely than all others. But these indeed require to be ranked.

If a scale of preferences be supposed, it is not a scale in any but an ordinal sense. One may prefer to relieve one's hunger, rather than to buy a theatre ticket; but the ends of gastronomical satisfaction and cultural satisfaction are incommensurable. Nor may any such scale be considered to be invariant through time for any individual. The relief, even the partial relief, of any strain changes the ranking of all strains and, therefore, of all ends. There is thus no such thing as an end in itself; there is no end which has an inherent value independent of the valuations placed on other ends. There is consequently no way by which an observer may derive the ends which any observed person will prefer to other ends at any time. Ends which *were* valued most highly may only be inferred from actions taken, that is, after the event. But the very fact that action was taken to attain a specific end makes it impossible for an observer to assert that the same end is ranked in the same position in the scale of preferences thereafter.

It is sufficient, and indeed observers have no other course, to regard specific ends of others as given and beyond inquiry.[1] But this in no way prevents the discussion of ends in general as the objectives of action in just the same way as any other class of things in general may be discussed. Neither does it interfere with the discussion of classes of ends which observation shows to be commonly preferred by specific classes of persons.

The object of each specific action is then the attainment of a specific end, or, in some cases, the attainment of several specific ends jointly. If one were free of all constraints on action, there would be no question of preferring one thing to another, of valuing one end more highly than another. There would be no occasion for choice. Every desirable thing could be desired and every desire could be satisfied. But there are constraints. All actions require the sacrifice of time and energy, and, in many cases, the sacrifice of other things; and the quantities of time, energy and other things available (or in prospect) to any person for the satisfaction of wants (and prospective wants) are limited. Where the quantities of these means are insufficient to satisfy all desires, one must choose. Thus, although those strains receive attention which are felt most intensely, and although their relief may be preferred to the relief of other strains, the choice of a course of action depends also on the sacrifices which the relief of each is expected to require, and on the quantities of time, energy, and other things available to be sacrificed.

This has several corollaries. One does not consider, as ends, effects which, however desirable, are clearly beyond one's means to procure. To hope for things beyond one's means is to dream. This is not to say that

---

[1] Our inquiry, like that of economics, "is entirely neutral between ends." Lionel Robbins, *An Essay on the Nature and Significance of Economic Science* (London: Macmillan & Co., Ltd., 1948 ed.), p. 24. "Ultimate decisions, the valuations and the choosing of ends are beyond the scope of any science.... Concrete value judgments and definite human actions are not open to further analysis." von Mises, *Human Action*, pp. 10, 17.

one may not strive towards an end, at present unattainable, by attempting to accumulate adequate means. But in the light of the possibility that one's ends will change as time passes, it is preferable, in seeking to explain choices to speak of the end in such a case as accumulation, for accumulation of means provides relief from some strains.

We have noted that the attainment of any end, in whole or in part, changes the ranking of other ends. The attainment of any end is, in fact, a means to the selection for attainment of another end.[2] There is thus a continuous chain of situations in which choice is exercised, as long as any uneasiness exists; and the persistence of uneasiness in one form or another—due to changes in one's preferences, or to changes in the environmental conditions—is a matter of common experience. It follows that, in choosing ends for attainment, one does not disregard the possibility that a sacrifice to be made in the pursuit of one end may gravely interfere with the prospect thereafter of pursuing another. One does not deliberately choose to devote to the procurement of any specific end more of one's time, energy, and other things than one believes to be worthwhile.

VALUATIONS

The sacrifice one is prepared to make in the expectation of attaining any end is an index of the worthwhileness or value attributed to that end. It is an index, not a measure. If the end were not more highly valued than the sacrifice, the sacrifice would not be made. Choosing is the selection of a course of action having expected future consequences. Valuation, which is part of the process of choosing, is likewise directed towards future possible consequences. What is past and present may be able to be measured. But what is future can only be evaluated.[3] Valuations are thus personal and entirely subjective. But valuation is nonetheless necessary. It is the only alternative to choosing at random. Furthermore valuations are always temporal. Any valuation is limited in time and context; it is made by a person in a given state, at a given time, and in a given environment. A valuation is an incident in a continuing stream of experiences and actions. It has no permanence; it may never recur. Valuations of ends, like ends

---

[2] Dewey, *"Theory of Valuation,"* Sec. VI.

[3] James C. Bonbright, *The Valuation of Property* (New York: McGraw-Hill Book Company, 1937) gives extended treatment to a wide range of occasions, temporal and circumstantial, on which valuation is undertaken. He refers to "the undeniable fact . . . that the process of valuation is one of prophecy" (p. 133) but goes on to speak of *measures* of value. Much of the literature of accounting and related types of economic calculation confuses valuation and measurement, values and measures. It is our position that the two are characteristically distinct categories, and that the distinction must be maintained in view of their different functions.

themselves, must be regarded as given at any given point of time and beyond inquiry.

Although choosing and valuation are subjective, their foundations are necessarily understandings of the relationships between events (actions) and their consequences in the environment of action. For an action, which expresses choice, is action taken in, or in respect of, the environment, and no expectation of satisfaction may be entertained in respect of any action which assumes relationships other than those which may be inferred from experience of the environment. If we wish to accommodate ourselves to circumstances which surround us, which affect us, and which limit us, of necessity we must discover as well and as reliably as we can the nature of those circumstances and the forces which shape them.

We ordinarily speak of these circumstances which surround us as "the facts" of a situation. The response to any situation is of course a response to that situation as it is understood by the respondent. We have indicated that beliefs are a function not only of the external stimuli to which we are or have been exposed, but also of the manner in which cognizance is taken of the impressions received. In the widest sense the effects of stimuli are influenced by the culture of the society in which one lives.[4] In a narrower sense, they are influenced by the status one enjoys or the role one fills in that society. In a narrower sense still, they are influenced by one's specific predisposition about the time an impression is received. It may seem therefore that impressions of the facts are the result of such a filtering process that what is "out there" has little to do with the responses one makes; that the selective influences of culture, role, existent beliefs, and so on, prevent us from discovering "the facts"; and that the values we place on culture, role, and existent beliefs prevent us from unraveling facts from values.[5]

Nevertheless, in any limited situation, and most action situations are limited, the wider reference systems in which we act and the valuations we attach to them may be taken as given. They may be regarded as implicit in the system; as being held in common, at least by those members of the society with whom one interacts; and as having a considerable degree of stability through time. In our present context, therefore, we speak of valuation with particular reference to the limited set of circumstances which constitute a problem situation, circumstances which do not occasion questioning our wider frames of reference but which do require a deliberate assessment of the immediate potentialities of action within those wider frames of reference.

Reference was made above to the sacrifice of time, energy, and other things. Every action entails some such sacrifice. And every such sacrifice

---

4 See Chap. 3.
5 Boulding, *The Image*, pp. 173–74.

represents the forgoing of some other end for the end actually pursued. If we devote labor time to some end, we sacrifice leisure time (itself an end) if nothing else. We may state a conclusion; action will be taken when the value of the expected sacrifice of attaining a selected end falls short of the value attributed to its attainment. But ends can never be considered in isolation; to be or not to be, to have or not to have, are always matters of choice; and choice is complicated by the limited availability of time, energy, and other things.[6] We require, then, a more general conclusion than the one above. Where there are limited means and competing ends, that action will be taken which is expected to yield the greatest satisfaction for a given sacrifice.

It will be apparent that choosing inevitably involves knowing one's present position or situation. If this is not known, one cannot imagine the direction in which one should act to procure a better situation. Choosing involves preferring some situation in the future to the situation which exists at the moment of choice; if the latter is not known, no other situation can be said to be preferred. Choosing also involves preferring some situation in the future to other possible situations in the future; without knowledge of one's present situation, and especially without knowledge of one's means of procuring any future situation, the range of possible future situations cannot be envisaged, the costs of procuring any one of them cannot be related to the means available, and no informed choice can be made. It is, for these reasons, beyond argument that the most universally useful information in any situation requiring choice is information as to one's present situation.[7]

As a point of reference, it will be useful to describe the preferred situation toward which an action is directed as optimal adaptation. Optimal adaptation does not mean the state of complete satisfaction or the state of rest where no further action is necessary, for we regard the attainment of one end as a means to the attainment of others. It means only that state of satisfaction the attainment of which would free one to seek other ends. The concept may appear to be lacking in precision; but this is in the

6 "Every valuation is a comparison; we have no conception of an absolute utility or an absolute standard of utility. The notion of value is meaningless except in relation to alternatives of choice." Frank H. Knight, *Risk, Uncertainty and Profit* (Boston: Houghton Mifflin Company, 1940), p. 63.

7 "Present problems should be worked out with reference to present events. We cannot rule the future. We can only imagine it in terms of the present. And the only way to do that is as thoroughly as possible to know the present." Jerome Frank, *Law and the Modern Mind* (Garden City, N.Y.: Doubleday & Company, Inc., 1963 ed.), p. 167. "Valuation is an essentially 'present' process arising out of the opinions, beliefs and sentiments of the owners of physical capital (including money) operating on the stocks of the various forms of physical capital actually in existence at the moment of valuation." Kenneth E. Boulding, *A Reconstruction of Economics* (New York: John Wiley & Sons, Inc., 1950), p. 194.

nature of the human situation. There are so many facets of being and so many forms of potential uneasiness that precise specification of the components of a state of rest is difficult to imagine. To speak of the pursuit of optimal adaptation is preferred to speaking of goal-seeking, simply because it comprehends the often implicit values one holds, of moral, aesthetic, and similar kinds, as well as the explicit goals of particular actions.

Now, as choice is directed towards a future action, and as there is always some element of uncertainty in respect of the future, and as understanding of the facts and forces of the environment may be incomplete or mistaken, one cannot know with certainty what actions will procure a given end. There always exists the possibility that, however carefully one may choose and act, the consequences of action will differ from the expected consequences. It is therefore convenient, even necessary, to speak of the "probability of optimal adaptation", when discussing the bases of choice.

RATIONALITY

Inasmuch as we are concerned with persons capable of deliberate action all action is deemed to be rational.[8] No person is obliged to go through the lengthy processes of building up his knowledge of facts, relationships, and possibilities before acting. Nor is he required to use all his knowledge in making choices. He may do both. But to do so itself involves sacrifices which he may consider to be greater than the increased knowledge is worth.

In particular, if a man chooses as between two courses of action by tossing a coin he is no less rational than another who chooses on the basis of long deliberation. Tossing a coin or any similar process of choice entails two things; that the actor is saved delay in taking some action, and that his expectations of either course of action in the then state of his knowledge do not warrant the effort of choosing by other means. An actor who proceeds, by diligent inquiry, to choose increases the probability that the action chosen will best serve his ends. This increase and the specific expectations in which it is embodied are his gains from the sacrifice of time and energy required in the process of deliberation.

It is a matter of experience that many actions fail to procure the effects sought. Roads we take lead elsewhere than our intended destination; goods we buy are found to be unsatisfactory; business firms fail. These effects are not intended. It cannot be said, if they eventuate, that the actions which brought them about were not rationally chosen. Subsequently, it may be possible to deduce that the knowledge available at the time of choice was inadequate, or that it was not all used. But to proceed on

[8] "Human action is necessarily always rational." von Mises, *Human Action*, p. 18.

inadequate knowledge or to use less than is available is, itself, a matter of choice. It is the function of knowledge, not to increase the rationality of action but, to increase the effectiveness of choices, to increase the probability of optimal adaptation.[9]

MEANS

Means are scarce goods which are believed to be serviceable in relieving a strain or strains. The belief that a thing is scarce arises only in respect of a conceivable strain. We do not consider ordinarily the air we breathe as a scarce good; we simply accept it as part of the environment. But if, in any situation we expect to find ourselves, the quantity or quality of air is insufficient for bodily functioning without strain, air is, by that very fact, a scarce good. To be in such a situation and to avoid strain requires the provision of air—for example, by ventilation systems and portable supplies of air under pressure. All elements of the environment are of the same nature. Where the supply is ample for all purposes, they are considered simply as environmental conditions. Only when the supply is scarce, in relation to the supply which would be necessary to avoid or to relieve all strains, does an element of the environment become considered as a means. Further, elements of the environment are only conceived as means if there is a strain in the relief of which they may be serviceable. The elements of the environment which are considered as means at any time depend, therefore, on the state of knowledge at that time.[10]

Generally, scarce goods include time, bodily and mental energy, some natural resources, and artifacts which are the combination of time, energy, and natural resources.

The utility of a good subsists in the belief that it will be serviceable in relieving a strain or strains. This belief, in turn, arises from knowledge of the technical properties of goods. It is a technical property of time that the passing of time is irreversible and that it cannot be stored simply by forgoing the present use of it in a purposeful manner. It is a technical property of human energy that it likewise cannot be stored simply by

[9] The term "rationality" is used with widely varying references. Herbert A. Simon, *Administrative Behavior* (New York: The Macmillan Company, 1949), pp. 75–77, gives a number of different types of rationality, by no means exhaustive of the senses in which the term is employed by others, and concludes that it should always be used with an adjectival qualifier. We take rationality as a general quality of human behavior, and regard all failures of actions to attain expected ends as the results of lack of knowledge, unforeseen events, conflicts of ends, and the like, each of which is open to further analysis.

[10] Mead, *Mind, Self and Society,* pp. 125 ff.

forgoing the expenditure of it. It is also a technical property of time and energy that they may be serviceable for a wide variety of strains, for they are undifferentiated as they become available. Clothing and houses keep the body warm, by reason of superior technical qualities. Some clothing and some houses attract to their users greater social esteem than other clothing and houses by reason of their technical properties. In general, all human wants of a material kind may be resolved into requirements of technical properties.

Apart from the more obvious technical properties of specific goods, there are some properties of a general kind which are particularly relevant to choices as between, and actions with respect to, different means. Means vary in *specificity* with respect to ends. Clothes and houses keep the body warm, but they have no technical properties which constitute them as means of relieving hunger or thirst. Means vary in *temporality*, that is to say in the point of time at which, or the period of time over which, they may be expected to yield satisfaction. Means vary in *divisibility*, that is to say in the size of the physical units in which they may be acquired. Means vary in *durability*, that is to say in the physical properties by virtue of which they maintain their form through time. Means vary in *convertibility* to other means, that is in their ability to be changed into other means. Means vary in their *substitutability* for other means. Means vary in *complementarity*, that is to say the extent to which they may be combined for the purpose of producing other means.

VALUATIONS OF MEANS

None of this discussion may be taken to imply that the utility of a means is a matter of technical properties only. Goods are desired because they have certain technical properties; their utility is greater or less because they have or are believed to have greater or less capacity for relieving strain. When we speak of utility being greater or less, we refer to relative utility; we contemplate the means in question relatively to the ends in view. As we may speak of the valuations of ends, so may we speak of the valuations of means with respect to ends. In relation to choice and action we are concerned with relative utilities of means, for which we may also use the terms "valuations" and "values." The valuations of means are derivatives of the values of ends. It is important to note that values are attributed on the basis of belief. A person may desire a thing intensely; it may have a high value for him relatively to other things. But when he acquires it he may find or come to believe that it has much less capacity for yielding satisfaction than he anticipated. There may be no difference whatever in its technical qualities; but there may be a great difference in the degree of satisfaction he expected before acquiring it and the degree of satisfaction he expects at a subsequent time.

Suppose that a person has at his disposal a limited amount of some undifferentiated means such as time and effort and that the environment provides resources which may be adapted to his ends. Suppose he has ends e_1, e_2, e_3, which he values in that order. He will first apply his time and effort to producing means, m_1, specific to e_1. But as each additional unit of m_1 reduces the value of e_1—because the strain associated with e_1 is progressively relieved—the valuation of each additional unit of m_1 declines. There will arise a point at which he prefers to direct his time and effort to m_2; for, as the value of e_1 declines, e_2 rises in value, provided nothing has influenced the scale of values other than the addition of units of m_1. At this point he prefers the addition of a unit of m_2 to the addition of a unit of m_1. The decision to sacrifice or forgo the production of an additional unit of m_1 for an additional unit of m_2 is based on the relative utilities of those units at the time, and at the time the relative utilities depend on the quantities of each then available.

In general, because the state of rest is sought, because there are competing ends, and because means are scarce, any choice involving addition to, or sacrifice of part of, a stock of specific means is based on the valuation of the marginal unit of the stock, the marginal unit being the unit, of whatever size, to be added or sacrificed. And, for any given scale of end values, the valuation of the marginal unit diminishes (increases) as the stock of a given means increases (decreases).[11]

Because the future (future strains and therefore future ends and their values) is unknown, because there are diverse contemporary ends, and because of the diverse specificities of means, persons will where possible hold a heterogeneous stock of means. If one has some means specific to some ends, the delay in relieving some strains is reduced. The greater the range of specific means the greater is the possibility of relieving potential strains

---

11 Economists have adopted various formulations of the criteria of choice. For example, A. Marshall, *Principles of Economics* (London: Macmillan & Co., Ltd., 1916), Bk. III, Ch. III resorted to description in terms of utility, marginal utility, and diminishing marginal utility. More recently the criteria have been formulated in terms of marginal rate of substitution of one good for another, and diminishing marginal rate of substitution. J. R. Hicks, *Value and Capital* (London: Oxford University Press, 1939). As we are not here concerned with a theory of consumers' demand, but only to establish the basis of choice in personal evaluations, these different formulations do not concern us. We use "valuation" and "utility" generally and "value" occasionally, but these terms are to be understood as subjective and temporal, in no sense as absolutes. Value used in this sense is not to be confused with mathematical value, the quantity assigned in a given case to a variable. It will be necessary to avail ourselves of the latter use in the sequel.

as they arise. But there are limits to the accumulation of means of any specific kind.

Because relief is sought from all strains, and because the valuation of the marginal unit of a specific means diminishes as the stock of it increases, a stock of heterogeneous means will tend to be so arranged that the marginal utilities of all specific means in the stock will be equal.[12] At this point no exchange of one means for another, or of one unit of one means for one unit of another or others, will increase or decrease the satisfaction of an actor.

EMPLOYMENTS OF MEANS

The characteristic actions of men in relation to means are production and consumption.

Production is the combination of means in the creation of things (other means) having a greater valuation than the valuation of the collection of means used. The process may involve any combination of time, energy, and material goods; the product may be valued more highly by reason of a change in form, location, or the passing of time, or any combination of these. The creation of means by the combination of other means is a technical process, subject to technical constraints only. For example, technically it may require eight units of a and four units of b to produce five units of c; we may write $8a + 4b = 5c$. But any decision to combine a and b in this way is predicated on the expectation that $5c$ will be more serviceable in terms of ends than the combined serviceability of $8a$ and $4b$. Where $8a$ and $4b$ are specific to $5c$, and have no alternative uses, there will of course be no occasion for choice. And where $(8a + 4b)$ is a perfect substitute for $5c$ in terms of ends, there will be no occasion for combining them in the form of c.

If a and b are not specific to c, other technically possible combinations exist. If $8a + 4b = 4d$, a and b will be combined in this way provided the valuation of $4d$ exceeds the valuation of $5c$. If $7a + 4b = 3e$, a and b will be combined in this way provided the valuation of $(3e + 1a)$ exceeds the valuation of $4d$.

It is the business of technology to discover the optimal, or most efficient, combination of means which will yield a given quantity of product. For if the combination of quantities of nonspecific goods is other than the optimum, some part of the effectiveness of one or more of the complementary means is wasted and is not, therefore, available for other ends. It is the concern of actors to decide whether to combine nonspecific goods

[12] Knight, *Risk, Uncertainty and Profit,* pp. 64–5.

in the manner which is technically optimal or in some other manner.[13] For whereas the optimum combination technically may be given by $8a + 4b = 5c$, it may happen that the valuation of $(8a + 4b)$ is exceeded by the valuation not only of $5c$ but also of $4c$. If this is so, clearly the combination is worthwhile. It follows that the technical service-yielding potential of a good is not the sole characteristic considered in employing it. Technical service-yielding potential explains only why a good is used at all. It does not explain the value of a good, nor choices between goods and between their alternative uses. What is pertinent to action is the relative valuations of the net advantages, of gains over sacrifices, of alternative courses of action. But unless the actor knows the technically optimum combination, he is in no position to arrange his means so that the maximum effect is obtained by their use where means have alternative uses.

The production process may involve the direct creation of goods which are immediately available for the relief of personal strains. Such goods may be called consumers' goods. The process may also involve the creation of goods which are not immediately available for personal use but which are combined in a further process or processes the outcome of which is consumers' goods. Such intermediate goods may be called producers' goods. The sole incentive to employing indirect methods rather than direct methods in the creation of consumers' goods lies in the superior capacity of indirect methods to produce the required quantities and qualities of goods in the form, place, and time in which they are required. The valuation of any producers' good is thus a derivative of the valuation of the consumers' good or goods to the production of which it is applied.

An actor will hold means through time if their possession or use at a later point of time is valued more highly than at any earlier time. The holding of goods is, however, subject to the risk that the ends of the holder may change. The expectation of the serviceableness of a good at a later point of time will, therefore, necessarily include consideration of this risk. Durable producers' goods, although employed in the creation of other goods, are also held through time. The holding of durable producers' goods is subject not only to the risk that ends may change, and that, insofar as they are specific to their products, their utilities may change; they are also subject to the risk that, through increases in knowledge, producers' goods which are technically more efficient may become available.

The end of all production is, as we have observed, consumption. Consumption is the employment of means in the relief of strains. Consumption includes, for any person, alienation by way of gift. The effect of consump-

13 "Economic action is primarily oriented to the problem of choosing the end to which a thing shall be applied; technology, to the problem, given the end, of choosing the appropriate means." Max Weber, *The Theory of Social and Economic Organization* (London: William Hodge & Company Ltd., 1947), p. 149. See also von Mises, *Human Action*, p. 208.

tion is to remove one or some means from the possibility of employment by the consumer in any other direction. The decision to devote means to consumption depends on the ends of the consumer at the time and these are beyond inquiry.

EXPECTATIONS AND ACHIEVEMENTS

It will be recalled that all valuations are subjective and are expectations. Writing V for valuation, if before the event,

$$V(8a + 4b) < V(5c),$$

then

$$V(8a + 4b + G) = V(5c),$$

where G is the expected gain in satisfaction. If nothing occurs during the interval of production to change the relative utilities of a, b, and c, and if the operation is technically optimal, the expectation will be achieved. But ends may change during the interval of production, affecting the valuations of a, b, and c, and their relation with one another. In this case the achieved gain will not equal the expected gain. Depending on the changes in the valuations of a, b, and c, the realized gain may be greater than G, or less than G but positive, or zero, or negative. In the first two cases, we may say a profit has been made, in the last case a loss, it being understood that we are concerned solely with the gain in satisfactions. In particular, if the satisfaction from consumption of a, b, and c were related thus:

$$V(8a + 4b) = V(4c)$$

the expected gain would be the marginal valuation of one unit of c. But if ends had changed, so that after the event the valuation of five units of c were equal to the valuation of four units of c before the event, there would have been no gain.

Our actor may choose whether or not to consume the whole of the product of the combination. If he does consume the whole of it and the realized gain is positive, he will be better off as consumer than if he had not engaged in the combination of means a and b. If he does not consume the whole of it in the interval, he will be better off as a potential consumer in some succeeding interval; he will enter the next interval with a stock.

INCOME, PRODUCTION, CONSUMPTION AND SAVING

A stock of means will only arise if production issues in durable goods (whether producers' or consumers' goods) and if consumption during the interval of production is less than the goods produced. A stock does not include the potential time and effort of the producer; it includes only such time and effort as have become embodied in things independent of persons. The difference between production and consumption is described as saving. For any interval of production, if there is no stock at the beginning the operations of the interval may be written:

$$\text{Production} = \text{Consumption} + \text{Saving} \qquad [\,1\,]$$

The terms relate to goods and services; thus goods produced are either consumed or saved. Whether savings arise by devoting more time and energy to production than is necessary for a desired level of consumption, or by curbing the rate of consumption, is immaterial.

A more general form of the above identity may be written to cover the existence of a stock at the beginning of an interval:

$$\text{Opening Stock} + \text{Production} = \text{Consumption} + \text{Closing Stock} \qquad [\,2\,]$$
$$= \text{Consumption} + \text{Opening Stock}$$
$$+ \text{Saving} \qquad [\,3\,]$$

Saving in the interval is the difference between the closing stock and the opening stock: if the difference is negative it is described as dissaving. Saving may only be reckoned from the point where the opening stock has been maintained.

Now from the beginning of the interval, goods and services in the quantity (consumption + saving), will have become available to the producer; we speak of this as his income during the interval—

$$\text{Income} = \text{Consumption} + \text{Saving} \qquad [\,4\,]$$

and $\qquad \text{Income} = \text{Production} \qquad$ from [1] and [4] above

Again the goods saved have certain forms; we may say the saving has been invested in these forms. Saving is thus equal to new investment in the interval, and we may write

$$\text{Income} = \text{Consumption} + \text{Investment}$$

The relationships between these terms hold both for anticipations and for actual events. Thus, there is a technically necessary quantity of means for any contemplated output of goods; a certain physical output requires a certain physical input. There is discoverable, after the event, the actual physical output and input. Comparison of the anticipatory (*ex ante*) form of the identity [2] and its discovered (*ex post*) form may indicate to an actor whether the planned quantity and the planned degree of technical efficiency were attained, and to plan future actions accordingly. Technical efficiency is an important element in choosing courses of action. However, the prime concern, from which pursuit of technical efficiency stems, is the attainment of satisfactions.

The actions of producing and consuming are clearly related to saving and are explicable, in part, in terms of saving. The incentive to save may be the expectation of the higher prospective satisfaction from future goods by comparison with present goods; it may be to match expected but unforeseeable strains. In this case, savings will take a form suited to consumption. Or the incentive to save may be the higher valuation placed upon the future product of present goods employed as producers' goods, by comparison with the valuation of goods as consumers' goods; that is to say, the expectation of a greater flow of income in the future.

In all such considerations, valuations of goods rather than goods themselves are the criteria of choice. Sacrifices for the purpose of production are sacrifices of things valued; they may be described as costs; their object is the production of things more highly valued, not simply other or more things. They may be discovered, after the event, not to have increased the stock of goods in the amount expected, for many efforts have no product. But, more significantly, they may be discovered not to have increased the potential for giving satisfaction in the amount expected; for, many goods, when produced, are found to have no value or much less value than was expected.

The uncertainty of the outcome of any action, and the consequent possibility that expectations may be disappointed, make the periodical assessment of position and results a necessary part of the adaptive process. One does not wish to pursue fruitless courses of action on the one hand, and one wishes to reconsider actions in the light of changed circumstances (stimuli and possibilities of action) on the other. An assessment of each of a series of consecutive actions and its consequences may be made at the termination of each; the interval between such assessments is then the duration of the action. Assessments of technical efficiency entail comparisons of physical inputs and physical outputs. But assessments of actions in terms of ends entail comparisons of positions, as well as comparisons of inputs and outputs. We have already indicated the necessity of knowing one's position in relation to strains and ends from time to time. No less necessary is the knowing of one's position for relieving strains and attaining ends from time to time, that is to say one's available stock of goods. For only if one knows one's available stock of goods is it possible to value them, singly or in combination, in relation to future ends in view.

The above discussion has contemplated a single actor as producer on his own behalf and consumer. Now valuations are instantaneous judgments; the valuations of each unit of a homogeneous good at a point of time differ; and because the values attached to different ends have different references they are incommensurable. So, also, are the items in a heterogeneous collection of goods. For these reasons the processes of addition required by the expressions of the relationship between production, consumption, income, saving, and investment, and by the discovery of a position at a point of time, are to be understood as notional or conceptual processes only. They could not be carried out except in the very simplest of circumstances. They, nevertheless, provide the foundation for methods of assessment to be developed subsequently.

ABSTRACTION AND THE ELIMINATION OF ALTERNATIVES

To every means and to every actual or potential course of action there is more than one property which may influence an actor's evaluation. The preceding discussion has suggested two such properties: the technical properties of things and their capacities for serving ends. But one's moral, ethical, and aesthetic codes, for example, may influence one's assessment of alternatives, even though they are unrelated to technical usefulness. In general, because the span of attention is limited, every property of a means or a course of action to which a person may attribute a value is considered, with reference to its value scale, independently. The judgments made in respect of each property enable the number of available alternatives to be reduced progressively as they are found to fall short of the optimum. Some alternatives may be eliminated on technical grounds, some on aesthetic grounds, some on the ground that they are beyond present means, some on the ground that their expected long-run consequences are intolerable and so on. Of those remaining, some will be eliminated on the basis of their relative disadvantages, on the same varied grounds, by comparison with others. A chosen course of action emerges from this process of elimination; but, at all points, the evaluations of actions in terms of the actor's ends determine the outcome of the process.

Argument

2.11   *Ends are preferred situations or effects.*

(*1.22, 1.24*)

2.12   A person may have a number of ends at any time.

(*1.21, 1.24*)

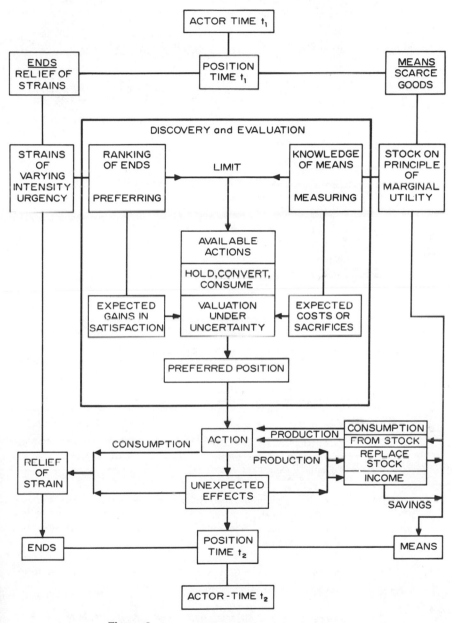

Figure 2
OUTLINE OF CHAPTER 2: ENDS AND MEANS.

2.13   Competing ends are ranked for attention according to the intensity with which they are desired.

(*1.22*, 1.36, 1.37)

2.14   The attainment of any end (in whole or in part) changes the ranking of other ends.

(*1.24*, 2.13)

2.15   Changes in stimuli change the ranking of ends.

(*1.32*, 1.37, 2.13)

2.16   Specific ends and the ranking of specific ends are beyond inquiry.

(*1.64*, *2.11*)

2.21   Every action is rational.

(*1.11*)

2.22   Every action defers other actions; every use of limited means precludes other uses.

(*1.17*, *1.18*, 1.37)

2.23   Every action involves a sacrifice or cost.

(*1.23*, 2.22)

2.24   Every action is specific to an end in view (or to a number of simultaneously attainable ends).

(*1.24*, 2.22)

2.25   Every action is based on a belief that it will procure a specific satisfaction in an expected measure.

(*1.22*, 1.66, 2.24)

2.26   Every action involves choosing.

(1.37, *2.11*, 2.25)

2.27   Valuation is preferring or ranking in order of preference.

2.28   Choice involves valuation; valuations are subjective, comparative, temporal, anticipatory, and beyond inquiry.

(*2.11*, 2.14, 2.15, 2.16, 2.25, *2.27*)

2.29   Satisfactions and sacrifices (the forgoing of other satisfactions) are evaluated in the light of the existing state of strain and the available means.

(1.65, 2.23, 2.25, 2.28)

2.30   That action will be taken which is expected to yield a given satisfaction for the least sacrifice or the greatest satisfaction for a given sacrifice. The situation sought may be described as optimal adaptation.

(*1.22*, 2.29)

2.31   The utility of an object subsists in the belief that it will be serviceable in relieving strains.

(*1.24*, 1.66)

2.32   Means are scarce objects (goods and services) having utility.

2.33   Means being scarce in relation to wants, an actor will prefer to have more rather than less means in general at any time, other things being equal.

(*1.22*, 2.12, *2.32*)

2.34   Means are valued for their utility.

(*2.27, 2.30*)

2.41   Utility arises from technical properties of goods, including the general properties:

(*1.21, 2.32*)

2.42   —*specificity,* or capacity for directly serving particular ends.

2.43   —*convertibility,* or capacity for serving ends indirectly.

2.44   —*divisibility,* or size of the unit good.

2.45   —*temporality,* or capacity for serving ends at different times.

2.46   —*durability,* or capacity for continued physical existence through time.

2.47   —*substitutability,* or capacity for serving ends, as alternatives to other means.

2.48   —*complementarity,* or capacity for serving ends when used in conjunction with other means.

2.49   Any good may be believed to have these properties in varying degrees and combinations.

(*1.41, 2.41*)

2.51   Given ends, the value of each unit added to a homogeneous stock of means diminishes.

(*1.24, 2.14, 2.34, 2.42*)

2.52   Any action involving adding to or sacrificing part of a stock of homogeneous goods is based on valuation of the marginal unit.

(*2.23, 2.51*)

2.53   Where possible a heterogeneous stock of means will be held.

(*1.21, 1.32, 2.12, 2.42*)

2.54   A heterogeneous stock of means will be so arranged that the marginal valuations of all means are equal.

(*2.52, 2.53*)

2.61   *Producers' goods are goods technically useful in production; consumers' goods are goods technically useful to consumers; some goods are both consumers' goods and producers' goods.*

2.62   *Production is the combination of means in the expectation of increasing total utility.*

(*1.24, 2.31, 2.48, 2.61*)

2.621   The end of all production is the creation of consumers' goods.

(*2.62*)

2.63   *Holding is deferring the use or disposal of means in the expectation of greater utility in the future than at present.*

(*1.24, 2.31, 2.45*)

2.64   *Consumption is the appropriating or disposal of means for the relief of immediate strains.*

(*1.24, 2.31, 2.42*)

2.65   Because of the indivisibilities of means, complementary means will tend to be arranged in a technically optimal manner which is a function of existing technology.

(2.30, *2.44*, *2.48*)

2.66   Holding for consumption is subject to the risk of changes in ends; holding for production is subject to the risk of changes in ends of consumers and in technology.

(*1.32*, 1.67, 2.14, 2.15, *2.62*, *2.63*)

2.67   As the object of all production is consumers' goods, the value of any producers' good is a derivative of the value of the consumers' good to which it is devoted.

(*1.24*, 2.34, *2.61*, *2.621*)

2.68   The achieved difference in utilities through production or holding is the gain from the process.

(*2.62*, *2.63*)

2.71   *In any interval, Production = Consumption + Saving*
= Consumption + Investment
= Income

2.72   The consequence of uncertainty is that expected effects of any action may differ from discovered effects.

(*1.32*, 1.67)

2.73   The adaptive process requires periodical assessment of one's present stock; the processes by which a past stock has become present stock; and the relationship between anticipated actions and consequences and attained actions and consequences.

(*1.24*, 1.65, 1.66, 2.72)

2.74   Elimination of alternatives in the process of choice involves separate assessments, serially and abstractly, of all relevant properties.

(1.36, *1.42*, *1.62*, 2.30, 2.73)

The Environment of Action

3

THE NATURAL AND SOCIAL ENVIRONMENT

The environment of action includes natural phenomena and events. Such phenomena and events provide, on the one hand, stimuli and incentives to action. On the other hand they provide materials having technical properties by reason of which they may be valued. Natural events and processes continually change the environment; the natural environment is fluid.

The environment of an actor living in a society includes all other persons. It is a commonplace that all persons differ. In particular, there are individual differences in susceptibility to strains, in knowledge and skill; and, therefore, there are differences in ends and valuations, differences in capacities for reasoning, and differences in capacities for action. These differences increase the problems of choice of any individual; for as the valuations of any individual are beyond inquiry, no single member of the society may know with certainty the manner in which the contemporary actions of his fellow members will interfere with the effects of his own actions. Individual differences thus tend to increase the uncertainty or the unpredictability of the environment for each actor. Because the ends and valuations of members are continually changing, the social environment is fluid.

Though there are differences, there are also similarities. The members of a society have similar creature needs, for food, clothing, shelter, and so on. In some respects, members may seek to express their individuality by demanding variation in the things they consume. In other respects, social living and the economies of producing wanted goods on a large scale tend towards uniformity in the things consumed.

In a society, individual persons may have or acquire ends other than those they might have as isolated individuals. They may value the respect of their fellows; they may value a status superior to that of some of their fellows; they may value the protection of others and the community at large against the possible depredations of more powerful fellows. If any of these ends is desired, the lack of them provides social sources of uneasiness. If it were possible, the social ends of any person are even less open to inquiry than material ends; but we have taken all ends to be beyond inquiry.

In a society, moreover, persons do not seek their ends in isolation only. Differences in aptitudes and knowledge and skills are found by experience to be capable of being employed, in combination, in ways which increase the supply of means. If each person is employed in the task for which his capacities are appropriate, he may be expected to produce more than if he engages in tasks which are beneath or beyond his capacities. The mere effects of learning also give rise to the expectation of an increase in the supply of means from specialization. And there are some tasks which, being beyond the capacity of any person, may only be performed by groups of persons acting in concert. Men cooperate in many ways to promote their ends. Social living is an expression of cooperation. Besides combining to increase the supply of goods, they combine to increase opportunities for enjoyment; they combine to procure better living conditions; they combine to secure mutual protection and the protection of their societies from other societies. The characteristic feature of persons living in societies is interdependence.

The associations they form—business firms, clubs, municipal, state, and national political units, workers' unions, trade associations, political parties —have utilities. They are formed because, and exist as long as, their members believe that they are capable of promoting the ends of individuals in a more effective manner than could the individuals acting each in his own behalf. Their members seek individual satisfactions jointly. Associations, like other means, have no values in themselves; they do not override individual ends.[1] In the case of voluntary associations, individuals join and retain membership only provided that, and as long as, they believe their ends are better served than by individual action or by some alternative association.

All such associations act through persons. Agents of associations may be members or employed servants. Associations as such may have committees and boards which deliberate upon the manner in which ends shall be served. Their decisions may or may not be deemed by the remainder of the membership to serve their ends most effectively. Thus, in any cooperative activity there lies the possibility of conflicts of interest. Beyond the point of deliberation is the discretion of the members or servants who act on behalf of the association. The actions of agents may be prescribed or proscribed by the association, but some discretion must be allowed if the association is to adapt its actions to its environment. The possibility exists that agents may act, at least in part, in the light of their personal values; here, again, is the possibility of conflicts of interest.

The same observations may be made of a society at large. It presents opportunities for cooperation, but there exists the possibility of conflict. Opinions will differ as to what goods shall be produced, as to the manner in which goods jointly produced shall be shared, as to the associations by which social ends shall be served, and as to the powers which shall be accorded to individuals to act on behalf of the society. It is generally recognized that there are both gains and losses from cooperation and conflict. Societies of the kind with which we are familiar seek, therefore, to provide against the losses by restraining what they believe to be oppressive forms of cooperation and harmful forms of conflict.

Cooperation entails the definition of roles, a role being any functional relationship of an individual to other individuals or associations, or the society at large. All members of a society are consumers; some are producers, some are heads of families, some are members of clubs, some of churches, some of business partnerships and companies, some of political parties. Some may voluntarily or contractually undertake tasks for others. Associations also have roles. Any member of a society may fill a number of roles. He may, at any time, be a consumer, a producer, a constituent of a city and a state and a nation, a member of one or more clubs and trade and professional associations, and so on.[2] Roles are defined by law, custom, or agree-

[1] See for example, Krech and Crutchfield, *Theory and Problems of Social Psychology*, pp. 380 ff.

[2] Barnard cites an acquaintance who, by virtue of his "membership" of communities, corporations, clubs, families, and so on, fills some eighteen roles. Chester I. Barnard, *The Functions of the Executive* (Cambridge, Mass.: Harvard University Press, 1947), pp. 71-2.

ment. As every role voluntarily assumed is assumed for the promotion of specific ends, a person will attach to a role the importance or value he attaches to the end it serves. The problems of choice of a person in a society are increased by the fact that he has social ends and by the fact that voluntary membership of associations˙is a matter of evaluating their prospective contributions to his ends. If a person in the process of selecting a course of action finds it necessary to consider abstractly each aspect of the expected sacrifices and results of alternative courses, then also in choosing actions appropriate to any role, where roles compete for attention, he will find it necessary to regard each role separately.[3]

Some conclusions may be stated with respect to expectations. The natural and social environment being fluid, an actor cannot know that any action which was efficacious in the past will be equally efficacious in the future. He can know that certain technical operations, if performed under stated conditions, will yield certain technical results. But he cannot know the future incidence of natural events or the future incidence of the choices of others. The dependability of expectations varies with the predictability of the environment. It is a matter of experience that some elements of the environment which serve as stimuli are fortuitous, some are recurrent, and some are persistent. The expectation that there will be future states of strain is thus highly dependable. But the expectation that there will be any specific strain at any specific time in the future is far less dependable. Further, given knowledge of the present structure or state of the environment, an expectation in respect of any time in the immediate future is more dependable than an expectation in respect of a distant future time.

THE LEGAL FRAMEWORK

Societies are structured in many ways by circumstance or by intention. In particular, the behavior of individual members is regulated by understandings, customs, and laws relating to interpersonal relationships, contracts, and bargains. The legal framework increases the predictability of the environment, but not to the point of certainty.[4] The legal framework sets only general bounds, leaving considerable freedom for persons to act within those bounds. If penalties for infringement are attached to any custom or law, the predictability of behavior is increased. But individual persons may be willing to accept the penalties for infringement: the

[3] Herbert A. Simon, "Theories of Decision-Making in Economics and Behavioral Science," *American Economic Review*, June 1959, Vol. XLIX, No. 3.

[4] There is much less certainty than is widely supposed. See Frank, *Law and the Modern Mind, passim.*

predictability of the behavior of any person is thus ʋɪ a lower order than the predictability of behavior of all persons. Laws, customs, and understandings are themselves responses to given sets of circumstances and given levels of knowledge, and are, therefore, susceptible to change. The greater the stability of the legal framework, the greater is the predictability of the environment. But the timing of changes in the legal framework is not predictable. There are, thus, at all points elements of uncertainty.

The employment of means by any person individually or as agent of an association entails control over those means. The legal framework provides for various forms of control. Because persons may assume many roles, the legal framework provides for control in respect of roles. The means controlled by a person may include means controlled in his own right, and means controlled by virtue of his relationships with others, for example, as agent or trustee. Control may take the form of possession or ownership.

Possession is a matter of fact; but the conditions under which one has possession are matters of law and custom. Freedom to use and dispose of means in possession is determined by the role in which one has possession—for example, as agent, trustee, or owner.

Ownership in means is a matter of law and custom. Ownership is the right under law to have the benefit of unrestricted and exclusive control over the use and disposition of means as against all others. The title or equity or property in such means is said to vest in the role in respect of which the means are owned. An owner may grant possession or user rights to others subject to remedies or reserved rights under the general law or the law relating to specific contracts. Ownership with possession is the most complete form of control. Ownership without possession entails that the owner's rights of use and disposition have been limited by the contract under which possession was granted. By contrast the rights of use and possession obtained by the grantee (possessor without ownership) are only those which have been ceded by the owner.

A person may, in respect of a given role, have generally restricted control of means. He may have acquired the title to means, but subject to the equity of other parties. He may, for example, have acquired title on the understanding that he would at some future time compensate the person or persons from whom the means were acquired. A person may, in respect of a given role, have specifically restricted control. On the one hand he may have possession as an agent, a lessee, or a bailee, in which cases control is specifically limited by the law or contract constituting the role. On the other hand he may have ownership but subject to the rights of others under contract to compensation in the form of repossession of the specific means acquired if he fails to give compensation in the form provided for in the contract.

Both goods themselves and limited rights in goods are means. Laws and customs establish the conditions under which ownership and possession may be transferred between persons. Generally, ownership and possession may be transferred gratuitously or for consideration. Ownership and possession in different degrees are properties which enter into deliberations antecedent to choice.

In a society which is governed in part by laws relating to the title to means, all means are the property of some person or association. There are no means which are unappropriated. Generally the means which have not been appropriated by persons or groups of persons smaller in membership than the whole society are deemed to be the property of the society at large. Exclusive or limited rights may be transferred to persons or private associations of persons by the society as a whole, just as transfers may be made between persons. But the title to means is distinct from means themselves. Means are physical objects and rights; title is a relationship which subsists between means and persons or associations.

SPECIALIZATION AND EXCHANGE

A society tends to arrange its productive processes so that the wants of its members may be satisfied to a greater extent than by the efforts of its members acting in isolation. It does so by the specialization of functions. The greater the expectation of increased product from specialization, the greater will be the differentiation of functions. But, as individuals have diverse wants, it is a condition of differentiation and specialization that each person shall have the possibility of exchanging what he produces for what he wants.[5]

Direct exchange is the interpersonal transfer of the ownership of goods for the ownership of other goods. It is a process by which each person, taking account of the marginal valuations of the goods he holds at any time and of the goods offered in exchange by others, endeavours to arrange that the marginal valuations of his holdings approach equality. The rate at which goods are actually exchanged is the ratio of exchange. An exchange occurs when both parties expect to gain in total satisfaction from the sacrifice of what they offer for what they receive. The sacrifice of the satisfaction which is expected to be obtained from the possession or use of the goods given is the cost of the goods received; the satisfaction expected to be obtained from the possession or use of the goods received may be styled the proceeds. As valuations are personal judgments, it cannot be said that the cost to one party is equivalent to the proceeds of the other; for

---

[5] For a general treatment of transactions as exchanges of power, see Alfred Kuhn, *The Study of Society, A Unified Approach* (Homewood, Ill.: Richard D. Irwin, Inc. and The Dorsey Press, Inc., 1963), Part V.

two different personal scales of evaluation are involved. And as both parties have different ends and different values, the ratio of exchange is a function of their preferences and stocks at the time of the exchange; as these change so will the ratio of exchange alter.

If the only method of exchange were direct exchange of goods for goods, every act of exchange would be unique. The personal exigencies of offerors and bidders, and their ignorance of the offers and bids of others, would limit the efficacy of exchange. Every bargain would be preceded by assessments of the values of the good offered and of the good to be acquired in exchange, in the temporal context of the contemplated transaction. Comparisons of this kind would be difficult to make, in view of the range of goods people ordinarily require for consumption, and calculations embracing stocks of varied goods and future capacities for giving satisfaction would be impossible. And as direct exchange depends on the willingness of the parties to exchange goods in the units in which they become available or in multiples of those units, the society would not benefit from the technical advantages of goods which are large in size or durable in character. These difficulties are obviated by the use of a generally accepted medium of exchange.

It is a necessary property of a medium of exchange that, like other means, it shall be scarce; for if it were not scarce no person would exchange other scarce goods against it. It is necessary that it shall be generally acceptable, or convertible into other means, in exchange; otherwise it would not be worth taking in exchange for goods having direct utility. It is necessary that it be available in small units; otherwise it could not serve as a means of facilitating exchanges of other means which have diverse quantitative ratios of exchange. It is necessary that it be durable; otherwise it could not be held and accumulated for the acquisition of goods having high ratios of exchange, or of goods at a time remote from the acquisition of media of exchange.

Media of exchange are means, in terms of the definition of means, having the above properties. In some circumstances, media of exchange are goods having utilities other than simply as media of exchange; we shall not be concerned with such media. Money is the most commonly used, and basic, medium of exchange. We shall be concerned with money only as a medium of exchange. In a monetary economy there is a specific unit of money or currency having legal status as a medium of exchange. The utility of money is a derived utility. Money is not desired for itself; it is desired because it is easily convertible into other means, and, in particular, into means having direct utility.

Exchange through the mediation of money is indirect exchange. For direct exchange is substituted two transactions, an exchange of goods for money, and an exchange of money for goods; and by reason of the durability of money the two need not be and seldom are simultaneous. In a monetary economy ratios of exchange do not express the rate at which goods are exchanged for goods. They express the rate at which goods are exchanged for money units. They are money prices.

In a monetary economy almost all exchanges are indirect; and even in those cases where direct exchanges occur, the ratios of exchange are expressed in terms of money prices or are based on calculations involving money prices. Buyers and sellers do not, therefore, have to compare the direct utilities of different goods. As money is an undifferentiated (non-specific) means, all prospective purchases or sales of goods and services may be referred to the common money scale. The sellers of labor-service and the final buyers of consumers' goods, it is true, have as one referent the disutility of labor and the direct utility of goods; but even in their cases the choices are simplified; they have simply to choose whether in their circumstances an addition to or a sacrifice of nonspecific means is warranted at the prevailing price.

The interposition of money in exchange makes possible a useful differentiation between the consumer-roles and the producer-roles of persons. A given person, as consumer, may be generous and self-indulgent to a fault; while, as producer (employee or manager) he may be shrewd and crafty to the point of rapacity. The goals of consumption and production are different in kind, and entirely different modes of behavior may be observed as a man's calculations shift from one role to the other. One counts the cost far less carefully in the case of consumption, because the direct satisfactions from consumption are personal, incommensurable and, therefore, not comparable with the money prices paid. But insofar as those who organize the processes of production expect a price for their services, it consists of the difference between the prices of goods and services acquired and goods and services sold. All such prices are expressed in the same terms; they may be related and compared with some nicety; and the magnitude of the difference between the prices of inputs and outputs represents the sum available to the organizers for consumption purposes. Entities engaged in trading, manufacturing, and ancillary operations may thus be deemed to have no consumer role. The criterion of choice of their managers is simply whether or not a given complex of actions will yield a larger or smaller increment in money than another complex of actions. Consequently, all goods and services acquired by such entities have for those entities only derived utility, measurable in terms of the common measure of derived utility, the scale of money prices.

No matter how roundabout or complex the production process may be, its object is the ultimate production of goods having direct utilities. But the evaluations of utilities by individual consumers do not determine the prices of such goods. They only provide the reason why such goods are demanded, and hence the reason why intermediate producers' goods and other factors of production are demanded.

MARKETS AND PRICES

Exchanges take place in markets. We speak of the wool market, the stock market, the money market, and other markets specializing in the exchange of limited ranges of means. In each of these cases there is a distinguishable set of institutions and operations by which sellers make offerings and buyers make bids. An important element of such organized markets is the information they make available—to buyers, as to the range of goods and qualities offered; to sellers and producers, as to the range of goods and qualities for which there are differing demands. Buyers are better informed than if there were no ready means of comparing goods offered; and sellers are able to take advantage of the demands of buyers for different qualities of the goods offered. These specific markets are, however, part of the whole system of markets of a community. A market is simply a set of arrangements by which exchanges are facilitated. It need have neither specific location nor distinctive form. In a community characterized by specialization of functions and interdependence of buyers and sellers, of producers and consumers, all markets are interrelated. Money paid for goods and services in one market is available to the recipients for the purchase of goods and services of other kinds. Purchases in one market reduce the money available to be spent in other markets.

Prices are established in markets. They may be established by the haggling and bargaining of buyers and sellers; or by sellers making general offers at prices which they expect the market will pay, and modifying their offering prices as stocks move more or less readily; or by regulation by governmental or other authorities. In all cases prices serve to ration available supplies among buyers and to direct the activities of producers. The price of any good at a given time depends on the interaction of the conditions of supply and demand, actual and anticipated, for the good itself and for substitute goods. Indeed, as all markets are interrelated, all prices in those markets are directly or indirectly related. For our purposes it is not necessary to consider in detail the conditions of supply (for example, the relative prices of factors of production, the state of technology) and of demand (for example, the relative prices of substitutes, the state of knowledge) and the determinants of changes in them. But the operation of the price mechanism may be briefly illustrated.[6]

[6] For extended treatments see, for example, George J. Stigler, *The Theory of Price* (New York: The Macmillan Company, 1946); Richard H. Leftwich, *The Price System and Resource Allocation* (New York: Rinehart & Company, Inc., 1958).

Other things being equal, if the aggregate demand for any means exceeds the aggregate supply, the price of that means will tend to rise. The rise will ration the supply available to those able to buy at the higher price. The production of the means in question will appear to producers to promise a higher income than before; they will tend to increase production (new producers may enter the market), and to bid higher prices for the goods and services they require once all factors of production are employed. If at the new level of production the aggregate demand falls short of the aggregate supply, prices will tend to fall, production will tend to be reduced, and the prices of factors of production will tend to fall or the surplus factors will be bid way by other industries. Relative changes in prices are the initiators of changes in the behavior of producers and consumers, of sellers and buyers.

Prices and changes in prices are the resultants of mass causes; for any single buyer or seller they are given as part of his environment, and he must adapt himself to them. Whereas the valuations arising from direct utilities are intensive and subjective, value in exchange is extensive and objective. Value in exchange, or price, is independent of the (subjective) judgment of the owner or possessor for the time being of any means. The value in exchange of a good is derived from the interactions of the judgments of all buyers and sellers of it, with respect to the utilities of marginal quantities in all employments. Except for means appropriated for consumption, no stock of means may be considered to be irrevocably committed to any purpose. Relative changes in prices and the expectations of such changes may make it preferable to abandon one course of action in favor of another at any time.

But to regard the market simply as a device by which actual exchanges are effected and the available goods and services are rationed would be to understate its functions. There may indeed be many offers and bids in the market which do not culminate in exchanges of goods or services. An important function of the market is to provide information to all operators in it.[7] In any short interval, the actual quantities available and demanded in the market and the offer and bid prices will have mutual effects on one another. But all the information on quantities and prices will be signals to those who expect to operate in the market beyond that interval. When we speak, as in preceding paragraphs, of prices or production tending to rise or fall, we do not refer to an impersonal mechanism; we refer to the actions taken by operators in the market in response to the information given by

7 L. M. Lachmann, *Capital and Its Structure* (London: G. Bell & Sons Ltd., 1956), pp. 21 ff., 61 ff. G. B. Richardson, *Information and Investment* (London: Oxford University Press, 1960), p. 30. Richardson is critical of classical theory on the ground of its disregard of the availability of market information.

the market. The response is not an automatic one. It proceeds from the expectations of operators, based in part on the information available. If and insofar as those expectations are proved to have been in error by the market in subsequent intervals, the signals of the market will produce cancelling or corrective responses in operators.

The market with its price mechanism may therefore be regarded as a homeostatic device, restoring to consistency with market conditions any distribution of productive resources which has diverged from consistency through error or mistaken expectations.[8] It maintains the viability of the system of specialization and differentiation of economic functions. But unlike organic homeostatic systems, it depends on the stimuli and responses of a collection of self-interested individuals who by one means or another may interfere with its working.[9] A society which depends on such systems will seek to moderate these interferences by statutory publicity, legislation, and regulatory devices (for example, restrictive trade practices legislation, rate-fixing tribunals, and so on).

MONEY

The primary form of money is cash or currency, the legally prescribed medium, or legal tender for the satisfaction of obligations and the settlement of bargains in a given community. It also includes bank deposits. The basic unit of a currency has a prescribed denomination; we may speak of it generally as the monetary unit. The general use of the monetary unit for the expression of prices, and in the case of deferred settlement for the expression of obligations, establishes the monetary unit as the unit of account, the unit in which economic calculations are made and in terms of which records of means, obligations, and transactions are kept. Under conditions of interdependence and indirect exchange, we may, therefore, redefine costs as the sacrifice of the command of monetary units entailed by any operation, and proceeds as the gain in the command of

8 Cannon, dealing with social homeostasis, proposed, as analogous to the "fluid matrix" which is an essential feature of bodily homeostasis, the systems of distribution, money and credit which are the common elements of advanced societies. Cannon, *The Wisdom of the Body,* Epilogue. Information is a no less significant element inasmuch as it is the initiating element in adaptive processes.

9 Norbert Wiener, observes that "In connection with the effective amount of communal information one of the most surprising facts about the body politic is its extreme lack of efficient homeostatic processes." Norbert Wiener, *Cybernetics* (New York: The M.I.T. Press and John Wiley & Sons, Inc., Second ed., 1961), p. 158. It is doubted that the lack is extreme in respect of economic operations, unless economic operations are narrowly defined to exclude social controls over economic processes. See Ch. 11.

monetary units. For any exchange, then, the costs of one party are equivalent to the proceeds of the other for both are expressed in the same number of units of a common scale.

The use of the monetary unit as a unit of account is a derived use, derived from the fact that money is a medium of exchange.[10] The usefulness of money as a medium of exchange is the only reason why men reckon in terms of monetary units. If it could not be expected that a money would continue in the future to be a generally accepted medium of exchange, reckoning in terms of monetary units would be pointless.

Like other means, money (and hence the monetary unit) has both a technical definition and a distinct economic significance. From the viewpoint of the market, a given sum of money has the same significance no matter who tenders it or who receives it. Its significance subsists in the fact that it can be offered in exchange for any collection of goods desired by any holder up to the amount he holds; it represents command over marketed goods and services generally, or general purchasing power.

Like other means, money as such is demanded. Men seek to have stocks of money adequate to meet their daily demands for goods, as a precaution against unforeseen events, including the possibility of taking advantage of relative changes in prices of the kinds of goods they want.[11] Holdings of the latter kind reduce the amount of money in circulation, that is the supply of money for transaction purposes. If, on the other hand, precautionary holdings are deposited in banks, the latter, taking advantage of the distribution through time of the withdrawals of depositors, are able to make advances to others, increasing the supply of money for transaction purposes. It is customary to speak of the price of goods being such and such a sum of money. It is equally possible to speak of the price of money as such and such a quantity of goods. As the demand for and the supply of money may vary in the manner suggested above, money does not have a fixed ratio of exchange through time with respect to other goods; the ratio of exchange will depend on the relative demands for money and goods.

The demand for money as such is not to be confused with the demand for wealth. Wealth may be considered to be the general capacity for satisfaction represented by the things owned by a person; so regarded, wealth is a subjective notion related to individual appraisals of utility. The significant concept and measure of wealth in a market economy is the monetary equivalent, or the sum of the market prices if sold, of all severable things owned. In this sense wealth does not include the skills or

10 "Money is the thing which serves as the generally accepted and commonly used medium of exchange. This is its only function." von Mises, *Human Action*, p. 398.

11 On the incentives to hold money and liquidity preference, see John Maynard Keynes, *The General Theory of Employment, Interest and Money* (London: Macmillan & Co., Ltd., 1942), Chaps. 13 and 15.

potentialities embodied in persons; for at any point of time these have not been delivered, and may never be delivered. Nor does it include things which a person has no intention, for sentimental or other reasons, of committing to the market. In a subjective sense, a person may consider himself to be well-off by virtue of such things; but in relation to the market and to his capacity for acting in the market, they have no significance. The demand for wealth, in the sense of money and vendible goods generally, diminishes at a much slower rate than the demand for specific goods; because one may always envisage unsatisfied wants, the rate of diminution may be regarded as almost infinitesimal. But the demand for money as such, for money holdings, is limited because money yields no direct satisfactions.

Whereas a rise in the price of goods tends to promote an increase in the supply, in the interest of some stability and predictability of the outcome of bargains at money prices, a rise in the purchasing power of money is not permitted automatically to increase the supply of money. The quantity of money is regulated by monetary authorities to serve the general ends of monetary policy; unlike the quantity of goods, the quantity of money is not increased by the diversion of factors from other employments in response to relative price movements.

Such regulation does not secure the perfect stability of the purchasing power of money, for exchanges and precautionary holdings are in a constant process of flux. In general, other things being equal, if the aggregate demand for money exceeds (falls short of) the aggregate supply, the price of money in terms of other means will tend to rise (fall). In other words, the purchasing power of money will tend to rise (fall), its counterpart being a fall (rise) in the general level of money prices.

Prices of non-monetary means are therefore subject to relative shifts, due to changes in the relationship between supply and demand, and to general shifts, due to changes in the purchasing power of money. Only under perfectly invariant conditions would the price of any means remain the same through time.

CREDIT

The satisfaction of both parties to an exchange may be simultaneous, as when money is transferred by one and goods are transferred by the other at the same time. The satisfaction of one party may also be deferred, as when one party transfers goods in consideration of an undertaking on the part of the transferee to perform his part of the bargain at some other time. Performance of any such undertaking is assured by legal rights of recovery and damages. But legal rights of recovery are limited by the extent of the unrestricted means of the transferee. Thus notwithstanding that a transferor acquires a claim against a transferee immediately on transfer, the claim is subject to risk of default. The risk is reduced by legal penalties against the transferee beyond the means under his control (for example, by restriction of the freedom of bankrupts) and by customary or legal provisions for inspection by transferors of the affairs of transferees. All transfers in advance of settlement by transferees are based on trust; credit is given by the transferor (or creditor) and received by the transferee (or debtor).

Credit extends also to the control of money. A person may place at the disposal of another a specific sum of money subject to agreement that at a future date or dates the sum advanced or some other agreed sum shall be repaid. The lender forgoes the immediate possession and use of money for a claim to money in the future for a price, designated interest, and stated as a certain percentage of the sum advanced per unit of time for which it is advanced. The amount of interest may by contract be embodied in provisions by which the sum advanced is exceeded by the lump sum payable on maturity; or in provisions by which the sum advanced is repaid on maturity and interest is paid periodically during the term of the advance; or by variants of these provisions. In general, any exchange which contemplates deferment of cash settlement includes an interest element, whether or not it is distinguished in stating the price.

Rates of interest are market prices. They are determined at any time by the relationship between the supply of and the demand for the use of money through time. Like other market prices they are also the means by which changes in the supply of and demand for money are effected from time to time. Different degrees of risk may be assigned by lenders to advances made to particular borrowers; and, in particular, the risk of long-term loans is generally deemed to be greater than the risk of short-term loans, due to the greater uncertainty of distant future events. Different rates of interest may, therefore, be found simultaneously, and in making calculations an actor will choose the rate of interest appropriate to the risk undertaken or to be undertaken. The pure rate of interest, for the use of money without special risk, may vary from time to time. By virtue of its relationship to the supply of money the rate of interest may be regulated by action of the monetary authorities.

VOLUNTARY AND INVOLUNTARY CHANGES IN A STOCK

Changes in the composition of a stock may be effected in several ways.

The first is by an interpersonal transaction or exchange at a money price. An actual price, as we have shown, says nothing very precise about personal evaluations or utilities of goods. An actual price merely expresses the fact that one party is or was willing to forgo the title to units of money, and the other was willing to forgo the title to goods, at the stated price. An actual price does not imply that it is the minimum which the vendor would accept, or the maximum which the buyer would be prepared to pay. If the vendor did not value so much money more highly than so many goods, he would not engage in the transaction; for the opposite reason neither would the buyer.[12]

The second way in which a change in the composition of a stock may be effected is by conversion in the process of production. A decision to acquire for the purpose of conversion is distinct and separate from a decision to convert. Two such decisions, being separate in time, are made in different contexts and are, therefore, independent. A decision to acquire means for subsequent conversion is predicated upon the expectation that the price paid (the cost) will be exceeded by the price obtained from the sale of the product. A decision to convert does not necessarily entail this expectation; for the price paid is by then a matter of history. A decision to convert is predicated upon the expectation that the product of conversion will yield a greater price than the means to be converted would yield if sold. In the case of durable producers' goods the product may issue over an extended period; the expected proceeds from the sale of the expected product must then be discounted for comparison with the price of the durable good if sold. As, during this extended period, relative prices may change, resale of the durable good may become preferable to continued conversion.

In both the above cases the change in a stock is a consequence of the actor's decisions. But there is a class of event which influences an actor's stock independently of decisions. These events are the actions of other persons or groups in respect of which the actor has no choice. The simplest example is an unconditional gift. A person may refuse a gift, but refusal is unlikely if the gift is entirely gratuitous. More common and more important examples are changes in the economic and technological environments which fall on the means of an actor, for good or ill. Changes in relative prices we have shown to be of this character; new inventions may render

---

[12] The tendency to use "valuation" and "measurement" interchangeably and the possibility of confusion therefrom have been mentioned. There is a tendency also to confuse "value" and "price." The tendency is strengthened by proposals for the measurement of utility and of value. Thus, supporting such a proposal, "If a surefire, expediting act exists, its cost is the value of the desired event." C. West Churchman, *Prediction and Optimal Decision* (Englewood Cliffs, N.J.: Prentice-Hall, Inc., 1961), p. 250. The additivity of values is possible if this is so, but if cost is value there is no explanation of why an event should be desired. The distinction between values (which are subjective) and prices (which are objective) is central to our argument.

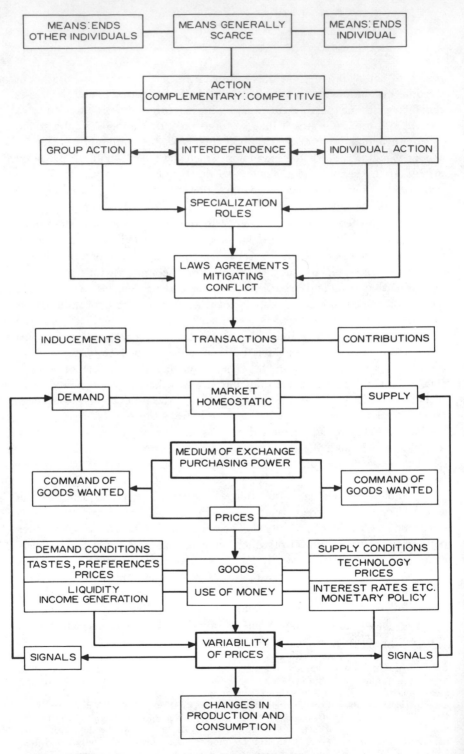

Figure 3
OUTLINE OF CHAPTER 3: THE ENVIRONMENT OF ACTION.

obsolete some of the means of an actor, so that although they are technically as useful as before their resale prices and the prices of their products may fall to the point where their use is abandoned. Such changes do not affect the physical composition of a stock; they do change the expectations of the holder and his capacity to engage in future exchanges. Knowledge of their effects is, therefore, necessary in the pursuit of optimal adaptation in the changed environment.

Argument

3.11   *The natural environment is fluid and, in part, unpredictable.*

3.12   *In respect of all properties (capacities, ends, valuations, and so on) attributed to persons, individuals differ.*

3.13   *Individuals in societies acquire social ends and are subject to strains on this account.*

3.14   The social environment is fluid and, in part, unpredictable.
(2.28, *3.12, 3.13*)

3.15   The demand for consumers' goods of all members of a society exhibits both similarities in kind and diversities in form.
(*1.21, 3.13*)

3.21   *Cooperation is the joint pursuit of individual ends, by individual actions of the same kind or by specialization (differentiation of functions).*

3.22   *An association is any combination, ephemeral or enduring, of persons pursuing their individual ends jointly.*

3.23   The incentive to cooperation is the expectation of attaining individual ends which are unattainable, or attainable only in an inferior measure, by individual action.
(2.30, *3.12, 3.21*)

3.24   Individuals will cooperate in voluntary associations only as long as they expect their share in the product and their status in such associations to be satisfactory in relation to the costs of membership and by comparison with alternatives.
(2.30, *3.13, 3.22*)

3.25   The greater the diversity of ends and the greater the differentiation of functions, the greater is the possibility of conflict.
(*3.12, 3.13*, 3.24)

3.26   *The characteristic relationship between individual members of a society is interdependence.*

3.31   *Cooperation entails the definition of roles, a role being any functional relationship with other individuals or associations.*

3.32   *Roles are defined by law, custom, or agreement.*

3.33   Individuals and associations may have many roles simultaneously.

(2.12, *3.22, 3.31*)

3.34   When roles compete for attention, the sacrifices and satisfactions relevant to each will be considered serially.

(1.36, 2.22, 2.74, 3.24)

3.41   *Laws, customs, and agreements define the rights of individuals and associations to the control and disposal of means, in respect of roles.*

3.42   The possibility of conflict in the case of joint production and investment is mitigated by the existence of such laws, customs, and agreements.

(3.25, *3.41*)

3.43   The dependability of expectations, and, hence, the probability of optimal adaptation, increases with the predictability of the environment.

(*2.30, 2.62, 2.63, 3.11*, 3.14, 3.23, 3.42)

3.51   Specialization in production is reconciled with individual wants by exchanges of means.

(*2.30, 2.62, 3.21, 3.26*)

3.52   *The rate at which means are exchanged for one another is their ratio of exchange.*

3.53   Ratios of exchange vary as preferences vary.

(2.30, 2.52, *3.52*)

3.61   *A medium of exchange is a means which is freely acceptable in exchange for other means. Money is a medium of exchange. Exchanges mediated by money are indirect exchanges.*

3.62   The exchange of means which differ in quantity, quality, and time or place of delivery is promoted by the use of a medium of exchange.

(*2.41*, 3.51, *3.61*)

3.63   Money prices are ratios of exchange expressing rates at which means are exchanged for money units.

(*3.52, 3.61*)

3.64   *The market is the process by which exchanges are effected, prices are generated and information on supplies, demands and prices is communicated between actual and potential buyers and sellers.*

3.65   Prices at a point of time are determined by the relationship between aggregate supply and aggregate demand, for goods and for money holdings.

(3.62, 3.63, *3.64*)

3.66   Prices paid or received are measures of sacrifices of or accretions to money holdings (command over goods and services in general).

(3.61, 3.63)

3.71 Production by roundabout methods and in anticipation of sale are possible by virtue of uniformities in demand, legal and customary rights, and the durability of money, money claims, and other means.

(2.46, 2.62, 3.15, 3.41, 3.61)

3.72 *The cost of any good acquired is the sacrifice of the satisfaction obtainable at the time from the good given in exchange. The cost of any good used is the sacrifice of the satisfaction obtainable at the time from its best alternative use.*

3.73 Costs may be generalized in terms of current market prices.

(3.00, 3.72)

3.74 The role of producer is assumed in the expectation that the money proceeds of sale will exceed costs of factors used by the greatest margin.

(2.30, 3.66, 3.73)

3.75 The achieved difference (profit) between proceeds and costs is the price of enterprise and risk-taking.

(2.72, 3.11, 3.14, 3.74)

3.76 Changes in relative prices of goods and services give rise to shifts in the use of resources, in the composition of production, and in the composition of demand.

(3.53, 3.63, 3.65, 3.74)

3.81 Command over goods and services generally limits capacity for obtaining future satisfactions through exchanges.

(2.30, 3.51, 3.61)

3.82 Command over goods and services generally is represented by the monetary equivalent, the market price if sold, of all severable means in an actor's possession at a point of time.

(3.63, 3.65, 3.66)

3.83 The purchasing power of money, the ratio of exchange of money for goods and services in general, varies from time to time.

(3.53, 3.63, 3.65)

3.91 The legal status of money and contracts makes possible the use of credit.

(3.41, 3.61)

3.92 *The price paid for the use of money through time is the rate of interest.*

3.93 The rate of interest varies from time to time.

(3.53, 3.92)

3.94 The use of money as a medium of exchange makes the monetary unit an appropriate unit of calculation in respect of all actual and prospective operations in markets.

(2.30, 3.61, 3.66, 3.91)

Monetary Calculation

4 NECESSITY OF MONETARY CALCULATION

The very nature of a monetary economy makes monetary calculation a process of perennial interest and use to all who buy and sell goods and services. Monetary calculation is not an artificial process; nor is it a subsidiary or inferior process to other forms of representation and calculation which concern themselves with physical or tangible properties of goods and services. The physical or tangible properties, sometimes described as "real" properties, are not the substance of which money prices are the shadow. Certainly goods and services are only bought and sold because they possess physical or tangible properties which are believed to be capable of serving ends. But, as we have shown, specialization and exchange through markets at money prices, break the link between direct utilities and prices, and prices are determined not by direct utilities but by the interaction of supply and demand. Any buyer or seller will concern himself with the technical properties of goods, with spatial dimensions, horsepowers, numbers of units. For all such properties, there are appropriate systems of calculation or ways of exercising judgment; but monetary calculation is not one of them. On the other hand, whatever technical calculations or judgments have been made, there remain the questions of when and whether to buy or sell. These questions may only be resolved by reference to money prices and one's control over or demand for money. Monetary calculation is, thus, a form of calculation standing in its own right as the only way of informing actions involving indirect exchange.[1] Monetary representations and monetary calculations, as they refer to one property only of goods and services, are abstractions; but they are abstractions which have a direct bearing on and relevance to operations in markets.

The emphasis on the importance of monetary calculation may predispose some to believe that purely material objectives are, thereby, raised to a status superior to other objectives; and this they may assert to be a distortion of the goals men seek. However, the use of monetary calculation involves no assumptions whatever as to the values men hold. Money units are a device only; they are counters in the same way as are numbers. Their use does not imply materialistic aims or a materialistic viewpoint.[2] One may calculate in money and at the same time value honesty, fairness, morality, and philanthropy. Among the associations men form are institutions which have cultural, aesthetic, charitable, and similar functions, none of which is materialistic. But, insofar as these institutions operate in markets, monetary calculation facilitates the selection of optimal courses of action in the same way as it facilitates the selection of courses of action in the case of purely commercial ventures. Monetary calculation does not concern itself with specific personal values or ends. On the other hand, in a market economy, no person can begin to select ends for attainment without knowledge of his ability, in terms of capacity to operate in the market, to achieve any given end.

[1] Compare: "Accounting in terms of money, and not its actual use is . . . the specific means of rational, economic provision." Weber, *The Theory of Social and Economic Organization*, p. 171. "Monetary calculation is the guiding star of action under the social system of division of labour." von Mises, *Human Action*, p. 230.

[2] Talcott Parsons suggests that the existence of noneconomic motives is not incompatible with economic reasoning; that self-interest may be interpreted very broadly; and that, in any case, the institutional patterns of industrial societies tend to make monetary or financial returns dominant tests, even of social behaviors which have only a partial economic orientation. Talcott Parsons, "Motivation of Economic Activities," *Essays in Sociological Theory*, rev. ed. (New York: Free Press of Glencoe, Inc., 1949). " . . . money is perhaps the strongest generalized secondary reinforcer [of responses] which is obviously not inborn." Kuhn, *The Study of Society*, p. 85.

RETROSPECTIVE, CONTEMPORARY AND
ANTICIPATORY CALCULATION

All actions are actions at points of time. An actor takes action in the light of his past experiences, his present constraints, and his expectations of the future. He may thus make calculations about past conditions and events, about present conditions, and about future conditions and events. The object of all such calculations is to provide beliefs on which a future course of action may be based. No calculation may have any bearing on past events. The past is past. It is a matter of fact. The facts of the past have a bearing on acts of the future (a) insofar as they have resulted in the present position, which is the position from which all future action is taken; and (b) insofar as they may be arranged or rearranged in the process of calculation and may thus supply the basis for inferences which are expected to be useful in forming expectations.

All calculations in monetary units are calculations in terms of prices, as they were in the past, as they are at present, or as they are expected to be in the future. As prices are subject to continual change under the influence of the supply of and the demand for all goods and money, no specific price is necessarily relevant to any time and place other than the time and place at which it is established. Furthermore the money unit, unlike a physical unit, is not invariant. It is always a unit having a significance at a defined time and place.

At any time and place, statements about monetary units and statements assigning monetary units to objects and events, are comprehensible to all persons at that time and place. They know the unit of currency and they are able to establish, by reference to contemporary prices, what any quantity of those units will purchase. But if, at any time, one is to make calculations of a kind requiring addition or relation of prices prevailing at different past points of time, the units employed will necessarily be converted to units of contemporary significance—necessarily, because the contemporary significance of the unit is the only significance relevant to action in the immediate future, and because calculations in terms of mixed units yield no useful information about past, present, or future.

Calculations are always made by or for a person or association acting in a specific role. As we have shown, the law defines rights, powers and obligations of persons in respect of a specific role; and to avoid confusing means and ends in respect of different roles an actor with many roles will reckon for each independently. For a person or association acting in a specific role we will use the general term entity. It will be necessary when dealing with particular entities or classes of entity to stipulate the rights, powers, and obligations which attach to it; but it is not necessary at this point.

Contemporary Calculation

Calculations about present conditions are essentially calculations about the immediate past. The present is for all calculations the nearest past slice of time, for observation and preparation for calculating take some time, however short. A present condition or complex of conditions is always ascertainable, even though it may not be ascertained at every point of time.

Of all contemporary conditions, the condition which bears most directly on the choices of an actor is his present position in relation to his environment. A person has only one position in relation to his environment at a point of time. This position is the determinant and predictor of future positions, as it is also the resultant of past positions. To know this position is not a sufficient condition of success in choosing or acting; but it is a necessary condition. This one position may require to be represented by a large number of relationships, one for each property for which there is a connection with the environment. But given these relationships, the actor's position is uniquely determined.

When dealing with an individual in isolation, it was stipulated that at a given moment of choice he will require to know his present stock of means. But we have shown that an individual in a market society adapts himself to prevailing circumstances through indirect exchanges. He will, therefore, require to know his stock of severable means expressed in terms of the unit medium of exchange.

As the possession of money and of other things convertible to money is a relationship with the environment, there is one position, in terms of money, in which an entity stands in relation to the environment at a point of time. We will call this its financial position. Financial position may be defined as the capacity of an entity at a point of time for engaging in exchanges. There is, then, an unequivocal financial position of an entity at a point of time. Either a person has or has not so much money; either he has or has not so many other goods or rights, each of which has a present market price, positive, zero, or negative; either he has or has not so many obligations to others designated by such and such sums of money; either he has or has not ownership in the goods and rights which he controls. Whether he has or has not such things is determinable by the legal title in rights and goods, for no two independent persons can have at the same time equal title in the same rights and goods. Whether or not a person knows his financial position at any time will influence the alternative actions he believes to be open to him. But whether or not he chooses to discover his financial position, that position is determinable.

An actor having no recollection of the manner in which his present position has resulted from past events, but knowing only what financial position means, can by direct observation at any time determine his position. A person having only money in his pocket can ascertain his present position simply by counting it. If he has other vendible goods he can discover their quantities and their present prices or monetary equivalents. No amount of reckoning about how he came to have so much will improve his knowledge of his position; and any reckoning which purports to tell him that he has a different quantity or that the monetary equivalent of what he has differs from the monetary equivalent ascertainable directly at the time will be false. The requirement of correspondence, the fluidity of the environment, and the variability of prices necessitate frequent reassessments of financial position by reference to the economic environment.

Retrospective Calculation

When dealing with an individual in isolation it was stipulated that adaptation requires periodical assessment of the processes by which a past stock has become a present stock and of the relationship between past actions and their consequences. For an entity acting in a monetary economy the analogous requirement is periodical assessments of past financial positions and of the transactions and events by which, between consecutive determinations, a financial position has been changed.

All past quantities and prices are ascertainable. Calculations about past financial positions and the transactions and events intervening can, therefore, be made with reasonable certainty. The calculations of an entity relating to its position at a point of time and to transactions to which the entity was a party can be made with greater certainty than calculations embodying inferences from events of which the entity was only a passive subject.

But certainty is relative. It may be discovered, after a past transaction, that through ignorance of the market an entity paid more than or received less than the generally prevailing price at the time of the transaction. Notwithstanding this, the quantity of money paid or received (or to be paid or received) at the time of the transaction is fixed. Nothing subsequently can change the amount of the bargain; that amount fixes the effect of the transaction on that part of the financial position which represents holdings of money or money claims and debts. But even though the original money amount of the bargain is fixed forever, the representation of the "goods" side of the exchange has not the same character. The price paid for any producers' good, if greater than the generally prevailing price, puts the buyer at a disadvantage in comparison with his competitors. Under the pressure of competition and demand he may have to recognize his error immediately. If he does not do so, he may come to the unwarranted conclusion that continued production of his product is not worthwhile, whereas production may well be worthwhile if he were to avoid errors of judgment or ignorance in the future. Again, if he does not recognize the error immediately, any subsequent reference to the experienced transaction may lead him to the conclusion that the margin between costs and proceeds will be, because it was in the past, insufficient to make production at that subsequent time worthwhile. Finally, the monetary equivalent of any durable good in possession may change from time to time as relative prices or the price level change; these events impinge on the entity's capacity to adapt through exchange and will necessarily be recognized in any assessment of financial position after such a change.

It will be clear that the certainty attaching to the price of any actual bargain, attaches only to the immediate effect on holdings of money or claims. There is no certainty that the price is or will be relevant to future comparisons, choices, or assessments in respect of goods.

The durability of goods and claims makes it inevitable that certain of these shall persist through intervals embracing many assessments of financial position. As the significance of the monetary unit may change through such intervals, no inference from differences in financial positions is legitimate which does not recognize the change.

Anticipatory Calculation

Calculations about future conditions and events are always and inevitably hypothetical. No proposition relating to the future is a statement of fact. One may use past experience and present knowledge of facts and relationships in forming propositions about the future. But those propositions are beliefs or expectations only.[3] In making monetary calculations about the future one employs hypothetical prices. These may be selected with care, taking account of current prices and the direction in which and the rate at which they have moved in the past. One may take into account also the extent to which technology and tastes, present and future, are expected to modify the observed trends of the past. But trends and rates of change may be variously interpreted. And the weights assigned to nonprice factors which may influence future prices will vary from person to person. However great the care exercised, future prices—as costs or proceeds—are subjective estimations; they are by

---

[3] "Any statement concerning the future is uttered in the sense of a wager ... It is the desire for action which necessitates this gambling. The passive man might sit and wait for what will happen. The active man who wants to determine his own future ... is obliged to be a gambler because logic offers him no better way to deal with the future." Reichenbach, *Experience and Prediction*, pp. 315–6. " ... never do we say that we are measuring the value of a quantity at a future time, even though it may be possible to *predict* that value on the basis of a measurement made at present." Margenau, *The Nature of Physical Reality*, p. 374.

nature not capable of independent corroboration at the time they are used in calculations.

This does not, of course, mean that future calculations are useless. Reasoned choice cannot be made without calculations embracing future demands and future prices. But all the results and inferences from them are individual and subjective. The choice of a future course of action is predicated upon hypothetical combinations of hypothetical quantities of means, for a hypothetical market situation, with hypothetical probabilities of achieving hypothetical results.

The necessity of calculations in anticipation of choice does not make calculations relating to the past and present of no consequence. Calculations relating to the past and present are the only calculations which are capable of independent corroboration. One may, therefore, attach to them greater dependability than to any anticipatory calculation. But they have value in two other directions.

First, if calculations relating to the past are continually made as their necessity arises and so arranged that they result in a full and complete representation of the financial position of an entity at any moment of choice the necessity of a comprehensive assessment at that time is obviated, the rapidity of response to any stimulus is increased, and the probability of optimal adaptation is improved. Whatever a man's position is at a point of time determines or limits his range of choices at that time. He may make the shoddiest or the most elaborate calculations about the future; that is his prerogative, for it is his resources that are to be committed and his expectations that are to be achieved or disappointed. But if he is uninformed or inadequately informed of his present position, only by chance will he make choices appropriate to it.

Second, if the events and transactions of the past are so represented and arranged that a full and complete representation of the financial position of an entity may be derived at any point of time, it is possible to deduce, for any interval between two such points of time, the rate and direction of the change in position which has resulted from any action or complex of actions and events. The discovered consequences of past actions will serve in making choices between future alternatives and the probability of optimal adaptation will, thereby, be improved.

CLASSIFICATION AND MEASUREMENT[4]

Merely to speak of monetary calculation implies that there are other forms of calculation; that we choose to classify objects

4 What follows is a development of R. J. Chambers, "Measurement in Accounting," *Journal of Accounting Research,* Vol. 3, No. 1 (Spring 1965).

and events into those which have monetary properties and those which do not, and to disregard the latter. It also implies that monetary properties are quantifiable, and that when quantified, there are certain operations, which go by the general name "calculation," which may be applied to the quantities obtained. Classification, quantification, and calculation are processes applied to all kinds of problems. They will be introduced to the present context by way of a general discussion of classification, the assignment of numbers, and measurement.

We have spoken of classification as a means by which men are enabled to consider diverse objects as members of sets of objects denoted by a conception. Objects *may* be classified only if they are perceived to have some property in common. Objects *will* be classified only if classification promotes the attainment of some purpose. Objects may and will be classified if they are perceived to have some property in common which is relevant to the attainment of some purpose. There are a potentially large number of properties which may be attributed to any object. As an example, every one of the roles a man fills may serve as a basis for classifying him; an illustration given in an earlier chapter alludes to eighteen such roles for one specific person; and the roles he fills constitute only a fraction of the properties which may be attributed to a man. As a further example, the different characteristics of means dealt with in a previous chapter may each serve as a basis for classifying any collection of goods. There are no natural classes. Classification is a purposive mental action. Its object is to economize cerebration. This it does by focusing attention on a single property of a collection of objects and disregarding others. It is selective and abstractive.

The simplest way of classifying objects is by qualitative description or definition. If the properties are stipulated which define the class of objects, "men," we may distinguish and classify objects which are "men" and objects which are "not men." (The purpose may be to anticipate the effects of our own actions on a number of objects.) To minimize confusion and to make the classifying process as simple as possible, we prefer a description or definition which unequivocally and in the fewest terms gives the basis for distinguishing men from other things. A collection of objects may be classified into more than two classes provided the qualitative descriptions do not overlap and the classes exhaust the collection. In all such classifications, the question is simply whether or not a given object possesses the stipulated property or properties.[5]

For some purposes, it is useful and necessary to rank objects in order according to the degree in which they possess a stipulated property. We

[5] Objects themselves are systems having many properties. See Warren S. Torgerson, *Theory and Methods of Scaling* (New York: John Wiley & Sons, Inc., 1958), p. 9.

wish to know not only whether or not a property is possessed, but also whether more or less of the property is possessed by the objects in a collection.[6] For reasons already given, more or less is a question inevitably associated with choice. We wish to rank objects in order—of size, weight, precedence, and so on—when all that it is necessary to know is their rank in a series, or when all that it is possible to know is their rank. An example of the former is sequential street numbering. It is useful to know that number 77 lies between number 75 and number 79, even though the numbering gives no indication of the linear distance between numbers, or the linear distance of number 77 from number 1. As an example of the case where only rank can be specified, there is the ranking of some wines as sweet, dry, very dry; or of cheeses, as bland, mild, tasty, sharp. In such cases ranking is clearly possible on the basis of properties affecting the palate; but a more precise designation of "dryness" or "sharpness," on a scale which is acceptable to all palates, seems to be unattainable.

In all such cases ranking is done in terms of one property only. Ranking in an ordinal scale is an advance on classifying by definition, or the naming of classes. It entails disregarding some properties which may be represented in a definition so that greater precision or more information may be obtained about a specific property. It may be useful to classify objects according to two or more properties simultaneously. But to do so involves two (or more) separate classifications. Objects may be classified as to color and as to shape; but there is no way of simultaneously ranking objects as to color and shape. Color and shape are independent properties; they are incommensurable.

An even greater degree of precision may be obtained if it is found to be possible to mark, on a linear scale, equidistant points the intervals between which represent equal differences in the property used as a basis for classification. Within the range between the upper limit of the highest interval and the lower limit of the lowest interval on the scale there may be many intervals, to describe each of which qualitative terms are inadequate. Commonly numbers in the ordinary scale of numbers are used to designate the marks or the intervals in the scale. Provided equal distances represent equal differences in the property, numbers may be assigned without regard for the meaning of zero in respect of the property.

---

6 Dealing with the evolution of the number concept, Dantzig observes, "The genesis ... of the cardinal numbers can be traced to our matching faculty, which permits us to establish correspondences between collections. The notion of *equal-greater-less* precedes the number concept. We learn to *compare* before we learn to evaluate. Arithmetic does not begin with numbers; it begins with criteria." Tobias Dantzig, *Number, The Language of Science* (Garden City, N.Y.: Doubleday & Company, Inc., 1954, Fourth Edition), p. 210. Emphasis in original.

Particular examples of such scales are the numbering of calendar years and the calibration of the Fahrenheit scale for measuring changes in temperature. But interval scales may likewise be used where zero has a definite meaning.

Finally the most precise means of assigning objects to classes is obtained if, in respect of a property, it is found to be possible to devise an interval scale with base zero such that the ratio of the numbers designating the classes in which any two objects fall remains constant whatever the size of the class interval or unit. Thus, suppose two objects, one twice as long as the other. The ratio 1:2 will remain constant for numbers designating the lengths of the two objects, whether those numbers are obtained by using a scale marked in inches, feet, centimeters or meters, provided the numbers are obtained by reference to zero on those scales. A scale of this kind takes the form of the scale of natural numbers; it is the kind of scale which is used for all operations which are, in ordinary usage, described as measurements. Such scales are used for the measurement of numerosity (the scale of natural numbers itself), of length (multiples of a unit—foot, meter—of length), of weight (multiples of a unit—pound, kilogram—of weight), to name only some of the commonest examples. The advantages of such scales will presently be indicated: one of them is that given the property to be used as the basis for classifying objects, and given the unit, every individual object may be classified uniquely, by the number assigned to it on the scale.

The four devices considered are in one sense simply means of classifying, of determining whether or not an object has a specified property, and to what extent such a property is possessed by, or may be attributed to, an object. In another sense these devices may all be considered as different scales of measurement. Suppose we define measurement as "the assignment of numerals to events or objects according to rule." Suppose further, we visualize the assignment of numerals (a) to objects identified by qualitative description (for example, model numbers or type numbers, where the numbers are distinctive symbols), (b) to the rank order of objects (street numbers), (c) to define equal intervals or differences, and (d) to designate the unique extent to which an object possesses a property. All such assignments of numbers are according to rule and the four scales may be styled scales of measurement. They have been designated nominal, ordinal, interval, and ratio scales.[7] Classifying and measuring are thus operations which are similar in kind in the sense that they are means of

[7] S. S. Stevens, "On the Theory of Scales of Measurement," *Science*, No. 103, 1946, pp. 677–80; and "Measurement, Psychophysics and Utility," C. West Churchman and Philburn Ratoosh, eds., *Measurements: Definitions and Theories* (New York: John Wiley & Sons, Inc., 1959), pp. 24 ff.

signifying similarities and differences.[8] But whereas we may classify objects according to measurements, the measurements are not of objects but of singular properties of objects. As we shall be concerned for the greater part with a singular property of many objects, our usage of "measurement" shall have reference to properties of objects, even though on occasion we speak of assigning numbers to objects.[9]

An Illustration

The resolution of traffic problems will provide an illustration of the application of these operations. For some purposes it is necessary to distinguish between pedestrian and vehicular traffic. The distinction may be drawn on the basis of qualitative description. For other purposes, it is necessary to draw finer distinctions. Some roads, bridges, ferries, and underpasses are unable to cope with vehicles of all sizes; the class "vehicular traffic" must be subdivided if any vehicle owner is to decide which routes he may use. He may, for example, only use those roads and bridges the width of which is greater than the width of his vehicle. "Greater than" implies an ordinal scale.

More precise designations are necessary if rules are to be made for the general safety of all road, bridge, and ferry users. It is not sufficient to say "Large vehicles may not use this road." Large is too indeterminate a description either as information to drivers of vehicles or as a test for enforcement of the rule. Large may mean wide, long, high, or heavy. And each of those is indeterminate; how high is high? We may visualize a set of signs to the effect: "no vehicle whose laden weight exceeds 5,000 (10,000, 15,000) pounds may use this road." Vehicular traffic is thus divided into classes according to an interval scale expressed in pound weight. The assignment of numbers, having definite positions in the generally known scale of numbers, to the weights of vehicles in pounds, where the pound weight is also a generally known and accepted unit, results in statements containing much more information than statements which refer to large vehicles or heavy vehicles. And they convey to all interested persons the same amount of information. Such a rule, therefore,

---

8 On the superiority of measurement over mere classification see Hempel, "Fundamentals of Concept Formation in Empirical Science," pp. 50 ff. "Classification is a half-way house between the immediate concreteness of the individual thing and the complete abstraction of mathematical notions." A. N. Whitehead, *Science and the Modern World* (Penguin Books, Inc., 1938), p. 42.

9 "Measurement is the process of assigning numbers to represent *qualities*." Norman R. Campbell, *Foundations of Science* (New York: Dover Publications, Inc., 1957). First published in 1920 under the title *Physics: The Elements* (Cambridge, England), p. 267.

predicts a whole series of actions—who shall be users of a given road, who shall be users of more sturdy roads, which road may be used for a given load.

Finally, if there is a scale according to which every vehicle and every load may be uniquely classified by a number designating its weight in pounds, it will have all, and more than, the advantages and predictive powers just mentioned. It will enable any vehicle to be classified according to any number of interval scales devised for different purposes.[10] It will enable any owner to determine how many pounds weight may be loaded on any vehicle so that it may still use a given road, and to determine what substitutions may be made, of one object for another, in loading a vehicle so that it may follow a certain route.

ORDER AND ADDITIVITY

The property "weight" used in the example is one of the class of properties measurements of which are made in ratio scales, scales corresponding to the scale of cardinal numbers, and having the same characteristics as that scale. The first of these characteristics is order. If there are objects a, b, c, ..., having a property, p, in different measures given by $m(a)$, $m(b)$, $m(c)$, ..., it is possible to arrange a, b, c ... in order according to their possession of p as measured in the scale m. Where precision is not necessary, that is to say where the number of uses to which a measurement is to be put is limited, ordinal and interval scales may so generate order. But mere ordering is insufficient for such problems as that of loading a vehicle. In these cases we wish to find what series of objects a, b, c ... in combination possess the property p in a given measure $m(n)$; or what is the measure, $m(n)$, of the combination of objects a, b, c ... each having the property p. The second characteristic of the class of properties of which weight is an example is that their measurements conform with the rules for addition.

A property only falls within this class if the combination of two or more objects possessing it has the same property, and if the degree of possession of the property by any combination differs from the degree of possession of the property by any constituent object.[11] The measurements of such a property only conform with the rules of addition if it can be ascertained,

[10] "Measurement, defined functionally, is the organization of experiences in such a way that they codetermine purposive decisions *in a wide variety of contexts—* where the organization is subject to control." Churchman, *Prediction and Optimal Decision,* pp. 101–102. Emphasis added.

[11] Norman R. Campbell, *What is Science?* (New York: Dover Publications, Inc., 1952), p. 111.

by observation or experiment, that when a and b having the property p are combined, the combination has the same property in the same measure as the sum of the individual measures of a and b; that is, $m(a) + m(b) = m(a + b)$. If the numerical value, one, is assigned to a chosen unit in the scale, in which the degree of possession of the property p by all objects a, b, c, $(a + b)$, ... is to be stated, then all numbers assigned to those objects in accordance with the scale will be capable of treatment (addition, subtraction, relation) in the same way as the cardinal numbers. Measurements of numerosity, weight, length, and time intervals conform with these rules. To the measurement of such properties the description "fundamental measurement" has been given.[12] It will be apparent that fundamental measurements employ scales which are members of the class, ratio scales.

It is also necessary to take account of other kinds of measurement, derived measurements. Two classes of derived measurements may be distinguished. In one case, the measurement of a property is derived by reference to a law or laws which establish that the required magnitude is a mathematical function of some other magnitudes for which methods of measurement have been established. Although the property in question may be measured directly within certain limits, beyond those limits recourse must be had to indirect methods of measurement. Distances may be measured between accessible points, for example, but the measurement of the distance between inaccessible points depends on laws relating distances to other magnitudes. The second class of derived measurements are measurements of new properties defined and obtained by relating other properties. Measures of efficiency (outputs per unit of input) or average speed (distance covered per unit of time) are examples. To these classes of derived measurement the designations "derived measurement by law" and "derived measurement by stipulation" have been given.[13]

APPLICATION TO MONETARY CALCULATION

The observations made in the course of this digression are to be applied to monetary calculation. As we have noted, monetary calculation is classificatory; all properties of objects other than monetary properties are excluded from consideration. The process of ordering or ranking is illustrated by the treatment of preferences and utilities; but for

---

[12] Campbell, *Foundations of Science*, pp. 267 ff. The criteria of fundamental measurements are more numerous than those indicated above. The notion of "fundamental measurement" seems serviceable, though it is not beyond criticism: see the discussion in Russell L. Ackoff, *Scientific Method: Optimizing Applied Research Decisions* (New York: John Wiley & Sons, Inc., 1962), pp. 196 ff.

[13] Hempel, "Fundamentals of Concept Formation," p. 70.

these there is no objective or nonpersonal scale; nor are direct utilities monetary properties. In a monetary economy, where alone monetary calculation is appropriate, buyers, holders, and sellers of nonmonetary means concern themselves with numbers of monetary units given or received, or to be given or received. The monetary scale is simply a scale of the numerosity of monetary units; it is a cardinal scale of the same kind as the scale of natural numbers. It is a scale in which zero has a definite meaning, and it is a scale equally comprehensible to all persons at a given point of time.

Numbers of monetary units are assigned to events and nonmonetary things by virtue of their being prices. Prices are measurements. They measure at a time and place the numbers of monetary units which may be substituted for the nonmonetary things to which they are assigned. As prices are determined in the market, they are objective measurements; whether one buys or not, market prices are objective measurements.

THE PROPERTY TO BE MEASURED

There are many prices which may be assigned to any nonmonetary object. For example, that number of monetary units may be assigned which represents (a) the number of money units given in exchange for any good at the date of its acquisition, (b) the number of units which could have been obtained in exchange, by resale, immediately after its acquisition, or (c) one year after acquisition, or (d) ten years after acquisition, or (e) the number of units which at present could be obtained by resale. All such assignments of numbers of monetary units are made or may be made by virtue of their being prices. All such numbers are ascertainable as at the date of each example, and can, therefore, be known at any point of time thereafter.

But at any *present* time all past prices are simply a matter of history. Only present prices have any bearing on the choice of an action.[14] The price of a good ten years ago has no more relation to this question than the hypothetical price twenty years hence. As individual prices may change even over an interval when the general purchasing power of money does not, and as the general purchasing power of money may change even though some individual prices do not, no useful inference may be drawn from past prices which has a necessary bearing on present capacity to operate in a market. Every measurement of a financial property for the

---

[14] "There is hardly any more subtle or corrupting fallacy in economics than that of misplaced concreteness as applied to values, the view that every good goes through its life with a birth-certificate in the form of a price-tag." Boulding, *A Reconstruction of Economics,* p. 194.

purpose of choosing a course of action—to buy, to hold, or to sell—is a measurement at a point of time, in the circumstances of the time, and in the units of currency at that time, even if the measurement process itself takes some time.[15]

Excluding all past prices, there are two prices which could be used to measure the monetary equivalent of any nonmonetary good in possession, the buying price and the selling price. But the buying price, or replacement price, does not indicate capacity, on the basis of present holdings, to go into a market with cash for the purpose of adapting oneself to contemporary conditions, whereas the selling price does. We propose, therefore, that the single financial property which is uniformly relevant at a point of time for all possible future actions in markets is the market selling price or realizable price of any or all goods held. Realizable price may be described as *current cash equivalent*.[16] What men wish to know, for the purpose of adaptation, is the numerosity of the money tokens which could be substituted for particular objects and for collections of objects if money is required beyond the amount which one already holds.

Suppose an entity (a private person, a business firm, or a charity) to have legal title at a point of time to the following:

	Cost at Date of Acquisition	Presently Realizable Sum, if Sold
Cash (notes and coins)		1,000 units
Automobile A	3,000 units	1,200 units
Automobile B	2,000 units	1,700 units
Equipment P	5,000 units	6,000 units
Equipment Q	3,000 units	2,000 units
Land	8,000 units	10,000 units

And suppose that a new piece of equipment becomes available in the

15 "In ordinary language, the numerical outcome of a measurement characterizes the state of the observed system at the time at which the observation was made. If the processes constituting the measurement require a finite time, the reference of the measured value becomes slightly inexact but it is usually taken to be the instant when the processes start." Margenau, *The Nature of Physical Reality*, p. 374.

16 "A man does not value money for its own sake, but for its Purchasing Power— that is to say, for what it will buy. Therefore, his demand is not for units of money as such, but for units of purchasing power. Since, however, there is no means of holding general purchasing power except in the form of money, his demand for purchasing power translates itself into a demand for an 'equivalent' quantity of money." John Maynard Keynes, *A Treatise on Money* (London: Macmillan & Co., Ltd., 1930), Vol. I, p. 53.

market at a price of 4,000 units. It must be decided, on the basis of anticipatory calculations, whether a new combination of goods, including the new equipment but excluding one or more of the existing goods, is to be preferred to the existing combination. However wide the range of anticipatory calculations there is one fact common to all: 4,000 money units must be made available if the new piece of equipment is to be acquired.

Now observe that the two money columns refer to different properties of the goods. The first column, acquisition cost, is quite irrelevant to the selection of a group of items which will yield at least 4,000 units if sold; only the numbers in the second column are relevant to this question. No combination of numbers from the first column and numbers from the second column will throw any light on the question; and no such combination may be added to obtain an aggregate which has a sensible meaning—simply because the two columns refer to different properties. Further only if all the units are identical in meaning will it be possible to select varying combinations of the numbers in the second column to represent alternative ways of procuring at least 4,000 units; identity of meaning at the time of calculation is implied by the description "presently realizable sum, if sold."

The situation and problem discussed is clearly an example of calculation as a guide to action in markets. The solution of the problem entails that the magnitudes entered in a summary statement such as the one used in the illustration shall be capable of addition and subtraction. Because the numerosity of monetary units is a measure in the scale of cardinal numbers, the individual magnitudes may be so added and subtracted. The illustration may be extended. If there are determinate obligations to pay to other persons sums of money, the measures of these obligations may also be set off against the numbers in the second column. The numbers in the first column have no relationship whatever to the measure of such obligations.[17]

THE UNIT OF ACCOUNT AND MEASUREMENT

A monetary unit becomes a unit of account by virtue of its function as a medium of exchange. It becomes a unit of measurement for the same reason. If singular measurements are to be added and sub-

---

[17] An early treatment of measurement rules in the literature of accounting is given by John B. Canning, *The Economics of Accountancy* (New York: The Ronald Press Company, 1929), pp. 199–202. It does not appear to have been followed up.

tracted, it is necessary that all measurements be made in terms of the same units. It is not sufficient that monetary units shall have the same name; measurements in terms of Canadian dollars, Hong Kong dollars, and United States dollars may not be added unless all the "dollars" stand at parity, or are freely substitutable for (that is, are equal to) one another. Dollar is not necessarily a common denominator. If it is necessary, in the process of choosing, to compare prices at a point of time in Canadian, Hong Kong, and United States dollars, they will be converted into prices in one of these currencies at the prevailing rate of exchange. The rate of exchange is a rule for transforming measurements in one scale into measurements in another scale. Like other prices, the rate of exchange may vary from time to time; the conversion rate will be the rate prevailing at any time at which a measurement is to be made.

Now suppose a merchant has branches in Canada, Hong Kong, and the United States, and that in each country he both buys and sells a certain good. There are thus statements of the cost price and selling price in the currency of each country. He may find it of interest to discover the rate of profit earned in each country and to compare the rates. This may be done without converting the different currencies into one currency, for each ratio of profit (the difference between cost and selling prices) to cost price is a ratio of measurements in the same scale. If he were to convert all the cost prices, selling prices, and amounts of profit to the currency of one country by use of the prevailing rates of exchange, he would get exactly the same ratios as if he used the three different currencies. This may, of course, have been anticipated by reason of the fact that the scale of the numerosity of money units is a ratio scale. If provides the foundation for the next step.

Any entity may endure over a period of time during which a given monetary unit has changing significance as a medium of exchange. The significance of money as a medium of exchange does not subsist in its power to command any specific good or goods. Holders of money or of claims to money or of goods convertible into money are concerned with the general qualities of money as a medium of exchange, with its capacity to command a wide range of goods; the collection which is accessible to them, and the collection which they will acquire, can only be decided when they have discovered the current cash equivalent of their holdings. If a monetary scale is to serve as a measurement scale at any time, the significance attaching to any unit of it is necessarily its general significance, its general purchasing power. If measurements are to be made in such a scale at different points of time, at each of which the monetary medium has a different general purchasing power, those measurements will be unique for each point of time. They will only be relevant to the choice of specific goods from all the goods available in the market if they represent command over goods generally at that point of time and at no other point of time.[18] Such judgments as "This is expensive" or "That is inexpensive" can only be made of the prices of this or that in the context of the level of prices generally prevailing at the time they are made.

The example given earlier of the use of different units in different countries may be applied to the use of different units across successive points of time. It is just as pointless to add monetary units representing different purchasing powers (dollars of 1950, of 1955, and of 1960, when the purchasing power of the dollar has continually changed) as it is to add Belgian francs and French francs when they do not stand at parity. To compare any absolute monetary quantities, such as the sales of a firm in 1950, 1955, and 1960 in the above circumstances, without correction for the changed significance of the money unit, would be plainly misleading.[19] It would nevertheless be quite proper to relate a profit margin (between a cost price and a selling price) to a cost price, and to compare such ratios for each of the three years, without first converting all prices to their equivalents in terms of the purchasing power of money in any one year.

It will be recalled that the characteristic of a ratio scale is that the ratio of any series of measurements in it remains constant for any change in the defined magnitude of the unit; the measurements of two lengths bear the same relationship to one another whether those lengths are expressed in inches or centimeters. The transformation rules from one scale to another are given by the defined relationships between these units. In the same way the measurements of two financial magnitudes bear the same relationship to one another whether they are expressed in units of the general purchasing power of 1950, 1955, or 1960. The transformation rules from one scale to another are given by the relationship between the general purchasing powers of the units at each of the stated dates.

That scales of linear dimensions and weights are ratio scales is important; conversions from one unit to another are now and then necessary. But that the monetary scale is a ratio scale is of far greater importance, for the

---

[18] "Of . . . the liability to variation of the value of money . . . the merchant, the accountant, and the commercial court, are alike unsuspicious. They hold money to be a measure of price and value, and they reckon as freely in monetary units as in units of length, area, capacity, and weight." Ludwig von Mises, *The Theory of Money and Credit* (London: Jonathan Cape, Ltd., 1934), p. 204. Even though the liability to variation is known it is very commonly ignored, in practical affairs as well as in theoretical discussion.

[19] "Now, the success of the whole system of business depends upon the truthfulness of reports. The truthfulness of reports depends mainly on the truthfulness of accounting. The truthfulness of accounting depends largely on the truthfulness of the dollar—and the dollar is a liar! For it says one thing and means another." Henry Whitcomb Sweeney, *Stabilized Accounting* (New York: Harper & Row, Publishers, 1936), p. xi.

significance of the unit is susceptible constantly to change. It is pointless to assign numbers according to diverse or mixed measurement scales and to suppose that they may be aggregated or related in a manner such that useful information will result.

THE DOMAIN OF ACCOUNTING

Retrospective calculations may embrace large numbers of past transactions and events. Anticipatory calculations may embrace large numbers of prospective transactions and events. As the capacity of the mind to comprehend the nature and effects of varied, isolated events and things is limited, devices for the systematic collection and ordering of the individual pieces of information are necessary in both cases. Now, any given set of anticipatory calculations, made with specific ends in view, may lead to the rejection of the course of actions which it represents; the expected consequences, as calculated, of that course of actions may be judged to be undesirable, or less desirable than the expected consequences of some other course of actions. There may be many or few such exploratory sets of calculations, depending on the actor's propensity to search, on the costs of making the calculations, and on the extent to which an actor is prepared, out of sheer optimism and "animal spirits," to back his intuition.[20] But any such set of calculations and the actions it entails, being hypothetical, cannot be regarded as present knowledge.

On the other hand, we have shown that present financial position is invariably relevant to adaptive choice; that, indeed, it circumscribes or predicts the range of choices available at a point of time. We have shown that singular measurements of the current cash equivalents of all means in possession and of all obligations may be made, and that those may be added, subtracted, and otherwise related. We have shown that the composition of a stock of means and of obligations is changed by transactions and involuntary events. We have shown that changes in financial position between two points of time represent the monetary effects of past courses of action and past events, and that inferences may be drawn from them which may inform future judgments. We have shown that where the dimension or significance of the monetary unit of measurement has changed between two points of time, it is possible, and necessary if addition or relation is contemplated, to transform measurements in the units of an earlier dimension to measurements in units of contemporary dimension.

We, thus, envisage a systematic arrangement of such pieces of information about the past and present, which will constitute present knowledge.

[20] Keynes, *The General Theory of Employment, Interest and Money*, p. 161.

On the ground that present knowledge—knowledge in the present, about the past, and the present—is the basis both of judgments about past events and of plans to procure future events, we regard the usefulness of such systematic calculation and arrangement as established. We adopt it as the domain of accounting.

The proposed limitation of the domain of accounting may be questioned in the light of earlier statements to the effect that (a) anticipatory calculations are essential to reasoned choice, and (b) both retrospective and anticipatory calculations entail systematic arrangement of monetary signs of events and transactions.

The usefulness of anticipatory calculations is not denied by the decision to exclude them from accounting as such. Anticipatory calculations may be made by any person regardless of the existence of retrospective information of the accounting variety; every new venture is predicated on such calculations. For the purpose one may seize upon every scrap of information which may influence one's estimation of the feasibility of a proposal. But because future actions are very much a matter of optimism and the impulse to push a chosen course of action to a successful outcome, and because their choice involves so much guesswork, it is difficult to say how useful any particular form of anticipatory calculation will be. There can on the other hand be no question of the usefulness of the particular form of calculation delimited by the above proposal for the domain of accounting.

The usefulness attributed to accounting information of the kind envisaged is not to be confused with use. One may use a device which for the purpose is much less useful than another. Again, it is not possible to predict the use which any user may make of an object; what may be produced as a useful kitchen utensil may be used by some as a decorative piece. Use depends on evaluations of ends, which we have contended are variable for any person and beyond the knowledge of other persons. On the other hand, usefulness may be predicted if we can observe or envisage a set of circumstances in which an object performs a function, and the larger the set of circumstances and functions performed the greater will its usefulness be judged to be. Judgments as to usefulness are in a sense anticipatory, but they are justifiable if it can be shown that the circumstances in which an object has been useful in the past will persist. The distinction drawn between use and usefulness is based on the subjective-or-objective test. We cannot say how people will use an object; we can make objective statements about the conditions in which an object is useful, for these are observable, environmental conditions.

In excluding anticipatory calculations from the domain of accounting, it is not implied that there is no similarity between the frameworks of calculation for retrospective and anticipatory calculations. There is, indeed, good reason why the general framework for both should be the same. One of the principal purposes of anticipatory calculations is to discover whether a proposed course of, action may be expected to produce results and a future position which compare favorably with past results and present position. And, one of the principal purposes of retrospective calculations is to discover whether a past course of action did, in fact, produce results and a present position of the same order as was expected at the outset. These things can be discovered most conveniently if the frameworks of calculation are similar.

Notwithstanding the above argument as to its subjectivity, there is a possibility that anticipatory calculation, because of its general orientation to the future, may be claimed to be a more important phase of accounting than retrospective calculation; it may be argued, therefore, that instead of being eliminated, anticipatory calculation should be accorded higher esteem, even to the point of being regarded as the preeminent form of accounting. One further reason for limiting the domain of accounting may be adduced in rebuttal of this claim. The word "account" has a commonly understood meaning which has persisted since its early appearance in the English language. It means to give a report of or to relate something that has happened. [21] Now no one can give an account of something that has not yet happened, and something, indeed, which may not happen even if one sets out to procure its happening. To speak about accounting for the future is abuse of the language. It has no justification on the ground that it is a mere extension of its presently understood interpretation; for, on the one hand, we have shown that the inputs are different in character for retrospective and anticipatory calculations, so that the latter are not extensions of the former; and, on the other hand, there are quite satisfactory words for describing anticipatory calculations, such as estimates, budgets, plans, forecasts, and so on.

The form of accounting we envisage may not be denigrated on the ground that it is purely retrospective. Insofar as it embraces the effects of transactions of, and events which impinge on, an entity, and represents these effects up to the point at which a statement of financial position is derived, it is directly related to all actions future to that point of time. To permit the inclusion of anticipated magnitudes would destroy the factual character of the results of calculation. To speak of accounting as if it included anticipatory calculations may lead to confusion among its exponents as well as its users. For it may result in the mixing of ascertained measures with hypothetical magnitudes in such a way that the mixture is deemed, mistakenly, to have the merit of objectivity.

---

21 *Shorter Oxford English Dictionary:* "(verb) to render account of; to answer; to explain. (substantive) a statement of moneys received and paid, with calculation of the balance; a relation, report or description." These are selected from a variety of other interpretations, but the sense of them all is that the subject matter of an account is something that has happened in the distant or the immediate past.

Nor may the limitation of accounting to the representation of one stated property of events, transactions, and things be challenged. All measurement systems are abstractive, representative of specific properties; the process of abstraction is justified by the variety of contexts in which, and problems to the solution of which, the results may be applied.[22]

We therefore define accounting functionally, as a method of retrospective and contemporary monetary calculation the purpose of which is to provide a continuous source of financial information as a guide to future action in markets.[23]

The definition is believed to be quite general. It applies equally to the monetary calculations of individual persons, business firms, eleemosynary bodies, governmental entities all persons or organizations, in fact, which get and spend money. It applies to entities which deal only in money and money claims, as well as to entities which acquire, hold, and use other goods. The full significance of the definition will develop as its terms are dealt with. It is offered here as an indication of the orientation of development. This applies particularly to the statement of purpose or function which it includes.

Argument

4.11   *An entity is any person or association acting a specific role.*

4.12   Associations assign powers to act on their behalf to agents who are persons.

                (*3.21, 3.31, 4.11*)

4.13   Monetary calculation is serviceable to all entities whose roles entail indirect exchanges, whatever their objectives.

                (3.51, 3.81, 3.82, *4.11*)

4.14   All monetary calculations relate to a defined entity.

                (3.33, 3.34, 4.13)

4.15   Money units and statements assigning monetary units to objects

---

[22] "Accountancy is, like all mathematical sciences which assume a correspondence between numbers and material things, essentially abstract. It chooses to neglect all aspects and quantities of the material things with which it deals, except the mere correspondence to money value." Arthur Stone Dewing, *The Financial Policy of Corporations* (New York: The Ronald Press Company, rev. ed., 1926), pp. 453–4.

[23] "By a 'functional definition' of a concept, we mean a definition which makes explicit the usefulness of the concept for certain purposes. One way of accomplishing this explication is to make clear what activities or things are denoted by the concept and what purposes these activities (or things) serve." Churchman, *Prediction and Optimal Decision*, pp. 96–7.

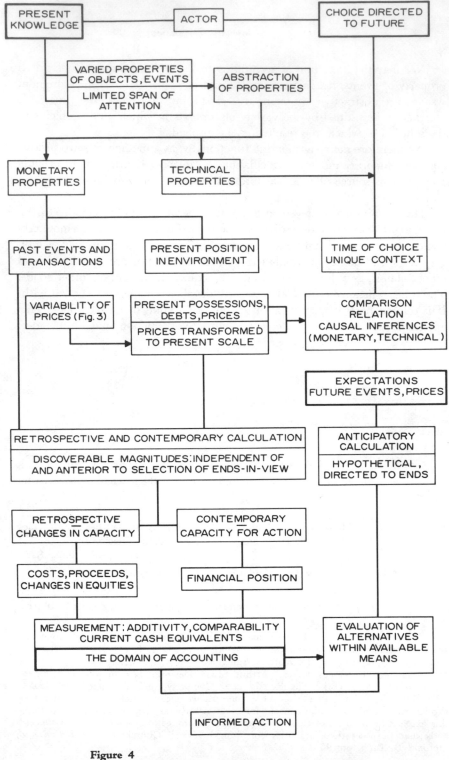

Figure 4
OUTLINE OF CHAPTER 4: MONETARY CALCULATION.

and events are signs comprehensible, at a given time and place,
to all persons acting in their own behalf or as agents.

(*3.61*, *4.11*, 4.12)

4.16   Numbers of monetary units assigned to objects and events for
the purpose of monetary calculation are so assigned by virtue
of their being prices. Monetary calculation has reference only to
money prices.

(*1.52*, 3.63, 3.94)

4.21   Monetary calculations may be retrospective, contemporary, and
anticipatory.

(1.63, 1.65, 1.66, *1.71*, 4.13)

*4.22   Financial position is the capacity of an entity at a point of time
to engage in indirect exchanges; it is represented by the relationship between the monetary properties of the means in possession
and the monetary properties of the obligations of an entity.*

4.23   Contemporary financial position is ascertainable objectively by
reference to the market, and is relevant to all choices.

(*1.41*, *1.64*, 3.81, *4.22*)

4.24   The monetary properties of past events are ascertainable objectively and verifiable.

(*1.64*, 4.16)

4.25   The function of retrospective calculation is to explain the
derivation of a contemporary financial position, and to suggest
causal relationships which may give rise to expectations.

(*1.41*, 1.66, 4.16, *4.22*)

4.26   The monetary properties of future events and objects are
hypothetical and subjective; they are neither measurable nor
verifiable.

(*1.64*, 1.67, 4.16)

*4.31   Measurement is the assignment of numbers to objects and events
according to rules specifying the property to be measured, the
scale to be used, and the dimension of the unit.*

4.32   Prices are measurements, made in the market, of the numerosity
of monetary units, paid or payable, and received or receivable.

(3.66, *4.31*)

4.33   In relation to financial position the prices assigned to means in
possession are realizable prices or current cash equivalents and
the prices assigned to obligations are current cash equivalents.

(3.81, 4.16, *4.22*, 4.32)

*4.34   The scale of numbers of monetary units of given dimension is
the scale of cardinal numbers; it is a ratio scale.*

*4.35   The dimension of the monetary unit at a point of time is its
general purchasing power.*

4.36   All measurements in the monetary scale are unique to a point
of time.

(3.83, *4.31*)

4.37   All numbers of units of given dimension being alike in relation to the market at a given time, current cash equivalents may be freely added, subtracted, and related.

(*1.43*, 4.33, *4.35*)

4.38   Measurements made on a ratio scale of stipulated unit dimension may be transformed into measurements of a different unit dimension by the rule relating the two dimensions.

(*4.31, 4.34*)

4.39   Where monetary measurements made at different times or places are required to be added, subtracted, or related, they shall be transformed into measurements in units of the same dimension.

(*1.43*, 4.21, 4.36, 4.38)

4.41   *The domain of accounting is the range of retrospective and contemporary measurements and calculations.*

4.42   *Accounting is a systematic method of retrospective and contemporary monetary calculation the purpose of which is to provide a continuous source of financial information as a guide to future action in markets.*

(4.23, 4.25, 4.26)

Financial Position

5 Every entity which acts or proposes to act by exchange has a financial position. We have observed that to describe the position of a person or object at any point of time, it is necessary to describe each property in respect of which the entity has a relationship with the environment. The same applies to the *financial* position of a person or other entity.

ASSETS

In respect of the possession of money and every good convertible into money, an entity has relationships with the environment. It is convenient to describe all such means under the control of any entity as its assets. An asset is defined as any severable means in the possession of an entity. The implications of the definition are to be made explicit.

By severable means is intended any means which, at any given time of action, may be converted to other means by exchange or the processes of production, or which may be alienated by way of gift. In respect of entities which are persons, the definition excludes all means which, for personal reasons (such as sentimental attachments to keepsakes), do not enter into calculations with respect to the market. It also excludes all potentials such as personal skills, of individuals *per se* or of individuals as agents of associations, which have not become embodied, by their exercise, in goods or services. Potential at a point of time inheres in a person. The market does not buy a man's potential; it buys his services, as his potential becomes an actuality.

By possession is intended the legal right to hold and use, whether or not the holding or use is subject to contractual or other constraints, in respect of the role for which a specific entity is defined. An individual *per se* cannot consider as an asset in respect of this role any means he possesses as a trustee, for example. Such an asset is an asset only in respect of the individual as trustee. Illegal possession is also excluded, for a man may base no firm expectations on what he holds illegally. But extra-legal possession, by right of custom or tradition, is included; for, insofar as the law respects custom and tradition, they are the law.

The term *asset* is thus to be used only in contemplation of some specific entity. *Asset* and *assets* are used of all means falling within the definition, singularly or collectively, as the case may be. The assets of an entity may include money, claims to money such as debts owing by others and bank deposits, transferable or convertible titles to rights, goods of all kinds, and titles to land.

It is important to distinguish assets from measurements of assets. Assets are objects, or titles to objects or rights. In relation to accounting, and to financial position in particular, measurements of assets are the current cash equivalents of assets, as these are established in current markets.[1] As we have shown, it is possible to add the current cash equivalents of all assets to obtain a measurement of their aggregate cash equivalent.

EQUITIES

In an earlier chapter, it was pointed out that possession may be unrestricted or restricted. It is necessary to develop this difference because of differences in the entities with which we will be concerned.

An entity in possession may hold means in its own right, being entitled to unrestricted use and benefit from them. The only class of entity in which

---

[1] "... measurement involves (1) an object or system upon which an operation is to be performed; (2) an observable whose value is to be determined; (3) some apparatus by means of which the operation can be carried out." Margenau, *The Nature of Physical Reality*, pp. 369–70. In our setting the subject is an individual asset or equity (or a collection of such assets and equities); the observable is its cash equivalent; the apparatus is the market.

this right subsists is the class of natural persons. They are the society. Whether singly or in association, they are the producers and consumers. The laws which provide the structure of a society concern themselves basically with the rights of natural persons; even when collections of natural persons cooperate to pursue their ends jointly, this is so.

Natural persons are able to pursue ends through associations by virtue of the powers of those associations, granted under law by the society at large, or granted within the law by those persons who constitute a given association. Among these powers are powers to buy, sell, and hold means, and to enter into many agreements and contracts of the kind available to natural persons. Many such associations endowed with these powers may exercise them in their own names, independently of the persons who constitute them for the time being; these corporations are recognized as having a distinct legal personality. The capacity of associations to engage in exchanges originates in contributions, of money or in kind, by natural persons. These constituents of an association acquire rights by virtue of their contributions, rights to determine what it shall do, how its affairs shall be supervised, and how its proceeds shall be divided. Subject to all these constraints, the association as such may be said to have the use and benefit of means acquired and held by it in its own name. This is analogous to the right of unrestricted use and benefit which we have attributed to natural persons. But it is analogous only; the rights and powers vested in associations are so vested for the benefit of their constituents.

Any entity may hold and use means subject to contractual obligations, usually to pay money, to the suppliers of such means. A natural person may create such obligations in favor of persons who, thereby, become his creditors. An association having any objective, the pursuit of which involves exchanges, can only exist at all by virtue of contractual obligations: but they are of two classes, obligations to constituents of the association and obligations to its creditors.

The several classes of rights or obligations referred to may be styled *equities*. The right of unrestricted use and benefit attributed to persons and the contractual rights of the constituents of an association will be described as *residual equities*.[2] Obligations to creditors, in either case, will be described as *liabilities*. As is the case with assets, it is necessary to distinguish between equities and measurements of equities.

Residual Equity

All means are the property of some person or other entity. An entity can hold no means in which there are no equities. Equities are,

2 After William Andrew Paton, *Accounting Theory* (New York: The Ronald Press Company, 1922), pp. 84 ff.

therefore, rights in the means in the possession of an entity. The measure of the aggregate means of an entity is the measure of the aggregate equities. As the settlement of any obligation requires that there shall be in the possession of the debtor entity money or other means convertible to money, the measurement of equities is necessarily a monetary measurement. And as obligations arise from exchanges, in respect of which settlement is deferred, the monetary measure of every liability is the contractual amount of the bargain established at the time of the exchange to which it gave rise. The difference between the aggregate monetary measure of the assets of an entity and the aggregate measure of its liabilities is the measure of the residual equity in its assets.

This may appear to be obvious in the case of personal entities, but not so obvious in the case of associations which depend on the creation of contractual obligations to acquire their initial means. In the latter case, the constituents pass the control of some of their means to the association as such, strictly to the control of the officers of the association whom the constituents have appointed. In the mere transfer there are risks; for example, the risk of future conflicts of interest between officers and constituents. And if such an association is formed for the purpose of production and exchange, there are the risks of changes in tastes and technology. There is, thus, no certainty that the means transferred to the control of an association may subsequently return in the same measure to its constituents, or that the aggregate amount of such means in the control of the association shall be maintained. And, although the incentive to such transfers is the expectation of a price for the services of bearing these risks and forgoing the use of money, there is no certainty that the difference between the proceeds and the costs of operations will be positive. The rules of an association may well stipulate the monetary amounts of the contributions of constituents and may stipulate the manner in which the difference between proceeds and costs shall be divided and distributed. But the application of these rules depends entirely on the outcome. For these reasons it is proper to speak of the rights of constituents in the assets of an association as residual rights.[3]

Liabilities

Notwithstanding that obligations to creditors are determinable with greater precision than residual rights, and that the relationship between a debtor and creditors is one of trust, there are risks to every

---

[3] We omit the case where the measure of assets is exceeded by the measure of liabilities, in which case the creditors' equity is the residual equity. On this point, and on residual equity generally, see George J. Staubus, *A Theory of Accounting to Investors* (Berkeley and Los Angeles: University of California Press, 1961), Chap. II.

transaction for which settlement is deferred. It is a legally established condition of the creation of obligations in favor of creditors that they shall have rights to the satisfaction of their claims in priority to other distributions of the assets of an entity. This condition is necessary to curb wanton abuse of the rights of creditors; it is reinforced by the threat of bankruptcy or insolvency in the event of default. Liabilities may, therefore, be called senior equities.

Beyond this general condition, creditors seek to minimize the risks in several ways. They may regulate the credit they grant to any entity on the basis of its residual equity. The amount of the residual equity is what a debtor has at risk. The greater the relationship between the amount of a residual equity and the amount of liabilities, the less is the risk of the creditor.[1] Again, creditors may regulate the credit they grant on the basis of the prospective income of an entity, where this can be judged satisfactorily. Further, they may augment their right to payment or repayment of amounts due by stipulating additional rights, by way of mortgage or bills of sale for example, against specific means of an entity. And, they may stipulate that their claims shall rank in a more or less senior position in relation to the claims of other creditors. They may support all these stipulations by requiring, as a condition, that the debtor entity shall inform them from time to time of its financial position.

STATEMENT OF FINANCIAL POSITION

The amounts of obligations and their due dates being determinable, it is possible to compute the current cash equivalent of these obligations, by discounting the sum payable in the future to a present sum using the rate of interest payable for the immediate use of the money necessary to enable immediate settlement to be made. The current cash equivalents of assets and liabilities being determined, their difference is the current cash equivalent of the residual equity. We thus have a system of measurements—one class being a residual, determined if the other two classes are determined—all of the same property, current cash equivalent. The aggregate of the current cash equivalents of assets is equal to the aggregate of the current cash equivalents of liabilities and residual equity. If a statement is drawn setting out the assets and the equities and their measurements, the number of monetary units assigned to any asset (equity) is freely

4 "(1) A person will fulfill a promise when he has a greater stake in fulfilling it than in not fulfilling it, (2) a person will normally incur costs on the basis of another's promise only when he is convinced that the second person has a greater stake in fulfilling the promise than in not fulfilling it, and (3) if a person wishes to acquire value on the basis of a promise he must be able to demonstrate convincingly that he has an adequate stake in its fulfillment." Kuhn, *The Study of Society*, p. 346.

substitutable for the number of monetary units assigned to any other asset (equity); and the number of monetary units assigned to any asset (equity) is freely relatable to the number of monetary units assigned to any equity (asset).

These substitutions and relations are not only logically and mathematically valid; they also correspond with the comparisons which it is necessary to make in choosing courses of action for any entity. In considering any possible action, an actor may wish to add the monetary units assigned to any collection of assets short of all assets, for, in the light of his knowledge and expectations, the conversion to cash of some such mixed collection may be preferable to the conversion to cash of any particular asset or other collection of assets. This can only be done if the monetary units assigned to all assets and liabilities are of equivalent significance. As many such combinations may yield an aggregate of the size necessary for the contemplated action and, as in any case, there may be many alternative actions in contemplation, an actor cannot choose in an informed manner unless all the items in every class of assets and liabilities are represented in common terms, so that substitutions of one item for another may be freely made when considering alternative possibilities and their potential consequences.

ORDERING OF ASSETS AND EQUITIES

One of the distinctive characteristics of means, in relation to adaptive behavior, is their liquidity or convertibility to other means by exchange. Money is the most readily convertible asset. The convertibility or liquidity of other assets depends on the characteristics of the markets in which they are bought and sold. Means for which there is a wide and active market are more readily convertible than means of a highly specific kind for which there is, consequently, a restricted market. In a general way, the higher the price of a vendible unit of a class of means, the less liquid are assets of that class. In a general way, too, the higher the price paid for units of a class of assets, the longer the period for which such assets are intended to be held, and the less, therefore, is the readiness to dispose of them. But these are general notions only. They are not to be considered as rules overriding the general view that changes in technology and preferences, and hence, changes in relative prices, may at any time make the sale of means of any class preferable to the sale of means of another class.

Further, in general, it is possible to rank assets in the order in which they may be expected to be converted into cash in the ordinary course of events. Such a ranking will conform approximately with rankings on the bases previously mentioned. Because, for immediately prospective exchanges, the rate at which cash will become available is relevant, liquidity may be considered to be a generally useful principle of ordering individual items in a list of assets.

Equities differ not only in legal priority; they differ also in date of settlement. Among the potential liabilities of any entity at a point of time are debts falling due in the near future and debts falling due within the more or less distant future. To distinguish the temporal priority of liabilities is critical; there is little time for maneuvering, for selling assets, or creating new debts to liquidate old ones, in respect of short-term liabilities; there is more time for preparing to meet long-term liabilities. But as failure to meet short-term liabilities may give rise to remedial legal action, even to the point of bankruptcy, by short-term creditors, the discharge of their claims when due is a condition of continued freedom. The adequacy of highly liquid assets to discharge short-term liabilities is thus a matter of continuing concern. There is, indeed, a parallelism between the term to maturity of debts and the expected term to liquidation of relatively liquid assets which a prudent actor will keep in mind. The listing of liabilities in order of term to maturity will thus run parallel to the listing of assets in order of liquidity. And in view of the importance of meeting obligations as they fall due, this order will be, for assets, from high to low degrees of liquidity, for liabilities, from short to long terms to maturity. The residual equity may be considered as an equity of indefinite term and will, therefore, rank last among the equities.

EQUALITY OF MEASURES OF ASSETS AND EQUITIES

As all means in the possession of an entity at a point of time are the subject of some equity we may, in a general way, write:

Assets = Equities

We quantify the terms by assigning to them numbers of monetary units; and, as equities are of different kinds, the difference is to be recognized. We, therefore, write:

$$A = L + R$$

where A is a monetary measure of all assets, L is a monetary measure of all liabilities and R is the monetary measure of the residual equity obtained by taking the difference $(A - L)$. The fact that R is a residual entails that the system is not a defined system in the same sense as $4 = 2 + 2$. It is possible to assign any numbers of monetary units to assets and liabilities, nonsensical numbers, or numbers assigned according to quite different rules; because

R is a residue, the above equation may be satisfied. But in these circumstances R will have no significance, mathematical or practical. Even if a common rule is adopted for assigning numbers of monetary units to assets and liabilities, errors and omissions will not prevent the equation being satisfied, for these will find their way into the residual R, and R will suffer in significance. The only way of obtaining a mathematical value for R which is of significance at the point of time at which it is derived is by obtaining the measures of A and L in monetary units of the same, and contemporary, significance at that time.

The above equation is to be understood as an expression of equality of magnitudes, not an expression of identity. By definition assets are different things from equities. Liabilities may not, therefore, be considered as negative assets; obtaining the difference $(A - L)$ is to be considered as a mathematical operation for deriving the magnitude of R, not as implying that assets and equities have substantive properties in common. The length of a piece of string and the length of a foot rule may be the same, but a piece of string is not a foot rule.

CHANGES IN FINANCIAL POSITION

The financial position of an entity at any time is the resultant of all transactions and involuntary effects in the past. Every such event changes the financial position in some respect. Liquid assets may be converted to less liquid assets; short-term liabilities may be converted to long-term liabilities; liquid assets and short-term liabilities may be reduced simultaneously, and so on. We have to consider the manner in which such changes affect the equation of assets and equities.

For illustration, consider a householder, whose role is that of a consumer, and who derives an income solely from the sale of his personal services. Every sale of his services increases his residual equity. We consider only such services as are sold to increase his residual equity; there is no market and there can be no price, for one's services to oneself, and such services do not increase the extent of one's severable means. Every act of consumption reduces his residual equity. Every exchange other than by sale of his personal services simultaneously changes the measure of his assets and the measure of his liabilities, or simultaneously changes the composition of his assets or the composition of his liabilities. We will assume that there are no changes in prices for the purpose of this example.

At an earlier stage income, consumption, and savings were described in terms of utilities. In relation to the ends of individuals this is quite proper. But in an interdependent society, these concepts must be reinterpreted in terms appropriate to market operations. We, therefore, use the terms I

(income), C (consumption), and S (savings) in a monetary sense hence forward.

Suppose that our householder's only transactions between two points of time, t_1 and t_2, are the sale of personal services for a money wage and the purchase of consumers' goods for cash; and suppose there are no lags between the giving of service and the receipt of the money wage, between the purchase of goods and the payment for them, and between the acquisition of goods and their consumption. In the specified interval, he will earn a wage which may be designated income, I, and receive cash, Mi, in the amount of it. He will incur expenditure, C, on consumption and pay out cash, Mc, in the amount of it. If I exceeds C, he will have acquired savings, S, and there will have been an increase in his cash holdings in the amount of it. If C exceeds I, he will have made dissavings and there will have been a decrease in his cash holdings in the amount of it. I, C, and S represent changes in his residual equity; changes equal in amount occur in his assets, in this case his cash holdings.

Now if we write

$$A_1 = L_1 + R_1 \qquad\qquad [\,1\,]$$

to represent his financial position at t_1, and

$$Mi - Mc = I - C \qquad\qquad [\,2\,]$$

to represent the events occurring between t_1 and t_2, these equations may be added to obtain the financial position at t_2:

$$A_1 + Mi - Mc = L_1 + R_1 + I - C \qquad\qquad [\,3\,]$$

Because Mi and Mc are changes in cash holdings, and $(I - C) = S$, we may write:

$$A_2 = L_1 + (R_1 + S) \qquad\qquad [\,4\,]$$

where $(R_1 + S)$ is his residual equity at t_2.

The demonstration may be extended by removing the assumption that there are no lags between the initiation and the consummation of any action. If the cash received is less in amount than the amount of I, he will have acquired a contractual claim, D, against his employer; A_1 will be augmented by the amount of it and cash receipts will be less than Mi in an equal amount, Md. But the effect on the aggregate assets of earning I will be unchanged. Similarly, if the cash spent on consumption is less in amount than the amount C, he will have incurred a liability in the amount Lc to another party; L_1 will be augmented by the amount of it and cash payments will be less than Mc in an equal amount, Ml. The assumption that there is no lag between the acquisition of consumers' goods and their consumption will be retained for the sake of simplicity, and because, in the case of ultimate consumers, the acquisition of consumers' goods is tantamount to consumption. The effects described above may be expressed as follows:

$$D + (Mi - Md) = I \qquad\qquad [5]$$

$$\text{and} \quad Lc + (Mc - Ml) = C \qquad\qquad [6]$$

The change in financial position between t_1 and t_2 may than be represented, by combining [5] and [6] in the manner of [2] above, thus:

$$D + (Mi - Md) - Lc - (Mc - Ml) = I - C \qquad [7]$$

Financial position at t_2 is obtained by adding [1] and [7]:

$$A_1 + D + (Mi - Md) - Lc - (Mc - Ml)$$
$$= L_1 + R_1 + I - C \qquad\qquad [8]$$

Because A_1, D, and all M items are assets, and both L items are liabilities we may transpose Lc and write

$$A_2 = L_2 + (R_1 + S) \qquad\qquad [9]$$

The example may be extended further. If our wage earner acquires assets by incurring liabilities in the interval, and there is no change in the cash equivalent of those assets in the interval, the relationship expressed in [9] will hold: A_2 and L_2 will simply be larger by equal amounts, but the amount of the residual equity will be unaltered. Again, if there is any change in the cash equivalent of any asset in the interval the relationship will hold; A_2 and $(R_1 + S)$ will simply be larger or smaller by equal amounts, for a change in cash equivalents falls on the residual equity, not on contractual creditors. Subject to appropriate related definitions of the components, the relationship holds generally for all entities and for all changes in the financial position of entities.

INCOME STATEMENT

Financial position at any time is the basis of action. But it gives no suggestion as to the mode of action one may pursue in the future. The rate of change of financial position, however, is knowledge which may provide some guidance. What has happened in the immediate past provides the basis of some expectations. It is not sufficient, however, to know simply that past income and past consumption resulted in a net addition to one's residual equity; unless the interval considered is very short there will have been many intervening acts and effects which have given rise to the change, actions which may or may not be taken in the future, effects which may or may not be sought or avoided in the future. Detailed knowledge will be useful. An actor will want to know the rate at which income is earned. If his sources of income are many, he will want to know the amount from each source, for if some sources provide a regular income while others provide a less regular, even an occasional, income, he will want to take these regularities and irregularities into account in the future. He will want to know his rate of consumption. If his consumption expenditures are varied, he will want to know the amount spent on recurrent, occasional but predictable, and unpredictable consumption. He will want to know whether the complex of income-earning and consumption actions of the past have resulted in savings and, therefore, additions to his wealth, or whether it has resulted in the consumption of part of his original wealth; for this will enable him to estimate the extent to which he must raise or may lower his rate of earning and the extent to which he may raise or must lower his rate of consumption in the light of his then present resources and his future plans.

Amounts representing income, I, and consumption, C, may be set down in a statement called an income statement. It will be apparent that the income statement is a description of the changes in the residual equity. It is quite possible to obtain the net amount of the change from two statements of financial position. Thus:

$$\text{from [1]} \qquad A_1 - L_1 = R_1 \qquad\qquad [1a]$$
$$\text{and} \quad \text{from [9]} \qquad A_2 - L_2 = R_1 + S \qquad\qquad [9a]$$

If we describe the terms on the left-hand side as net assets, and subtract [1a] from [9a], the change in net assets is equal to S, the change in residual equity.

If there is no detailed statement of the transactions of any period, it is thus possible, by obtaining the financial positions at beginning and terminal dates, to deduce the change in residual equity. If, on the other hand, there is a detailed statement of transactions intervening between the opening and closing dates of a period, its net effect will necessarily be the same. Changes in residual equity and in net assets are essentially derivatives of financial positions at two points of time. To the amount of net assets at any time we apply the term *capital*; measurement of changes in capital by reference to an initial capital stock is said to be based on the maintenance of capital.[5]

CAPITAL AND THE MAINTENANCE OF CAPITAL

The term *capital* as it is used here relates to that part of the assets of an entity over which its command is unrestricted by liabilities. The measure of the capital of an entity at a point of time is, thus, the current cash equivalent of all its assets less the current cash equivalent of its liabilities. It will be apparent that the measure of the capital and the measure of the residual equity are equal; that, given the aggregate amounts of assets and liabilities, the amounts of the residual equity and the capital are simultaneously determined. But although the magnitudes of capital and residual equity are the same, the conceptions of capital and residual equity are different. Residual equity subsists in rights in assets; capital or a capital stock subsists in assets. It will be apparent, too, that, unless the aggregate amount of the assets exceeds the aggregate amount of the liabilities, there can be no residual equity and no capital.

In relation to any collection of assets in respect of which there are both liabilities and residual equity, neither residual equity nor capital refers to any specific subcollection. Except by express contract, liabilities are equities to be satisfied out of the collection generally, not out of any specific part of it; one may not attribute any specific liability to any specific asset, even though a specific asset may be charged as security for a specific liability, or a specific liability may have been created for the purpose of acquiring a specific asset. The parallelism suggested above, between the term to maturity of liabilities and the term to final liquidation of assets, may not be supposed to imply that any asset may be linked with a specific liability or with the residual equity in the ordinary course of events.

It follows that capital and the maintenance of capital have reference only to a general property of a collection of assets, regardless of the composition of the collection. The maintenance of capital does not, therefore, mean the maintenance of any given physical good. Some may suppose that if an entity is to continue to engage in a given activity the continued possession and replacement of some specific goods must be assumed. But changes in relative prices may make any given activity no longer worthwhile; and they may make the same activity worthwhile only if a different group of specific goods is employed than was formerly employed. Readiness to change the composition of a stock of assets may, therefore, be a condition

---

[5] "Capital is the sum of the money equivalent of all assets minus the sum of the money equivalent of all liabilities as dedicated at a definite date to the conduct of the operations of a definite business unit." von Mises, *Human Action*, p. 262.

necessary to the maintenance of capital in the present sense; and readiness to change the composition of liabilities may be a no less necessary condition.

The use of the notion of the maintenance of capital as a basis for measuring changes in wealth does not imply that an entity will intend always to maintain its capital. To add to their capitals or to consume them is a matter of choice for individuals; to add to their capitals or to run them down is a matter of choice for associations, subject to the general law and their own rules. Entities may at some stages add to, at other stages run down, their capitals, in accordance with their ends for the time being. But measurement processes are unconcerned with specific ends; and the measurement of changes in financial position is concerned only with the capital at the beginning of a period insofar as it provides the basic magnitude about which changes may have occurred.[6]

EFFECTS OF CHANGES IN PRICES

The preceding demonstration was simplified by the assumption that there were no changes in prices during the interval. Changes in relative prices and changes in the general level of prices have effects on holdings of money and other assets which are quite involuntary in respect of all holders. But they cannot be ignored. They are facts to be reckoned with in discovering whether, during any past period an addition has been made to the magnitude of the assets and hence to the wealth or capital of an entity. The calculation of a change in assets proceeds from the assets as stated at the beginning of the period; that position is expressed in monetary units having the purchasing power prevailing at that date. If, at the end of the period, the current cash equivalent of all assets is a greater number of monetary units the increase will only represent an increase in command over resources generally if the level of prices has not risen at the same or a faster rate. If the level of prices has risen at the same rate, the entity will have no greater command over goods generally than it had before; it will be no better off with respect to the market. The same conclusion follows from consideration of the measurement process. If at the

6 The maintenance of capital, in economic analysis, is not regarded as an end in itself. "We are interested in the magnitude of capital because, *ceteris paribus,* a change in it will cause a change in the income to be expected from it, and because in consequence every change in it may be regarded as a symptom of such a change in the really relevant magnitude: income." F. A. Hayek, *The Pure Theory of Capital* (London: Routledge & Kegan Paul Ltd., 1941), p. 298. Capital accounting is seen as a means of avoiding using up unintentionally parts of the sources of income. At a general level, in an interdependent society the importance of capital and the maintenance of capital arise from effects on the incomes of others than those simply having legal rights in capital and its product.

end of the period the dimension of the monetary unit is different from its dimension at the beginning, the latter must be subjected to transformation to the dimension at the end before calculation in homogeneous terms is possible.[7] In the circumstances cited, the result of the transformation will be identical with the number of monetary units designating the capital at the end of the period; the difference will be zero.

If may be suggested that the purchasing power of money will be different for different persons, because ends differ and, consequently, what different persons will do with a given sum of money will differ. In the first place, however, what any person will do with a given sum of money depends on him discovering the current cash equivalent of his stock of means. He cannot begin to formulate plans to buy without knowing this. What is more, it is quite unnecessary in a market economy employing a monetary medium of exchange to think of what one will do in the future when calculating what one has. All goods have market prices; surpluses of one kind may be sold to provide the means of acquiring what one wants. The only significant thing about money or the monetary equivalent of a mixed stock, in the face of the diverse offerings of the market and the diverse and constantly changing preferences of buyers, is its capacity for commanding goods generally. There cannot, therefore, be different "purchasing powers of money" for different entities.

Changes in relative prices are quite different in effect. Suppose that there is no change in the general level of prices, but that the price of one good in possession has risen in a period. It follows that the price of one or more other goods has fallen; we suppose that the entity has none of these goods. By virtue of the rise in price the entity is better off at the end than at the beginning. In general, any change in relative prices gives rise to a change in the magnitude of capital, and, hence, of residual equity. It is possible that during any period there may be both changes in the general level of prices and changes in relative prices. The magnitude of the effects of the latter may only be discovered after first making general trans-

---

[7] Discussions by economists of the behavior of individuals with respect to income are concerned primarily with expected income (income *ex ante*), for this is the income which is "significant for conduct." Thus, in a frequently quoted passage, Hicks suggests "we ought to define a man's income as the maximum value he can consume during a week, and still expect to be as well off at the end of the week as he was at the beginning." Faced with the expectation of changes in prices, income "must be defined as the maximum amount of money which the individual can spend this week and still expect to be able to spend the same amount *in real terms* in each ensuing week." Hicks, *Value and Capital,* pp. 172, 174. In both cases the consequence "and still . . ." has reference to maintaining a level of potential consumption "in real terms." We are not hindered by the difficulties Hicks finds in quantifying *ex ante* income, for our calculations are *ex post*. The position we have taken corresponds with an *ex post* version of the above *ex ante* definitions.

formations, in respect of all nonmonetary goods, to correct the opening stock of assets to monetary equivalents at the closing date.

INCOME, COST, GAIN, AND LOSS

The example of the householder postulated as the only source of income the sale of personal services. This income may be considered as discretionary or predictable income, for, subject to there being opportunities for the sale of his services, a man may sell more or less of his services and regulate his income from this source as he chooses. Most people prefer discretionary income to be regular for there is a regular level of expenditure on consumption which is necessary to their standard of living as they see it.

There may also be occasional (irregular) events which fall on assets and residual equity beside the shifts in relative prices mentioned above. One's assets and residual equity may be increased by the receipt of legacies or gifts, and may be decreased by accidental loss or destruction of assets. To such involuntary effects we apply the term windfalls. One's attitude towards windfall gains and losses will differ from one's attitude towards discretionary income and expenditure. A man may feel free to dissipate a windfall gain in a manner quite different from the careful manner in which he plans to lay out his regular income. He may accept philosophically or as a disaster a windfall loss, whereas ordinary expenditure on consumption is regarded simply as necessary. One cannot plan on windfalls. It is a matter of ordinary wisdom therefore, in calculating changes in residual equity and in assets, to distinguish windfalls from other items. The assets arising from or dissipated by planned actions and by windfalls are, of course, the same in kind; they simply form parts of the pool of assets generally. The distinction is of importance only in designating the sources of gains and the causes of losses; it is made so that erroneous expectations may not be formed.

Although the example used is of the simplest kind, it embodies most of the characteristics of other entities. It has been used to demonstrate that the process of calculating a financial position at a point of time and of changes in financial position through an interval is relevant to adaptive behavior at the personal level. In subsequent chapters, examples of other entities will involve developments of the notions and processes presented so far. The types of changes in the monetary representation of residual equity may, in general, be summarized thus:

(a)   Changes in the purchasing power of money, which necessitate transformations of measurements from units of one scale (the scale appropriate to the beginning of a period or the date of purchase) to units of another scale (that appropriate to the end of a period or the date of sale). The amounts of such adjustments neither add to nor diminish command over resources generally; they are adjustments for the change in the scale only.

(b)   Changes which add to or diminish command over resources generally:

(1)   Discretionary incomes and costs

(2)   Windfall gains and losses

Involuntary changes of type (a) are not directly discoverable from the transactions of an entity. Nor indeed may the magnitude of changes of type (b)(2) be readily discoverable in this way because they are not exchanges at a price. If any event falls on the financial position of an entity one-sidedly, so to speak, its magnitude must be ascertained by reference to observable facts, at the time or at the end of the period; in particular, by reference to the actual liabilities and assets, and to their current cash equivalents as these are evidenced in the market. There is no experience privy to an entity which will enable it to distinguish the magnitudes of these changes, in a manner relevant to future action, without reference to observable facts in this way. An income statement is derived, fundamentally, by inference from two successive statements of financial position. An income statement in the derivation of which effect is given to the above types of change is dependent on inferences of the same kind as to gross amounts and on inferences from additional market information where the several types occur concurrently.

But what are discretionary income and cost? It is possible, conceptually, to distinguish between incomes and costs which arise from short-run events and those which emerge in the longer run. If one sells one's labor, for example, for a money price, the income and the cost are immediately discernible and the income is measurable. But if one buys a good, holds it for some time and sells it at a greater price than the purchase price, is the difference income (assuming no change in the general level of prices)? The difference between the purchase and selling prices may be an ordinary seller's margin or it may arise from changes in relative prices in the interval of holding. The first alternative may indicate that the difference is to be regarded as discretionary income; the second that it is involuntary income. But it is difficult to say objectively, without relying on the assertion of the actor, whether the difference arose because his anticipation of a seller's margin was realized or because his anticipation of a rise in relative prices was realized. Although the gains (or losses) from changes in relative prices are not at the discretion of a given actor, the choice as between goods whose prices are expected to rise and those whose prices are not expected to rise is at the option of the actor. At any time, though certainly more so at some times, it may be supposed that gainful transactions are deemed to be gainful whether the expected gains lie in seller's margins or in relative price changes or in both. The same applies with appropriate changes to expectations of falls in prices. We, therefore, regard both these sources of a change in residual equity as discretionary.

Generally, then, we regard discretionary incomes and costs as gross increases and gross decreases respectively in the measure of residual equity, the incidences of which are capable of being expected in advance, even though the specific expectations may not have been realized. We regard windfall gains and losses as gross increases and gross decreases respectively in the measure of residual equity due to fortuitous events, the incidence of which in time or magnitude could not have been evaluated in advance.

In the case of an individual as consumer, total income is the sum of all gains, discretionary and windfall alike. Total costs are all costs of consumption. The difference between total income and total costs in a period is the measure of the savings of the period. We may generalize the exposition, to represent all types of entity, by interpreting costs as costs of consumption for consumer entities and costs of operations for other entities; and by interpreting the difference between total income and total costs as savings for consumer entities and as net income for other entities. In all cases the magnitudes are those obtained after eliminating the effects of changes in the dimension of the monetary unit during the period.

STATEMENT OF CHANGES IN FINANCIAL POSITION

The rate of change of financial position, as financial position has been defined, comprehends more than the rate of change of capital and residual equity. Changes may occur in the composition of assets and liabilities whether or not changes occur in the magnitude of the residual equity; the parallelism between terms to maturity of liabilities and terms to liquidation of assets has been shown to be of importance. The income statement of itself is inadequate to describe fully the change or rate of change in financial position. What is required is a statement of all changes in financial position—changes in residual equity, in the composition of liabilities (as between those of different maturities), and in the composition of assets (as between those of different liquidity).

By incorporating in one statement the amounts of income and costs, and the amounts of receipts and payments by which changes in assets and liabilities have been effected, an indication is obtained of gross changes in resources and obligations during the income period. The items in the statement may be arranged to show, by sources, the gross cash or cash equivalent inflows and their disposition over the period. The gross rate of change is useful both as a basis for judging the relative significance of any specific change of a past or a future period, and as a condensed and classified summary of the financial features of all operations. The general orientation of the statement to changes mediated through cash movements gives rise to its abbreviated description, funds statement.

Like the income statement, the statement of changes in financial position is a derivative. The determination of financial position from time to time is the basis of inferences both as to income and as to other changes. The three statements—statement of financial position, income statement, and statement of changes in financial position—may be said to be articulated; meaning that the general import of both the latter statements is entailed in any consecutive pair of statements of financial position, by virtue of the definitions of financial position and of change in financial position.

Argument

5.11   *An asset is any severable means in possession of an entity.*
(2.32, 3.41, 4.11)

5.12   *An equity is a right to the beneficial use of assets, or a right to the satisfaction of a claim out of assets, of an entity.*
(3.41, 4.11)

5.13   *A residual equity is the right to unrestricted and beneficial use of assets in the case of entities which are persons, or the contractual rights in assets of the constituent group in the case of entities which are associations of persons.*
(3.41, 4.11)

5.14   *Liabilities are rights of creditors to the satisfaction of claims against the assets of an entity in priority to the residual equity.*
(3.41, 4.11, 5.13)

5.15   The monetary measurement of an asset or a liability at a point of time is its current cash equivalent at that time.
(4.33, 5.11, 5.14)

5.21   As all means in the possession of an entity at a point of time are the subjects of some equity, Assets = Equities.
(5.11, 5.12)

5.22   If A is the sum of the monetary measurements of all assets, L is the sum of the monetary measurements of all liabilities, and

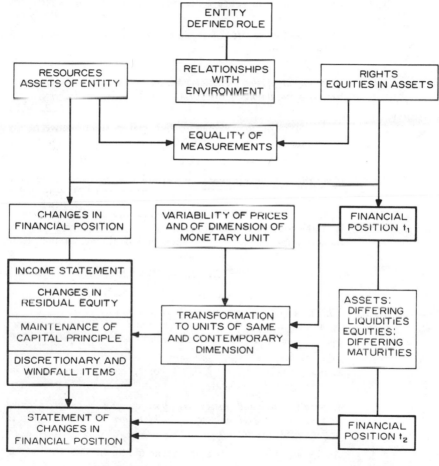

Figure 5
OUTLINE OF CHAPTER 5: FINANCIAL POSITION.

R is the monetary measurement of the residual equity, $A = L + R$.

$$(5.13, 5.14, 5.15, 5.21)$$

5.23   The measurement of the residual equity is obtained by inference from the measurements of the assets and liabilities.

$$(5.13, 5.22)$$

5.24   *The capital of an entity is its unrestricted stock of assets.*

$$(5.11, 5.14)$$

5.25   The measurement, K, of capital is equal to the measurement of residual equity.

$$(5.22, 5.23, 5.24)$$

5.31   *A statement of the financial position of an entity at a point of time is a statement of the form,* $A = L + R$.

$$(4.22, 5.22)$$

5.32   A statement of the change in financial position between any two points of time, t_1 and t_2, is a statement of the form

$$(A_2 - A_1) - (L_2 - L_1) = R_2 - R_1$$

given that all measurements are in units of the same dimension.

$$(2.73, 4.39, 5.31)$$

5.33   If, for a given period, I is the monetary measurement of income, C is the monetary measurement of consumption, and S is the monetary measurement of savings, and if all measurements are in units of the same dimension,

$$I - C = S = R_2 - R_1 = K_2 - K_1$$

$$(2.71, 4.39, 5.25, 5.32)$$

5.34   *The measurement of savings, and generally of income, by reference to changes in the measurements of capital in a given scale is said to be based on the maintenance of capital.*

5.41   *Discretionary incomes and costs are positive and negative changes respectively in residual equity arising, directly or indirectly, from exchanges.*

5.42   *Windfall gains and losses are positive and negative changes respectively in residual equity which are unilateral, that is, not induced by exchanges.*

5.43   An income statement is a statement of the form

$$I - C = (R_2 - R_1)$$

where I and C include both discretionary and windfall elements.

$$(5.33, 5.41, 5.42)$$

5.44   The separate representation of discretionary and windfall elements in an income statement is a condition of informed action.

$$(1.53, 1.66, 5.43)$$

5.51   The ranking of assets in order of liquidity and equities in order of maturity in a statement of financial position increases the interpretability of the statement.

(1.37, *1.41*, 1.66, *3.41*, *5.31*)

5.52   Changes in the dimension of the unit of measurement are not, of themselves, incomes or costs.

(4.38, 5.33)

5.53   All transformations of measurements shall be transformations up to the terminal date of the period for which summary statements are prepared.

(1.68, 2.29, 4.39)

The Formal Framework
of Accounting

6   Changes in financial position are continual; changes in the state of satisfaction are continual; adaptation or its pursuit is a continual process, or, more strictly, a continuous cycle of processes. Man acts; he observes, reflects on, and appraises the consequences of his action. He refers his new state to his ends, which, by virtue of his latest action and of other stimuli, will have changed in composition or rank; he makes a new decision and acts again. He is not necessarily self-conscious of the repetition of this cycle for every aspect of his behavior. But by it he inches towards the satisfaction of his wants, the attainment of his ends.

RECORDS AS MEMORY

An individual person acting on his own behalf depends on his memory and on his immediate observations as to the operating stimuli and the means at his disposal when considering future courses of action. His memory is a store of signs of past experiences; his recollections are, in effect, communications between himself at the time of a former experience and himself at the time of recollection. If his experiences are of limited number, variety, and consequence, his memory and immediate observations may suffice as premises of action. Memory and immediate observation interact, the one serving to sharpen the other.

But the capacity of the memory and the capacity for recollection are limited. The greater the number and variety of experiences upon which an actor may wish to draw when considering future courses of action, the greater will be his need to supplement his memory with a formal record. The capacity for observation and the time available for observation are also limited. So that even for experiences which are remembered, not all aspects of them may be recollected; for all aspects may not have been observed with such attention that recollection is assured. Again, every past experience is an experience in a particular setting; each has a time dimension, reference to which is necessary, as indicating its setting, for the subsequent interpretation of past experiences as guides to action. But the time and setting of experiences is less readily remembered than the events experienced themselves. A formal record is the surest safeguard against faulty recollection in this respect, and, hence, against the misinterpretation of past experiences.

If the assets and liabilities of an entity are numerous and varied, it may be difficult for an actor to ascertain them by immediate observation at a particular time. A record of past transactions up to a point of time will serve as a check on immediate observation. For the record is itself an observable object, capable of evoking responses when the natural memory fails.[1] It will therefore serve to prompt inquiry and direct observation at any particular time, tending to circumvent the oversight of specific assets and liabilities.

It is the function of formal written records to supplement the memory and to provide communications between an actor at antecedent points of time and himself at a time of choosing. As change is continual and future events are, at least in some respects, unpredictable, it may become necessary at any time to appraise past actions and events and their consequences. The demand for knowledge is continuous. If this demand is met in part by formal records, these records will necessarily be of a continuous kind.

[1] "Symbolization constitutes objects not constituted before, objects which would not exist except for the context of social relationships wherein symbolization occurs." Mead, *Mind, Self and Society*, p. 78.

ISOMORPHISM

The record will also have other properties. An entity of which the financial affairs are the subject of an accounting system may not be considered independently of its environment. It is an integral part of the community in which it exists. Its financial position is not a position it has to itself; it is a position it has in relation to its environment. An entity is a part of the working system which is the society. It is a sub-system of the system which is the society. Its relationships with the society exist whether or not it keeps a record of its transactions and their consequential effects. Many individuals, as such, have no record, certainly no continuous record, of financial relationships with the rest of their society, but they have such relationships nevertheless.

Now, it has been observed that the greater the correspondence between objects and beliefs in respect of them, the greater is the probability that actions taken on those beliefs will procure expected effects. It follows that, if an actor depends on a continuous record as a source of guidance, every transaction and every event which changes the relationship with the environment shall be represented in the record; and the monetary magnitude by which every such transaction and event is represented shall be the magnitude of its effect on the objective financial position.

An accounting system is, thus, contemplated which is isomorphic with the system of actual events which impinge directly on an entity.[2] It is sufficient that the accounting system concerns itself with direct effects on the entity. This does no violence to the notion that the entity is an integral part of the whole society, for the entity may act in response to proximate stimuli even though it has little or no knowledge of distant causes.[3] For reasons already given, direct effects include both voluntary and involuntary effects.

Systems which are identical in structure or form are isomorphic systems. Isomorphism is the principle of all systems of instrumentation and theories.[4] The most obvious example is a map, in which the relationship between the points of the map correspond with the relationships between the points on the terrain mapped. Speedometers, odometers, pressure and temperature gauges are systems which are isomorphic with other systems, the events or conditions which they represent. Their value subsists in their capacity to

[2] On isomorphism see, for example, Cohen and Nagel, *An Introduction to Logic and Scientific Method,* pp. 137 ff. Torgerson, *Theory and Methods of Scaling,* pp. 14–5.

[3] "The whole acts as one market, not because any of its members survey the whole field, but because their limited individual fields of vision sufficiently overlap so that through many intermediaries the relevant information is communicated to all." F. A. Hayek, "The Use of Knowledge in Society," *The American Economic Review,* Vol. XXXV, No. 4, September 1945.

[4] On theories as maps see Stephen Toulmin, *The Philosophy of Science,* (London: Arrow Books Limited, 1962), Chap. IV.

represent the properties of events and conditions at a distance, on a smaller and, therefore, more convenient scale for supervision of those events and conditions. In a complex system (for example, an automobile, an airplane, a blast furnace), there are many variable properties, and to each there is a specific instrument. As the failure of any single instrument to represent its particular aspect of the state of the system may endanger the system as a whole, care is taken to ensure that the instruments are reliable.

A business firm, likewise, is a complex system, supervised by the aid of a number of instruments. It has a number of distinctive properties— financial, legal, economic, psychological, social—each of which requires to be kept under observation. The accounting system is the instrument by which financial properties are observed. It is not, of course, the only source of financial information. The driver of an automobile responds to visual and tactile sensations as well as to his instruments. A person conducting a business may, likewise, rely on his own observations as well as on his instruments. It is indeed quite possible for an entity having limited operations, assets and liabilities, to be managed without recourse to complicated instrumentation.

But the importance of isomorphism as a principle of instrumentation increases as the difficulty of direct observation increases. The pilot of a modern aircraft depends on instruments for many types of information about matters at a distance. It is virtually impossible for a business entity to be managed without recourse to a formal information system if its operations are varied and continuous and its assets and obligations are numerous and widespread.

Further, past events and conditions are not observable at all—they are at a temporal distance. Their variety tends to confuse the memory, if it does not overtax it altogether. Their numerosity tends to reduce the sharpness of recollections of specific events and to confuse the subsequent relating of events and their consequences. The importance of a record isomorphic with past events will be apparent. Its importance may be supported on other grounds. The numerosity of operations, events, and things makes it more probable that current events and conditions will have similarities with past events and conditions. The sacrifices involved in keeping records may then be justified on the ground of better informed choosing in the future.

That a formal information system shall be an isomorphic system follows also from the fact that individuals themselves undergo mental modifications through experience. $Smith_{1960}$ is quite a different person from $Smith_{1963}$.[5] Likewise Smith's $environment_{1960}$ is quite different from Smith's $environment_{1963}$. The probability that $Smith_{1963}$ will interpret an action taken

5 Reichenbach, *Experience and Prediction*, pp. 281–2; Alfred Korzybski, *Science and Sanity* (Lakeville, Conn.: The Institute of General Semantics, 1958), p. 263.

in the environment$_{1960}$ in the same manner as Smith$_{1960}$ would have interpreted it in 1960 is low indeed; for his capacity for interpretation will have been modified by every intervening circumstance. If Smith$_{1963}$ requires to interpret an action taken in the environment$_{1960}$, the probability of a valid interpretation will be increased if the context of the action (particularly his financial position) and its effect on him in 1960 has been preserved; that is to say, if the information system recording all such events has been an isomorphic system. To interpret any such action as if it were taken in isolation or with no particular time dimension would be to disregard a significant element of the requirement of correspondence.

That time of occurrence is a significant element of all transactions and events provides the ground for a further property of a systematic information system. Changes in financial position occur in a certain order. It is a matter of importance that the order be preserved if at any time the position at an earlier time or the interpretation of any earlier action may be required to be known. We may say the record shall be isochronic, that the separate entries in the record shall be entered as the events they represent occur and shall be identified by the dates of occurrence of those events. Isochronism may be regarded as a specific aspect of isomorphism; it is distinguished here by reason of its importance for the identification of events with periods of time and for the effect of sequence on causal inferences.

FORMAL RELATIONSHIPS OF THE PRINCIPAL CATEGORIES

The objective of the process of accounting will thus be the development of a continuous systematic record of the financial properties of transactions and events which will make possible the derivation, at any time, of a summary statement of financial position and a summary statement of changes in financial position over any preceding interval. A procedure for doing this is to be specified. For the sake of simplicity, it will be assumed that there are no changes in prices.

The following relationships have been established for any entity:

$$\text{at any point of time,} \quad A = L + R$$

$$\text{for any interval,} \quad S = I - C$$

Suppose a point of time, t_0, at which the entity has neither assets, liabilities nor residual equity. If, in any subsequent interval, $(A - L)$ becomes greater than zero, it will be because costs have fallen short of income. A residual equity will have arisen. It is necessary to be specific as to the dates and intervals to which all the above magnitudes refer. At any time, t_1, after the base point of time, t_0,

$$A_1 - L_1 = I_{0\to1} - C_{0\to1} = R_1 \qquad [1]$$

where the suffixes to A, L, and R denote the time of measurement, t_1, and the suffixes to I and C denote the interval between t_0 and t_1. Similarly,

$$A_2 - L_2 = I_{0\to2} - C_{0\to2} = R_2$$
$$= R_1 + I_{1\to2} - C_{1\to2}$$

In general,

$$A_n - L_n = R_{(n-1)} + I_{(n-1)\to n} - C_{(n-1)\to n} \qquad [2]$$

and, transposing the terms having negative signs,

$$A_n + C_{(n-1)\to n} = L_n + R_{(n-1)} + I_{(n-1)\to n} \qquad [3]$$

Now, A, C, L, R and I are aggregations of the numbers of monetary units assigned to particular events and transactions. The rules for recording these particular events and transactions systematically are entailed in the preceding discussion. Every event and transaction produces an incremental effect upon the position preceding it; every entry in the record is, thus, to be regarded as an incremental entry, impinging on the position shown by the record at the moment preceding the entry. The object of transposing items as in [3] is to enable all entries to be recorded as increments to one or another of the variables. The justification for this procedure lies in the facts, (a) that absolute magnitudes are of importance in choosing, for choosing means deciding as between more or less of a given operation or thing, and (b) that if in any interval only the net effect of two or more operations was recorded it would be impossible to assess the relative significances of different operations at any time after the event. The method of quantifying increments is disregarded, and discussion is limited, for the moment, to the (mathematical) signs to be attributed to these increments.

RECORDING RULES

The formal equation relating measures of assets and equities implies that the two classes are of opposite mathematical sign. To derive a system in the form represented by [3], the following rules are sufficient:

1.   Measures of assets at any point of time shall be denoted by signs mathematically opposite to the signs denoting measures of equities.

2.   Positive (negative) changes in measures of assets and costs shall be denoted by signs mathematically opposite to signs denoting positive (negative) changes in measures of equities and income.

3.   Positive changes in measures of assets, costs, liabilities, income, and residual equity shall be denoted by signs mathematically opposite to signs denoting negative changes in measures of assets, costs, liabilities, income, and residual equity respectively.

4.   The signs "debit" and "credit" shall be used as mathematically opposite signs, "debit" being used of measures of asset holdings, of increments to asset holdings and costs, and of decrements to liabilities, income, and residual equity. The contrary usage of "credit" is implied by the above rules.

The use of the terms *debit* and *credit* requires justification in view of the well-established usage of the signs + and − to denote mathematically opposite characteristics. These terms have a distinctive origin related to financial position, which has become generalized to cope with the treatment of all changes as increments. The usage is retained because, although the numbers assigned to assets and equities may be treated formally as of opposite sign, assets and equities have quite different properties. An asset is not a negative equity; an income is not a negative cost. Debit and credit may be regarded as technical terms or terms of art, signifying mathematical oppositeness within a system in which other features than simple mathematical oppositeness require to be recognized.

The above set of rules, taken together with the definitions of the terms and the relationship [3], has the following merits. Given the measures of the aggregates of any four of the five variables, the measure of the aggregate of the fifth may be deduced; this is of value because of the difficulties of quantifying directly some of the variables under conditions to be discussed. The aggregates may be obtained directly in respect of each variable and of each element in a class of variables; derivation of aggregates is not confused or encumbered by items bearing different signs.

The formal equation relating measures of assets and equities implies also that no change in financial position is an isolated change. Every event and every transaction have two effects of equal magnitude but of opposite sign. If we use Dr for debit and Cr for credit in accordance with the above rules, and a, c, l and i for measures of particular components of A, C, L, and I respectively, then all transactions and events will fall into one or a combination of the following classes:

> Dr a = Cr l : assets acquired on credit at a price equal to the amount owed;
>
> Cr a = Dr l : assets alienated in settlement of an obligation;
>
> Dr a = Cr a : assets acquired at a price equal to the price of other assets sacrificed;
>
> Dr l = Cr l : an obligation settled by conversion to another obligation;
>
> Dr a = Cr i : assets acquired for services given or windfall gains;
>
> Dr c = Cr a : assets consumed (costs) or windfall losses.

Here i and c are changes in residual equity. If we contemplate an entity other than a person as consumer, it is necessary to provide for other changes, r, in the residual equity; for an association, for example, we may add the following:

> Dr a = Cr r : assets contributed by constituents;
>
> Cr a = Dr r : return of contributions or proceeds to constituents;
>
> Dr r = Cr l : creation of an obligation to constituents out of residual equity;
>
> Cr r = Dr l : conversion of an obligation to a residual equity.

These illustrations are sufficient to indicate that every transaction and event are fully described within the framework given by [3], only if the changes in the stock of assets and the changes in equities are simultaneously recorded. An accounting system which requires as one of its rules that for every debit there shall be a corresponding credit of equal amount is described as a double-entry accounting system. Double-entry accounting rests simply on the fact that all goods are the property of, or are subject to the equity of, some entity. Double-entry accounting gives expression to this empirically verifiable fact. It is dictated by the very nature of the process of exchange and of the rights in means.

CASH AND ACCRUAL ACCOUNTING

Income and cost are concepts ordinarily considered in terms of temporal bounds. However, they may be made to denote whatever specific collections of events and transactions of a period are found to be useful or necessary as guides to action. For example, income may be used to embrace windfall gains; for the purely formal demonstration of the simultaneous effects of events and transactions on financial position given above it has been so treated. But it has been shown that to do this, in summarizing the effects of the transactions of a period, would result in the loss of a significant piece of information.

Now to procure information is costly: the more refined the information the more costly it is to produce. Any person, concerned only to regulate his personal financial affairs, may well consider the cost of refinements unwarranted by reason of the simplicity or the uniformity of his economic actions. He may adopt, as a guide to action, the actual amounts of cash received and cash disbursed during a period, notwithstanding that there may be lags between the dates on which he becomes entitled to receive cash (or incurs obligations to pay cash) and the dates on which he receives cash (or pays cash in settlement of obligations). An accounting system in which events and transactions are recognized and made the subject of entries in the record, when cash is received or paid is said to be conducted on a cash basis. Accounting on a strict cash basis clearly precludes the recognition of all events which are not cash transactions, and is, therefore, inadequate to represent the changes in financial position which arise from shifts in prices. Such a system is isomorphic only in respect of cash movements. Nevertheless, such a system may have it uses in certain specific situations such as the simple case mentioned above and other cases later to be discussed.

An accounting system in which events and transactions are recognized and made the subject of entries in the record, when they effect changes in assets and equities, even though cash is received or paid at other dates, is said to be conducted on an accrual basis. This is the basis adopted throughout the preceding demonstration. It is the only system which can be isomorphic in respect of all economic effects on an entity. It will, necessarily, record all cash movements, so that it embodies all, and more than, the information yielded by accounting on a cash basis.

There may also be systems which are a mixture of the two, aiming to produce more information that a cash based system at less cost than an accrual system. The aggregates obtained from such a system, however, being of mixed parentage, are of little use except in the case of the simpler entities. The double-entry principle may be applied equally well to systems having cash, accrual, or mixed bases, subject of course to quite different conceptions or definitions of the five classes of variables. Double-entry accounting thus embraces a family of systems and of itself is inadequate to describe any specific system.

TEMPORAL ORDERING—THE JOURNAL

It has been shown that the incidence in time of any economic event is required to be known if the event is to be interpreted.

Likewise it has been shown that the position of an entity at any point of time influences the capacity of the entity to engage in further actions and the willingness of others to permit it to engage in further actions. It has also been shown that transformations of measures in the unit dimension operative at one point of time to measures in the unit dimension operative at another are frequently necessary. It is apparent, therefore, that a recording system will have, as one of its elements, a chronological record of events and transactions. Such a record may be described as a journal.

A journal may consist of a series of formal "translations" of the properties of each event or transaction into signs of the accounting system. Thus suppose an entity sells goods for cash in the amount of 200 monetary units on January 1, 19x1. In effect an addition is made to the asset, cash; and an addition is made to income from cash sales, in the same amount. The double-entry is made, by convention, thus:

Jan. 1, 19x1	Cash	Dr	200
	Cash Sales	Cr	200

The chronological record may occupy one journal, or, where transactions are numerous, there may be many journals each serving a particular class of transaction. Or, again, the detailed chronological record may be the original documents evidencing a series of like transactions, the formal journal entries being in respect of aggregates only. Where the details are abstracted in the record, and where the nature of the event represented is unusual, the entry will be accompanied by a brief narration, so that subsequent authentication and interpretation may be facilitated.

SUBJECTIVAL ORDERING—THE ACCOUNTS

The record giving the temporal sequence of events is primarily an intermediate device preparatory to a more significant ordering of the original entries. This ordering is a subjectival ordering or classification. The general framework of classification has already been given—it subsists in the categories: asset, liability, residual equity, income, and cost. But among the assets there may be means having widely varying characteristics (different specificities, divisibilities, convertibilities, and so on); among the liabilities there may be obligations having different maturity dates and different degrees of security; among the causes of changes in residual equity there may be incomes and costs of differing kinds and different degrees of regularity. All of these differences may be of consequence to an actor. But during any period there may be many events of the same kind—many receipts of cash, many payments of cash, many receipts from and payments to a particular person or class of persons. For every group of events, transactions, or relationships of the same kind there will be a separate "account." The account is the basic element of an accounting system.

For many purposes the ways in which the information yielded by individual accounts will be aggregated and related may be known in advance; for example, certain groupings are dictated by the need to derive statements of financial position and of changes in financial position. But occasions may arise when an unusual grouping or regrouping is necessary to inform some particular choice. Unless the individual accounts are of known and limited character, it would on these occasions be necessary to reconstruct the accounts concerned making finer distinctions, necessary for the purpose in view, than had previously been made. If, for example, an income account were to include all income items of discretionary and windfall character alike, the aggregate would later have to be broken down if a decision of the actor is to turn on the magnitude of either the discretionary or the windfall components. It follows that an account shall not contain statements about materially different kinds of events, transactions, or relationships.

The account has a conventional form. As in the prototype journal entry given above, the account is divided in columnar fashion, debit entries being made on the left hand side and credit entries on the right hand side. All entries are "posted" to accounts from the journal. The journal entry

| Jan. 1, 19x1 | Cash | Dr | 200 |
| | Cash Sales | Cr | 200 |

signifies that a debit entry shall be made in the Cash Account (an asset account) in the amount of 200 monetary units, with the narration that the sum derives from Cash Sales; and that a credit entry shall be made in the Cash Sales Account (an income account) in the same amount, with the narration that Cash was provided by such Cash Sales. If all journal entries are thus posted to their appropriate accounts, the totals of the debit columns and the credit columns of the set of accounts which constitute the system will be equal. This equality provides a purely arithmetical check on the process of posting; but it provides no check on the propriety of the original journal entries and no check on the substantive meaning of the information contained in the accounts.

An account may take the so-called "T" form illustrated below, in which the first entry is a posting from the above journal entry:

Dr				Cash Account				Cr
Jan.	1	Cash Sales	200		Jan.	7	Salaries	300
	5	Cash Sales	500			9	Rent Paid	200
	10	Cash Sales	600			14	Salaries	300
	14	Cash Sales	500			14	Balance	1000
			1800					1800
Jan.	14	Balance	1000					

Or the account may take the following tabular form in which all entries appear in strict chronological order and the balance at any time is readily ascertained:

Cash Account

			Dr	Cr	Balance
Jan.	1	Cash Sales	200		200 Dr
	5	Cash Sales	500		700 Dr
	7	Salaries		300	400 Dr
	9	Rent Paid		200	200 Dr
	10	Cash Sales	600		800 Dr
	14	Cash Sales	500		1300 Dr
	14	Salaries		300	1000 Dr

High-speed processing devices, such as punched card equipment, have given rise to further modifications in which an account consists of a series of cards or other units of information, one for each entry, a formal statement in the tabular form being produced as and when required.

The account serves to bring together all entries indicative of changes in that aspect of an entity's affairs which it represents. A system of cross-references as between journal entries and individual entries in accounts provides a means of tracing effects on the state of each account to the original evidence for the purposes both of authentication and interpretation.

SUMMARIZATION OF ACCOUNTS

At any point of time at which it is required to discover the financial position and the change in position since the last previous discovery of financial position, appropriate adjustments for accrued and deferred costs will be made insofar as they have not already been recorded. The balances of the accounts will be computed. The balances of all the accounts of the categories cost and income will be brought together in an income account, the balance of which will represent the net income for the period intervening between two "balancing" dates.

The balances of all the accounts of the remaining categories, assets, liabilities, and residual equity will then be brought together with the balance of the income account (itself the increment to the residual equity) into a statement which is styled a balance sheet. The sum of the debit balances will, in aggregate, equal the sum of the credit balances.

The mere equality of the two types of balances indicates nothing more than that the entries in the original records and all adjustments and aggregations have been followed through the system so that for every debit there is a corresponding credit. It is no guarantee against the omission of any transaction; it is no guarantee against entries being made in the wrong accounts. And most significantly it is no guarantee that any balance of an asset or liability account does in fact represent an actual asset or liability in the amount of that balance. It will be recalled that early in the present chapter it was assumed for the purpose of the demonstration that there are no changes in prices. This assumption is plainly contrary to all experience; the method of treatment is for the moment deferred. But unless the effects of these changes are brought into the record, the balance sheet will not correspond with independently determinable current cash equivalents of assets or liabilities. Further still, the recording process and the equality of balance sheet aggregates provide no guarantee against purely fictitious entries in the accounts or against wilful or accidental loss to the entity of part of its assets.

It is of no consequence to an actor making use of financial summaries that the books of account have been kept in impeccable order. He wishes to be assured that the information given by the accounts represents, or is consistent with, his financial position and results. Hence, it is necessary periodically to ascertain that the goods which the accounts represent him as possessing are, in fact, in his possession, and the obligations which the accounts represent him as owing are, in fact, owed; and in each case that the monetary representations are, in fact, reliable representations. Only by such authentication may the record be freed from inadvertent or deliberate misstatement.[6]

If, and only if, all events and transactions, and only those events and transactions, which have a bearing on the financial position of an entity have been duly represented by entries in the accounting system, the balance sheet will represent the financial position of the entity as at the date for which it is drawn.

Given two balance sheets drawn at opening and closing dates according to the above conditions, a summary statement of the change in the financial position during the interval may be prepared.

The processes of summarization involve condensation or reduction of the number of separate balances appearing in the accounts to the principal significant classes of balances. The object of reduction is to facilitate the comprehension of the general effect, for, as we have observed, the span of attention of potential users is limited. But reduction may not be carried

[6] "There are two ways of constructing the balance sheet ... by actual investigation ... the *inventory* method ... and by tracing the changes ... thru the accounts ... the method of *derivation* .... In practice, the two methods ... must cooperate." Charles E. Sprague, *The Philosophy of Accounts* (New York: The Ronald Press Company, 1918), p. 27. Numerous failures and frauds since Sprague wrote testify to the failure to ensure correspondence between the two. See also Kenneth MacNeal, *Truth in Accounting* (Philadelphia: University of Philadelphia Press, 1939), *passim*.

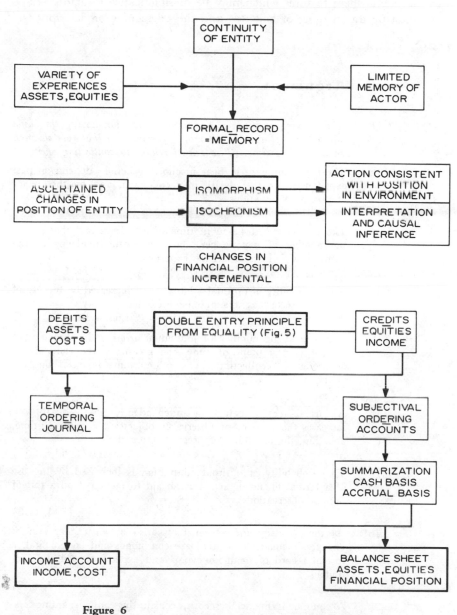

Figure 6
OUTLINE OF CHAPTER 6: THE FORMAL FRAMEWORK OF
ACCOUNTING.

to the point where features which may be of significance to actors escape attention by the merging of balances and the telescoping of descriptions.

Argument

6.11   *A continuing entity is a person or association having the same role and therefore a number of experiences in that role through an interval of time. (The sequel relates to continuing entities.)*

6.12   The beliefs brought to bear in choosing actions depend on past experiences, on the clarity of recollection, and on the extent of present observations.

(*1.12*, *1.14*, 1.63, *6.11*)

6.13   The greater the distance in time of an event, and the greater the number of experiences, the greater the tendency of the memory to fail or to confuse experiences.

(*1.14*, 1.36, *6.11*)

6.14   The probability of optimal adaptation is increased by the use of a formal record as a supplement to the memory.

(1.68, 2.30, 6.12, 6.13)

6.15   The greater the number of individual assets and obligations of an entity at a point of time, the greater is the difficulty of observing or recollecting them to determine financial position at that time.

(*4.22*, 6.13)

6.16   A formal record, being an independently observable object, increases the number of observable objects at a point of time, and thus, the reliability of present observations.

(1.74, 6.12, 6.15)

6.17   The probability of optimal adaptation is increased by the use of a formal financial record as an aid to memory and a test of present observations.

(6.14, 6.16)

6.18   As the necessity for action may arise at any time, and as changes in financial position are continuous and incremental, a formal record of financial events and experiences will be continuous.

(*1.32*, *6.11*, 6.17)

6.21   A continuous financial record, constituting an accounting system, shall be isomorphic with the financial aspects of the relationships and things of a continuing entity, if it is to serve as a means of increasing the probability of optimal adaptation.

(*1.32*, 2.29, 4.23, 6.18)

6.22   Time being of the essence of all events and transactions having financial aspects, a continuous financial record shall be isochronic with such events and transactions, if it is to serve as a means of increasing the probability of optimal adaptation.

(2.29, 3.76, 4.22, 6.18)

6.31   Income and cost being defined in incremental terms with reference to the residual equity,

$$A_n + C_{(n-1)\to n} = L_n + R_{(n-1)} + I_{(n-1)\to n}$$

where the suffixes denote successive points of time.

(*5.31, 5.34, 5.43*)

6.32   As incremental changes affect the ranking of courses of action, the aggregate of increments (relatively small in themselves) in any of the categories A, C, L, R, and I may at any time be required in the course, and for the purpose, of adaptation. A continuous record of the form 6.31 will satisfy this requirement.

(2.14, 2.15, 2.51, 6.31)

6.33   *The following rules are sufficient to produce a systematic record of the form 6.31:*

6.331   *Measures of assets at any point of time shall be denoted by signs mathematically opposite to the signs denoting measures of equities.*

6.332   *Positive (negative) changes in measures of assets and costs shall be denoted by signs mathematically opposite to signs denoting positive (negative) changes in measures of equities and income.*

6.333   *Positive changes in measures of assets, costs, liabilities, income, and residual equity shall be denoted by signs mathematically opposite to negative changes in measures respectively of each class.*

6.334   *The signs "debit" and "credit" shall be used as mathematically opposite signs, "debit" being used of measures of asset holdings, of increments thereto, of costs and of decrements to liabilities, income, and residual equity. The contrary usage of "credit" is implied.*

6.41   Every event or transaction which changes the measure of any component of A, C, L, R, and I simultaneously changes the measure of another component of A, C, L, R, or I, in an equal amount but in mathematically opposite direction.

(6.31, *6.33*)

6.42   *An accounting system in which the dual effects of every event or transaction are simultaneously recorded will be described as a double-entry system.*

6.43   As the aggregate of increments in any component of the categories A, C, L, R, and I may be required in the course of, and for the purpose of, adaptation, there shall be a separate record for each component of these categories which is significantly different in relation to choice.

(6.32, 6.41)

6.44   *An account is a record of the debits and credits in respect of a significant component of the main categories, or a record summarizing the net effects of other accounts.*

6.45   *The balance of an account at a point of time is the mathematical difference between the debits and the credits entered in it.*

6.46   The sums of the debit balances and of the credit balances of the accounts in a double-entry system at any time will be equal.

(6.41, *6.45*)

6.51   *An accounting system in which events and transactions are recognized and made the subject of entries in the record when cash is received or paid is said to be conducted on a cash basis.*

6.52   Discovery of financial position, when accounting on a cash basis, requires *ad hoc* adjustments for unpaid claims and obligations and other noncash changes.

(3.91, *6.51*)

6.53   *An accounting system in which events and transactions are made the subject of entries in the record when they effect changes in assets and equities, even though cash is received and paid at other dates, is said to be conducted on an accrual basis.*

6.61   A record of the dual effects of all events and transactions in chronological order makes possible the subsequent tracing of entries in accounts to original documents (for authentication) and original circumstances (for interpretation). Such a record is styled a journal.

(*1.41*, 1.68, 6.22, *6.42*)

6.71   The balances at any time of all accounts of the categories, cost and income, may be brought together in a single account which will be styled an income account for the period ended at that time.

(5.43, 5.44, *6.45*)

6.72   The balances of all accounts of the categories *A*, *L*, and *R* together with the balance of the income account at a given time may be brought together into a statement (containing debit balances and credit balances, equal in aggregate), which will be styled a balance sheet.

(6.46, 6.71)

6.73   If all events and transactions bearing on the financial position of an entity have been duly represented by entries in the accounting system, the balance sheet will represent the financial position of the entity as at the date for which it is drawn.

(*5.31*, 6.72)

Information and
Information Processing

7
FUNCTIONAL SPECIALIZATION

An actor may employ another to keep his financial records and to carry out his accounting processes because his own time and effort can be employed more effectively otherwise, because of the greater skill the other may have or may develop, or for both reasons. This is a common form of differentiation and specialization of functions. In such a case, the keeping of the record and the processing of financial information are divorced from the making of decisions bearing upon the financial position and results of an entity. To speak of the two roles, information processing and decision-making, suggests that there are two classes of decisions; decisions relating to information processing and bearing on actors, and decisions relating to the entity and bearing on its relationships with the world at large. In this chapter, we shall be concerned with the former class, but always having in mind the relationship of information to the operations of the entity on behalf of which the actor decides.

In the simple case where a single actor engages a single person to process financial information, most of the transactions and events to be reflected in an accounting system pass as singular facts under the notice of the actor himself. He buys and sells; he is familiar with the fluid character of the environment, with the variability of prices and of the purchasing power of money. Even in this case, as we argued in the previous chapter, detailed recollection of past transactions and events for the purpose of informing impending choices may not be possible; and in complex cases it is quite impossible. In complex cases also, by reason of geographical dispersion, an actor may not be able to apprehend directly all the singular facts which are relevant at any time. But, further, the actor is, in general, unable to reduce a variety of singular facts to a resultant or aggregative effect by direct apprehension. Aggregative or resultant effects of a multiplicity of actions, events, objects, and relationships may only be ascertained by the manipulation of the singular pieces of information which represent them individually. This applies even when the terms and units have an invariant significance. It applies for greater reasons to financial information, which not only must be collected and arranged in a manner related to its expected use, but also may require to be transformed as time passes due to changes in relative prices and in the dimension of the monetary unit.

To the extent that any of his decisions are based on processed financial information, an actor relies on the information processor and the process. Now, we have observed that the probability of optimal adaptation varies with the correspondence between objects and beliefs in respect of them. But where reliance is placed on processed information, the processor and the process are interposed between the actor and at least some of the objects and events relevant to optimal adaptation; and the actor's beliefs as to those objects and events will arise from the processed information supplied to him. It follows that the probability of optimal adaptation varies with the correspondence of processed information with the actions, events, objects, and relationships it represents.

The actor's reliance may be based on the reputed skill of the processor and the reputed propriety of the process. It will tend to be so based, for unless an actor spends an inordinate amount of time supervising the recording and processing operations (incidentally defeating the object of specialization), he will not have direct knowledge of the processor's skill, the processes used, or the relevance of the resulting information. But, consider some of the possibilities.[1]

---

[1] See, for more general features, Victor A. Thompson, *Modern Organization,* (New York: Alfred A. Knopf, Inc. 1963), Chap. 3.

Some Consequences of Specialization

A consequence of the development of a specialism in recording and processing information is that the design of information processing systems becomes the concern of others than actors themselves. Now, information processors are persons having the same general properties as actors. They have limited capacities for observation, for perception, for discrimination, for recollection; they have personal ends and value systems; their experience and knowledge are limited, and they will have more experience and knowledge of their specialism than of the particular acts which represent the role of the actor. In all these respects, an information processor will differ from the actor he serves. It is quite possible, indeed it is almost inevitable, that a processor will see, understand, and interpret things in a different light than does the actor. But if he does so, it is unlikely that the results of his operations will be as serviceable as the actor may, and is entitled to, expect.

Again, a specialist may well entertain the notion that the products of his services are ends in themselves. This notion may arise from the distinctive character of a technique and from the nonpecuniary satisfaction obtained from mastery of a technique and the expression of that mastery as expertise. But this is a personal satisfaction. It has no necessary value to the actor served by the specialist. Expert specialist performance only has value to an actor if the technique is deliberately designed to be of service; that is, if the processor envisages that what is to him an end product is to the actor a means to his ends.

And, again, it may happen that either or both the actor and the processor confuse the functions of the product of an information processing system. Some kinds of information are used directly by those for whom it is prepared, and used by others altogether as a basis for quite different decisions. It is possible to confuse these two uses, to such an extent that even when a system fails to serve directly those it was intended to inform, its continuance may be accepted because it still serves secondary and remote users.[2]

2 Even in the absence of secondary and remote functions a system may persist. "Not only can we build purpose into machines, but in an overwhelming majority of cases a machine designed to avoid certain pitfalls of breakdown will look for purposes which it can fulfil." Wiener, *The Human Use of Human Beings,* p. 38. "It is typical rather than exceptional to find that conventionally labeled institutions do not in fact perform the function that the label implies. If the function continues, it may no longer dominate." Harold D. Lasswell, "Strategies of Inquiry: The Rational Use of Observation," *The Human Meaning of the Social Sciences,* Daniel Lerner, ed. (New York: Meridian Books, Inc., 1959), p. 97. At the psychological level, the social needs of individual members of functional or institutional groups makes desirable to them the survival of the function or institution. "This need becomes an autonomously functioning one without any reference to the services that the group can perform." Krech and Crutchfield, *Theory and Problems of Social Psychology,* p. 384.

THE INFORMATION PROCESSOR'S ROLE

For all these reasons it is possible that the product of an information processing system may fail in its function. This possibility may be obviated by a clear understanding, on the part of the processor, of his role. He acts as an extension of the actor's sensory and calculatory apparatus. But, as such, he is not part of or an extension of the actor's selective apparatus; the problem of evaluating the information produced, by reference to the actor's strains and goals, remains the problem of the actor—otherwise there would be no differentiation of functions. What the processor observes, he observes for the actor. What he records and calculates, he does for the actor, as if he were the actor. He may do some of these things with greater skill than could the actor, but always within the constraint that he does them for the actor. He can have no independent, personal viewpoint in his role as information processor without damaging the effectiveness of his product as a means by which an actor seeks his ends. He is an agent having a specific functional brief.

This does not, however, entail that the processing technique shall follow the express dictates of a specific actor. We have observed that, for the purpose of mentally grasping the nature of a complex situation or process, men resort to abstractions which simplify the facts. Models or conceptions are formed, the elements of which represent only significant or manageable properties of the actual situation or process, as these are perceived at the time to be significant or manageable. An actor may resolve a problem, or a certain class of problems, on one occasion in a coldly deliberate manner, on another occasion in quite a cavalier fashion; on one occasion in a mood of pessimism, on another in a mood of optimism; and these differences may depend on the objective context as well as on the subjective state of the actor. There exists, then, the possibility that what is, in general (that is, for the whole class of problems), significant, may be disregarded in any specific situation, and may, thereafter, come to be regarded as insignificant in general. If an actor demands information of a certain kind, on the basis of such singular experiences, it is manifest that it may not serve his purposes on other occasions when problems of the same class arise.

An actor acting on his own observations and on his own behalf is solely responsible for errors which arise as a consequence of unwarranted generalizations from his experiences. But an information processor may not, as an expert, adopt the view that the possibility of erroneous action, due to over simplification and misinterpretation of experiences by an actor, absolves the processor from care in selecting and processing information. Indeed, the engagement by an actor of an agent to process and supply information is a step by which the actor seeks to avoid erroneous action due to his own inadequacies, when the separate tasks of collecting information relating to the progress of his affairs and of making decisions and acting upon them become complex.

WHAT IS INFORMATION?

If an information system is to be designed it is necessary to make explicit what is to be considered as information. Information is something newly apprehended. It may consist of objects, configurations of objects, or statements about objects. But when it is used in connection with choice, information does not refer to everything which is newly apprehended; it refers to signs or signals bearing on the situations in which choice is to be exercised. When information is used with reference to a particular kind of information producing system, the things which constitute it are further circumscribed.

Within any circumscribed field, we do not regard any commonplace statement as information; to be regarded as information an object or a statement is required to be more specific than a commonplace. An actor whose mind is made up, who has no intention of being "confused by the facts," has no alternatives from which to choose. But an actor who envisages alternative ways of proceeding from a present situation to a future situation experiences doubt. He lacks knowledge of at least some, and often of many, of the facts which will enable him to adapt himself optimally. It is because of the existence of doubt that we consider as information objects or statements that are not mere commonplaces. Only if an actor is in doubt will he seek, and receive, information. The function of information, and hence of an information processing system, is to increase the knowledge or to reduce the doubt of an actor.

Now, generally, there are many pieces of information which influence an actor's response to a stimulus in a given situation. Some may arise from his own observations; some may arise from information processing systems concerned with different facets of his affairs. Some may, in any event, be disregarded. Of any given object, statement or message, we may say that its information content is its potential for selecting responses in the actor.[3] By the potential for selecting responses we do not mean that a given piece of information shall direct an actor what to do. This is ruled out by two considerations: that choice may be made on the basis of many pieces of information, apprehended directly or emanating from different kinds of information processing systems; and that doing depends on the actor's specific ends at the time and the ranking of these depends on all the information then available to him. By the potential for selecting responses

[3] Colin Cherry, *On Human Communication* (New York: Science Editions, Inc., 1961), pp. 9, 169.

we mean, rather, capacity for modifying the actor's predisposition to act in a certain way by virtue of increased knowledge or reduced doubt.

To speak of modifying the actor's predisposition to act is to recognize that he has already some predisposition. He knows the strains to which he is subject; he knows, in a general way, the strains to which he may become subject. He knows at a point of time the strain he would choose to relieve if he were not subject to financial or other limitations of capacity. He knows the valuations he would place on courses of action and on the means of carrying them out, if those means were in his possession or he could acquire them. But all this knowing is of the nature of private knowledge. Private knowledge is personal to its possessor. It is subjective. Useful as it may be to him, it can be of no use except unilaterally in his dealings with others. It may influence his behavior; but he cannot expect the behavior of others to be influenced by it.

The modification we refer to is a modification of the predisposition based on private knowledge in the light of objective reality; the instrument of modification we may describe as public knowledge. Public knowledge is knowledge which is the common property of many men, and may be the property of all men.[4] Now the market place is a public place in which many actors have commerce with one another. The only knowledge useful to any actor in commercial intercourse with others is knowledge which is equally useful to all others. If an actor has at a point of time so many monetary units, or by reference to market prices the means of acquiring so many monetary units, knowledge of this quantity is useful to the actor and to all other actors with whom he may deal. One cannot expect others to assent blandly to one's private evaluations in dealings with them in the market place. To be useful in the market, information as to one's means will be of the kind to which one's counterparts in the market would give assent. And as one's next transaction may be with any one of a number of different kinds of actors, information as to one's means will be such as would command the simultaneous assent of many kinds of one's counterparts in the market. In short, the financial information which is useful in relation to potential operations in markets must have the character of public knowledge. Information based on the notion of current cash equivalents has such a character.

ACCOUNTING AS CONTINUAL RESEARCH

The search for public knowledge, of knowledge which will be useful in any situation requiring adaptation through the market, is

---

4 "What we call objective reality is, in the last analysis, what is common to many thinking beings and could be common to all." Henri Poincaré, cited in Dantzig, *Number, the Language of Science,* p. 242.

essentially no different from the search in which scientists of every variety are engaged. A physical scientist, for example, may want to discover the characteristics of light or of electromagnetic force; he wants to be able to state those characteristics in such a way that his statements may be used in any and every situation in which light or electromagnetic force plays a part. But in enunciating the laws or principles which appear to describe the phenomena of physics, the scientist is concerned with their general utility, not with the aims, objects, or wishes of any person who may subsequently make use of those laws or principles. Only if he maintains his independence of the specific users of his discoveries is it possible to formulate them in such a way that they are generally useful.

In the same sense the processes of accounting are processes of research and discovery. The financial position of an entity at a point of time represents the "laws" under which at that time it must operate, which define and delimit the extent of the operations which are financially possible. Financial position does not predict the precise forms which subsequent actions may take; neither do the laws of physics predict the precise actions of any person who makes use of them. But a statement of financial position which represents the objectively determinable relationships of an entity predicts the general limits—the financial limits—of all immediately future actions. It may, of course, be objected that this use of the notion of laws is strained; for the laws of physics are believed to be generally applicable continuously over long periods of time and over wide ranges of specific objects within their compass. But for any particular application of a physical law, the parameters require to be quantified. In the same way, for any particular application of the laws represented by a statement of financial position, the parameters require to be quantified. The only difference between the two fields then is one of degree; in the field which accounting informs there are no constants and there are no fixed standards of measurement.[5]

For this reason accounting is a process of continual research, of continually discovering the laws which temporarily predict the scope of future actions. This being its character, its procedures will follow the same procedures as other forms of research or scientific inquiry. The information it produces will be information in a strict, scientific sense, uncolored by any presupposition regarding its specific use. Though the processor is an intermediary between objective reality and the actor, the statements which embody the information generated are required to be objective or intersubjectively testable statements. Particular singular statements will be such that, given the same opportunity for observation, an actor himself would make them. They will be such that any other processor would make them;

[5] Economic propositions relating to specific behaviors are likewise constrained. See Robbins, *The Nature and Significance of Economic Science*, pp. 131 ff.

for an actor may successively engage different processors, and, if the statements of any one of them were not objective statements, they could not be compared with or related to statements made under the tenure of another. They will be such that auditors and other investigators would make them.

The role of the processor, the accountant in the present context, is thus a scientific role; he is constrained by the common constraints of scientific inquiry; his problems are amenable to the same kinds of observation and analysis as are those of other scientists; and his function is, in relation to financial matters, no different from that of the researcher in other fields.

OBJECTIVITY AND RELEVANCE

Having outlined the accounting process and having introduced the accountant as an expert intermediary between the environment and the actor, it will be useful to recapitulate some points already developed in Chapter 4. In that chapter it was contended that an actor may discover his financial position by reference, at the time, to market prices which, it was argued, are objective measurements. If a continuous recording process is employed, there may well arise a belief that the recorded statements representing transactions are a series of objective statements, and the mere fact that they are objective statements warrants their processing without any modification.

Now we have observed that the mere equality of balance sheet aggregates at the conclusion of the accounting process provides no guarantee against fictitious entries in the accounts or against wilful or accidental loss of assets. If this is disregarded and the account balances are carried forward without corroboration by reference to other direct evidence, the recording process may perpetuate and compound errors. As to the mere existence of particular assets and obligations, therefore, a continuous record requires authentication, and may require modification, from time to time in order that its statements shall be objective statements.

Similar problems arise in respect of the numbers of monetary units assigned to assets and liabilities which persist through a series of balancing dates. In the absence of a continuous record, an actor would have to determine his financial position by reference to market prices. For a given asset, for example, he may accept, in turn, each of the following statements at the stipulated points of time: "it cost 400 monetary units" (three years ago); "its market selling price is 300 monetary units" (two years ago); "its market selling price is 200 monetary units" (today); "an asset of the same kind in new condition is priced at 500 monetary units" (today). All of these are objective statements; and, if each statement were appropriately dated and recast in the past tense, each could, thereafter, be regarded as an objective statement. Their character, as objective statements, is unaltered by the introduction of an accounting process as an aid to the actor. If objectivity were the only criterion, every such statement would qualify for reporting by the accountant at any present moment. But not all statements have equal potential for selecting responses of an actor at any present moment. The only one which has any bearing on the actor's capacity for adaptation is: "its market selling price is 200 monetary units today." We shall describe such a statement as a relevant statement. Relevance of information is the property by virtue of which information is serviceable in the adaptive process at a point of time. Relevant statements, being objective statements, do not relate to or contemplate any specific potential choice or future situation of an actor. Relevance is a general property; its reference is any and all of the actions available to an actor at a given time. It will now be clear that the first two statements of the above example are excluded because they are not contemporary; and that the fourth is excluded because its reference is to a specific future action which the actor may or may not take.[6]

We contemplate, then, an hierarchy of statements: objective statements, which are subjective but intersubjectively testable; objective statements which have been corroborated; and objective statements which have been corroborated and are relevant. It is this latter subclass which shall be the end product of an accounting system if it is to be serviceable in the adaptive process.[7]

Relevance After Aggregation

The statements generated by an accounting system are more complex than the singular statements used as an illustration in a preceding paragraph. The singular statements which are account balances at the end of a period are reduced in number by aggregation; each such aggregative statement represents the combined or resultant effects of numbers of events and transactions, all of which are represented by dated and objective statements when they first entered the record. These aggregative statements are also required to be objective and relevant statements at the point of time for which they are made. But these characteristics may be lost in the aggregation. Suppose that on January 1 an automobile was acquired for an outlay of 2000 monetary units; that on July 1 a similar

6 We agree with the view: "Accounting is concerned with 'price,' however greatly the businessman may be concerned with 'value.'" A. C. Littleton, "Value and Price in Accounting," *The Accounting Review*, Sept., 1929. And with the notion of "price-aggregates," as in W. A. Paton and A. C. Littleton, *An Introduction to Corporate Accounting Standards* (American Accounting Association, 1940), pp. 24–5. But subject to price being understood as contemporary price or current cash equivalent.

7 See also R. J. Chambers, "The Formal Basis of Business Decisions," *The Australian Accountant*, April, 1956.

automobile was acquired for the same outlay; and that appropriate dated entries were made in the record. Both dated statements in the record may be described as objective statements. Suppose now (disregarding wear and tear, for the sake of simplicity) that a balance sheet dated December 31 includes a statement "Automobiles, at cost, 4000 monetary units." By the omission of the dates of purchase, this statement has lost the objective character of the original statements in the record. It is not a testable or an interpretable statement, unless the date of the balance sheet is presumed to be the date to which "cost" refers, and this is clearly a false presumption. It would make a great deal of difference to an actor if the date to which cost refers were ten years ago; but the statement leaves him entirely without a reference.

Note that the example given is free of any complication which may arise from shifts in relative prices or in the price level; if such shifts supervene, it is even more necessary to state the dates of acquisition if a statement in the above form is to made. This, of course, would prevent the reduction of account balances by aggregation. But aggregation is a necessary device if overtaxing of the span of attention is to be avoided. The way out of this dilemma has been indicated. If the only relevant statement at a point of time about a particular asset is its market selling price at that time, the only relevant statement about a group of assets is the sum of their market selling prices at that time. An aggregative statement bearing a single date will be an objective statement only if its components are objective statements at that date; and at that date the aggregative statement will be relevant. If the only step in the processing of originally recorded statements were aggregation and the consequent omission of dates of occurrence, some modification would be necessary to make good the loss of information. But we have shown that modification is also necessary for other reasons.

Some Objections to Modification of the Record

Now it may be objected that modification entails the intrusion of subjective or personal influences into the system. No more so than proceeding without modification. A statement entered in the record of a past transaction is, itself, a subjective statement; but it qualifies as an objective statement if other persons could independently make the same statement; it qualifies by being intersubjectively testable. But we have shown that a whole series of similarly objective statements could be made through time; the mere fact that a transaction took place at a specific price established by an arm's length bargain does not constitute a statement to that effect the only possible objective statement about the asset or liability arising from the transaction. Objections to changing statements of record on the ground of the subjectivity of the modification cannot stand. Nor, further, can the objection be sustained on the ground that modification reduces the relevance of the products of the system. For this would entail the belief—a subjective belief to which no other person would give assent—that an objective statement once made is forever after relevant to adaptation.

It may be objected, however, that if one seeks to discover the presently realizable market price of any asset in possession, one may obtain many different quotations, and that the selection of any one of these as a basis for modifying the record involves a personal judgment. This is true, if the selection of one from a series of quotations is seen as the solution. But this problem like many others may be illuminated by reference to the sciences. It is generally accepted that no empirically determined measurement, no single measurement obtained by observation, represents the "true" value of the property measured.[8] All such single measurements are regarded as members of a class of measurements which, if a sufficiently large sample were taken, could be represented by a frequency distribution having a central tendency. If such a distribution is discovered, the value about which the distribution is clustered is regarded as the most acceptable, because it is the most probable, value of the property measured.[9] Reverting to the problem of finding a measure of realizable market price, it will be clear that solution by selection of one from a series of quotations rests on a belief that there is a single "true" value, a belief which is inconsistent with the imperfections of the measurement apparatus in the exact sciences, and for greater reason in the field of economic phenomena. If, on the other hand, quoted prices are regarded as instances of a collection of prices, and the problem is regarded as one of discovering the price which has the greatest probability, its resolution along statistical lines will be freer of subjectivity than any other process of selection. If, of course, only one quotation can be obtained, that must be accepted.[10]

Whatever the disabilities of an information processor in referring to market prices for information, exactly the same difficulties confront the actor. A market may be imperfect; one may believe prices quoted are not "fair" prices. But the market with all its imperfections is in the last resort

---

8 "An empirically 'true' value of a measured quantity does not exist. What passes for truth among the results of measurement is maximum likelihood, a concept that attains meaning if a sufficient statistical sample of differing measured values is available." Henry Margenau, "Philosophical Problems Concerning the Meaning of Measurement in Physics," *Measurement—Definitions and Theories*, C. West Churchman and Philburn Ratoosh, eds. (New York: John Wiley & Sons, Inc. 1959), p. 165.

9 It is not intended to suggest that the problem of discovering the most probable value of a series of measurements is simple of solution; the difficulties are dealt with in the literature of statistics.

10 "... a single measured number is devoid of significance except as a tentative indication, acceptable only under the duress of conditions that forbid the repetition of a measurement." Margenau, "Philosophical Problems...," p. 165.

the only source of information which is free of subjective and speculative elements. Inasmuch as an actor must accept its verdicts, so must the accountant.

UNIFORMITY

If relevance is accepted as a principle in the design of information processing systems, and of accounting systems in particular, certain uniformities are entailed. Note that we do not say universalities. A physicist does not apply the principles of gravitational systems to the study of light. There are entities which have quite different financial constraints and objectives, and it will be shown that the requisite accounting systems for different classes of entities will differ. But it is reasonable to expect that the accounting systems of all entities which are members of a class of entities having similar generic operations, environments, constraints, and ends shall be substantially uniform, yielding information of uniform quality. In rebuttal of this presumption, it may be contended that every entity is different from every other entity of the same class; for example, among the class of entities which are trading firms, some are retailers, some wholesalers, some deal in perishables, some in durables, and so on. A uniform process or set of rules requires to be justified.

One reason for uniformity lies in the interdependence of actors. Any actor acts in contractual cooperation or in competition with other actors over a wide range of particular actions. Under contractual cooperation, each of the contracting parties may wish to assure himself of the financial capacity of the other to perform his part of the contract. If resort is to be had to the financial statements of another, as being more reliable than the mere assertions of that other, one will expect that the information they contain will be interpretable in the same manner as the information contained at the same time in one's own statements. If the statements are not so interpretable, there can be no consensus between the parties; the situation leaves the contractors open to every abuse from simple secretiveness to gross fraud. The classes of action we contemplate here are extensive; they include all transactions involving the giving and receiving of credit and all transactions by which two or more entities engage in a common task. Under competition, each of the competitors will require to know the extent to which he can withstand or counter the moves of another. Each may seek to outwit the other—to increase his share of the market, to strike a more favorable bargain—but he would not wish to outwit himself, to be under any delusion as to the limits of his financial capacity for meeting competition. If, for the moment, we consider information processors as a class to stand aloof from this competitive struggle, they will see that each of the competitors will require information of the same contemporary and relevant kind—whether the age of the competing entities is the same or disparate, informed competition depends on this. If the information required is the same in kind, uniform in quality, the principles and rules by which it is derived will necessarily be uniform.

A second reason lies in the fact that comparison is a process antecedent to or incidental to all perceptions, judgments, and choices. For the present purpose, we will disregard the external actions and relationships used as examples in the previous paragraph and consider judgments made as to the effectiveness of past courses of action. To make any such judgment on the basis of financial statements requires that successive accounting summaries shall have been compiled according to the same principles and rules. For suppose they have not been so derived. If the actor does not know this he will make comparisons which are invalid. If he does know, he will be obliged to make *ad hoc* adjustments so that he may make comparisons. But as these adjustments are made in close temporal proximity to the evaluation of future courses of action, the tasks of getting at the facts and evaluation may be confused, to the detriment of objectivity and relevance. These adjustments do not become part of the record, so that such adjustments made when interpreting successive accounting summaries may be inconsistent, defeating comparison. And as they do not become part of the record, the record does not provide the full context of the immediately following decisions, and cannot, thereafter, provide an adequate basis for judging the effectiveness of past decisions.

A third reason for uniform processing rules is related to processing itself. If one were to suppose that, all actors being unique, the quality of processed information relevant to a given actor is not relevant to any other actor of the same class, there could be no general rules capable of being taught and learned, no transfer of processing skill and experience. There could be nothing expert about information processing. Each processor would come to the service of an actor with no pertinent knowledge or experience, and would be subject to whatever rules the actor, wisely or foolishly, knowledgeably or ignorantly, may impose. Uniform rules are the fruit of expert understanding of the uniformities underlying apparent diversity. Diversity of rules is evidence of a very rudimentary, particularistic understanding; indeed, diversity is evidence of observation without understanding.

Further, uniformity makes for ease of application, an advantage to processors as a class in terms of simplicity of formal processes, but no less an advantage to actors in terms of economy of processing costs. More importantly, it operates as a safeguard against the undisciplined exercise of discretion by processors, and against unwarranted interference with the process by actors. Suppose, for example, a processor were to imagine that it is in the best interest of an actor that he should have a conservative view of the state of his affairs and of his results; or suppose, even, that an actor were to require that the processed statements should give a conservative view, and that the process were modified to procure such an effect; or suppose, that a confident or optimistic view were required. The intrusion of any such modification involves (subjective) tampering with the objectivity of the statements.[11] And in a continuous process through time, tampering once entails distortion thereafter, unless the effect is corrected. But if such interference is acceptable, the effect will not be corrected. Further, there is no measure of what is meant by, say, conservatism; its effects may be modest or extreme; they may be slight individually, but extensive cumulatively; they may vary in extent from year to year. They will confuse all efforts to profit from comparisons. This is not to say that an actor may not, given the facts, appraise them conservatively or optimistically, or act conservatively or optimistically. But if the facts are recorded he will, thereafter, be able to discover whether and when he acted one way or the other and with what effects.

Clearly, uniformity is not to be considered as simply a device for coercion, a straitjacket or a systematist's whim. Its necessity stems from the assumptions of informed adaptation under conditions of interdependence.

RELEVANCE—GENERAL AND PARTICULAR

What is generally relevant to a class of actors is discoverable by examination of the circumstances in which they act, of the general bases of their choices, and of the kinds of action they may take; but without any supposition or presumption that a given actor will take any specific action. The environment, the role, and the available actions of an actor are the primary data for the design of an information processing system; this is the reason why these matters have received attention in preceding chapters.

If an actor is obliged to accommodate himself to information generated on principles other than those which emerge from the above considerations, the information processing system is less efficient than it can be. If the

11 " . . . any . . . tampering with messages decreases the amount of information they contain, unless new information is fed in, either from new sensations or from memories which have been previously excluded from the information system." Wiener, *The Human Use of Human Beings*, p. 94.

process is technical and the particular rules are the upshot of decisions by the processor, the obligation to accommodate himself and the process rests on the processor. The processor may not choose to omit from the record a representation of any event or fact which is relevant; nor may he choose to introduce representations of events and facts which are irrelevant or which produce irrelevancies. The processor can have no personal criteria of relevance; what is relevant to an actor is determined by reference to the actor's objectively determinable interactions with his environment.[12]

The term "relevance" may be used of much information other than systematically processed information, and even of propositions which are not strictly information. The whole of his environment is continually conveying messages to an actor. He becomes aware of numerous pieces of information by direct observation, whether or not he has access to processed information. His judgments or decisions are products of the appraisal of information of many kinds and from many sources. In choosing between conflicting ends, quite different pieces of information directly observed may be relevant to the available courses of action severally; in choosing, say, between poverty and honesty, quite different considerations are relevant in respect of each separately. We may even say that a hypothetical proposition or calculation is relevant to the evaluation of a course of action, even though hypothetical propositions are argumentative and exploratory rather than informative.[13] These usages of "relevance" are not to be overlooked; but neither are they to be confused with relevance as a property of processed information. The latter has been defined as a general property, related to every course of action but to no course in particular; whereas the usages illustrated above have reference to particular actions.

But note that the selection of particular actions for evaluation is at the option of the actor, not of the information processor. What is relevant to any particular potential course of action depends, therefore, upon whether that course is selected for evaluation. The actor selects courses for evaluation, searches the environment, and makes his exploratory and anticipatory calculations in the light of his present strains and

[12] For some reflections on principle arising from experience of the introduction of a computer and a standard costing system—both information processing systems—see P. L. Smith, "What is Relevant? Some Initial Problems in the Production of Quantitative Data," *The Journal of Industrial Economics,* Vol. VII, No. 3, July 1959.

[13] If *B* tells *A*, an actor, that "income for a forthcoming period is expected to be 10,000 monetary units," we do not consider this statement to be information. What *is* information to *A* is: "*B has estimated* that income for a forthcoming period is expected to be 10,000 monetary units." In short, the usage of the term *information* is restricted to corroborable statements.

capacities; he does not search at random. Insofar as knowledge of financial strains and capacities influences the selection, it- is antecedent to, and a necessary condition of, deliberate selection. An information processor, being only a limited agent of an actor, cannot know during the process, the financial or other strains to which the actor is subject. The financial condition only becomes apparent at the conclusion of the accounting process, and all other strains are either the subject of other information systems or personal to the actor. The financial information processor cannot know, therefore, what may be relevant in the particular sense, for the actor himself cannot know during the interval of processing.

The anticipation of a future state, or the selection of specific actions for evaluation, even by the actor himself, does not alter his present state and can provide no basis for ascertaining his present state. The impropriety of permitting anticipations to influence the processing of information is greater still. Any conceivable action may become an action selected for evaluation; and any conceivable end may become an end selected for attainment. Processed information, part and whole, will, thus necessarily be generally relevant to every such possible action and end, but particularly relevant to none.

Independence of the possible ends of actors may be described as the neutrality of information. The relevance of processed information depends on its neutrality with respect to the ends of the actor.

The criteria of objectivity, correspondence, relevance, and neutrality all tend in a similar direction; they reinforce one another. But it seems to be worth emphasizing that they arise from quite different considerations. Objectivity is necessary as a protection against the intrusion of private statements and potentially biased and untestable statements. Correspondence is necessary by virtue of the possibility that formal records may cease, without correction, to represent the independently discoverable relationships of an entity with its environment. Relevance is a necessary criterion because it provides the means of selecting from the multiplicity of possible objective statements those which inform an actor at a specified time. And neutrality is a necessary criterion because of the variety and unpredictability of the specific courses of action and ends which an actor may entertain.

RELIABILITY

We observed at the beginning of this chapter that an actor is in many respects obliged to rely on the processor, the process, and the information it generates. But he is not altogether without the means of discovering whether or not his trust is well placed. Acting in the market place, he may discover whether or not particular statements of record are consistent with his observations.[14] If any such statement is not consistent with his observations, he will be disposed to doubt the veracity at the time of the processed information. Doubting any such statement entails doubting any aggregative statement of which it is a component or on which it has an effect—the balance sheet and the income statement, for example. If he is sufficiently critical or if such inconsistencies occur frequently, the discovery will tend to weaken, if not to destroy, his confidence in the process and, or, the processor. He may, thereupon, abandon reliance on their product and seek other means of informing himself. Instead of producing information which will tend to the reduction of doubt, the process will have increased the area of doubt; for the actor will still entertain doubts about his relationship with the environment, and will, in addition, doubt the reliability of the process or the processor. The processor will, in fact, have destroyed his function.

On the other hand, an actor is not able to test by observation every singular statement arising from the process. If he discovers some inconsistencies he may regard them as excusable or random errors, supposing that, in general, the information he is given is of better quality. His confidence may not then be destroyed, but it may, nevertheless, be misplaced. In the second place, the aggregate effect of a multiplicity of events is not a matter of direct experience. An actor, therefore, has no means, if there is effective specialization of functions, of discovering whether an aggregative statement is reliable and pertinent to his future actions. For this reason, too, his confidence may not be destroyed, but it may be misplaced. In these circumstances, it is obviously possible for an actor to act with great astuteness and wisdom in respect of particular actions which have modest and readily discernible costs and effects, simply because he may directly observe the immediate costs and effects; but he may yet act quite foolishly in matters of great consequence, if these depend on assessments of aggregates of which he can have no direct experience, and if the processed information on which he depends is an imperfect representation of objective and relevant facts.

The problems of ensuring reliability and relevance may be explored

---

[14] Reichenbach speaks of the attachment of "weights" to all unverified propositions and reports. "The highest initial weights concern the immediately observed concrete objects .... All reports of the past, transmitted by other persons or by myself, appear with an initial weight which is referred to what I know and observe just now. The world of the immediate present, itself bearing the highest weights, is the center of reference for all other weights coordinated to propositions about other things ... This is what we call the *superiority of the immediate present*." Reichenbach, *Experience and Prediction*, pp. 23, 280–1. Emphasis in original. See also Keynes, *The General Theory of Employment, Interest and Money*, p. 148.

by considering actors singly and entities of a more complex kind as purposive systems or machines.[15]

ACTORS AND ENTITIES AS SYSTEMS

An actor having means and acting in his environment constitutes a system for serving his ends. His capacities for acting are limited by his means and the other constraints of the environment. His actions have effects which, after an interval, short or long, become apparent to him; he receives information; the receipt of information as to effects is described as feedback. But, as the expected effects may differ from the discovered effects and as the action and the discovery of its effects take time, the effects of any course of action may exceed the limits set in advance and represented by the expected effects. On discovery of the excess effect, action will be necessary to compensate for the deviation and this, for the same reason, may produce excessive effects in the opposite direction. The system is capable of wide oscillations in effects, their extent depending on the time taken for actual effects to become apparent as marked deviations from the desired effects. For a single actor engaging in a series of actions which work themselves out concurrently, the time may be considerable and the dissipation of effort or other resources may be considerable. The system may be represented as follows:

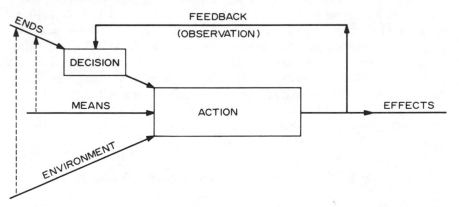

Now consider a more complex entity of the kind discussed in this chapter. The division of labor which expresses specialization of functions entails that an entity consists of an actor and at least one other agent;

[15] Following the usage of "machine" as in, for example, Stafford Beer, *Cybernetics and Management* (London: The English Universities Press Ltd., 1959), pp. 24–5.

but the entity has one orientation, the set of goals of the entity. Actor and agent, and the information system which links them, constitute a single "machine" or purposive system. The system involves at least two independent intelligences, but they are to act as one.

Simple as a two-person system may seem it is much more complicated than a single person acting purposively in the same environment. Where specialization is warranted, the transactions of the entity and the events impinging on it are numerous. They are observed or experienced, sometimes by the actor, sometimes by the agent, and sometimes by both parties. Each having experiences, memories, capacities for observation and action, and so on, different from the other, the possibility of different interpretations being placed on transactions and events is considerable. The agent may have no direct experience of the strains which act as stimuli to the system (or, more specifically, to the actor); and the indirect experience he may obtain through signals—discussions, explanations, instructions—from the actor may be incomplete and, therefore, not invariably reliable as guides. The actor may have no experience of the processing system as such, and may, therefore, be unaware of the degree to which its products are relevant, or are affected by preconceptions of the processor or by defects of the process.

As a whole the system is, in relation to the goals of the entity, a probabilistic one; and not only by reason of the unpredictable effects of the environment, but also by reason of the fact that two or more persons are involved having different specific goals, experiences, and competences. The system may be represented thus:

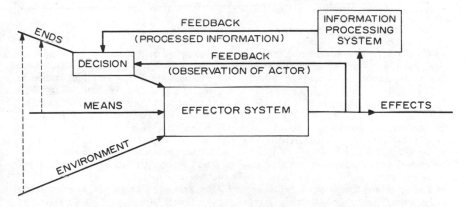

Several things may yet happen. Observations of effects and the treatment of these observations in the information processing system may be such that what appears as a feedback is distorted information and inconsistent with the functioning of the system. If distortion is not discovered, the system will continue to function only by a fortuitous combination of favorable circumstances. If the distortion is discovered, the discovery will have one or both of two consequences. The actor will be obliged to regulate the system in terms of expected effects only, and as expected effects do not constitute new information, the system is left open to the oscillations previously mentioned. Again the actor may resort to an additional observational feedback where this is possible, depending on the information processing system where observational feedback is not possible. In this case the information in the total system will be conflicting and confusing, tending to dissipation of the energies of the system, if not to its destruction.

Any such complex system, left to its own devices or allowed to develop without deliberately selected principles, is subject to the law of increasing entropy.[16] If in any collection of components constituting a system, there is clear differentiation of functions and clear definition of the relationships between the components and between the functions, the system may be said to be organized. The clarity of differentiation and definition enables each component to concentrate its specific energy on its specific function. But if functions are not defined, or become mixed or unrelated, the tendency to nondifferentiation results in the dissipation of "local pockets of high energy," increasing disorganization and increasing entropy.[17]

It is the function of new information to prevent this degeneration.[18] But an additional loop in the system is necessary to secure that the observation and information processing component is aware of what the system requires. Including this loop the system may be represented thus:

[16] The concept of entropy and the law of increasing entropy are derived by analogy from thermodynamics. Entropy being interpreted as a measure of disorganization, or nondifferentiation of the energies of the particles in a system, the second law of thermodynamics may be formulated: "In *natural processes* taking place in *isolated systems* the entropy never decreases." Henry Margenau, William W. Watson, C. G. Montgomery, *Physics, Principles and Applications* (New York: McGraw-Hill Book Company, 1953), p. 308. (Italics in original.) The analogy is supported by observable tendencies in social affairs. The analogue of an isolated system is a system cut off from the energizing effect of new information (for example, by a faulty information subsystem). The analogue of natural processes is the undirected interrelationships and discretions of persons who are components of the system but have also other ends. Among those who have recourse to the notion in the context of human affairs are Beer, *Cybernetics and Management;* Cherry, *On Human Communication;* Joshua Whatmough, *Language, A Modern Synthesis* (London: Secker & Warburg, 1956); Wiener, *Cybernetics* and *The Human Use of Human Beings.*

[17] Beer, *Cybernetics and Management,* p. 26.

[18] Wiener, *The Human Use of Human Beings,* pp. 21, 25. "Messages are themselves a form of pattern and organization ... it is the function of these [feedback] mechanisms to control the mechanical tendency toward disorganization; in other words, to produce a temporary and local reversal of the normal direction of entropy."

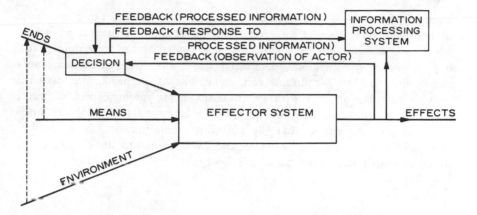

The effect of the new loop is twofold. It serves to put the information processing system on the footing of knowing what effects are expected, and hence of activating observation. And it serves to correct the flow of information from the process if the information shows a tendency to wander from what is relevant. An information processing system itself is subject to increasing entropy if isolated from the total system of which it is a part. The loop now inserted is a feedback imposed on a feedback to avert this tendency.

The system as a whole will now have the characteristic of stability in performance of its function. It will have the characteristics of a homeostatic machine. There are limiting conditions under which it will continue to function, represented by the constraints of the environment and the ends of the entity; these are known to the system. It is energized by decisions of the actor. The effects are continually under observation. Any tendency for the effects to exceed the limits of its viability is observed and serves to modify the inputs, to give rise to new decisions and actions. Whether or not the causes of such a tendency are known or discoverable is immaterial for immediate adaptation. What serves to modify the inputs is information as to the effects of past actions. The modification takes place by negative feedback, that is to say, the information has the potential for selecting responses which tend to prevent effects exceeding the limits of the system's viability.

RELIABILITY AND RELEVANCE

It will now be clear that feedback provides the solution to the problem of securing the reliability and relevance of processed information, and that the adaptive process which is taken as fundamental to the behavior of actors is equally fundamental to the operations of auxiliary processes. There can be no presumption that an actor can, out of his experience, instruct an accountant as to the information he needs which an accounting system can produce; nor that an accountant can, out of his experience alone, determine the information which an actor needs; nor that an accountant can, by means of an accounting system, provide information of the range that any actor might expect of him. There is no other solution of questions relating to the reliability and relevance of information than by constant communication between the actor and the information processor and by reference to the environment in which the system they constitute operates.[19]

Argument

7.11   *Information subsists in signs—objects or statements—having a potential for selecting responses in an actor at a point of time; the information content of a sign is its potential for selecting responses.*

7.12   The function of information is to reduce the doubt of an actor, to order his expectations, and thus to modify his subjective state.
(1.67, 2.72, *7.11*)

7.13   Direct apprehension by an actor of signs of aggregative effects is impossible when an entity is affected by many acts and events distributed through space or time.
(*1.12*, 1.36, 6.13)

7.14   *Information processing is purposive and abstractive collection, arrangement, aggregation, and transformation of singular signs.*

7.15   Acting and information processing will be functionally differentiated when detailed recollection or direct apprehension, by the actor, of singular or aggregative effects becomes impossible and when the time available for acting prevents the allocation of time to searching.
(*1.14*, *1.18*, 3.23, 7.13)

7.16   The information processor's role is as an extension of the actor's sensory and calculatory apparatus.
(*3.31*, *7.14*)

---

19 " . . . the relations between knowledge and action . . . cannot be adequately mastered unless each kind of specialist develops an extensive knowledge of the other's mental processes. Indeed, the most important task for both policy-makers and researchers is a more communicable definition of the problem to be solved." Max F. Millikan, "Inquiry and Policy: The Relation of Knowledge to Action," in Daniel Lerner, ed., *The Human Meaning of the Social Sciences* (New York: Meridian Books, Inc., 1959), p. 168.

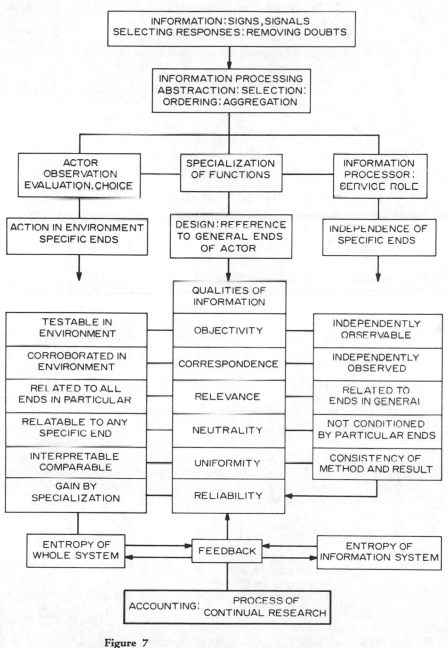

Figure 7
OUTLINE OF CHAPTER 7: INFORMATION AND
INFORMATION PROCESSING.

7.17   Differentiation does not remove the actor's capacity for observation or the functions of evaluation and choice.

(*1.12*, 2.26, 2.28, 7.15)

7.21   As action in markets entails relationships of an actor with another or others, only objective, or intersubjectively testable, statements will qualify as information. Objective statements representing singular objects or events necessarily include the times of occurrence of those events.

(*1.64*, 1.68, *3.26*, 4.15)

7.22   All objective statements which meet the criterion of correspondence (that is, which have been corroborated) at a point of time qualify as information at that time.

(1.68, 1.74, 7.21)

7.23   *The independence of an information processor subsists in his disregard, as processor, of specific ends or values, his own or what he believes to be the actor's.*

7.24   The probability of correspondence varies directly with the independence of the processor.

(1.68, *7.14*, *7.23*)

7.25   *Relevance is the property by virtue of which a statement, singular or aggregative, has potential for selecting responses in an actor at a point of time.*

7.26   *Neutrality is the property by virtue of which a statement, singular or aggregative, is relevant whatever ends are selected by the actor for consideration.*

7.27   The product of an information processing system from time to time shall be that class of statements which meets the tests of objectivity, correspondence, relevance, and neutrality.

(1.45, 1.68, 2.30, *3.12*, 7.17)

7.31   Statements representing financial properties of events and objects require processing not only by reason of the diversity and distribution through space and time of those events and objects, but also by reason of the variability of prices and of the dimension of the monetary unit.

(3.53, 3.63, 3.83, *7.13*)

7.32   Accounting is an information processing system.

(*4.42*, *7.14*, 7.31)

7.33   Accounting is a process of continual research, directed to the discovery of the consequences of past actions and events, and of the laws which at a point of time state the financial limits of all immediately future actions.

(*4.42*, 7.27, 7.32)

7.34   Where a process entails aggregation of singular statements at a common point of time, the aggregative statement will be relevant only if each component statement is relevant at that time.

(*1.43*, 6.22, *7.14*, 7.21)

7.35   Modification of a continuous financial record in the light of changes in the observable facts is a condition of optimal action on the basis of processed financial information.

(2.72, 7.31, 7.34)

7.41   In respect of all similar entities under interdependence, conformity with the principles of objectivity, correspondence, relevance, and neutrality entails processing rules which are either uniform or equivalent in effect.

(7.21, 7.27)

7.51   *Complex effector systems (systems in which there are many variables) operating in isolation are subject to the law of increasing entropy or disorganization.*

7.52   Effector systems and information sub-systems are complex systems, isolable from environmental conditions by defects in sensory or observational or communicatory apparatus, and by continued operation on the basis of expected effects only.

(*1.12*, 2.72, *3.12*, 7.15, *7.51*)

7.53   *Feedback is the process by which the future behavior of actor or agent is informed by the effects of immediately past behavior.*

7.54   Information systems are negative feedback mechanisms, operating against the tendency for entropy to increase.

(*7.11*, *7.51*, *7.53*)

7.55   *The reliability of processed information subsists in the actor's belief in its correspondence; the reliability of an information processing system subsists in its capacity to produce information having the property of correspondence.*

7.56   The reliability of processed information as a basis of choice, and, hence, the reliability of the process, may be assessed by the actor in respect of singular statements, by observational feedback.

(7.17, 7.52, *7.53*, *7.55*)

7.57   The reliability of aggregative statements may be assessed by observational feedback in respect of the singular component statements, but at the cost of at least some of the gains from differentiation of functions.

(*1.42*, 7.15, 7.56)

7.58   The reliability and relevance of processed information and of the process are controlled by feedback, from the environment and the actor to the processor.

(*7.25*, *7.53*, *7.55*)

Communication

8 THE COMMUNICATION PROCESS

A system in which separate persons have distinctive but complementary roles gives rise to problems in communication. In the previous chapter we considered some of the general characteristics of information and information processing systems. But information and information processing systems are only parts of larger systems—communication systems—in the case of multiperson entities. We have now to consider the structure of information or messages, and the conditions under which communication is possible.

Communication, as a physical process, takes place when signs or signals are transmitted from a source to a receiver through a channel linking the source with the receiver. In our present context, the source is a series of economic events and effects. The signs or signals are representations of properties of those events and effects. The channel is the whole process of observing, describing, recording, and summarizing descriptions of a particular aspect of those events and of transmitting the result. The receiver is an actor. But communication may not be considered simply as a physical process. An actor has no use for signs as such; he has use for signs having meaning or significance in the circumstances in which he finds himself. Communication between persons is a matter of transmitting significances, of establishing in the mind of another what one has observed, or the product of what one has observed, recorded, and otherwise processed. In view of the personal element inherent in all perceptions, interpretations, and evaluations it is necessary to demonstrate that transmission is possible.

Between the observable facts and the actor are many points at which losses of financial information may occur. At the simplest level, evidence of actual transactions may be mislaid. The translation of actual transactions into double-entry statements may be in error, either of a mechanical kind or through failure to distinguish significant features of either or both aspects of the transaction. Events other than transactions may not be regarded as relevant, and no statement representing them may appear in the record. Defects of these kinds may be remedied by relatively simple means. At a more serious level there may be misunderstandings of the events observed (on the part of the information processor) and of the signals received (on the part of the actor). Many of these arise from the fact that ostensible objects and events are not equivalent to the statements which represent them. Such correspondence as objects have to statements about them arises from habitual or instantial association of signs with objects. Associations of signs with objects being subjective, there is no necessary relationship between the associations of any two persons, even if they are components of the same system. The potential difficulties may be illustrated by reference to the adjacent diagram.[1]

An observed event or thing (the designatum) is associated with a sign: the dotted line represents association, which is a product of learning and memory provoked by direct apprehension. The sign, in conjunction with the environment and other memories of the processor, organizes responses or thoughts in the latter; the processor translates what he observes into statements capable of treatment in the system he operates—for example, an automobile purchased by an actor is treated by his accountant as an asset; its style, horsepower, and other properties, not being amenable to translation into accounting signs, are disregarded. The result of this process is transmitted as a signal to the actor. The actor, in turn, associates the signal with something and interprets the signal, in the context of

---

[1] The diagram extends the application of the triangle of reference of Ogden and Richards, *The Meaning of Meaning*, p. 11, in a manner suggested by Cherry, *On Human Communication*, p. 110. An earlier form of the diagram and of the following argument was given in R. J. Chambers, "The Role of Information Systems in Decision Making," *Management Technology*, Vol. 4, No. 1, June 1964.

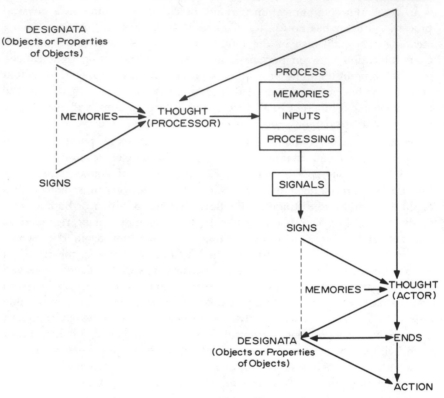

INFORMATION PROCESSING AND COMMUNICATION.

his environment and *his* memories as designating that thing. Ideally his response to the signal will be the same as would be his response to the thing which was the experience of the processor, if he had apprehended it directly.

The diagram serves the above case of a single event; but it has been drawn in contemplation of the complex overlapping sequence of events which is commonly the subject of accounting signals. In this case, there is a number of designata—each associated with its sign, each organizing thoughts in the processor—which as signs enter the formal record system where there is already a store of signs, a "memory." This store of signs, representing the situation of the actor-entity before the events to be recorded, is augmented by signs representing those events. The result of the process is a signal, or signals, indicating to the actor the consequential effect of the events recorded and the position of the entity after those events. As before, the actor interprets the signal, in conjunction with his environment and his memories. Ideally, his response to the signal will be the same as if he were to have direct knowledge of the events and their effects.

Clearly, there are many points at which interference may arise. Contrast the associations of objects and signs by the two parties; and the effects of the different environments and memories of the two parties. Even if there were uniquely interpretable signs, the system would still involve some loss of information; for processing takes time, and the passage of this time entails that the actor is always behind time in appraising effects, by comparison with appraisal after direct observation. We merely observe this loss; as long as operations are complex and processing takes time, it is inevitable to some extent. We will, however, consider whether and under what conditions the response to a sign, a signal, or a message may be expected to be the same as if the actor had direct knowledge of what it represents.

SEMANTICAL RULES

The signs commonly used in person to person communication are words and numbers. In accounting, use is made of both—to designate the time of occurrence of an event, to designate its character, and to denote the magnitude of its monetary properties. All three elements occur in the concatenations of signs which are the singular or aggregative statements produced by accounting processes.

Neither words nor numbers are unequivocal signs of objects, events, relationships, or of the properties of any of these. The word used as a sign for any object depends at least on the language system being used. It also depends on which of the several properties of the object is considered by the user sufficient to differentiate the object from other objects; one may refer to a ball as a sphere; but the use of "sphere" does not suggest that the referent is a ball. In natural languages there are understandings governing the usage and interpretation of word-signs at any time. These are given by dictionaries. But the greater part of the signs commonly used, notwithstanding that they usually procure effects which their users intend, are not uniquely defined in dictionaries.[2] The referents of such signs are at any time ambiguous. Not only that; a natural language is continually

2 "The dictionary is a list of substitute symbols. It says in effect: 'This can be substituted for that in such and such circumstances.' It can do this because in these circumstances and for suitable interpreters the references caused by the two symbols will be sufficiently alike. The dictionary thus serves to mark the overlaps between the references of symbols rather than to define their fields." Ogden and Richards, *The Meaning of Meaning*, p. 207.

evolving; words acquire new meanings, lose old meanings; words which at one time have unique referents come, by figurative, euphemistic, or analogical use, to have many referents. Meanings become less specific to signs; signs become more diffuse in meaning.[3]

Though this tendency adds to the richness and capacity of a language in its everyday use, in relation to situations requiring signs having more or less precise referents the tendency is an instance of the application of the law of increasing entropy. The tendency may be reversed in particular areas by the introduction of new energy represented by the effort of devising new unequivocal terms, or the effort of defining (of indicating the designata of signs) and the effort of submitting to the discipline of defined terms.[4] Most discussions and negotiations at some point require the introduction of such effort; and in scientific and technical discourse it is almost mandatory. Indeed, in the latter case, technical languages are developed, which are sign-systems designed to facilitate communication by preventing diffusion of meaning. The signs denoting mathematical operations and relationships, and logical operations and relationships are examples of such systems. The rules governing their use are explicit and clearly understood among their users. The signs denoting the chemical elements, their compounds, and the reactions between them constitute such a system. They serve to rationalize the diverse descriptions and symbols employed prior to the time of Berzelius and Dalton.[5] The object of all such exercises is to make possible the intersubjectivity of meanings and to establish consensus between the users of terms. The effect is to make explicit the semantical rules which determine the applicability of a word or other sign to certain situations under certain conditions.[6]

[3] It has been alleged that an English Act of Parliament relating to finance contained twenty-seven different definitions of the word "value." *Proceedings of the International Congress on Accounting,* London, 1933, p. 135. An inquiry to discover the "multiple meanings of words which are most confusing to grammar school pupils and foreigners who are studying English" revealed thirty-four meanings of the word "account." Harold A. Larrabee, *Reliable Knowledge* (Boston: Houghton Mifflin Company, 1945), p. 264. And, in another field, "Perhaps an extreme form of the tendency to rob the term 'scientific' of all definite content is illustrated by the earnest use that advertisers sometimes make of such phrases as 'scientific hair-cutting,' 'scientific rug cleaning,' and even 'scientific astrology.' " Nagel, *The Structure of Science,* p. 2.

[4] " . . . when a writer creates or modifies a concept he ought also to coin a new word to denote it, rather than corrupt the language and spread confusion." Fritz Machlup, "Statics and Dynamics, Kaleidoscopic Words," *The Southern Economic Journal,* Vol. XXVI, No. 2, October 1959; reproduced in *Essays on Economic Semantics* (Englewood Cliffs, N.J.: Prentice-Hall, Inc., 1963), p. 12.

[5] Bernard Jaffe, *Crucibles, The Story of Chemistry* (New York: Simon and Schuster, Inc., 1957), Chaps. VI, VII. Leonard Bloomfield, "Linguistic Aspects of Science," *International Encyclopedia of Unified Science* (Chicago: University of Chicago Press, 1955), Vol. 1, pp. 260 ff.

[6] Morris, "Foundations of the Theory of Signs," pp. 102, 125.

Where the originator of a message and the receiver of it are specialists in different fields—in the present case, the actor and the accountant are specialists in different fields—consensus may not be established, or if it is established, it may break down. This will occur if terms are used which have quite different referents in two or more fields. We have already observed that, in a given system, common use and interpretation may be established by feedback. But this in itself provides no rule for deciding which specific usage of the available competing usages shall prevail.

The actor has relationships with a potentially extensive range of other actors, in the course of which he may wish to make reference, for his own information or for the information of others, to accounting statements, singular or aggregative. If the terms of those statements are employed in a technically defined manner which is at variance with common understandings in the market place, it is unlikely that consensus will be established between actors during negotiations. And because the actor has to cope with the external environment, the common understandings of the market place will carry such weight with him that consensus may not persist between himself and his accountant. The forces tending to the ineffectiveness of any such technical usage are numerically and functionally much greater than the forces which could be mustered to support it. The appropriate general rule governing the semantical rules in the circumstances under discussion, therefore, seems to be that terms shall be so defined and used as to evoke the same references as their use would evoke in the market place.[7]

Consider some possible deviations from this principle. It would be confusing to speak of "financial position" if the position designated is not a position in the sense of financial capacity for acting at the time for which it is given. It would be confusing to speak of "gains" when one holds more money but one's command over goods is less than at some previous time. It would be confusing to speak of the "costs" of doing something if cost means something other than the sacrifice at the time of doing

7 Such a rule was proposed in respect of the usages of political economists by T. R. Malthus, *Definitions in Political Economy* (London, 1827). "When we employ terms which are of daily occurrence in the common conversation of educated persons, we should define and apply them so as to agree with the sense in which they are understood in this ordinary use of them." Cited in Machlup, *Essays on Economic Semantics,* p. 3. Compare also: "Fruitful intellectual activity... draws its strength from the common knowledge which all of us share... whenever the culture of a people loses contact with the common life of mankind... it is becoming a priestcraft. It is destined to end... in superstition. To be proud of intellectual isolation from the common life of mankind... is the end of progress in knowledge." Lancelot Hogben, *Mathematics for the Millions* (London: George Allen & Unwin, 1951), p. 19. The literature of accounting is liberally seasoned with assertions that the public should be "educated" in the limitations of accounting terms and statements; even if the attempt were made, it is improbable that common sense usages and understandings could be unsettled.

that thing. It would be confusing to assign to assets and liabilities the same numbers of monetary units as were appropriate at some other time, if there had been, in the interval, a change in their monetary equivalents. Any expectation that communication can be effective if uncommon usages are accepted is doomed to disappointment; and any expectation that a technical usage can be established by justification against the well-entrenched and constantly reinforced usage of the laity cannot but fail.

SYNTACTICAL RULES

Insofar as they are pertinent to human behavior, signs never occur in isolation. They occur, in the first place, in temporal and spatial contexts; in the second place, they occur as parts of a sign-system; and, in the third place, they usually occur in conjunction with other signs of the system.

Whether signs occur singly or as part of a complex sign, statement, or message, the functioning of a sign is conditioned by its context. The context is itself a sign, qualifying all signs appearing in that context. The road sign "SLOW WORKERS AHEAD" causes amusement because it may be interpreted in two ways. But its location leaves the observer in no doubt that the reference of SLOW is to the speed of traffic, not to the diligence of the WORKERS. Similarly, in spoken language, the occasion of speech sets the framework for interpreting the word-signs uttered. We do not ordinarily expect wisdom in soapbox oratory, truth in debate, or objectivity in political speeches; we interpret the words uttered accordingly. Further, in spoken language, a speaker has recourse to inflections and intonations, grimaces and gestures, and other rhetorical devices, all of which qualify the words actually used. Inasmuch as these auxiliary signs or qualifiers are forgone in written records and messages the signs of the system themselves are the only vehicles of communication. A greater burden, the necessity of greater precision, is, thus, cast on signals consisting only of written signs.

The sign-system in which a given sign is used is also a qualifier. The technical languages, to which we have already referred, employ signs which are used in other languages (other technical languages or the vernacular) with quite different referents. Such a sign within such a system has reference only to the usage permitted by the semantical rules of the system.

But of all qualifiers, the most common is the set of signs of the system which are used in conjunction with a given sign. Every statement is a complex of linked or combined signs. In natural languages, there are understandings as to the manner in which signs are combined to form complex signs or statements. They are generally accepted, as conventions, because they reduce the effort and increase the efficiency of communication. They are syntactical rules. They are made explicit by grammarians (rules for forming sentences) and logicians (rules for forming sentences on the basis of or by derivation from other sentences). If communication is to be effective, it is no less necessary that the signs employed shall be related to one another in accordance with syntactical rules than that they shall individually conform with semantical rules.

Consider an example. It is generally accepted that the operation of summation is only possible if the separate objects or properties to be aggregated are alike. This is a logical rule. The recipient of a message purporting to designate a sum will respond to the message as if the operation of summation had satisfied the rule. If, however, the operation of summation did not satisfy the rule, the derived statement would be logically false. Given that the component statements were empirically or factually true, the derived statement cannot be factually true, and the response cannot, therefore, be the response which the designata themselves would evoke. Again, consider a balance sheet which purports to represent a state of affairs at a stipulated date. Stipulation of the date implies that there are certain existent things, those set out in the balance sheet, as at that date, and not at any other date. This is a logical rule. If in such a balance sheet there appears a statement, "Asset A (at cost) 2,000 monetary units," or "Asset A (at valuation) 3,000 monetary units," cost or valuation as the case may be will evoke a response of the same kind as if the balance sheet date were part of each such statement. If it is not factually true that the asset cost 2,000 monetary units at the stated date, or if the valuation was, in fact, made at some other date, the logical rule will have been violated. Nevertheless, the recipient of the message, which is the balance sheet, will respond as if the rule had been satisfied; his response cannot be the response which the designata (properly including the date of purchase or valuation) themselves would evoke.

FORM AS A SIGN

The form or structure of a statement is a functional property. Form is, itself, a sign. It predisposes the receiver to interpret a message in the manner in which he customarily or habitually interprets messages in the same form. Consider some lines in the "Jabberwocky" of Lewis Carroll:

> "Twas brillig and the slithy toves
> Did gyre and gimble in the wabe:
> All mimsy were the borogoves,
> And the mome raths outgrabe."

This has the form of verse, and its grammatical and metrical structure predisposes us to interpret it as a statement in the English language—if only we could find the semantical rules for the unknown terms. (Humpty Dumpty did later explain the rules to Alice.) The form of a balance sheet predisposes the reader to believe, without close inspection, that its two money columns will be equal in total and that the operations of addition have been correctly carried out.

As a sign, form may have different effects. In natural languages, the preferred form is one which leaves the least doubt as to the intended associations of substantives, adjectives, and verbs. In some languages, the syntactical rules provide for agreement, in number and gender, of substantives and qualifying adjectives, and agreement, in number, of substantives and verbs. These rules tend to avert the possibility of unintended associations or responses to written verbal forms or sounds being made by the reader or the hearer of a sentence. The existence of such rules additional to the rules for ordering terms in a message is described as redundancy. Simple repetition of a message is a form of redundancy, exemplified by the repetition of numbers appearing in telegrams or cables at the end of the message. By virtue of redundancy an ungrammatical message may evoke the same response as the corresponding grammatical message, provided the syntactical errors are not numerous.[8]

Technical sign-systems, as we have seen, seek to avoid mistaken responses by definition of the terms used. And, generally, the forms in which statements are expressed are such that a given message requires fewer signs than an equivalent statement in a natural language. Both definition and form tend to the elimination of redundancy, to economy in the use of terms, and to the reduction of doubt about the referents of the terms used. Consider, again, a balance sheet as a message. A balance sheet consists of a number of statements cast in a specific form. The singular statements which are its constituent parts are shorthand statements abbreviated from sentences in the vernacular. Abbreviation is possible by the setting of those statements under the rubric: "balance sheet as at (a specified date) ;" and by virtue of the habit of readers to respond to the singular statements as if they were in the vernacular. Thus, "Cash, 1,000 monetary units" evokes the same response, in its setting, as the sentence: "There was, at the stated balancing date, a sum of 1,000 monetary units in currency, or bank deposits, in possession of the entity." The form in which all such statements commonly appear makes it possible for the *designer* of the message to adopt the abbreviation.

The economy of terms which the casting of singular statements in a common form permits may, however, induce in *recipients* of a complex

8 Cherry, *On Human Communication*, pp. 18, 19, 180 ff.

message responses quite different from the responses they would make to full singular statements in the vernacular. As we have indicated earlier, the reader of a balance sheet as at a specified date will be disposed to interpret all singular statements in it as designating money measures as at that date, notwithstanding that, to non-monetary items, there are appended qualifying words such as "cost" or "valuation" (implicitly at some other date). He will be so disposed for two reasons. The general heading or caption will be believed to set the framework of the contents, to indicate that all statements in the form are of the same temporal class; and this will be reinforced by the items which, having no qualifying words, appear to relate to the balancing date. In general, the reader will not suppose that the transmitter would state a specific date at the outset and then in the body of the statement include statements relevant as at other dates. In the second place, the reader finds himself in a context, of time and circumstance, to which he will suppose the balance sheet and its components to be relevant. He will suppose that the message is intended and designed to be of use to him at or about that time, for he can imagine no reason why the designer and transmitter should have other intentions or follow rules with other effects.[9] Even if he were given statements relevant at some other time, he could interpret them when he receives them only with reference to the time and circumstance in which he receives them; he cannot recreate himself, in his imagination, as he was at an earlier time, nor the circumstances of an earlier time, for the purpose of interpreting the statements he has before him at any present time.[10]

These common sense responses are understandable. They stem from the need to systematize, to classify, to reduce diversity to order. The information processor is subject to the same kind of responses. If a man says, "These shoes cost me twenty monetary units," and we observe that the shoes have a new appearance, we will interpret "cost" as present or recent cost; and from our own knowledge of present or recent prices, we will interpret the statement as a whole. If we cannot observe the shoes, to interpret the statement we will have to ask "Cost, when?" That this is a pertinent question may be overlooked when dealing with a collection of assets. Consider an entity having a collection of assets of which the following are a sample:

---

9 "... the ... lay reader of a balance sheet ... assumes that here are the *present* values of the assets owned by the concern and here is stated the *present* net worth [that is, residual equity]." H. C. Daines, "The Changing Objectives of Accounting," *The Accounting Review*, Vol. IV, No. 2, June 1929, p. 97. See also Reichenbach, *Experience and Prediction*, pp. 23, 280–1.

10 It may be asked, upon what grounds may the suppositions here made be justified? There is an extensive literature on financial statement analysis the authors of which, accountants and non-accountants alike, implicitly entertain the views here supposed, notwithstanding that the financial statements they discuss include singular statements which are relevant at quite different dates.

Date of Acquisition		Asset	Cost at Date of Acquisition
December	31, 19x9	Cash	1,000 units
January	1, 19x5	Automobile A	3,000 units
January	1, 19x8	Automobile B	2,000 units
March	1, 19x5	Equipment P	5,000 units
July	1, 19x9	Equipment Q	3,000 units
February	1, 19x5	Land	8,000 units

The characteristics of cash, automobiles, equipment, and land, as means, are sufficiently distinctive to provide an obvious basis of classifying all assets and showing four sub-totals. But for the purpose of interpreting the figures in the last column, the dates of acquisition provide another and necessary basis of classification. If the full collection is to be classified both by types of asset and by dates of acquisition, no reduction in the number of separate statements would occur on bringing account balances to balance sheet form. Yet reduction is desirable. Now it may appear that the one thing common to all the above singular statements is that they express cost at date of acquisition; and it may, therefore, seem that, if the dates are disregarded, the figures in the final column are homogeneous. So to regard the singular statements would permit classification by types only, and the desired reduction to four sub-totals would be possible. But the effect is to represent, as homogeneous, groups of items which are not homogeneous. This, of course, the recipient of the balance sheet will not know; his interpretation of the message will be mistaken; he will be misinformed. The reduction of singular statements to abbreviated and aggregated statements may be supposed to have improved the comprehensibility of the message, for fewer terms imply less strain on the attention. But in the above case it will have seriously diminished the potential of the message for selecting responses in the recipient. The effect described would not, of course, arise if all items were shown at their current cash equivalents as at the balance sheet date.

Form may come to occupy such a dominant place in the minds of authors and users of statements that the meaning and relevance to recipients of statements cast in a given form receive scant attention. Form tends to habituation, to ease of engagement by transmitter and receiver alike. It is conducive to ritual, and, therefore, perfunctory responses. The Procrustean operation of making the facts fit an habitual form is easier than the retention or restoration of significance; for the latter is a matter of deliberate intention, strain, and effort, which in the absence of constraints tends to be avoided. Yet only by the latter effort may the tendency for entropy to increase be reversed.

The full advantage of habituation may, of course, be retained if habits are formed on the basis of functionally effective principles. It is not suggested that all processors of information or all recipients of messages shall necessarily be committed to the self-conscious and critical consideration of the quality of the signals generated or received. Complex systems—whole organizations or their information processing units—require the exercise of routine skills on a much larger scale than the critical and constructive skills by which those systems are designed, directed, and modified. Much of this routine acting is not of the deliberate kind but a stimulus-response behavior of the nature of a conditioned reflex.[11] Without it, the speed of performance of routine operations would be reduced, action would be inhibited, the system would grind to a halt. But the design of a communication system requires, at the outset and subsequently, deliberate thought by some persons. Functionally effective principles of signals design do not emerge from singular experiences of the generator or of the recipient of messages. They emerge only from consideration of all the elements of a communication situation taken as a whole.

THE COMMUNICATION OF MEANING—
PRAGMATICAL RULES

It is possible to study the semantics and the syntactics of a language or sign-system as such. But in the context of a discussion of human communication, semantical, syntactical, and pragmatical considerations are necessarily interwoven.[12] The taking account of, or responding to, things by the use of signs (as in a recording or reporting process) or by the mediation of signs (as in acting upon messages) is the distinctive concern of that branch of the theory of signs designated pragmatics. The recurrence in the preceding sections of such terms as response, interpretation, convention, usage, is indicative of the primary preoccupation with pragmatical considerations, and a number of pragmatical rules have been suggested. But the general question of the communicability of messages remains to be answered.

In view of all the potential differences and idiosyncracies of actors and information processors as individuals, it may seem that the possibility of establishing communication of meanings or significances by complex messages is remote. But this is not so, given appropriate pragmatical rules. If, as we have argued, the message is to evoke the same response in the actor as the designata themselves would evoke, the author of the message has

11 Mead, *Mind, Self and Society,* p. 102.
12 For general treatments see Rudolf Carnap, "Foundations of Logic and Mathematics," *International Encyclopedia of Unified Science* (Chicago: University of Chicago Press, 1960); Cherry, *On Human Communication;* Morris, "Foundations of the Theory of Signs."

simply to discover what statements will serve as surrogates for direct experience or observation on the part of the actor, and to employ those statements and no others. It is immaterial that the actor and his accountant may have different individual experiences of a given object; and it is immaterial that each does not experience the direct experience of the other. Given the feedback stated to be necessary in the preceding chapter, it is possible for each to designate by signs "the experience relations in which the other stands," for this entails only the discovery of the rules of usage of both. As it is desirable to standardize the rules of usage where both parties are components of one system, the meaning of all signs, simple or complex, is potentially intersubjective.[13]

Feedback is not to be considered as a mechanical process, however. Nor is the discovery of the rules of usage a simple process. An independent observer may be expected to discover rules of usage by observation of the two parties in a communication situation. It is less easy for the parties themselves to specify their own rules of usage, for each in his own particular environment is subject to the overlay or accretion of associations with terms of objects or properties beyond the communication situation.[14] In the absence of an independent observer—a catalyst, as it were—the process of discovery will necessarily be disciplined and self-conscious. If, of course, the communication situation is common to a large number of multiperson entities (and this is the case in accounting) the problem of discovery is simplified, and standardization of rules of usage may be effected, not only as between functionally differentiated persons in one such situation, but for all persons of both functionally differentiated classes of persons, actors and information processors.

INFORMATIVE AND OTHER COMMUNICATIONS

The discussion has been oriented to only one of the variety of functions which languages perform. Among the other functions, there have been suggested dynamic, emotive, and aesthetic; prescriptive, appraisive, and incitive; and more elaborate classifications.[15] The function which has been the focus of attention is the informative function—setting forth the facts. An information system has no political, hortative, directive, or

13 Morris presents the argument at length; "Foundations of the Theory of Signs," pp. 123–5. See also Ayer, *The Problem of Knowledge,* pp. 205 ff.; Reichenbach, *Experience and Prediction,* pp. 248 ff.

14 " ... the true meaning of a term is to be found by observing what a man does with it, not what he says about it." P. W. Bridgman, *The Logic of Modern Physics* (New York: The Macmillan Company, 1960), p. 7, and generally Chap. 1.

15 For example, Ogden and Richards, *The Meaning of Meaning, passim;* Reichenbach, *Experience and Prediction,* pp. 59 ff.; Whatmough, *Language, A Modern Synthesis,* Ch. VI.

aesthetic functions. No denigration of the other functions is implied. Any two persons in close relationship, such as an actor and his accountant, will have occasion to resort continually to other than informative communications. But the lack of constraint in ordinary conversation may not be permitted to spill over into technical communications if the informative function is to be served. A man may say his wife is an asset, or his secretary is a liability, or that "to the credit" of another, there is his honesty. These are metaphorical uses, borrowing technical terms from a technical sign system; they are not likely to be misunderstood, even though one's wife may not be sold in the market, one's secretary is not a debt, and one's honesty is a property in possession and, therefore, if anything, a debit balance.

A technical sign-system, however formal, depends for the definition of its terms on the words and other signs of a natural language. The commonest response of an observer to an object is to think in terms of the signs of his natural language; a physical scientist most of the time thinks "chair" or "table" in response to objects called by those names, he does not think "a differentiated collection of atoms conforming with certain laws." And if for technical purposes natural language terms require to be translated to technical language terms, the latter require retranslation to natural language terms if persons other than the technically proficient are to be informed, and, indeed, even if the technically proficient are to respond outside of the technical sign-system.[16]

This very necessity, coupled with the previously mentioned tendency for people to press technical terms into everyday use, makes possible confusion in technical discourse and formal messages. Under such influences functionally limited sign-systems may be expected to do more than they can; measurement may be confused with valuation; and hypothetical statements may be granted the status of information. Economic actions and experiences, being such a common class of events in interdependent societies, the possibilities of confusion are considerable if the constraints of informative communications are relaxed or disregarded.

UNIFORMITY IN OBJECT LANGUAGE AND METALANGUAGE

The general import of these observations is that the verbal and numerical signs used in the messages emanating from the accounting process should, as far as possible, have unique referents, and that the usage

16 " ... our formal systems serve merely as written or mechanical mediations between utterances of language .... The interpretation, initial and final, of the procedure is made in terms of some natural language (such as English), and the system as a whole is meaningless to a reader to whom it has not been interpreted in these terms." Bloomfield, "Linguistic Aspects of Science," p. 262.

of verbal and numerical signs should conform with lay usages. In an earlier section the terms "financial position," "costs," and "gains" were mentioned as examples which occur in financial communications.

The conclusions are equally valid for statements made as between technical people on the subject of their technique. Accounting is being treated as a method of acquiring financial knowledge. This book, however, is also an exercise in acquiring knowledge, not financial knowledge, but knowledge of *accounting as a method of acquiring financial knowledge.* We are thus concerned with two language systems. The system which communicates financial information or knowledge may be described as the object language of accounting. The system which communicates knowledge of accounting methods and principles may be described as the metalanguage of accounting, a metalanguage being a "language about a language."[17] The importance of the difference lies in the fact that the object language has reference to objects external to the accounting process, whereas the metalanguage has reference to the process itself. Thus, for example, there are no "objects" such as "objectivity," "neutrality," and "uniformity" to which the object language may be applied. The use of such terms in this book marks it as dealing with the metalanguage of accounting.

That the terms of a metalanguage should have unique and defined referents is a condition of communication in that metalanguage. The difficulty which arises from the fact that most of the referents of terms in a metalanguage are abstract concepts can only be overcome by definition. These definitions may conflict with usages in the vernacular language and with usages of different theorists or users of the metalanguage. The function of definition within the metalanguage is, thus, not only to enable the implications of a concept to be discovered with the object of making inferences from them, but also to secure consistent usage of terms throughout a particular discourse and consistent responses to those terms by the recipients. Ideally, these usages shall be consistent with the function of the recipients of communications in the metalanguage, in the same way as usages in the object language are to be consistent with the function of the recipients of communications in the object language. And ideally the whole system—of object language and metalanguage—shall have an integral quality related to the action system in which substantive events occur.

Some examples may be given of the application of these principles in preceding chapters. We have restricted the use of "value" generally to the result of a valuation process which is distinct from and subsequent to the process of discovery. The act of valuing or preferring is peculiar to the actor. Value is, thus, a term appropriate in the metalanguage, as giving an orientation to the design of the object language; it is inappropriate as a term of the object language, except in the purely mathematical sense. We

17 See for example, Carnap, "Foundations of Logic and Mathematics"; Cherry, *On Human Communication,* pp. 79 ff.

have referred to the process of discovering the magnitudes to be assigned to assets, equities, costs, and incomes as a "measurement" process, both to distinguish it from the valuation process and because we have shown measurement to be necessary if statements in the object language are to be useful over a wide range of potential choices. Rather than say we are measuring assets and equities, leaving the property measured open to question, we have said we are measuring a specific property of assets and equities, namely their monetary or cash equivalents at stated points of time. Rather than leave it open to be supposed that any price, past, present, or future, may be used in the assignment of monetary magnitudes to assets and equities from time to time, we have selected and given reasons for selecting contemporary prices as the basis to be used in deriving financial position. These refinements are necessary in the metalanguage; they make it possible to design an object language but they do not necessarily occur as terms in the object language.

Now, if, as our analysis suggests, mutual understanding and reciprocal interaction depend on conventional usages, and if there are conventional usages already in extensive circulation, it may be asked on what ground alternative usages which are more precise, or in which the terms used have unique referents, are to be preferred. It may be answered: principally on the ground that existent usages are supposed to be conventional but, in fact, they are not so. A terminology which is vague, which implies diverse and conflicting principles or processes—as, for example, the indiscriminate use of "cost" to signify cost at widely divergent points of time without specification of those points of time—cannot be said to give a conventionalized message, in the sense that the understanding of it will be general because the conventions are known. Where alternative usages are open to selection according to the circumstances of the case, it cannot be said that any given usage is conventional.

But suppose particular usages were widely, even universally, accepted and known. There still exists the possibility of there being better usages, which by virtue of their ostensible connection with the realities they represent and of their pertinence to the situations to which they are applied appeal to the reason of experienced people.[18] The objective of inquiry,

18 "The less a science has advanced, the more its terminology tends to rest on an uncritical assumption of mutual understanding. With increase of rigor this basis is replaced piecemeal by the introduction of definitions. The interrelationships recruited from these definitions gain the status of analytic principles; what was once regarded as a theory about the world becomes reconstrued as a convention of language. Thus it is that some flow from the theoretical to the conventional is an adjunct of progress in the logical foundations of any science ... It is valuable to show the reducibility of any principle to another through definition of erstwhile primitives, for every such achievement reduces the number of our presuppositions and simplifies and integrates the structure of our theories." Willard V. Quine, "Truth by Convention," *Philosophical Essays for Alfred North Whitehead* (New York: Longmans, Green & Co., Inc., 1936), pp. 90, 124.

redefinition and reexamination of existing conventions and theories is, thus, the establishment of superior conventions. There are, within the methods of inquiry, no absolute criteria for what is superior, but if others are to be able to judge the superiority of one usage over another, the semantical and syntactical rules require clear statement.[19] The judgment of superiority rests with the general body of informed people and rests on the relative usefulness of alternatives. The suspension of judgment by the general body of informed people—by the acceptance of inconsistent alternatives as equally useful—implies that there are no conventions. Yet without conventions, there can be no communication.

That an approach to unique usages is to be sought may be supported on grounds laid in the previous chapter. To a receiver in great doubt about a matter, any statement about the matter within a wide band of possible statements will improve his situation. If, therefore, a transmitter believes that a receiver is in great doubt, he may justify the transmission of some information without regard for relevance. But we have contended that an actor is not necessarily in great doubt, because he has potentially some recollection or some opportunity for direct observation of recent events in the market place. The smaller the doubt of the actor, then, the greater will be the demand for highly selective information. But the processor and transmitter will not know on which matters or to what extent an actor entertains doubts. We may stipulate then, as an attitude of the processor and transmitter, that he may not suppose the doubts of the actor to be other than minimal.

INTERFERENCE

Every factor which tends to impede the free flow of signals in a channel of communication is a potential source of "noise" or interference. Much of this chapter has been concerned with the elimination of "noise," so that a mere listing of these factors will provide a summary of the matters raised. Interference occurs if the observer-transmitter permits his personal ends or values to influence the encoding of signs, their processing, or their decoding; or if the signs do not have or cease to have unique referents or if a given message includes mutually inconsistent signs; or if the processing of signs is logically illegitimate; or if the signs in the memory of the system fail to be modified on the occurence of events which make the original signs irrelevant. An efficient communication system will be protected against interference by screening devices at the point of entry of signals and by rectifiers in the channel where necessary.

[19] Carnap's "Principle of Tolerance," "It is not our business to set up prohibitions, but to arrive at conventions." Rudolf Carnap, *The Logical Syntax of Language* (London: Kegan Paul, Trench, Trubner & Co. Ltd., 1937), p. 51.

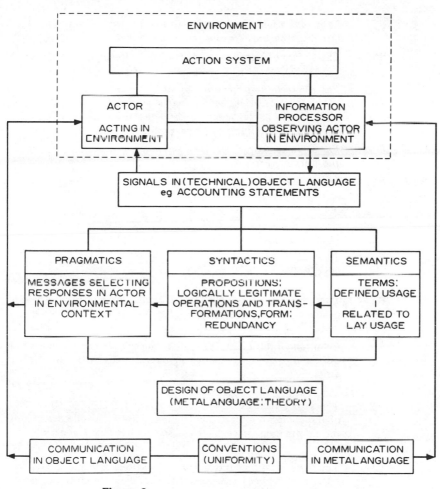

Figure 8
OUTLINE OF CHAPTER 8: COMMUNICATION.

Argument

8.11   *Communication is the transmission of signals from a source through a channel linking source and receiver.*

8.12   The source of signals having financial referents is the market.

(3.64, 6.18, *8.11)*

8.13   *The channel comprises the observer-transmitter, the processes of encoding observations in the language of the accounting system, of manipulating the signs and statements of the system, and of decoding and transmitting the result.*

8.14   *The signs are words and numbers, and the forms in which words and numbers are cast.*

8.15   The receiver is an actor responding adaptively to changes in his relationships with his environment through the market.

(7.11, 7.15, 8.11)

8.16   *The efficiency of communication is the capacity of the signals received to evoke in the receiver the same responses as would direct experience of the events which are the subject of the communication.*

(1.68, 7.11, 8.14)

8.21   The efficiency of communication varies directly with the independence of the observer-transmitter (or information processor).

(7.23, 8.16)

8.22   Actor and information processor being different persons, their associations of objects with signs and signs with objects may differ.

(1.42, 1.51, 3.12)

8.23   The actor's habits of associating objects and signs of objects and of responding to objects and signs of objects are discoverable by the information processor by observation or by feedback.

(1.12, 7.53, 8.22)

8.24   The signs of an accounting system constitute a technical language interposed between economic events and the responses of actors.

(1.51, 7.15, *8.14)*

8.25   The efficiency of communication varies directly with the capacity of the terms of the technical language to designate uniquely objects or properties of economic events, that is, with adherence to semantical rules.

(1.41, 8.16, 8.24)

8.26   The efficiency of communication varies directly with the capacity of the syntax of the technical language to generate statements such that the relations between the signs used in those statements correspond with the relations between their designata, that is, with adherence to syntactical rules.

(*1.41*, 6.21, *8.16*, 8.24)

8.31   *A component sign of a complex message is redundant if an equivalent sign occurs also in the message.*

8.32   The greater the redundancy of signs in any message, the less is the possibility of misinterpretation.

(1.44, 1.74, 8.26, *8.31*)

8.33   The form of a message is a sign, conducing to economy in the use of other signs, that is, reducing redundancy.

(8.26, *8.31*)

8.34   The greater the dependence on form, the easier is the construction of messages, but the greater is the necessity that all other signs shall have specific referents.

(2.30, 8.25, 8.33)

8.35   In sign-systems subject to increasing entropy, the greater the dependence on form, the greater the "energy" input (definition and submission to defined usage, on the one hand, and transformation by new information, on the other) necessary to preserve the potential of messages for selecting responses.

(*7.51*, 7.54, 8.25, 8.33)

8.36   Accounting is subject to the above proposition, inasmuch as the referents of the number signs of the system are continually changing due to shifts in relative prices and prices in general.

(3.53, 3.63, 3.83, 8.35)

8.37   The greater the uniformity of association of specific signs with unique referents the greater is the number of individuals by whom messages in a technical language are interpretable. (This applies equally to object languages and metalanguages.)

(*1.51*, 8.23, 8.35)

8.41   The greater the doubt of an actor, the greater is the possibility that any message will have some potential for selection.

(*7.11*, 7.12)

8.42   The greater the doubt assumed by the information processor to assail the actor, the less the stimulus to produce information having a high potential for selection.

(*1.22*, *1.23*, 8.35, 8.41)

8.43   The information processor being ignorant of the degree of doubt of the actor on any matter, and of the number of matters about which the actor entertains doubts, may not assume that the actor's doubts are other than minimal.

(*1.21*, *3.12*, 7.15, 8.42)

Trading Ventures

9 Trading ventures are entities which acquire and dispose of money and other means, subject to prevailing property rights, in accordance with the demands, influences, and criteria of choice of the market alone. Commonly, the goods and services bought and sold by such ventures are bought and sold at a price per unit; and the money or money claims which make their operations possible are acquired at prices under the same kinds of influence. Any such venture will be described as a firm. Firms operate in a market matrix, exercising and being exercised by operations made effective in markets. The definition excludes entities which are instruments for providing the members of a society with goods and services financed out of tax revenues which are not sold by the unit but are consumed jointly. Thus national defense, social health, law enforcement agencies, for example, are excluded from consideration.

FIRMS AND THEIR PARTICIPANTS

Firms are voluntarily established entities. They arise from the decisions of persons to devote part of their personal resources, in money or kind, to productive or trading functions. We have spoken of such persons as the constituents of firms. A firm may have one or more constituents. The role of the constituents is to decide whether firms shall be established, and when established, whether and to what extent firms shall be permitted to grow, and whether or not they shall be liquidated. The incentive to divest oneself of resources, to forgo temporarily their availability for consumption, is the expectation of gain. That is to say, it is expected that the future flow of satisfactions or means of obtaining satisfactions will, when appropriately discounted to the present, exceed the satisfaction presently expected of the resources divested. In a monetary economy, money is the generalized means of acquiring goods believed to be capable of yielding satisfactions. But, one does not simply want to have more monetary tokens if his command over goods in general is less.

A firm may, thus, be considered as an instrument by which its constituents seek increased command over goods in general. It is not the same thing as its constituents, even if there is only one such constituent. It has no function with respect to its constituents other than the functions they attribute to it. It has no ends other than those of the individual persons associated with it.[1] As an instrument it can have no wants and can obtain no consumer satisfactions such as those of natural persons. Consideration of the modes of operation of firms need not, therefore, be confused by the difficulties of evaluating satisfactions from consumption or by the difficulties of diverse personal ends of its constituents.

But inasmuch as other persons than constituents are associated with firms—as agents, employees, customers, financiers, and so on—a firm is also a social instrument. The resources devoted to its function are resources available to the society in which it operates, though the possession and use of those resources is assured to the firm, through its constituents and by other contracts under property laws. The goods and services it produces and the income which it generates become available to the society in which it operates, though their division among members of the society is secured likewise under property laws and contracts.

As a voluntarily established entity, the firm operates, therefore, under the constraints imposed by society at large; more directly it operates under

---

[1] "People (i.e., individuals) have goals; collectivities of people do not." Richard M. Cyert and James G. March, *A Behavioral Theory of the Firm* (Englewood Cliffs, N.J.: Prentice-Hall, Inc., 1963), p. 26. "... there is nothing in social psychology that is not logically explicable at the level of the psychology of the individual.... There is nothing superordinate to the individual, no 'group mind.'" Krech and Crutchfield, *Theory and Problems of Social Psychology*, pp. 366–7.

the constraints of its constituents and all other persons associated with it. We will speak of all such persons—constituents and others—collectively as participants in the firm.[2] It is a condition of the existence of a firm that the expectations of all participants shall be satisfied. Where the freedom to contract subsists in all participants and where there are many possible firms in which a person may participate, these expectations will subsist in the belief that the yield to each from participation will be greater than the yield from alternative engagements. In particular, constituents participate not simply in the expectation that the future flow of purchasing power will exceed the purchasing power of the resources divested, but that the future flow will exceed the expected future flows from known alternative employments of the same resources.

FINANCIAL EFFICIENCY: RATE OF
RETURN ON CAPITAL

There is required, therefore, a scale for measuring actual flows from a given investment which shall be comparable with estimated future flows from the same and alternative investments. An indicator of relative efficiencies is necessary, efficiency being understood as the relationship between outputs and inputs. A firm buys, converts, and sells. Each operation employs labor service and the service of other factors. A series of measures of efficiency embodying service inputs and outputs is conceivable. But we have observed that the firm is an instrument of gain, and that the monetary scale is the only scale in which measurements or calculations of diverse inputs and outputs are made. Also, the monetary scale is common to the beginning and the end of all cycles of buying, converting, and selling. We seek, therefore, a measure of gain in the monetary scale as one component of the measure of the efficiency of a firm as an instrument. But a measure of the absolute gain is meaningless of itself.

As different alternatives may involve the use of more or less of the resources available to any person for investment in a firm, a measure of relative efficiency will take account of the amount of the investment in each case. As from any point of time, the expected future inputs consist of the current cash equivalent of assets held and of all future services necessary to employ those assets; the outputs consist of the current cash equivalent of the proceeds to termination of the enterprise. For the life of a given enterprise the difference represents the expected gain; the ratio of gain to the investment is a measure of efficiency in the monetary sense. Constituents will choose the firm which they expect will yield the better aggregate, in periodical divisions of gains or on withdrawal from or termination of the

2 After Simon, *Administrative Behavior,* p. 16.

venture, or partly in one way and partly in the other, all such receipts being appropriately discounted at the time of choice.

The aggregate gain over the whole life of a continuing venture is not ascertainable during that life. Yet, if constituents are to choose whether or not to continue their association, or if they are to exert any influence on the efficiency of the venture, a measure of efficiency during the life of the venture is necessary. A measure of efficiency which will be comparable with measures for alternative opportunities involving investments of different magnitudes is the periodical rate of return on capital. This is the percentage of periodical income to the capital employed in earning it. Because the measure of capital is equal to the measure of residual equity, the measure of efficiency is also the rate of change of residual equity. The expected rate of return from an investment in a continuing venture will be estimated on the basis of the actual rate of return in the immediate past. For convenience in comparing rates of return with rates obtainable from alternative investments, and in particular with the pure interest rate on riskless investment, rates of return are expressed as percentages per annum. Rates of return, actual or prospective, may be computed for investments in individual assets or for investments in firms as wholes. The rate of return on the capital of a firm takes into account the effects of all operating and financing arrangements undertaken in the interest of residual equity holders, the one class out of all participants which bears the risks and whose interest is primarily in the monetary return.

This position does not presuppose that constituents are concerned solely with monetary considerations. It regards non-monetary considerations as constraints. In some cases constituents may obtain direct satisfactions from firms in which they are participants. In particular, a person who conducts a venture as a sole trader or as a partner is both a constituent and an agent or manager. In either or both roles, he may value his independence and his achievement; and he may prefer to engage in one class of trade than in another. But those are personal, subjective, and immeasurable elements of the case. Further, they depend on the capacity of the firm to generate cash, both as a means of settling obligations to others and as a means of remaining independent and demonstrating achievement.[3] Nor does our position presuppose that the firm has no other functions in relation to other participants, its suppliers, customers, agents, and employees. But its capacity to attract and retain the participation of these groups depends also on its capacity to generate cash by the sale of unit quantities of goods or services. Our position implies only that insofar as monetary tests are significant to constituents as a basis of choice, the rate of return on capital is relevant. And on the ground that the specific ends of constituents which will compete

---

[3] "Man does not live by bread alone, but he lives by bread at least." George C. Homans, *The Human Group* (London: Routledge & Kegan Paul Ltd., 1951), p. 401.

for attainment at any future time are unknown, it is reasonable to suppose that, given knowledge of the purchasing power of money at a point of time, constituents will choose between alternative employments of their resources very largely on the basis of the expected future flows of money.

It should be apparent that there is no measure of absolute efficiency, that absolute efficiency is not conceivable. One firm, one policy, one course of action, may only be more efficient for its purpose than another. Judgments of efficiency are always relative; the spur to improvement is always comparison.

Trading firms are no less adaptive entities than are persons as such.[4] Whether their expected span of existence is short or long, the expectations of constituents may only be satisfied if their modes of operation, and their particular operations, are such that they take advantage of their resources in the environmental conditions as they prevail from time to time. The arrangement of operations with this objective we will suppose to be in the hands of an agent or agents of the constituents. We will consider the overall arrangement at this stage and a single agent or manager. The manager will be directly informed of the expectations of the constituents and of their responses to the effects procured as a consequence of his decisions. He will, as manager, act for the constituents in the same way as we considered an information processor to be an agent of an actor. In some cases, one person will be both constituent and manager; in other cases different persons assume the two roles. In general the manager may be considered as manipulator of the instrument which is the firm in the interest of its constituents.

FINANCIAL TESTS IN ADMINISTRATION

The rate of return on capital is no less significant as a guide to actions of the manager than as a guide to actions of the constituents.

---

[4] The notion of adaptive behavior applies as well to firms as to individuals. The postulated objective of optimal adaptation avoids the fallacy of a "single goal," such as profit-maximization for example; it avoids debate on the relative merits of the postulation, as goals, of profit-maximization and satisficing on the basis of aspiration levels, e.g., Herbert A. Simon, *Models of Man* (New York: John Wiley & Sons, Inc., 1957), Chap. 14; and "Theories of Decision-Making in Economics," *The American Economic Review,* Vol. XLIX, No. 3, June, 1959. It permits the inclusion of such objectives as the maintenance of liquidity and the maintenance of control. W. W. Cooper, "Theory of the Firm: Some Suggestions for Revision," *The American Economic Review,* Vol. XXXIX, No. 6, December, 1949). It permits the intrusion of the specific goals of all classes of participant and particularly of that class which at any point of time occupies the dominant position in relation to the survival of the firm. Optimal adaptation may appear thus to be an imprecise notion, but of all the customary criteria of choice it alone provides an explanation of liquidation. For our purposes, the generation of financial information, all more specific financial goals are subsumed by it.

As the relative attractiveness to constituents of alternatives changes, the specific lines of action of a given firm will require reexamination, because managers will be held accountable by constituents for shifts in the attractiveness of the firms they manage. Many factors contribute to the relative attractiveness of the rate of return on capital of different firms. One firm may have a superior management, another a superior source of supplies, another a superior labor force, another a superior marketing organization. In every firm, there are factors which contribute to its relative superiority in any one of these directions: individual drive, initiative and insight, individual desires for reward, recognition or respect, individual recognition of standards of professional competence. None of these factors is capable of measurement or calculation in the monetary scale. Only their consequences are so measurable. There are, nevertheless, a number of features of the financial consequences of operations which are capable of assessment and which may evoke changes in the style of operating.

To have anything but a short life, a firm will necessarily meet its short-term liabilities. These are monetary obligations and require to be met by money payments in the near future. It is, therefore, necessary to know what money sums will become available in the ordinary course of business in the near future. This may be judged from the cash already in hand, the short-term claims against debtors, the marketable securities in possession, and the completed inventories of vendible products. This class of assets may be styled short-term assets; their current cash equivalents individually and in total are ascertainable. The ratio of the measure of short-term assets to the measure of short-term liabilities is an indication of the capacity of the firm to meet shortly maturing obligations. But clearly the ratio is only logically valid and practically significant if the short-term is in both cases the same, and if the measures are taken in scales of the same unit dimension. A ratio of this kind is commonly called the current ratio.

To take advantage of the residual equity in its assets, a firm may have raised or may seek to raise additional cash by incurring deferred liabilities, giving charges over the assets or some of them as collateral security. The relationship between the residual equity and the total liabilities of the firm we may style the equity-debt ratio. It is of consequence when contemplating the choice between further contributions from constituents and contributions from lenders; a high ratio may indicate the possibility of further borrowing, a low ratio is suggestive of further contributions from constituents. Other things being equal, the lower the equity-debt ratio, the greater the risk borne by creditors. Again, the ratio is only logically valid and practically significant if the measures are taken in the same scale. And as the measure of the residual equity is the difference between the sums of the measures of all assets and all liabilities, it follows that all assets and all liabilities shall be measured in the same scale.

Whether a firm is able to justify the expectations of constituents and creditors turns on the expected rate of return, the nearest experienced approximation to this being given by the net income plus interest on debt related to the aggregate measure of the assets held, on a per cent per anuum basis, for the most recent accounting period. This rate is a measure of efficiency in the use of resources however they are financed. But to be logically valid and practically significant, the measures must be taken in the same scale. And as net income is the difference between total revenues and total expenses, these, likewise, must be in the same scale, individually and aggregatively.

The demonstration of the usefulness of ratios of monetary measures of classes of assets, equities, incomes, and costs may be extended. The ratio of net income from sales to sales turnover is indicative of the profitability of the particular combination of goods sold. The ratio of commodities inventory to the cost of sales is indicative of the effectiveness with which inventory holdings are coordinated with demand. The ratio of receivables to sales is indicative of the effectiveness of credit selling and collections policies. The illustrations given are sufficient to indicate that any systematic analysis of the financial characteristics of a firm will extend, directly or indirectly, over every class of items found in balance sheets and income statements; and that the components of the ratios are so interlocked that the monetary properties of all items in those financial statements are required to be measured in the same scale if inferences from those ratios are to be themselves valid and are to be related to the general test of the rate of return on capital.

This conclusion has already been established on other grounds, namely the necessity of a common scale if measurements are to be added, and the necessity of addition if the large number of individual account balances are to be reduced to a convenient number of class subtotals. The conclusion is reinforced here by reference to the practical necessity of comparing absolute magnitudes by the use of ratios and percentages in the pursuit of preferred courses of action both by constituents and by managers of firms.

INTERTEMPORAL AND OTHER COMPARISONS

In the first period of operation, the only guides a firm will have to the expected relationships between financial magnitudes arise from the past experience of its officers in other firms or from observation of the habits and conventions of the trade in which it operates. But every firm is unique—in respect of its personnel, its relationships with constituents and creditors, and in the composition of its assets. The earliest opportunity will, therefore, be taken to establish its own bases of comparison.

Given the financial statements of a firm for two balancing dates, the most obvious comparisons are those between the measures of corresponding items in the two sets of statements. But any such direct comparison is nugatory if there are reasons for supposing that, relatively to one another, the magnitudes of the specific obligations and assets of the firm will have changed in the interval. On the assumption of adaptive behavior, the grounds for such a presumption are high. Changes in expectations and in actions to bring about those expectations will inevitably produce changes in the composition of assets and obligations. And whether a surplus or a deficit has arisen from the operations of the interval, this in itself will have affected the composition. Comparisons of measurements of cash holdings, of inventory holdings, of durable goods holdings, of net incomes for successive dates or intervals are of themselves meaningless.

An alternative mode of comparison is to relate certain measurements made in or in respect of one interval to other measurements for the same interval. This avoids the defects of the intertemporal comparisons mentioned above. It is possible to assign a meaning to the ratio of equity to debt at a point of time, or to the ratio of receivables at a point of time to sales revenue for a preceding interval, or to the ratio of short-term assets to short-term obligations at a point of time; for in each case the two components are logically or practically related. But, again, these ratios, standing by themselves at a given point of time are meaningless; like all isolated comparatives, they are simply large or small.

The questions which confront the managers of firms are not of the kind "large or small?" but of the kind "larger or smaller?" or "more or less?" In the case of continuing ventures, an obvious basis for judging such questions is the expectations held at some prior time or the state of affairs as it existed at some prior time. Having discarded the intertemporal comparison of fundamental measurements, we may consider only the intertemporal comparison of ratios.

If a firm's ratio of net income to sales revenue, or to capital, is less than was expected at some prior time, or less than was attained in some prior period, it may seek to improve one or more facets of its operations. It may discover that the current ratio has risen, that its inventory turnover rate has fallen, or that its receivables recovery rate has fallen, and so on. Each of these changes in rates has some bearing on a particular group of actions, and each has potential for selecting adaptive responses. The latest rates may, of course, be no less than are possible in the changed circumstances; but the change in a rate may be expected to stimulate inquiry as to the determining facts and to lead to a modification of future expectations.

Though the numerator and denominator of any ratio or rate are logically required to be measurements in the same scale, ratios or rates are pure numbers or no-dimensional magnitudes.[5] It is logically possible to compare

[5] Campbell, *Foundations of Science*, pp. 373–4.

these numbers as they are discovered from time to time, regardless of changes in the scale of operations of a firm. The interpretation of changes in ratios and rates, like all interpretations of signs, depends on the contextual circumstances. Thus, if a firm earns the same rate of net income to capital during two periods, when, in the interval, its capital has increased by 50 percent, an unfavorable interpretation will be made if economies to scale were expected. However, we are concerned here with the logical possibility of comparison and the validity of inferences from the comparison. It appears, then, that the prime basis for inferences as to the prospects of firms and of their particular policies is the series of ratios indicative of their structure and performance from time to time.

The no-dimensional characteristic of ratios opens up two other possible bases of comparison. It is possible, validly, to compare ratios for two or more firms at a given time. This is of importance to constituents who have the option of disinvesting and investing in alternative firms. It is equally important to the managers of particular firms, if, by general publication or through trade associations, information permitting the derivation of ratios becomes available. And it is of importance to the managers of horizontally integrated firms, for it may enable one branch of such a firm to be made more efficient out of the experience of another. Secondly, it is possible validly to compare ratios for two or more firms at a given time, even though they operate in communities having different monetary systems, without conversion of the original monetary measures to a common scale.

But more important than these possibilities is the possibility of intertemporal comparison when the purchasing power of the monetary unit has changed. Direct comparison of magnitudes—of holdings of cash and receivables, or of sales revenues—is clearly uninformative when the dimension of the monetary unit has changed. But a change in the dimension of the monetary unit does not automatically effect a change in the technical conditions of operation, such as the processing time of materials or the trade terms of credit; hence it does not affect the validity of comparisons of ratios.

Superficially it may appear that, if the trends in the affairs of a firm are to be examined for the purpose of forming expectations, the sets of financial statements for successive periods or dates will require to be converted to monetary units of the same dimension. This may be necessary in the case of some specific magnitudes. For example, if periodical sales revenue is regarded as an indication of growth, uncorrected magnitudes would suggest growth when prices rise even if the physical volume remained unchanged. But such isolated examples do not represent a case for restating previous financial statements throughout. On the contrary, in the first place, to restate previous statements would reduce their contents to magnitudes which were not relevant at the time of occurrence; and inasmuch as the restatements would involve differential effects on monetary and non-monetary asset measurements, the derived ratios would differ from the ratios which were effective at the previous balancing dates. In the second place, readers of the adjusted statements would be confused if they still had access to the original statements. Thirdly, and conclusively, the argument of the previous paragraphs has shown that generally such transformations are unnecessary, for the pieces of information relevant as indications of trends are rates or ratios which are independent of the scales employed. Recasting of previous balance sheets and income statements is, therefore, unnecessary.

This examination of some of the uses capable of being made of accounting information suggests that trading ventures require an accounting system which yields, periodically, statements of financial position and of changes in financial position, the components of which at any time are all measured in terms of the same contemporary scale. It is no impediment to interpretation that the scale changes from time to time; for, the monetary scale being a ratio scale, ratio analysis is unaffected. However, the fact that assets and obligations may persist through periods of time in which the monetary scale changes in significance constitutes one of the principal difficulties in maintaining a continuous record so that the requirement stated above is met. This problem is central to the ascertainment of measures which are, at a stated point of time, relevant and interpretable in the light of market prices and conditions then prevailing. It will occupy the greater part of the next chapter.

EQUITIES, MONETARY AND NON-MONETARY ASSETS

The differential effects of changes in prices and price levels on the measurement from time to time of assets and equities makes it necessary to distinguish between monetary and non-monetary items.

All liabilities are monetary items. They represent monetary expressions of the magnitudes of the claims of others against the assets of an entity. Obligations to, or equities of, creditors arise out of legal contracts which fix the nominal monetary amounts of bargains in the general unit of currency regardless of changes in the dimension of the monetary unit.[6] If by reason

---

6 In a number of countries "indexed bonds" have been issued to overcome the long-run attrition of bondholders' equity in terms of purchasing power when price levels rise. This is explicit recognition of the differential effects of price level changes on different kinds of investment. See Peter Robson, "Index-linked Bonds," *The Review of Economic Studies,* Vol. XXVIII, No. 1, October 1960, p. 75; and John Hein, "A Note on the Use of Index Clauses Abroad," *The Journal of Finance,* Vol. XV, No. 4, December 1960. The accounting treatment we are to propose would be modified slightly if a firm borrows under any such contract.

of such contracts the firm is able to borrow when the price level is lower than it is at the time of repayment, the lender will have suffered a loss in purchasing power and the firm will have gained. The gain accrues to the residual equity holders. Residual equity is not a monetary item; being a residue its measurement emerges from the measurement of other equities and assets and is, therefore, variable in amount through time.

Among the assets, cash holdings and contractual claims to cash against debtors are also fixed in nominal amount. In Chapter 5, it was suggested that all claims to cash by or against an entity may be reduced to current cash equivalents by discounting from expected dates of receipt or payment to the present when determining financial position. On the continuity assumption, given at least a short period for recovery or payment of debts, we may regard nominal amounts as adequate representations of the magnitude of short-term claims.[7]

Liabilities, cash, and contractual claims to cash will be described as monetary items, and monetary items may be defined as assets and equities the measures of which are fixed contractually regardless of changes in the dimension of the monetary unit.

All other items are non-monetary items. Their measures are continually being reassessed in the market. All holdings of goods or titles to goods are non-monetary assets. The debentures, notes, and bonds of corporations and of governmental bodies are generally fixed in nominal amount. But if any such securities are held as assets, if they are readily negotiable, and if there remains some time to maturity, the measure of the holdings of these securities will be given by their market prices. Holdings of interests in the residual equity of other firms (shares or stock) are likewise measured by reference to market prices.

The importance of the distinction lies in the fact that monetary assets and non-monetary assets are subject to quite different risks. Holdings of monetary assets are subject to the risk of changes in the purchasing power of money. If, for whatever reasons, the general level of prices rises, the purchasing power of a unit of money tends to fall; a greater number of units is required to buy a given good. Clearly then, non-monetary assets are subject to the same influences, but in an opposite direction. If the price level is expected to rise, it is clearly preferable to hold goods and to incur fixed obligations than it is to hold monetary assets. This applies generally to firms as well as to persons, for a rise in the level of prices implies a prospective rise in the rate of cash inflows to a firm, an effect which the holding of cash will not procure. Non-monetary assets are subject also, however, to the risks of changes in customers' preferences, in technology, and in the

---

7 As also, Robert T. Spouse and Maurice Moonitz, *A Tentative Set of Broad Accounting Principles for Business Enterprises*, Accounting Research Study No. 3 (New York: American Institute of Certified Public Accountants, 1962), pp. 25, 57.

demands, therefore, both for producers' goods and their products. The expectations which gave rise to their purchase may be more or less than fully realized; what is realized, in fact, is only discovered when goods have been converted to monetary assets through the market. If one wishes, one may hedge against the risks of holding monetary assets by incurring obligations; the practice is eminently exemplified by firms whose assets are principally monetary assets.

INVESTMENTS OF FIRMS

We have noticed that, where possible, individual persons will tend to hold a heterogeneous stock of means. To hold a mixed stock is obviously necessary to firms. A firm will hold means of differing specificities, divisibilities, durabilities, and so on. That combination of means will be chosen which in the particular context of technical knowledge, market opportunities, and total means available is expected to meet the tests of liquidity and rate of return on capital of both classes of equity holders.[8] The combination will vary from time to time.

There are no technical rules by which a firm in any trade or industry is obliged to invest its resources in any specific combination of assets. Its scale of operations and the manner in which it operates at or about that scale are matters of choice. In a given trade, one firm may buy and another may lease its premises; one may buy and another may lease its plant; one may manufacture the whole of the components of its finished goods, another may merely assemble bought parts manufactured by others. The productivity of any asset or combination of assets is not uniquely determined by physical properties; the skill with which assets are employed bears directly on it. For such reasons as these, all firms will differ. But any chosen combination of assets may be supposed to have been chosen because, in the state of available techniques and resources and in the state of market expectations at the time, it was believed to offer the prospect of a better rate of return than alternatives.

There is, thus, no principle on the basis of which assets may be ranked by usefulness in the process of operation. It may be just as necessary to have so much cash as so much plant. If the knowledge available to a firm, or the general state of technology, or the supply of its necessary materials and services, or the demand for its products, or the price of what it buys and

---

8 An extended treatment of the factors determining the types and amounts of the assets of a firm and the optimum method of financing them is given in Friedrich and Vera Lutz, *The Theory of Investment of the Firm* (Princeton: Princeton University Press, 1951). The analysis of the determinants of each class of item appearing in the balance sheet parallels our concern with the discovery of the monetary magnitudes of each class.

sells, changes, it may be no less necessary to change its investment in plant than its investment in inventories or in any other type of asset. To meet its debts, it may incur other debts, run down its inventory, or sell part of its plant. In general, the possibilities of a change becoming necessary in the composition and amount of assets and liabilities are extensive; every conceivable change is possible.[9] The changes that do, in fact, occur are the consequences of choice; they depend on the valuations of existing and alternative assets and obligations made by the firm's agents. There is, thus, no foundation in business or economic reasoning for drawing a distinction between "fixed assets" and current assets on the ground that the former are "not held for sale or for conversion into cash."[10] It is incontrovertible that non-monetary assets are acquired and held only so that they may be converted into cash through the sale of the product of their services, and, or, their resale.[11] Holdings of non-monetary assets can have no intrinsic value to firms. Their value subsists only in their expected power to generate cash. In this sense, we may speak of the utility of holdings of goods by firms; goods are acquired and held not because of their technical capacity but because of the belief that they will be serviceable directly or indirectly in generating cash.

PRICES AND VALUATIONS OF PRODUCERS' GOODS

All goods bought, held, and used in the process of manufacture or trade are, in those uses, producers' goods. Goods of the same kind may, in other uses, be regarded as consumers' goods. The distinction

[9] Boulding makes use of the notion of "homeostasis of the balance sheet" meaning presumably that the balance sheet represents the consequence of the homeostatic principles of a firm at any time. Boulding, *A Reconstruction of Economics,* pp. 27 ff.

[10] The distinction is expressed in the words of the *Report of the Committee on Company Law Amendment* (London, H.M.S.O., 1945), p. 58. The formula is general. "Fixed assets are assets of a relatively permanent nature used in the operation of a business and not intended for sale." H. A. Finney and Herbert E. Miller, *Principles of Accounting, Introductory* (Englewood Cliffs, N.J.: Prentice-Hall Inc., 1963), p. 200. Judicial opinions in which the distinction is drawn seem to have contemplated that fixed capital and circulating capital are separate immiscible funds, possibly on the precedents of railroad, canal, and similar undertakings. But the degrees of mobility of resources and complementarity of assets cannot be satisfactorily accommodated in such a bipartite classification. " . . . any sharp division into two distinct categories of capital goods, such as circulating capital and fixed capital, is likely to do more harm than good" by creating the impression that one part "must be regarded as given in unalterable form" in the short-run, while the other "adapts itself practically instantaneously to any change in conditions." Hayek, *The Pure Theory of Capital,* p. 329. See also Roland Bird, "The Use of Published Accounts, The Viewpoint of an Economist," *The Accountant,* 3 February 1951.

[11] The evidence is extensive and varied. There is the common admission of a putative scrap or salvage value in the calculation of depreciation allowances. But more cogent is the extensive sale of producers' goods before their technical capacity has been exhausted; and the planned (e.g., Vance Packard, *The Waste-Makers,* Penguin Books, 1963) or accidental obsolescence which gives rise to sales by some firms to other firms which can still employ so-called obsolete plant economically.

is one of employments, not of kinds. The valuation of an automobile by a private user turns on his direct satisfactions; but the valuation of a similar automobile by a firm turns on its capacity—in conjunction with other services—to generate cash.

The product of any firm may itself be a producers' good. It is easy to imagine a long chain of producers and producers' goods, more or less distant from the final goods in the hands of consumers. But the sole justification for this chain, this roundabout method of producing final goods, is the demand by consumers for consumers' goods. The prices of all producers' goods are thus derivatives of the expected prices of the consumers' goods the demand for which gives rise to their use.[12]

Specifically, the price paid for any producers' good is, at the time of purchase, a derivative of the expected future proceeds of its product, whether the product is itself a producers' good or a consumers' good. The purchase by a firm of any good or service is evidence that the then present (discounted cash) equivalent of the expected future proceeds from its sale in one form or another is not less than the price paid. A firm geared to the expectations of its constituents does not buy producers' goods without consideration of the expected prices of its products or in the simple hope that the product will be vendible whatever its cost turns out to be. To operate in this manner is to disregard the constraints of the environment. Whether or not firms are established and goods are acquired by them depends on the prices at which their outputs are expected to be sold. If the margin between expected input prices and expected output prices is, in relation to other opportunities, insufficient to compensate for the delays and risks the process entails, any proposed venture will not be undertaken and any proposed investment in goods will not be made.

Trading ventures are surrounded by, and themselves contribute to, the ceaseless ebb and flow of technical and economic change. To hold some assets of low specificity and high convertibility is, thus, justifiable. But roundabout methods of production involve the investment of large sums of money in assets, or collections of complementary assets, of high specificity; and the proceeds of such investments are recoverable through the sale of the product over lengthy periods. These investments are predicated on expectations as to future supply conditions, including changes in technology, and future demand conditions—expectations both as to quantities and prices. The more distant the time for which any such expectation is entertained, the less certain are the matters about which it is entertained.[13] And,

---

[12] "The first and ultimate valuation of external things refers only to consumers' goods. All other things are valued according to the part they play in the production of consumers' goods." von Mises, *Human Action*, p. 94.

[13] "If we speak frankly, we have to admit that our basis of knowledge for estimating the yield ten years hence of a railway, a copper mine, a textile factory, the goodwill of a patent medicine, an Atlantic liner, a building in the city of London amounts to little and sometimes to nothing; or even five years hence." Keynes, *The General Theory of Employment, Interest and Money*, pp. 149–50.

the more distant the periods for which estimates are made, the greater is the extent to which expected events are discounted. The present value of a sum of money to be received 10 years hence at a discount rate of 10 per cent is only 38 per cent of its nominal amount, for example. It follows, for both reasons, that in making investment decisions in respect of durable goods, the recovery of outlays over moderately long to short intervals will be contemplated; in general the shorter the better, for the recovery of the outlay over a short interval will reduce the risks of the investment and facilitate adaptation over that interval.

In a very real sense, the operations of a firm consist of an overlapping sequence of short-term investments, the test of each being the expected cash proceeds, discounted to the time of purchase, by comparison with the proceeds of alternative investments. Every purchase of an asset is potentially a short-term investment. We speak here of expectations. This does not mean that, having acquired a durable good, a firm will use it only for the period represented by the period over which the expected proceeds are expected to become available. Nor does it mean that, subsequently, the costs of its use should be reckoned at the rate, through time, embodied in anticipatory calculations.

REVOCABILITY OF INVESTMENTS

By acquiring a good, particularly a durable producers' good, a firm changes its capacity for adaptation. The reduction in its cash holdings, if the good is bought for cash, reduces its freedom to lay out cash on other things. The increase in liabilities, if the good is bought on credit, reduces its freedom to obtain further credit. But as fluidity is the dominant feature of the environment, so adaptation, not constancy or adherence to a past decision, is the dominant mode of economic behavior, of persons and firms alike. No investment may be considered as having been made irrevocably. A building, a machine, a vehicle will be considered a worthwhile investment only as long as the present value of the expected net cash proceeds from its use exceeds the present value of the expected net cash proceeds from investing its current resale price in an alternative manner. However "fixed" the original intention to use an asset over a long period, it is economic wisdom, on discovery of an opportunity for greater returns, to dispose of it and invest in another.

Any consideration or reconsideration of an investment necessarily involves contemporary prices. The initial price of a good purchased is acceptable to the buyer because no superior opportunity of using the sum represented by the price is known. But once the good has been acquired, the initial price has no more bearing on adaptation than the price twenty years before its purchase or twenty years thereafter.[14] The only prices then relevant are the contemporary price obtainable for the resale of the asset as it is, and the price of obtaining some other asset in its place. We may speak of all such prices as opportunity costs, for insofar as any good is purchased or held, other opportunities are forgone to the extent of its current cash equivalent. And as long as any good is held, it is implied that the most recent appraisal or evaluation of alternative opportunities has ranked the existing investment ahead of others in the judgment of the firm or its agents. In relation to adaptive behavior the relevant price of goods in possession, their opportunity cost, is the present market resale price.[15]

OPPORTUNITY COST AND REPLACEMENT PRICE

The argument may seem to suggest that long-run holdings of assets by firms would be rare. But this does not follow. The roles of opportunity cost and evaluation are complementary, but they may not be confused. A good may have no present market price because there is no potential buyer; in such a case, the opportunity for adaptation through its resale is closed. The opportunity cost of the good itself (apart, that is, from the additional costs of using it) is zero. It follows that the expected rate of return on such an existing investment, even if the amount of the return is modest, is infinite and its long-run retention is, thus, very strongly indicated. Or take a less extreme case. A good once purchased, will have a smaller, often a much smaller, resale price than the sum laid out on its purchase, except in extreme inflationary conditions. Suppose that an asset is purchased for 1,000 monetary units and that after one year's use, its current resale price is 800 monetary units; and suppose that at both points of time a rate of return of 20 per cent per annum is expected. To satisfy the expectation in the first year, the required net cash proceeds will be 200

---

[14] "In commerce, by-gones are forever by-gones; and we are always starting clear at each moment, judging the values of things with a view of future utility. Industry is essentially prospective, not retrospective . . . ." W. Stanley Jevons, *The Theory of Political Economy* (London: Macmillan & Co., Ltd., 1871), p. 159. "Acting man is faced with the problem of how to take best advantage of the available supply of goods . . . . The actual sacrifices made and the time absorbed in their production are beside the point. These belong to the dead past." von Mises, *Human Action,* p. 491.

[15] See Edgar O. Edwards and Philip W. Bell, *The Theory and Measurement of Business Income* (Berkeley and Los Angeles: University of California Press, 1961), Chap. III. The authors establish a strong case for opportunity cost ("exit prices") in accounting, but, giving inadequate weight to the principle of adaptation, reject opportunity cost in favor of current cost ("entry prices"). In the following chapter we adopt current cost *as an approximation,* necessary owing to the inadequacy of markets and the supply of price information.

monetary units; but to satisfy the expectation in the second year, no more than 160 monetary units will be required. If an asset of the same kind is technically necessary to the firm, the old asset will not be replaced if it is expected to produce 160 monetary units or more, unless, of course, for a smaller sum than 800 monetary units at least the same net cash proceeds can then be expected. It is the decline over time in the net resale price of durable goods—in response to technological or economic changes—that explains the tendency for assets to be held, even past the time when they have become technically obsolete.

It should be noted that the criterion of choice is opportunity cost not replacement cost. Suppose, for the moment, that a certain asset is to be put out of service and that its replacement by a similar asset is being considered. The price of the replacement, discoverable in the market, provides the basis for its evaluation as an investment. If the expected proceeds are such that alternative investments will yield a higher rate of return to the firm (as a whole, if the asset is complementary to other assets of the firm, or as a solitary investment if it is not complementary), the asset will not be replaced. But, in any case, unless the available liquid assets (including the proceeds from sale of the old asset) are adequate, the asset will not be replaced. The opportunity cost determines, in part, the sum available to finance replacement and provides the basis for calculating the discounted expected returns from retention of the asset. The replacement price provides the sum to be found to finance the replacement and provides the basis for calculating the discounted expected returns from replacement. Both are necessary to the replacement decision. In general, no assumption may be made to the effect that a going concern will replace any specific asset. For accounting purposes, therefore, no difficulty is encountered in respect of such questions as replacement with identical assets, or as to what part of the outlay on a new asset may be regarded as merely replacement and what part as new investment.

LONG-TERM AND SHORT-TERM VENTURES

Trading ventures may be undertaken for varied expected intervals of time. Some are intended to perform specific functions for short periods. In this case the investment in durable producers' goods will be minimal, unless favorable movements in resale prices are expected. Even though, technically, some necessary durable goods may have longer potential lives than the contemplated period of the venture (as in the case of mining equipment used in places remote from resale markets), they will be considered to have no greater lives than the venture. Resale prices will be heavily discounted. Generally in short-term ventures, the incentive in the form of net cash proceeds is clear.

It may not be so clear for ventures which are established for a potentially wide range of functions to be performed over an indefinite period. Yet in such cases adaptability is most important; for over an indefinite period substantial changes may occur in the firm's conditions of supply and demand. Whatever changes occur in the commodities markets, and despite those changes, the firm will be expected, as long as it is continued, to meet the demand for cash proceeds on the part of its constituents; and this it will only do by securing cash proceeds adequate in the first place to adapt itself to the commodities markets.

The expectation of an indefinite life does not entail that every operation selected to carry out its functions shall be carried on indefinitely. Nor, consequently, does it entail that every investment in durable goods shall continue until their exhaustion. A firm may change the lines in which it deals, the processes it employs, the means it uses, even to the point where its general character differs materially from its initial character. The end products, and, therefore, the producers' goods required and the processes employed, of the petroleum industry have developed from medicine oil, through paraffin and gasoline to industrial chemicals. A sugar processor may become also a manufacturer of building boards (to exploit its wastes) and of industrial chemicals (to exploit its by-products). A ready-mixed concrete manufacturer may become also a dairy farmer, to exploit the river flats over which it holds gravel leases. The most common general form is vertical integration of distinctive stages in commercial and merchandising operations, as, for example, a manufacturing firm which extends its business backwards to raw materials production, and, or, forwards to finished goods merchandising. Every such change may involve the reconsideration of existing assets for disposal to make possible new investments, either from the proceeds of the sale of those assets or from the proceeds of borrowing on the security of those assets.

Again, it is an easy step, but a mistaken one, to suppose that the expectation that a firm shall have an indefinite life will be held indefinitely. Expectations as to the life of a firm as well as expectations as to the holding of its durable assets are constantly being revised. This is attested by the frequency with which firms lose their identity, either by being absorbed by others or by being liquidated in their entirety. The revision of expectations as to a firm's life takes the same course as the revision of decisions as to particular assets of the firm. To the firm's constituents the present cash equivalent of the whole of its assets minus its liabilities is the opportunity cost of being in business. If the only alternatives available to the constituents are to remain in business or to liquidate the firm, it is necessary to know the opportunity cost, (a) because the net present cash equivalent, of assets less liabilities, determines which alternatives are available without introducing additional resources, and (b) because comparison of the expected proceeds of existing and alternative investments (both being hypothetical or valuations) cannot otherwise be made with a common reference, that is, the sum presently available.

This may seem to imply that liquidation of a firm in its entirety is an ever present assumption. But this is not so. A distinction is to be drawn between forced liquidation and liquidation in the ordinary course of business. In a forced liquidation, the initiative lies with the firm's creditors; its assets are sold more or less under duress. This kind of duress is not in the ordinary course of business. It may, and frequently does, happen that assets sold under such conditions are bargains to their buyers. Liquidation in the ordinary course of business is a very different matter. Generally, non-monetary assets are continually being converted into cash, or liquidated, by the sale of the products of their services. They are being liquidated under conditions which allow of some choice between different methods and times of selling. This is orderly liquidation. It is in the very nature of the trading business that assets are being liquidated in this manner. When, therefore, we refer to the present cash equivalent of particular assets or of a collection of assets and liabilities, we mean the present cash equivalent as determined, not on the basis of forced liquidation, but on the basis of orderly liquidation. We may speak of any firm which is not in the process of forced liquidation as a going concern. Unless a firm is in the process of orderly liquidation it can scarcely be described as "going." The designation of a firm as a going concern will imply that it has at least some future, even though we do not know at the time how far that future will extend.

It follows that forms of adaptation which involve the sale of durable goods formerly employed in the processes of production and trade are actions taken in the ordinary course of business. The proceeds are available for any purpose of the firm, and the net gain, the difference between the resale price and the latest recorded opportunity cost, is available for disposition in the same way as other gains made in the ordinary course of business.

LONG-RUN AND SHORT-RUN CONSIDERATIONS

The objection may be raised that the emphasis on present cash equivalents disregards a notorious fact, namely, that in the conduct of firms attention is widely given to long-run considerations. It may be urged, therefore, that short-run prices (present cash equivalents) are not pertinent. But we do not deny that business firms or their agents take account of the long-run. They do not take actions which are expected to impair their capacities in the long-run; they invest in assets which are expected to serve well into the future. But they are not content to have returns only in the long-run. They prefer returns in the short-run. Indeed they must have returns in the short-run, for only by meeting the circumstances of the short-run will firms survive in the long-run.

Whatever consideration one gives to the long-run, adaptation in a fluid environment cannot be deferred. Adaptation is action here and now. A state of adaptation in the long-run is the consequence perhaps of a series of actions taken at various moments of time. But every such action is taken in the context of a specific here and now. Long-run considerations are of no concern in ascertaining financial position at any moment; but ascertaining financial position here and now is a necessary condition of reasoned action at every present moment.[16]

The long-run is simply a rather vague and general form of orientation. One may make calculations about events expected to occur in the long-run; but they are all hypothetical and, at least, tentative. The gradual modification of long-run expectations may create an illusion of consistent pursuit of long-run ends; but the folly of consistency in pursuing long-run ends is evidenced by the numerosity of short-lived enterprises. Whatever calculations one makes and whatever consideration is given to the long-run, long-run expectations will only be approached by policies for the immediate future which are possible within the framework of the position here and now. There is no long run position which does not arise out of short-run decisions and operations, whatever long-run may mean.

The process of determining financial position, the accounting process, can take no cognizance of expectations in respect of the long- or short-runs. Until the manager of a firm discovers its present position, he does not know whether he is able to take a long-run view or must be content with short-run adaptation. There are notable examples of firms which have crashed while their managers were protesting that they were taking a long-run view. A long-run view is sheer fantasy unless it is disciplined by present facts, and, in particular, by present financial constraints. If any of the financial facts are colored by long-run considerations, they may lead to mistakes in the short-run which may abort all expectations about the long-run.

COSTS OF ACQUISITION AND USE OF ASSETS

All trading and production processes take time. The acquisition of any non-monetary asset is the initiation of a process which is consummated only when the asset is converted into cash, by the sale of the services or products of the asset or of the asset itself. Every acquisition of

16 "... so long as the environment of the firm is unstable (and unpredictably unstable), the heart of the theory [of the behavior of the firm] must be the process of short-run adaptive reactions." Cyert and March, *A Behavioral Theory of the Firm,* p. 100. See also, for example, Walter W. Heller, "The Anatomy of Investment Decisions," *Harvard Business Review,* Vol. 29, No. 2, March 1951, 99; Albert Gailord Hart, *Anticipations, Uncertainty and Dynamic Planning* (New York: Augustus M. Kelley, Inc., 1951), Chap. IV.

assets (except by way of gift) involves a sacrifice or cost. Costs are incurred by firms on the principle that the total stock of utilities will thereby be increased, utilities subsisting in beliefs that goods will be serviceable in generating purchasing power. Now as the total stock of assets, in combination and in amount, varies from time to time, the sacrifices which a firm will make for a good not in possession will also vary. As the markets in the firm's supplies and in its products vary from time to time, the utility of any good which may be technically useful if acquired also varies.

Every cost is a cost at a point of time. The cost of acquiring an asset at a point of time is the sum of money forgone, or the money obligation incurred, to acquire it. But the cost of an asset of a given kind is not necessarily the same at one time as at another, even if the quality has not changed, the level of prices has not changed, and the two moments are relatively close together. A firm will not add to its stocks of any good of which it believes it has ample stocks without compensation by way of reduction in price. But when additional stocks have been acquired, they are not distinguishable from other stocks of the same kind, even if different parcels have been bought at different prices. If the firm disposes of any unit of a homogeneous stock, by sale or use, the sacrifice then made is the same whether the unit came from the older or the newer stock. Whatever unit is used, the opportunity cost is the same at a given point of time. If the opportunity cost (the market resale price at the time) differs from the money laid out on acquisition of any unit (assuming no change in the level of prices) a gain or loss since acquisition will have occurred; this will necessarily be recognized as a gain or loss, irrespective of use.

The use of an asset occurs at points of time or over intervals of time subsequent to its acquisition. For reasons given in the previous paragraph, the cost of using an asset varies from time to time. Only in perfectly static conditions will it be the same as or directly related to the cost of acquisition; and there are, in the real world, no perfectly static conditions. If the market price of the end products of a firm rises or falls by comparison with the purchase price of an asset employed in its production, the derived price of such producers' goods will also rise or fall. Suppose the cost to a firm of acquiring a good is 100 money units when the selling price of each unit of its product is 2 money units. If the selling price of the product rises to 3 money units, because, for example, the supply falls short of the demand at a price of 2 money units, the producers' good will have greater utility than it had before and its price will tend to rise to, say, 150 money units. The holder of a producers' good which cost 100 money units will be immediately better off (given no change in the general level of prices) in terms of the market price obtainable for that good; but every additional unit of product which that good yields will also involve an increased cost or sacrifice.

An alternative view of the process of adjustment between product prices and producers' goods prices might be noted. It may be supposed that, in the above illustration, the unit selling price of the end product rises from 2 to 3 money units under the pressure of the supply price of the producers' good rising from 100 to 150 money units. But this is not so. The price of the latter will only rise to 150 money units, if there is some firm which has expectations of the price obtainable for the end product being 3 money units, or if there are firms producing other end products (with the same producers' good) which are expected to yield a price of the same order. The belief that rises in costs are the proximate stimuli of rises in prices disregards the fact that rises in costs in some cases force firms to abandon the production of some goods, and in other cases force firms to discover compensating economies; and it disregards the fact that these responses are evoked because there are other users of the same producers' goods whose market expectations justify their paying the higher price. It is the relationship between opportunity cost and market expectations (that is, evaluations of the future proceeds) which determine whether a firm engages in trading in a particular product; neither alone is sufficient. As the supply conditions of producers' goods are discoverable by all potential buyers and users, the proximate stimulus of any investment subsists in expectations, not in facts except the facts representing financial position; in expectations of prices in the future, not in prices paid in the past.[17]

It will be clear that in the case of any venture, the operations of which extend over time, acts of investing in assets must be regarded as distinct and separate from acts of use or disinvestment. For empirical evidence, we have the fact that use of producers' goods may be, and is constantly being, terminated before the technical capacities of such goods have been exhausted by a given firm. Such terminations are recognitions of the change in the status of an asset between the date of acquisition and the date of disposal.

We have contended in Chapter 5 that gains or losses through changes in relative prices are not objectively distinguishable from gains or losses arising from successful or unsuccessful anticipation of seller's margins. Our present conclusion is complementary; the measure of the cost of using any asset at a point of time is the diminution, through that use, of the current cash equivalent of the asset.

---

[17] The argument that costs are the basis of prices of end products purports to be supported by evidence collected by, for example, R. L. Hall and C. J. Hitch, "Price Theory and Business Behaviour," *Oxford Economic Papers,* Vol. 2, May 1939; reproduced in *Oxford Studies in the Price Mechanism,* T. Wilson and P. W. S. Andrews, eds. (London: Oxford University Press, 1951). Notwithstanding that the firms examined gave general rules suggesting a cost basis, in most cases the general rules were subject to provisos which indicate the determining role of market expectations. For an examination of the cost argument see Fritz Machlup, "Marginal Analysis and Empirical Research," *The American Economic Review,* Vol. XXXVI, September 1946.

DEPRECIATION OF DURABLE ASSETS

Many producers' goods and services are exhausted by conversion to vendible products in a short interval. Durable goods may persist through intervals during which many assessments of financial position may be required. The problem arises, therefore, of deciding what part of the investment should be regarded as exhausted or lost, in one way or another, between any two balancing dates. To such losses by way of wear, tear, and technical obsolescence the term depreciation is commonly applied. In this usage, depreciation is not wear, tear, and obsolescence. It is the diminution in the measure of the investment due to these factors. It may be of some technical consequence that wear and tear differs from technical obsolescence; for wear and tear arises from use and the magnitude of its effects depends on the adequacy of forms of physical protection and the rate of actual use, whereas obsolescence arises from technological developments.

But there is also a secondary form of obsolescence. This arises from changes in the market's evaluation of the product of a producer's good and, hence, of the good itself. A machine may be technically the most perfect machine devised for a particular process; but if the demand for the process has vanished, the machine is economically obsolete. The measure of economic obsolescence in a period would be the difference between the market's evaluations of an asset in the same condition at opening and closing dates of the period.

If there were no change in the general level of prices, and no change in the price of the good relatively to the general level of prices, and if the initial cost less the expected disposal price of a durable good were distributed in some formal way over its expected life, no provision for obsolescence would have been made. Both forms of obsolescence would be recognized only at the time of disposal. But obsolescence is a continual threat to the status of assets, and should, therefore, be recognized as a factor affecting the measure of the remainder of an investment continually.[18] If a formal process were relied upon, without recurrent reference to the market, no *measure* of the diminution in the investment would be obtained; and the resultant representation of the remaining investment may deviate materially from the measure obtainable by reference to the market.

However, the market does not discriminate between wear and tear, technical obsolescence, and economic obsolescence. It takes account of them all, but it generates only prices of goods in a certain state at a certain point of time. If we wish to determine the magnitudes of the several kinds

---

[18] " . . . any suggestion that [physical depletion through wear and tear] is in any sense more fundamental than [obsolescence, or the losses in value which occur without a corresponding change in physical substance] is baseless." Hayek, *The Pure Theory of Capital,* p. 301.

of effects, we may do so only by inference or imputation. Given the resale prices of a good at opening and closing dates of a period, the effects of any change in the general level of prices is eliminated firstly. The difference between the two prices expressed in the same scale may be apportioned between other factors and economic obsolescence if we can discover the change in the price, during the interval, of the same good in the condition it was in at the beginning of the period. Further consideration of these measurements and estimates is deferred to the following chapter. But it may be observed that for the purpose of discovering financial position at a point of time, the reference is to the market, whatever interpretation is placed on the differences between opening and closing market prices. Any basis other than market prices involves recourse to fictions, which may be convenient and as a last resort unavoidable, but which may also be misleading.

GOODWILL

Hitherto we have, by implication, considered the assets of a firm to consist of money holdings, claims to money payments against debtors, and various classes of producers' goods—commodity inventories and durable goods such as plant, buildings, and land. We may speak of all such things collectively as tangible assets.

A going concern is commonly said to be something more than a mere collection of tangible assets, liabilities, and residual equity. A firm which has or is expected to have a rate of return on its capital which is relatively superior to the rates of return available from alternative investments is valued more highly by its constituents than the current cash equivalent of its capital. The difference between this higher valuation and the current cash equivalent of the firm's capital is generally described as goodwill. The question arises whether goodwill is an asset of a firm.

Now, first, the goodwill of a firm or a division of a firm is not severable from that firm or that division.[19] The capacity to earn the rate of return which a firm, in fact, earns subsists in its collection of assets and liablities and the advantages which flow from them as they are arranged among themselves and in relation to the market; it does not subsist in any separable thing. As the property of severability was stipulated as a defining characteristic of assets, goodwill does not, therefore, rank as an asset. If it were only a matter of definition, however, the definition may be considered suspect. But the definition arose from the necessity of considering the capacity of an entity to adapt itself to changes in its state and its environment.

[19] Compare the qualities of "nontransferability" or "lack of independent realizability" attributed to goodwill in *Accountants Handbook,* Rufus Wixon, ed. (New York: The Ronald Press Company, 1962), p. 193.

Adaptive behavior implies that the goodwill subsisting in any collection of assets and liabilities is so susceptible to variation as to have no enduring quality, such as durable assets, nor any exchange value to a going concern, such as money or claims to money have. And as goodwill subsists in a certain collection and arrangement of assets and liabilities it cannot be sold separately from that collection for adaptive purposes.

Second, in ascertaining financial position, we have stipulated that the assets and liabilities are to be measured. But the goodwill of a going concern is the subject of evaluation, not of measurement. A going concern has, by definition, some future as such; and it is only with reference to the future that it has any goodwill. If the evaluation of the constituents did not exceed the current cash equivalent of the firm's capital, they would prefer the return of their investment. But clearly this value can only be calculated anticipatively. It may be obtained by estimating the future net cash inflows of the firm over some hypothetical period, discounting these at some hypothetical rate to the present, and deducting from this the figure obtained by similar calculations for a "normal" firm having the same capital. Or, assuming the maintenance of capital and, therefore, reducing the calculation to future changes in capital, the value of goodwill may be obtained by estimating the excess of the present value of expected future income over the "normal" return on the investment in tangible assets.[20] In making these calculations one may use, but as a basis only, the past performance of a firm, if it has a past; but the whole calculation, and the norms used for comparison, are hypothetical, subject to changes in expectations and not open to independent corroboration. Such a valuation is not the same in kind as measurements and cannot, therefore, be added to measurements in any statement of financial position.

The difference may be demonstrated by reference to durable assets. A durable asset is acquired because it is valued more highly for some purpose than the cash laid out on its purchase. But the measurement of any such asset is not considered to be the amount of this higher valuation. The expectation represented in the valuation may never eventuate in respect of the asset; equally the value placed on goodwill may never eventuate.

Third, the position is supported by a *reductio ad absurdum*. Suppose that there are a number of going concerns open to acquisition as alternatives by a group of potential constituents. And suppose that their balance sheets all contain an item, goodwill, found by obtaining the present value of expected future incomes over an indefinite period and deducting from this the present value of expected future incomes from a "normal" investment over the same period; suppose, that is to say, that the incomes are per-

20 Eric L. Kohler, *A Dictionary for Accountants* (Englewood Cliffs, N.J.: Prentice-Hall, Inc., 1963), p. 246.

petuities. The value of the goodwill in each case will be the present value of a perpetuity at the difference in the rates of return on the actual investment (as discovered) and on a normal investment. If this is added to the current cash equivalent of the actual investment, in each case the rate of return on the augmented "capital" (that is, including goodwill) will simply be the normal rate.[21] All opportunities would seem to be alike and the potential constituents could not choose between them. The process is circular and self-defeating. If the goodwill valuations were made by different persons (for example, information processors) having different notions of the normal rate of return, comparison would be rendered ineffective as far as the constituents were concerned. Inasmuch as the assessment of opportunities rests with constituents, it is their affair to choose their own capitalization rates and time horizons, and in fact they do so, disregarding any valuation of goodwill interpolated in the financial statements.

Finally, the goodwill of a going concern runs to the constituents, not to the firm. It is they who put valuations on expected superior returns. It is they who have the right to dispose of going concerns or of their interests in them. To regard goodwill as an asset of a going concern is to confuse two entities—the constituents as persons and the firm as an instrument. If the constituents accept an offer for a going concern in excess of the current cash equivalent of its capital, the difference is simply a gain to them. It arises only when the firm *ceases* to be the same firm by becoming the instrument of a new group of constituents. The new constituents, having laid out a sum in excess of the current cash equivalent of the old firm's components, may regard the advantage acquired as an asset of the new firm. But this excess, though represented by a money payment, is no different from the amount by which the subjective valuation of any single asset exceeds the price paid for it; and no such excess is regarded as part of the current cash equivalent of an asset. That cash has been paid may be recognized in the record; but its effect is in no way to increase the adaptability of the firm, and the indicated treatment of it is to reduce the amount of the residual equity from the price paid to the current cash equivalent of the new firm's component assets less its liabilities.[22]

21 Suppose that 100 units invested in a firm gives a return of 8 units and that the normal return, however determined, is 5 units. The present value of a perpetuity of 5 units at 5 per cent is 100, and of 8 units at 5 per cent is 160. The value of the goodwill is, therefore, 60 units. If this is added to the 100 units invested, the return on the resulting 160 units being 8 units is at the same rate as the normal expectation. And so for all opportunities. Paton makes the same point but apparently in respect of non-purchased goodwill only; Paton, *Accounting Theory*, pp. 317–8.

22 A similar conclusion is reached by J. E. Sands, *Wealth, Income and Intangibles* (Toronto: University of Toronto Press, 1963), p. 83.

We conclude, therefore, that goodwill is not an asset of a firm.[23] The firm may well have the capacity to justify the expectations of its constituents and of its creditors. But this capacity subsists in the superior rate of return on the current cash equivalent of its capital, by comparison with other alternatives; and the actual return and the current cash equivalent of capital are provided by the accounting procedure already outlined. It is not the function of accounting to determine the going value of a firm as a whole; this function rests with constituents and potential constituents—those who are in the market for investments in going concerns.[24]

THE ACCOUNTING PERIOD

Hitherto, we have referred, generally, to the periodical preparation of statements of financial position, of income statements, and statements of change in position, but without giving attention to the frequency or occasion of such statements.

A going concern engages in transactions and operations which have widely varying intervals between initiation and consummation. Commodities and labor service purchased commonly find their way into vendible products the investment in which is liquidated over relatively short periods. Durable goods yield their services over much longer periods. Some liabilities mature in relatively short periods; others may run long terms to maturity. The residual equity runs as long as a firm continues, though the interest of any constituent may, subject to the rules governing constituents, change hands at shorter intervals.

Many classes of transactions and operations pursuant to any chosen policy are repetitive in form, but they are not necessarily repetitive in consequence due to changes in markets and techniques. Although a general course of action, involving a sequence of similar acts, may be selected for a future interval, it will be varied in details if not in major respects if the expected consequences change. But it is clearly impossible, before every single action, to ascertain the present position and evaluate the consequences of alternatives if there are many single actions following one another in close succession and working themselves out concurrently.

We may suppose that certain actions of themselves will not appreciably

---

[23] "Goodwill ... cannot under any circumstances be called an 'asset', unless that term is confessedly meant to include at least two kinds of things which have no common attribute peculiar to them." Canning, *The Economics of Accountancy*, p. 43. Canning refers to goodwill as a catchall for "values" not specifically shown elsewhere in a balance sheet.

[24] For an early treatment tending to the same conclusions see Paton, *Accounting Theory*, Chap. XIII; and recently, Leonard Spacek, "The Treatment of Goodwill in the Corporate Balance Sheet," *The Journal of Accountancy*, February 1964.

alter the position and expectations of a firm, but that the cumulative effects
of a series of such actions, and of the series of concurrent market changes,
through some interval of time, will give rise to appreciable alterations both
in position and expectations. In general, there will be a point of time,
t_n, such that a material change may be expected to have occurred since the
last previous assessment of position (at, say, time t_m), or at which a
material change is about to occur. It is a necessary condition of informed,
adaptive behavior, that the financial position of the firm shall be determined
at each point of time, t_n, and that the rate of change of position shall be
then determined for the interval, $t_n - t_m$. This interval may be described
as the accounting period.[25]

The accounting period is defined by reference to the exigencies of the
firm. If any external set of circumstances which impinge on the firm is
changing at a rapid rate, the period will be relatively short. Such circumstances include the availability of credit, the rate of technical advances in
the firm's industry, the rate of change in style or fashion or taste on the
part of customers. Similarly, if any aspect of the firm itself is changing
rapidly—its sales, its inventory, its investment in durable goods, its indebtedness—the period will be relatively short. On the other hand, if there are
relatively few or minor changes in the firm or its environment, or if the
rate of change is not such as to raise doubts about cumulative effects, the
period may be relatively long. The period, as it has been defined, is thus
related to the predicated goal-oriented and adaptive character of business
behavior. There is no ground for presuming that accounting periods shall
be the same in length for different firms or for a given firm at different
stages in its life.

But the preparation of periodical financial summaries and statements
of position involves costs additional to the costs of keeping a continuous
record. As costs deliberately incurred are incurred in the expectation of
gain, the length of an accounting period may be supposed to be determined
on the consideration that the marginal utility of the information content
of summarized information shall exceed the marginal cost of deriving it.[26]
But information content is not a vendible commodity; we have contended
that it is simply a potential for accomplishing changes in the expectations
of a receiver of a message. This intangibility makes difficult the assessment
of marginal costs and gains.

There are two potential consequences of this difficulty. Periodical summarization may become simply a recurrent formal procedure, the accounting
period being of fixed duration regardless of the circumstances through
which a firm is passing. The operation will be regarded as a more or less

---

[25] For a more elaborate demonstration see R. J. Chambers, "Detail for a Blueprint," *The Accounting Review*, April 1957.
[26] See Hart, *Anticipations, Uncertainty and Dynamic Planning*, Chap. V.

necessary evil, passively accepted, rather than as an integral component of the adaptive mechanism. On the other hand, the costs of the exercise may be considered as necessary and fixed, regardless of the information content of the product. Despite major developments, past and prospective, decision-makers will be left to assume no material change in the firm's capacity over considerable intervals. Both consequences are in violation of economically adaptive behavior.

Notwithstanding the relation of the accounting period to the firm's exigencies, some purposes may be served by adopting accounting periods of equal length. Planning for periods of equal length and reviewing position and performance at regular intervals makes it possible to build up a stock of "period experiences" which are similar in at least some respects and which may be supposed to be comparable. Weeks, quarters, years are comparable periods, at least in length; and years are comparable inasmuch as they embrace the recurrent range of seasonal and social events. The technical problems of deriving financial summaries are made easier by the use of a period of fixed length. Nevertheless, any firm subject to marked seasonal variations may find it useful to consider its year as broken into, say, summer and winter seasons of disparate length; and any firm having contracts or commitments over several years may find it useful to adopt a period longer than one year for some purposes.

We thus contemplate the possibility that accounting periods shall be determined by reference to the nature of a firm's business, that for some purposes the period may be shorter than, equal to, or longer than the calendar year, and that for some purposes statements of changes occurring over several shorter periods may be combined to give a statement of changes over a longer period. In general, the shorter the accounting period, the greater is the probability of optimal adaptation. But as all processed information involves processing costs, the comprehensiveness and frequency of periodical reporting will ideally be determined on the basis of the relationship between the marginal cost and the marginal utility of information additional to that presently available at any time.

REVIEW

In this chapter we have isolated some of the features of firms and their operations which bear on the form of accounting appropriate to them. Some of the matters considered have been selected because clarification seemed necessary; others for the purpose of showing the application of conclusions already reached; others for the purpose of providing additional evidence for the propriety of those conclusions. No attempt has been made to elaborate on the theory of the behavior of firms, but the argument and conclusions are believed to be consistent with the tenor of the economic theory of the firm as far as it relates to our purposes and with the observable operations of firms. The object of the chapter has been to lay some of the foundations for consideration, in the next chapter, of the methods by which the financial positions and incomes of firms are quantified.

Argument

9.11   *Trading ventures (firms) are adaptive entities engaged in buying and selling goods and services at a price per unit and financing their operations otherwise than by taxing powers.*

9.12   *The constituents of firms are persons who divest themselves of personal assets in exchange for residual interests in firms. (They are residual equity holders in firms).*

9.13   *The participants of firms are all persons for which the firm is the focus of one or more of their interests. (Participants include, for example, constituents, financiers, workers, suppliers, customers).*

9.14   The objectives of firms embrace the satisfaction of all participants to a greater degree than would alternative participations.
(3.24, *9.11*, *9.13*)

9.15   *The rate of return on capital is the time rate of change in capital, both capital and the increment to it being measured in units of the same dimension.*
(5.25, *5.41*, 5.52)

9.16   The rate of return on capital is a measure of the relative financial efficiencies of alternative uses of capital, within a given firm and as between firms.
(*9.12*, 9.14, *9.15*)

9.17   Ratios of monetary magnitudes representing particular financial features of firms are indicative of directions in which the rate of return on capital may be improved.
(2.54, *2.62*, *2.63*, *9.11*, 9.16)

9.18   All measurements of the financial features of firms which occur as terms in financial ratios shall be in units of the same dimension.
(*1.43*, 9.16, 9.17)

9.21   Judgments of the past efficiency and future capacity of a firm are comparative; no judgment may be based on absolute magnitudes.
(*1.42*, 2.28, 9.16)

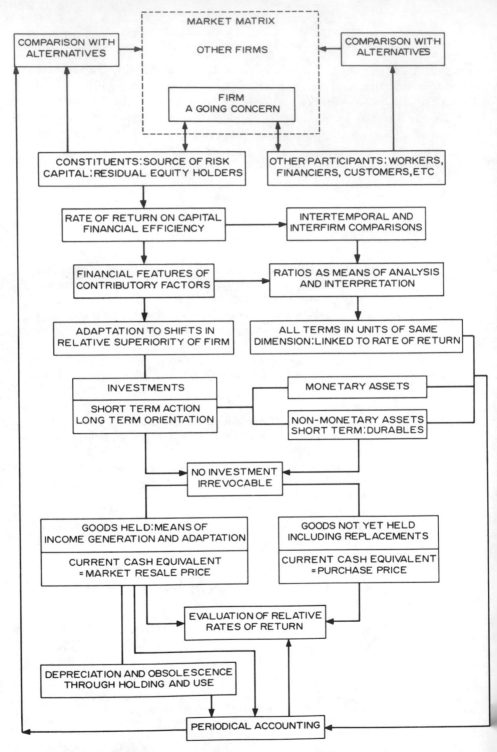

Figure 9
OUTLINE OF CHAPTER 9: TRADING VENTURES.

9.22   *Ratios expressing comparisons of absolute magnitudes are no-dimensional magnitudes.*

9.23   Comparison of ratios at successive points of time does not require that measurements at those points of time be transformed to units of the same dimension.

(*4.34*, 9.17, *9.22*)

9.24   Comparison of ratios of monetary magnitudes for different firms of the same kind and at a given time does not require that absolute measurements of the characteristics of those firms shall be of the same order.

(4.36, 9.16, *9.22*)

9.31   The differential effects of changes in the purchasing power of money on holdings of money (and money substitutes) and on holdings of goods necessitates classification of assets and equities into monetary and non-monetary items.

(3.53, 3.83, *5.11*, *5.12*)

9.32   *Monetary items are assets and equities the measures of which are fixed contractually regardless of changes in the purchasing power of money.*

9.33   *Non-monetary items are assets and equities the measures of which through time are not contractually fixed.*

9.41   Firms act through agents or managers appointed by constituents.

(*3.31*, *9.11*)

9.42   As agents, managers are accountable for the performance of firms in terms of the criteria of participants.

(9.14, *9.41*)

9.43   The continued existence of a firm, as from any point of time, depends on the superiority of the expected future returns from the firm over the expected future returns from alternative uses of the capital employed in it (that is, on valuations by constituents).

(*9.12*, 9.14, 9.16)

9.44   The continued use of a good by a firm, as from any point of time, depends on the superiority of the expected future returns from its use over the expected future returns from alternative uses of its current cash equivalent (that is, on valuations by managers).

(9.16, 9.17, 9.42)

9.45   No such valuations may be made unless the current cash equivalents of assets, singly and in aggregate, are known.

(4.33, 9.43, 9.44)

9.46   Capacity for adaptation depends on the amount of, and knowledge of the amount of, the current cash equivalents of assets, singly and in aggregate.

(3.24, 3.66, *9.12*, 9.14, 9.42)

9.47   *The current cash equivalent or market resale price of any good held is its opportunity cost.*

9.48   All investments of firms are revocable; the rate at which market resale prices decline through time tends to the stability of holdings of durable goods but not to the stability of their monetary equivalents.

(3.76, *9.11*, 9.44)

9.51   Firms take account of the long-run consequences of decisions but as a general orientation and subject to discounting.

(2.25, *3.92*, 4.26, *6.11*)

9.52   The long-run position of a firm is a consequence of a time series of short-run decisions, to which the contemporary position is always relevant.

(1.68, 2.72, *4.22*)

9.53   *A going concern is a firm which adapts itself by the sale of its assets, short-term and durable, in the ordinary course of business; that is, a firm which is not in the process of forced liquidation.*

9.54   The current cash equivalents of the assets of a going concern are the sums obtainable in the short-run in the ordinary course of business; that is, market resale prices in the short-run.

(4.33, *9.53*)

9.55   The measure of the cost of using an asset is its then market resale price; the measure of the cost of using up any part of an asset is the appropriate proportional part of its current market resale price.

(*3.72*, 3.73)

9.56   *Depreciation of a durable asset is the diminution in the monetary measure of the asset due to the effects of wear, tear, and technical obsolescence.*

9.57   *Economic obsolescence of an asset is the change in the monetary measure of the asset induced by changes in the demand for the asset or in the demand for its product.*

9.58   The measure of depreciation and obsolescence through a period is the difference in its market resale prices, reduced to the same and contemporary scale, at the beginning and end of the period.

(9.55, *9.56*, *9.57*)

9.61   *The goodwill of a going concern subsists in the superiority of its expected rate of return by comparison with alternatives.*

9.62   Goodwill is not an asset of a firm, being neither severable nor measurable. It subsists in expectations of constituents and is, therefore, capable of evaluation; such evaluations, being comparative, will vary from time to time.

(2.28, *5.11*, 9.43, *9.61*)

9.71   The accounting period conducive to optimal adaptation is the period defined by the last previous balancing date, t_m, and a time t_n, t_n being a point of time at which it is believed that a significant change in the aggregate position may have occurred in the period (t_m, t_n), or at which a significant prospective change in the aggregate position is to be considered.

(2.30, 2.73, 9.52)

9.72   In the absence of significant changes in the rate of change of position, the accounting period will be a fixed and regular interval, on the ground that the marginal cost of additional information exceeds the marginal valuation of that information.

(2.52, 3.43, 9.71)

Accounting for Trading Ventures

10 In stipulating that no investment of a firm is irrevocable, we imply that investments and obligations of every kind shall be open to examination and shall be reexamined from time to time. The investments of constituents in firms, no less than the investments of firms, are to be considered as revocable from time to time; constituents are not committed to one firm indefinitely. Commonly, constituents expect periodical divisions of the net returns from operations, as the price of risk-taking and deferring consumption, during the life of a going concern. On the basis of these returns, their knowledge of a firm's financial position, and their knowledge of developments in the firm's industry and in other industries, constituents may revise their expectations and switch their investments. For informed action, on the part both of constituents and managers, periodical summarization of the financial records is, therefore, necessary. It is true that the final outcome of a firm's operations is not discoverable until it has ceased to be a firm. But it is also beside the point, for, over any future interval, investments, obligations, and constituents may change materially, and constituents and others will wish to reconsider their valuations in the light of these changes. Periodical accounting is not arbitrary; the period is a matter of choice, and as we have suggested, of deliberate choice. But the necessity of periodical summarization and reporting arises from the principle of adaptive behavior.

In this chapter we consider the general problem of the discovery of financial position and periodical income. Little attention is given to specific assets and obligations as such; it is sufficient to consider the principal classes, for given the principles upon which classes shall be treated, the treatment of items which fall within each class follows.

PERIODICAL MEASUREMENTS UNDER STATIC PRICE CONDITIONS

The periodical recurrence of summarizing processes cuts across the more or less continual inflows and outflows of goods, services, and money. Periodical assessment of financial position and of the rate of change of position is a device for measuring past flows, but it does not interrupt them. The continuity of these flows poses some problems of measurement; but there are few real difficulties in the case where there are no changes in relative prices or the general level of prices.

Consider a trading firm which has as its assets at two points of time cash, amounts receivable, short-term inventories (commodities to be sold or processed) and durables inventories (plant equipment), and has as its equities, liabilities (amounts payable), and a residual equity. Cash, receivables, and payables are freely interchangeable at their measured amounts. Following the earlier discussion we call them monetary items, and the difference between the measures of cash and receivables and the measure of payables we will call the measure of net monetary assets (M). We will designate the sum of the measures of short-term and durables inventories as N (non-monetary assets). These designations represent simply a reclassification of assets and liabilities, by comparison with the expression for financial position given in Chapter 5. If, as in that chapter, R is the measure of residual equity, financial position at a point of time t_0 may be expressed by the equation

$$M_0 + N_0 = R_0$$

If we disregard new contributions or withdrawals by constituents, the income of the period (t_0, t_1) will be given by

$$(M_1 - M_0) + (N_1 - N_0) = (R_1 - R_0)$$

On the ground that a continuous record is necessary so that measures of particular assets or obligations may be obtained at any point of time, the process of measuring income by taking differences in the above manner may be modified. Monetary receipts, payments, claims, and obligations are specific in amount and generally definitive as to time; their amounts during any interval may be obtained by cumulating the monetary measures of particular events. It is less reasonable to rely on simple cumulation in respect of the short-term and durable goods which pass through the hands of agents of the firm or remain under their control for periods of time. There is no external check—such as customers and creditors, in the case of monetary claims and obligations—on the product of the record. It is therefore preferable to obtain the measures of these assets periodically by counting and pricing the inventory, of short-term and durable goods, by reference to market resale prices.

If non-monetary assets are divided into the two classes, short-term and durables inventories; and

if MRI, MRD represent the monetary receipts in a period from sales of short-term and durables inventories respectively (monetary receipts including cash and claims to cash); and

if MPI, MPD represent the monetary payments in a period for purchases of short-term and durables inventories respectively (monetary payments including liabilities incurred); and

if I_0Q_0, I_1Q_1 represent the opening and closing measures of short-term inventories; and D_0Q_0, D_1Q_1 represent the opening and closing measures of durable inventories; where I's and D's represent quantities, and Q's represent unit market resale prices; then

$$(M_1 - M_0) = MRI + MRD - MPI - MPD$$
$$(N_1 - N_0) = I_1Q_1 - I_0Q_0 + D_1Q_1 - D_0Q_0$$
$$\text{and}\quad (R_1 - R_0) = (MRI - MPI + I_1Q_1 - I_0Q_0)$$
$$+ (MRD - MPD + D_1Q_1 - D_0Q_0)$$

The change in the residual equity comprises two expressions of the form in which the income accounts of traders are customarily cast, viz.,

Sales proceeds	MRI	MRD
Plus Closing inventory	I_1Q_1	D_1Q_1
Less Opening inventory	$<I_0Q_0>$	$<D_0Q_0>$
Less Purchases	$<MPI>$	$<MPD>$
Income		$R_1 - R_0$

The grounds for treating transactions and changes in the measurement of durables in the same way as transactions in short-term inventories were established in the previous chapter. Assuming that no durables were bought or sold in the period, $(D_1Q_1 - D_0Q_0)$ expresses the measure of depreciation of durables in the period.

The items in this equation which give rise to difficulty are the measurements of inventories. For short-term inventories the difficulty is not great, for there is a reasonably ready market in which the prices of short-term inventories may be obtained. Inventories of durable goods may be considered the most difficult of measurement for the market in durable goods is much thinner, and subject, therefore, to greater variations in quotations than are short-term inventories. Notwithstanding the difficulties, as the measures of inventories enter into the statement of financial position, the attempt must be made if the effects of events in any particular period are to be assigned to that period, and prevented from spilling over into subsequent periods.

PERIODICAL MEASUREMENTS WHEN PRICES CHANGE: COMPARATIVE STATICS

Changes in General Level of Prices

Consider the more complicated case in which there has been a change in the general level of prices, but not in relative prices, between the balancing dates. Such a change is the obverse of a change in the purchasing power of money and, hence, in the dimension of the unit of measurement and account.

Measures taken at the beginning of a period are, in this case, not directly comparable with measures made at the end of the period. Though we have spoken generally of the measurement of monetary properties of assets and equities hitherto, it will be useful to distinguish measurement from mere counting. To discover one's money holdings at a point of time, whatever their purchasing power, one merely counts the monetary tokens held. The same process applies to receivables and payables; for by virtue of the legal rights they vest, they are equivalent to money tokens. It does not matter whether the receivables and payables arose at a time when the purchasing power of money was greater or less. At any time their nominal amounts represent the numbers of tokens then to be received or paid. Debtors obtain no relief when the purchasing power of money rises, and attract no additional monetary burdens when the purchasing power of money falls.

On the other hand, the monetary tokens which are equivalent to nonmonetary assets at any time cannot simply be counted. Their number is obtained by the application of the monetary scale in the market. If a greater number of money tokens is offered in the market at one time than at another, and the quantity of goods offered in the market changes less than proportionately, prices generally will tend to rise; all goods will be represented by a greater number of units of money than before.

The consequences of a shift in the level of prices will be demonstrated for a case in which between two balancing dates, t_0 and t_1, there are no transactions: hence, the designation of this and succeeding sections as "comparative statics."

Let M be the measure of net monetary assets, N the measure of non-monetary assets, R the measure of the residual equity, all at times t_0; and let p_0, p_1, represent the general levels of prices at time t_0 and t_1. Let p (without suffix) represent $(p_1 - p_0)/p_0$, the proportionate change in the level of prices between t_0 and t_1, so that, in effect, the price level changes from p_0 to $p_0(1 + p)$. The financial position at t_0 is given by

$$M + N = R \qquad [1]$$

As a formal operation, multiply throughout by $(1 + p)$:

$$M(1 + p) + N(1 + p) = R(1 + p) \qquad [2]$$

Now, by hypothesis, the holdings of assets are the same at both points of time; in particular, the "count" of the net monetary items is the same. Transpose the term Mp to the right-hand side; the position of the firm at the end of the period will then be given by

$$M + N(1 + p) = R(1 + p) - Mp \qquad [3]$$

Thus, if the price level rises ($p > 0$), and if the prices of non-monetary assets rise in the same proportion, any given position will, in respect of those assets, be represented by a greater number of monetary units than before. But at t_1 these will be interpreted in the light of the price level p_1, not in the light of the previous level of prices p_0. It is of no use to contemplate the current cash equivalent at t_0 of any asset held at t_1. If $M = 0$, there will have been neither gain nor loss in command of resources generally, even though the position is represented by larger numbers of monetary units.

But when prices rise, so long as monetary assets exceed liabilities ($M > 0$), the measure of the residual equity, the right-hand side of [3], will represent a smaller command over goods and services generally than did R at t_0, by the amount Mp. A loss in this amount will have occurred. If $M < 0$ a gain will have been made. This accords with the known principle that if prices are expected to rise it is better to acquire goods and incur debts than to hold monetary assets. The perfect hedge against losses of purchasing power through holding monetary assets is to have liabilities in an equal measure, so that $M = 0$; its effect is also to preclude gains should the level of prices fall.

Changes in Relative Prices

Consider now the consequences of a shift in the prices of goods held, relatively to the general level of prices, between t_0 and t_1.[1] We assume again a static firm, and that, in the community generally, the relative change in the prices of goods of the class held by the firm is compensated by other price changes which leave the general level of prices constant. Suppose that there is a proportionate change, q, in the prices of non-monetary assets held by the firm through the period. The position of the firm at t_0 (given by [1] above) will become, at t_1,

$$M + N(1 + q) = R + Nq \qquad [4]$$

Nq is an increment in the purchasing power of the firm. Unlike p in the former case, q is not a means of transforming measurements in one scale to measurements in another scale; it produces an increment measured in the same scale. Nq is a gain $(q > 0)$ or a loss $(q < 0)$. The new current cash equivalent, $N(1 + q)$, of non-monetary assets is the amount to be taken into account when the firm is considering changes in the composition of its assets and equities. For example, if $q > 0$, the change in relative prices may make it preferable to sell the relevant asset and to replace it with some other asset which has not risen in price (or with an asset which has risen in price by a smaller proportion, in the more general case where all prices are subject to change). And if $q > 0$, clearly the ratio of equity to debt will have improved, the current measure of assets will have improved, and consequently the capacity to borrow and the collateral security available for borrowing will have improved.

Changes Both in the General Level of Prices and in Relative Prices

But market prices are constantly subject to the effects both of relative changes in demand and of changes in the general level of prices

---

[1] Sweeney proposed two methods of "stabilization" or approximation to contemporary measures, stabilization on the basis of original cost and stabilization based on replacement cost. The former disregards the effects of relative changes in prices; the latter is dealt with only in relation to durable goods. We propose a procedure having neither of these limitations. Sweeney, *Stabilized Accounting*, Chaps. II and III.

(that is, in the general purchasing power of money). As the effects of both on a residual equity are quite different, they are required to be distinguished. Consider a static firm, the initial position of which is given by

$$M + N' + N'' = R \qquad [5]$$

and suppose that between t_0 and t_1 the proportionate changes in the general level of prices and in the specific prices of the two classes of goods are p, q, and r respectively.

The position at t_0 is first to be restated in terms of the dimension of the monetary unit at t_1, thus

$$M + N'(1 + p) + N''(1 + p) = R(1 + p) - Mp \qquad [6]$$

The change in relative prices is only significant at t_1, in terms of the then dimension of the monetary unit. If the prices of non-monetary goods have risen in the proportion $1 + q : 1$ while the general level of prices has changed in the proportion $1 + p : 1$, only the difference between the effects of p and q remains to be considered as the effect of a change in relative prices. The new position will therefore be:

$$M + N'[(1 + p) + (q - p)] + N''[(1 + p) + (r - p)]$$
$$= R(1 + p) - Mp + N'(q - p) + N''(r - p) \qquad [7]$$

or, on simplification,

$$M + N'(1 + q) + N''(1 + r)$$
$$= R + Rp + [N'(q - p) + N''(r - p) - Mp] \qquad [8]$$

The several sources of the change in the residual equity may be summarized:

Rp represents the transformation due to the change in the dimension of the monetary unit;

$N'(q - p) + N''(r - p)$ represents the change due to shifts in relative prices;

Mp represents the change due to holdings of net monetary assets.

Rp is not thus a substantive change in command over resources, while the other expressions are; it is simply the effect of the transformation of the units of one scale to units of another. To the measure $[N'(q - p) + N''(r - p) - Mp]$ we assign a symbol V, the net effect of relative changes in goods prices and of changes in the purchasing power of holdings of net monetary assets. The treatment of these apparently different changes as of one class is justified on the ground that they are not independent changes.

If we suppose the resources of a firm to be given by $(M + N)$ monetary units at any time, M and N are not independent variables; each is determined by the amount of the other. The magnitude of V is just as much a consequence of the initial magnitude of N as it is of the initial magnitude of M, in terms of the act of choosing.

By the magnitude of V, the firm has greater or less command over resources in general than it had at the beginning, for $(R + Rp)$ represents the same command over resources at t_1 as R represented at t_0. In this transactionless case, V represents a substantive increment to the residual equity which is the same in effect as an increment derived from any other operating source; we designate all increments of this kind (that is, exclusive of transformations having effects Rp) as income or a part of income. The transformation of R to $R(1 + p)$ is made to secure that income shall be measured by reference to the maintenance of capital, as capital is measured in the new scale.

THE INDEX NUMBER PROBLEM[2]

The preceding demonstration is highly simplified and abstract. But it has enabled the discovery of the elements with which a method of recording events as well as transactions must cope. Some particular points may be elaborated.

The natures of p, q, and r are not to be confused. The symbol p relates to proportionate changes in the general level of prices. It is not determinable by the firm itself from its own experiences. Insofar as a firm has holdings of monetary assets and owes obligations, and insofar as it may wish to acquire any of an extensive range of goods and services, a general measure of p is necessary to reflect the changed dimension of the monetary unit—not just the change in respect of the prices of the goods and services customarily bought, held, and sold. To use a limited index of the latter kind would make nonsense of any adjustment in respect of monetary items.

On the other hand, the symbols q and r are not to be considered at this stage as general price indexes of the classes of goods to which they are applied. They are discovered measures, derived by obtaining for each item of goods the prices at t_0 and t_1. Thus for each item of an inventory, its $q = (q_1 - q_0)/q_0$, where q_0 and q_1 are given by actual prices. Where an

---

2 To lampoon index numbers is entertaining sport. For example, M. J. Moroney, *Facts from Figures* (Penguin Books, Inc., 1953), pp. 48 ff. The facts remain that the dimension of the monetary unit does change; that at any time there is a specific dimension however difficult its discovery may be; and that men require some device to enable comparisons through time to be made however imperfect the device.

inventory is extensive and varied, it may seem that a general index of the prices of the classes of goods held may be used to obtain closing inventories. Such an index is eschewed on the following ground. A price index is an average of the prices prevailing for all members of the class of items to which it applies. If the index is computed externally, the prices of some items will have varied less, and the prices of other items will have varied more than the proportionate change represented by the index. Indeed it is possible that, as the construction of an index involves sampling and weighting, the goods in which any firm deals are not included in the sample or are weighted in a manner entirely irrelevant to the firm. If, on the other hand, an index is constructed for goods specifically used by the firm, the processes of adaptation will make the index useless; for the component items of an inventory are always open to variation in composition; and if the firm constructs an index on the basis of prevailing market prices of goods in new condition, it may be vitiated by the fact that some of the component items are no longer marketed. An internally constructed index is subject to greater deficiencies in this respect than an externally constructed index, because the latter extends over a wide range of commodities of the class and is a better representation of trends in the prices of items of that class. But adaptive behavior subsists in discovering the particular items, within a class of items, which promise greater prospective advantage than other items of the class; firms buy particular assets, not those represented by the "basket" selected for index-making purposes. In measuring an inventory at any time, t_1, therefore, only by recourse to the market will the averaging effects of an index be avoided, and will an objective statement of financial position be obtained in respect of non-monetary goods. We state here the general principle. In view, however, of the characteristics of markets, we shall find it necessary presently to adopt specific indexes in circumstances which prevent the discovery of actual prices.

But is not the use of the index of the general level of prices subject to similar objections? No, for reasons already given but which are worth repeating.

At any point of time the purchasing power of money, or the dimension of the monetary unit, is the reciprocal of the level of prices generally, whether or not an index number is computed to represent this level of prices compared with some previous level. A unit of currency at that time is freely exchangeable at the prices then ruling for other goods, not at the prices ruling at any other time. We do not know which particular monetary or non-monetary assets a firm will hold, acquire, or dispose of in the near future, or whether it will run into debt or discharge existing debt. All these possibilities, if they are considered for the selection of an end in view, will be evaluated in terms of the prevailing level of prices expressed in terms of the monetary units then circulating and these evaluations will be the basis of choice. The monetary scale of the *prevailing* unit dimension is the only scale commonly interpretable and, therefore, usable by all persons operating in markets.

Notwithstanding the difficulties of discovering the dimension of the unit and the imperfections of any index used in the process, some such device is necessary when complex combinations of goods at varying prices through time must be considered. The exercises in comparative statics have shown that, even though the prevailing prices of an inventory are given, the proportionate change in the general level of prices is required to enable the substantive increment in residual equity to be measured; and the amount of this increment is an element in choosing between existing and alternative employments of means on the basis of expected future increments.

Since there are many conceivable collections of prices which may be used in computing such an index, what is the appropriate index of the general level of prices? An index of consumers' goods prices seems to be indicated.[3]

First, as we have seen, all production and trading operations are geared to the final objective of making available consumers' goods. Directly or indirectly, the expected prices of consumers' goods determine what production processes and what producers' goods are worth employing by firms and at what prices the necessary factors of production will be exchanged; and whether consumers' goods prices may be expected to rise, fall, or remain the same over the interval of production, the first approximation to expected prices is the level of consumers' goods prices then prevailing.

Second, as we have also seen, the role of the firm in relation to its constituents is to provide them with gains or incomes. Whether these incomes will be devoted to consumption or to further investment, we do not know; nor, indeed, do we know what the magnitudes of those incomes will be, for the constituents may choose not to withdraw in any year the whole of the increase in the firm's residual equity. But insofar as any part of this increase withdrawn is to be devoted to consumption, a consumers' goods index is relevant; and insofar as any part is left in the firm or invested in other forms, the considerations of the first argument above make a consumers' goods index equally relevant.[4]

ACCURACY AND APPROXIMATION

All measurement processes yield approximations. Only in the case of the counting of discrete items or in the abstractions of mathe-

3 Keynes, *A Treatise on Money*, p. 54.
4 For other reasons for the choice of such an index, see, for example, Ralph Coughenor Jones, *Price Level Changes and Financial Statements* (n.p., American Accounting Association, 1955), p. 3.

matical symbolization is precision possible. We have deferred consideration of some of the difficulties of measurement until, as at the present stage, a range of examples may be cited. We have observed that there may be difficulties in obtaining a measure of the current cash equivalents of assets by reference to the market; there are thus consequential difficulties in ascertaining the measure of depreciation of durable goods if in any way the environment is not static. We have noticed that if the dimension of the monetary unit is to be discovered at a point of time and used in transformations of measurements from one scale to another, there are difficulties in sampling and weighting the components from which a price index is derived. It may appear then that the products of an accounting system of the kind we are elaborating will lack the degree of accuracy which some may expect of, and others may like to impose on, a system of accounting.

Some objections arise from the presumption that in the so-called exact sciences it is possible to make and use measurements which are paragons of accuracy. But this presumption is false. If it were true, there would have been no occasion for the origin and growth of the well-developed theory of errors.[5] The physical sciences are not concerned with accuracy as an absolute. They are concerned with measurements having varying degrees of accuracy, which ideally would be specified in each case. There are always limits to the degree of accuracy with which properties of objects are measured. These limits arise first from the properties themselves and the states under which they are measured.[6] Properties and states are concepts, and concepts may change. Atomic weights were assigned in whole numbers, until the existence of isotopes was recognized; the theory of relativity involves quite different concepts of the state or condition under which certain measurements are made than the Newtonian concept. Second, limits are imposed by the capacity of the hand, the eye, and the brain to devise, construct, and use satisfactorily calibrated scales as standards of reference. The invention of measuring devices depends on the state of technical and conceptual knowledge, and such inventions in turn promote developments in technical and conceptual knowledge.[7] And, third, pragmatical limits are imposed by the uses to which measurements when made are to be applied, and by the costs of measuring to greater or smaller

[5] See for example Campbell, *Foundations of Science,* Chaps. XVI, XVII.

[6] For a fuller treatment of errors due to "(1) the observer, (2) the instruments used, (3) the environment, and (4) the thing observed," see Ackoff, *Scientific Method: Optimizing Applied Research Decisions,* p. 206 ff.

[7] "However far we go in the pursuit of accuracy we shall never get anything other than a finite series of discrete results which are *a priori* settled by the nature of the instrument." Erwin C. Schrödinger, *Science, Theory and Man* (New York, Dover Publications, Inc., 1957), p. 73. "... physics progresses by successive approximations ... there is every reason to suppose that however far we go, we shall always be dealing with approximations." d'Abro, *The Evolution of Scientific Thought,* pp. 384–5.

degrees of accuracy.[8] These limitations, however, in no way interfere with the pursuit of better approximations and higher degrees of accuracy; nor do they interfere with decisions as to what should be measured if any given purpose is to be served.[9]

The problem of accuracy of measurement in accounting is a problem of choosing devices which will yield measures having the greatest possible potential for selecting responses, given that the unit of measurement varies in dimension and given the character of the market in which the measurement is obtained.[10] The problem is not solved by assuming that the dimension of the unit does not change or by assuming that such changes as occur in relative prices are irrelevant. Such assumptions ignore the very facts which influence and determine the economic responses of actors. Nor is the problem solved by assuming that the prices obtainable in any actual market, however thin, are not "normal" or "true" prices. A man may, by taking thought, conceive the value of a certain good to him; but he may not conceive a "normal" or "true" price of the good. There are no other prices than those yielded by the market, whether it is monopolistic, oligopolistic, or competitive. When business firms buy and sell products or durable producers' goods, new or partly used, no price is obtainable other than in the market as it exists, whatever its imperfections. And if, for the purpose of relating measures taken with scales of different unit dimension, transformations are necessary, the technical imperfections of indexes as they exist must be accepted. In making his choices, the manager or agent of a firm can have no better prices or indexes than are available to his accountant; indeed, his prices or indexes may well be poorer without aid, for he is thrown upon the limitations of his memory and upon a lay understanding of measurement processes. Any attempt to cope with the difficulties of measuring a property known to be relevant is preferable to any attempt to measure an entirely different property instead, unless the measure of a different property is the closest possible approximation to the measure of the desired property.

SHORT-TERM INVENTORIES

With these limitations explicitly recognized, we turn to some of the difficulties which arise in dealing with specific assets. The

[8] "The problem of accuracy is the problem of defining the allowable limits [in the construction of measurements]. These allowable limits must be defined in part in terms of the uses to which the measurement is put." Churchman, *Prediction and Optimal Decision,* p. 127.

[9] d'Abro, *The Evolution of Scientific Thought,* p. 354.

[10] C. West Churchman, "Why Measure?," *Measurement: Definitions and Theories,* Churchman and Ratoosh, eds., pp. 85 ff.

discussion will be limited to two classes of assets, short-term and durable goods inventories. There is no substantial problem in dealing with initial transactions in any asset or obligation; it is a matter of discovering the prices at which bargains are made and the times at which they become effective. The treatment of goods inventories involves additional problems of measurement from time to time and of identifying, if possible, the factors contributing to changes in measured magnitudes.

Consider first, the ascertainment of the current cash equivalent of finished goods inventories. We have defined a going concern as a firm having some future, in which it may liquidate its inventories, not under duress but in the ordinary course of business. It may seem, therefore, that the current cash equivalent of finished goods may be obtained by applying the ruling resale price at the balancing date; not the price obtainable by dumping all the inventories on the market at that date, but the price obtainable by sale in the customary parcels at the customary rate. But the ruling market price will, if the goods in question are sold at a profit, include the profit margin which will become income only when the goods are, in fact, sold. This margin is the price of waiting during the interval between investment and sale and of risk-bearing during that interval. These functions will not have been completed at balancing date, and it may not be anticipated that their expected price will be received. The resale price of the goods will, therefore, necessarily be reduced by any amount which represents this margin. But the margin is strictly a residue; it may on sale be greater or less than the expected margin. This uncertainty makes it necessary to attempt the measurement from a different direction. Resale price less the expected margin represents the current cost of the product or of the services embodied in it. This is the sum of money which at the time the firm would have to hold if it had not the goods on hand, but was in a position to acquire those goods; it represents the opportunity cost at that time of a decision already taken to hold goods. We may, therefore, take as the current cash equivalent the initial prices of the goods or services sacrificed in production, transformed to contemporary prices, and aggregated. If this sum exceeds the prevailing price of the finished goods, of course, the latter will be used, for in this case there is no doubt about the profit margin; there is no margin.[11]

Notice that measurement of the current cash equivalent does not turn on sale in the market. The facts of the market—resale price and the present prices of the goods and services embodied in the product—are used in

___

11 It will be clear that in terms of the discovery of present cash equivalents the rule "cost-or-market whichever is the lower" reduces to resale price less expected margin. It has, therefore, a definite rationale unrelated to "conservatism" by reference to which it is commonly justified; but it has this rationale only in the context of the system of ideas being developed here.

making an approximate measurement. All the facts upon which the measurement is based are ascertainable and the measurement is capable of corroboration.

If we were to resort to resale prices, work in progress inventories would be even more difficult to treat. Working backwards would entail estimating the costs of the remaining processes to completion; and as these processes are internal to the firm, there is no market measure of their extent. And if we were to seek resale prices for partly processed goods, as would be necessary on a total liquidation basis, they may have no current cash equivalent whatever. But on the assumption that the firm has some future, the pricing of work in progress may be carried out on the same principle as has been suggested for finished goods inventories, by transforming acquisition prices of the goods or services sacrificed to prices at present ruling for those goods and services, provided their sum does not exceed the market resale price of the finished product. The pricing of raw materials inventories according to the same principle is relatively simple.

The process of discovering the current cash equivalent of short-term inventories in the above manner involves only the use of prices actually paid and prices currently discoverable in the market. But we wish to discover the effects of various types of transactions and events when they occur in series in a time period of some length. For illustration we take a numerical example of a firm having net monetary assets and short term inventories; the data for a period (t_0, t_5) are given in the adjacent Table A.

TABLE A
Transactions in Short-term Inventories—Period (t_0, t_5)

Price Data		Net Monetary Assets Money Units	Inventory		Residual Equity Money Units
			Qty·Price	Money Units	
$p_0 = 100, q_0 = 20$	Position t_0	1,500	60×20	1,200	2,700
$p_1 = 105, q_1 = 24$	Inventory repriced		60×4	240	240
$p_1 = 105, q_1 = 24$	Position t_1	1,500	60×24	1,440	2,940
	Purchases	$\langle 720 \rangle$	30×24	720	—
$p_2 = 110, q_2 = 24$	Position t_2	780	90×24	2,160	2,940
	Sales	1,400	40×24	$\langle 960 \rangle$	440
$p_3 = 110, q_3 = 24$	Position t_3	2,180	50×24	1,200	3,380
$p_4 = 108, q_4 = 24$	Position t_4	2,180		1,200	3,380
$p_5 = 117, q_5 = 30$	Inventory repriced		50×6	300	300
$p_5 = 117, q_5 = 30$	Position t_5	2,180		1,500	3,680

The general price level data are index numbers on the base $p_0 = 100$; the inventory price data, $q_0, q_1, \ldots q_5$, are actual prices. For the purpose of illustration the number of transactions and events in each period is limited. The effects of the changes in prices and of transactions are to be obtained for the periods ended $t_1, t_2 \ldots t_5$; the whole series is to be linked in such a way that the periodical effects are in aggregate equal to the change between t_0 and t_5.

In this table, the residual equity at each point of time $t_0, t_1, \ldots t_5$ is the sum of the measures of net monetary assets and inventory, and these are obtained by count and by pricing inventory at current prices. The measures of all three components of financial position are, thus, objectively determined. To obtain this effect by continuous recording, the inventory on hand is repriced whenever a change occurs in the market price, for example, in periods ended t_1 and t_5. But throughout the period (t_0, t_5), the dimension of the monetary unit is continually changing. It would be useful to trace the effects of these changes on the residual equity. The tracing is carried out in the following table, by means of the continuous repetition of the result obtained for the transactionless case when the general level of prices changes and the prices of the specific inventories change relative to the general level of prices:

viz., $$R_1 = R + Rp + N(q - p) - Mp$$ (see p. 226)

TABLE B
Changes in Residual Equity—Period (t_0, t_5)
Based on Table A

Period Ended	t_1	t_2	t_3	t_4	t_5
(i) Opening Equity, R	2,700	2,835	2,970	2,970	2,916
(ii) Rp	135	135	—	⟨54⟩	243
(iii) $R(1 + p)$	2,835	2,970	2,970	2,916	3,159
(iv) Opening Retained Income, S	—	105	⟨30⟩	410	464
(v) Sp	—	5	—	⟨7⟩	39
(vi) $S(1 + p)$	—	110	⟨30⟩	403	503
(vii) $N(q - p)$	180	⟨69⟩	—	21	200
(viii) ⟨$-(Mp)$⟩	⟨75⟩	⟨71⟩	—	40	⟨182⟩
(ix) Realized Surpluses			440		
(x) Income, s	105	⟨140⟩	440	61	18
(xi) Closing Equity (iii) + (vi) + (x)	2,940	2,940	3,380	3,380	3,680

(i) R is the measure of the opening residual equity for the period expressed in units of the dimension effective at the opening date of each period.

(ii) Rp is the amount of the measurement scale adjustment for each period; it is the number of units to be added to the opening measure of R to obtain the number of units, in the scale effective at the closing date, which will at that date have the same substantive significance, or purchasing power, as R at the opening date. Applying the basic formula to the period ended t_1,

$$Rp = R(p_1 - p_0)/p_0 = 2,700(105 - 100)/100 = 135$$

(iii)   is the effect of the transformation from one scale to another; it is the sum of (i) and (ii). In substantive terms it represents the maintenance of the purchasing power of the opening residual equity in each period.

(iv) S, the opening retained income, is the sum of (vi) and (x) of the preceding period. S is analogous to the savings of individuals.

(v) Sp is the amount of the measurement scale adjustment in respect of the opening retained income for each period; it is calculated in the manner of (ii) above.

(vi)   is the effect of the transformation of the opening retained income from one scale to another; it is the sum of (iv) and (v).

(vii) $N(q - p)$, is the measure of the change in prices of inventory relative to the general level of prices. In the case of the interval ended t_2, for example, it is obtained from Table A as follows:

$$N = 1,440 \text{ units}$$
$$p = (p_2 - p_1)/p_1 = (110 - 105)/105$$
$$q = (q_2 - q_1)/q_1 = (24 - 24)/24$$
$$N(q - p) = <69>$$

(viii) $<(Mp)>$, is the number of units to be added to or subtracted from the number denoting the measure of net monetary assets in the opening scale, in order to give the number of units in the closing scale having the same purchasing power as the initial measure in the opening scale. In the period ended t_4, for example, it is the opening balance of net monetary assets multiplied by the appropriate value of p;

$$2,180(p_4 - p_3)/p_3 = 2,180(108 - 110)/110 = <40> \text{ units}$$

In this period, as the general level of prices fell, a smaller number of money units will have the same purchasing power as 2,180 units in the scale of t_3. For the purpose of the table the absolute amounts are multiplied by $<1>$, for they represent amounts by which other increments must be reduced if the net increment to residual equity is to be obtained.

(ix)   Realized surpluses are the actually obtained differences between the proceeds of sales and the current costs of goods sold.

(x)   Income, is the sum of (vii), (viii) and (ix).

(xi)   Closing equity, is the sum of opening equity, opening retained

income, and income of the period, for each period, all in terms
of the scale effective at the close of each period.

It will be observed that the sum of the scale adjustments (ii) and (v)
and the income (x) of any period is equal to the change in the residual
equity given in Table A for the same period, and that consequently the
closing residual equities are the same as those shown in Table A.

The measure of the aggregate residual equity at any time is the sum of
the measures of the initial residual equity of the firm and of all subsequent
increments up to that time. The latter components are separated in Table
B so that at any time the contributions of each to the then residual equity
may be ascertained.

SOME CONCLUSIONS

The magnitudes used in the example simulate, in abbreviated and exaggerated form, types of transactions and events which may
occur. Suppose, now, that the five periods are telescoped into one accounting period. It will be clear that none of the incremental or measurement
scale adjustment factors, other than Rp for the whole period (459 units),
can be derived by a simple calculation or conversion factor applied to the
data of Table A. When transactions and events are numerous, the operations of Table B could only be carried out at all by computers.

In anticipatory calculations of expected incomes, it is permissible to
assume regularities of rates of change in the general level of prices, in
specific prices, and in sales, purchases, and inventory holdings. The magnitudes used are hypothetical only and there are limits to the usefulness of
refinements in hypothetical data. But such regularities occur only by chance
in the experience of firms. If, for the purpose of obtaining separate
measures of the effects on a moving inventory of actual changes in inventory prices relative to the general level of prices, or the effects on a
changing net monetary asset holding of changes in the general level of
prices, hypothetical regularities are applied to ascertained data of the kind
given in Table A, the results will only be as accurate as the hypotheses are
realistic.[12] For special purposes, on some occasions, it may be useful to
obtain *ad hoc* approximations to the separate incremental factors. But the
major elements of the incremental factors $N(q - p)$ and $< (Mp) >$ are
the magnitudes of N and M; and, as we have already pointed out, these are
mutually determined by any decision on the deployment of given resources

---

12 Most, if not all, proposals for isolating the effects of price variations make
assumptions about underlying regularities; as an example see Edwards and Bell,
The Theory and Measurement of Business Income, p. 144. The conclusion we reach
avoids any distortion from the use of such assumptions.

between monetary and non-monetary assets. The separate identification of the incremental factors mentioned is thus unwarranted.

We are left with the following solution of the problem of denoting the periodical changes in a residual equity. The gross change is the difference between the aggregate measures (or current cash equivalents) of net assets at opening and closing dates, each such measure being in terms of monetary units of contemporary dimension at the time measurement. These measures are determined by reference to markets at those dates and are, therefore, objective and corroborable. From the gross change is to be deducted the measurement scale transformation adjustment in respect of opening residual equity, both initial equity and retained income.[13] The remainder is the income of the period. If the amount of realized surpluses is ascertainable (which reduces to the condition: if the current costs of goods sold are ascertainable), their amount may be deducted from the measure of income to obtain the aggregate effect of changes in relative prices of inventory and of changes in the general level of prices on holdings of net monetary assets.[14]

In case some uneasiness is felt about applying the general price index to the opening residual equity, it should be emphasized that in this scheme the opening and closing residual equities are obtained not by a process of aggregating book entries, but by reference to prevailing discoverable prices. The correction is, therefore, quite proper. It would be improper to proceed thus if the measures of residual equities were mixtures of measures of specific assets made at different times.

The procedure outlined has some self-correcting principles through time. The opening and closing inventories are priced by reference to the

---

[13] "... we hold to the view that there can be no recognition of income for a period unless the capital employed in the business at the beginning of the period has been maintained, that is to say, after it has been established that the purchasing power of that capital at the end of the period is equal to that at the beginning of the period." A. Goudeket, "An Application of Replacement Value Theory," *The Journal of Accountancy*, July 1960, p. 38. We hold to the same view, though the above statement is made in respect of a replacement price method, a method we reject in principle but accept as an approximation. See below p. 249.

[14] It is of interest to note the result which would be obtained if only actual transactions were recorded and at their actually paid or received measures:

Sales		1,400 money units
Opening inventory, t_0	1,200	
Purchases	720	
	1,920	
Less Closing inventory, t_5	1,200	720
Increment to residual equity		680

The increment for the period (t_0, t_5) given by Tables A and B is 521 units, for if the period is treated as a whole the increments (v), Sp, would be merged with the increments (x), s.

market. Errors of estimation of the gross change in assets and equity may occur; but they will not be accumulated or distributed through successive periods, as may occur if frequent reference to the market were not made. Given an external basis for measuring changes in an equity, the aggregate change in a period is determined. The division of this change between an adjustment for the change in scale and an increment designated *income* may be subject to errors of estimation, however, which do accumulate through time; the running character of the residual equity account makes this inevitable, and requires that no relaxation of the search for a high degree of accuracy be permitted. Whatever the defects, it is preferable to attempt to distinguish the effects of changes in the measurement scale rather than to regard the gross change in residual equity as income.

As a test of the potential for selecting responses of the information provided by the method outlined, consider the quality of the result. The method yields measures of the income of the period and the closing residual equity in the measurement scale of the balancing date, and, therefore, of the opening date of the following period. The rate of return represented by the ratio of these measures is a mathematically valid rate. It may be considered as an indication of the prospective rate of return in the succeeding period. But it understates the rate of return on the average capital employed, which, by definition, is equal to the average residual equity, during the period. The method, however, also yields the measure of the opening residual equity in the scale of the closing date. The rate of return calculated on this basis is also a mathematically valid rate; but it overstates the rate of return on the average capital employed. A closer approximation to the effective rate of return may be obtained by relating the measures of income and average capital employed, the latter being also mathematically valid, for opening and closing measures of capital are expressed in the same scale. It would be a quite fallacious operation to relate income measured in the closing scale to capital employed measured in the opening scale.

DURABLES INVENTORIES

Consider the ascertainment of the current cash equivalent of durable goods inventories. In general, investments in durables are less readily revocable than investments in materials inventories, though they are always to some extent revocable, even if this means abandonment. Generally, they involve larger outlays per unit than short-term inventories and, in some cases, very large outlays indeed.

Ideally, what is required is the current resale price of each item at each balancing date. The determination of such prices is not subject to the same difficulties as those of short term inventories. A durable good, if it is to be sold, has not to be processed, other than by removal. But there are other difficulties. To determine a selling price requires that there be a market; and to determine the selling prices of all durables requires that there be a market in all severally, or at least in the technically useful combinations in which small collections of durables may be sold without changing the character of the firm (for example, a lathe with its motive system). The more highly specialized producers' goods become, the smaller the market; to the point where, in some cases, there is no market. Treatment of this case will be deferred. We consider first the problem where there is an active secondhand market.

An active secondhand market will readily supply a resale price. The question to be resolved is the significance of the difference between two such prices obtained at the beginning and end of an accounting period. The treatment differs little from the treatment of short-term inventories; but it does differ because of the incidence of wear and tear, if for no other reason.

Let X represent a durable good in a certain condition at t_0;

X' represent the same good in a different condition at t_1;

x_0 represent the unit resale price at t_0 of X;

x'_1 represent the unit resale price at t_1 of X';

and suppose there is no change in prices through the period (t_0, t_1). Then the change in the measurement of the current cash equivalent of the good is given by $(x_0 \quad x'_1)$; this is the measure of wear, tear, and obsolescence.

Now suppose that there is no change in the general level of prices, but that there is a change in the price of X. Let x_1 represent the price of X (in its original condition) at t_1. The change in the measurement of the current cash equivalent of the good is compounded of the change in its relative price and the change due to wear, tear, and obsolescence. The effect of the change in price is $(x_1 - x_0)$; it is a substantive increment in the amount of the residual equity. The effect of wear, tear, and obsolescence is $(x_1 - x'_1)$. The initial measure augmented by these effects gives the final measure of the good:

$$x_0 + (x_1 - x_0) - (x_1 - x'_1) = x'_1$$

Suppose, now, that there has been a change in the dimension of the monetary unit; p_0, p_1 representing the general level of prices at t_0, t_1 respectively. We have the following terms:

x_0 converted to the scale at t_1	$x_0(p_1/p_0)$
$U(x)$, Change in number of units due to this transformation	$x_0(p_1/p_0 - 1)$
Price of X at t_1	x_1
$V(x)$, Change in measurement due to relative price change	$x_1 - x_0(p_1/p_0)$

$W(x)$, Change due to wear, tear and technical obsolescence $x_1 - x'_1$
when $x_0 + U(x) + V(x) - W(x) = x'_1$

These elements are to be incorporated in the accounting system of a firm in the manner suggested by the general formula for changes in financial position. As with short-term inventories, we take a numerical example, in this case of a firm with net monetary assets and two durable asets, X and Y, which are employed in the earning of income. The data for a period (t_1, t_3) are given in the adjacent Table C.

TABLE C
Transactions in Durables Inventories—Period (t_0, t_3)

Price Data		Net Monetary Assets Money Units	Durables X Money	Durables Y Units	Residual Equity Money Units
$p_0 = 100$ $x_0 = 900$ $y_0 = 1,200$	Position t_0	1,500	900	1,200	3,600
$p_1 = 110$ $x_1 = 900$ $y_1 = 1,350$	$x'_1 = 700$		⟨200⟩		⟨200⟩
	Y' sold at t_1 ($y'_1 = 1,100$)	1,100		⟨1,200⟩	⟨100⟩
	Revenue received at t_1	1,000			1,000
	Position t_1	3,600	700	—	4,300
$p_2 = 115$ $x'_2 = 650$	$x''_2 = 600$		⟨100⟩		⟨100⟩
	New Y purchased t_2	⟨1,600⟩		1,600	
	Revenue received at t_2	500			500
	Position t_2	2,500	600	1,600	4,700
$p_3 = 120$ $x''_3 = 600$ $y_3 = 1,750$	$x'''_3 = 600$; $y'_3 = 1,400$		—	⟨200⟩	⟨200⟩
	Revenue received at t_3	1,500			1,500
	Position t_3	4,000	600	1,400	6,000

Table C is prepared on similar principles to Table A. The general price level data are index numbers on the base $p_0 = 100$; the other price data are actual prices. Note that for each interval we require the price of the good at the beginning (for example, for X in the interval ended t_1, x_0), the price of the good in the same condition at the end of the interval (for example, x_1), and the price of the good in its actual condition at the end of the interval (for example, x'_1); and that, for example, the symbol x''_3 is to be read as: the price of X in its used state after two intervals, at t_3. Given all such prices, the financial position at any time is objectively determined.

As before, we wish to trace the effects of these changes on the residual equity in terms of their distinctive characteristics; this is done in Table D after the manner of Table B, by continuous application of the general formula, augmented by measures of realized surpluses and of depreciation.

TABLE D
Changes in Residual Equity—Period (t_0, t_3)
Based on Table C

Period Ended		t_1	t_2	t_3
(i)	Opening Equity R	3,600	3,960	4,140
(ii)	Rp	360	180	180
(iii)	$R(1 + p)$	3,960	4,140	4,320
(iv)	Opening Retained Income, S	—	340	560
(v)	Sp	—	15	24
(vi)	$S(1 + p)$	—	355	584
(vii)	$V(x)$, relative price variation, X	⟨90⟩	⟨82⟩	⟨26⟩
(viii)	$V(y)$, relative price variation, Y	30		80
(ix)	⟨(Mp)⟩	⟨150⟩	⟨163⟩	⟨108⟩
(x)	⟨$W(x)$⟩, depreciation, X	⟨200⟩	⟨50⟩	—
(xi)	⟨$W(y)$⟩, depreciation, Y	⟨250⟩		⟨350⟩
(xii)	Realized surpluses	1,000	500	1,500
(xiii)	Income, S	340	205	1,096
(xiv)	Closing Equity (iii) + (vi) + (xiii)	4,300	4,700	6,000

(i) to (vi) are in substantially the same form and are derived in the same way as the corresponding items in Table B.

(vii), $V(x)$, is obtained in the manner already indicated. The opening price is converted to the closing scale and the result is subtracted from the closing price of a good in the same condition. Thus, for X in the period ended t_2, the opening price x'_1 (= 700 units) ; converted to the scale of t_2 by application of p_2/p_1 (= 115/110) this becomes 732 units; subtract this from the closing price of a good in opening condition x'_2 (= 650 units), and we obtain $V(x)$ for the period (<82> units). In the same manner (viii), $V(y)$, is obtained.

(ix), <(Mp)>, is obtained in the same manner as in Table B. The sum of $V(x)$, $V(y)$ and <Mp> is equivalent to the measure of V which was described in the section on comparative statics.

(x), <$W(x)$>, is obtained in the manner already given. From the closing price of the good in opening condition is deducted the closing price of the good in actual, closing condition. Thus, for X in period ended t_2, the closing price of the good in opening condition is x'_2 (= 650 units) ; the closing price of the good in actual condition is x''_2 (= 600 units), and the difference is the absolute measure of depreciation (50 units). It is given a negative sign throughout as representing a reduction of the increment to residual equity. In the same manner (xi), <$W(y)$>, is obtained.

Items (xii), (xiii), and (xiv) are obtained in the same way as their counterparts in Table B.

It will be observed that the sum of the scale adjustments (ii) and (v) and the income (xiii) of any period is equal to the change in the residual equity given in Table C for the same period, and that, consequently, the closing residual equities (xiv) are the same as the residual equities given in Table C. But the net effects shown in Table C are clearly extreme simplifications of the effects isolated in Table D. In respect of the good X in the period ended t_2, for example, the difference between the opening and closing prices shown in Table C (100 units), which might superficially be considered a measure of depreciation, resolves itself into a scale transformation adjustment of 32 units, taken up in the adjustment Sp for the period, a relative price variation of $<82>$ units and a depreciation measurement of $<50>$ units.

The separate measurements of V ($= V(x) + V(y) - (Mp)$) and W ($= W(x) + W(y)$) are only possible if it is possible to obtain at any time the present price of a good in the same condition as it was at the beginning of a period. It is not impossible to conceive such a price being available, but it is quite unlikely that such a price could be found in practice due to the difficulty of specifying the meaning of "condition." Goods even of the same age and production batch do not long retain the same condition. Is it permissible then to avoid this difficulty by merging V and W? Insofar as the price of a good declines relative to the general level of prices, it may be said that the decline represents economic obsolescence. The good is desired less, presumably because the market assesses the prospects of employing other goods more highly. Even though wear, tear, and technical obsolescence may be conceptually distinct from economic obsolescence, the effects of both on the current cash equivalent of a good and on the financial position of a firm are the same in kind. As was contended in the previous chapter, it is quite legitimate to merge V and W, regarding their sum as the general effect of all factors, economic and technical, having an impact on financial position. The term *depreciation and obsolescence* may be adequately descriptive. In the case of the good X for the period ended t_2, then, there would be simply the correction for the change of scale ($+ 32$ units) and the measure of depreciation and obsolescence ($<132>$ units), the difference being equal to the change represented in Table C. It is quite possible that in some cases the measure of depreciation and obsolescence will have a positive sign, due to changes in relative prices offsetting the effect of wear, tear, and technical obsolescence. But, if the accounting system is to be isomorphic with actual transactions and events, such effects are no less pertinent than the more common negative effects.

There are several possible indicators of the current cash equivalent of those durable goods which have a resale price. There is clearly the second-hand market. It may be imperfect; but the imperfections of single quotations may be mitigated by obtaining a number of quotations and selecting as an adequate approximation a mean or modal price. It is possible to resort to the prices of technically analogous goods, if prices cannot be obtained for identical goods, estimating the resale price on their basis. It is possible to obtain the replacement price of similar goods in the second-hand market in the same way as resale prices may be obtained. (Note that the reference is to the replacement price of goods in the same condition; replacement by the new goods is ruled out by the ignorance of whether physical replacement would in fact occur). In all cases a measure of the objective assessment of prices in the market is required; given a series of such readings an estimate of the probable current cash equivalent may be made. The result would be no more subjective than every scientific estimate made on data of the same kind, and it may be independently corroborated or falsified by reference to the data. Adjustment of initial purchase prices by internally established rules provides no objective measure of the change in the current cash equivalents of assets, and no measure, therefore, which is, by design, relevant in the contemporary environment.

NONVENDIBLE DURABLES[15]

The preceding discussion of durables deals with the case where there is a ready secondhand market, so that market prices of a durables inventory can be ascertained. Many firms, however, will acquire and hold some assets which are so highly specialized that there is no used goods market. To this extent the short-run adaptability of the firm is reduced. When this is indeed the case, it seems that the information given by the accounts should reflect it. A firm which makes outlays on specialized, nonvendible goods forecloses the opportunity of adapting itself by resale of those goods. The goods have no opportunity cost. There seem, therefore, to be grounds for assigning no current cash equivalent to them.

The effects of so doing will be twofold. The amount of the outlay would not appear among the assets, unless by a notation with no monetary units assigned for the purpose of aggregating the current cash equivalents of all assets. The aggregate current cash equivalent of assets and of

---

15 The problem of nonvendible durables has received little attention. The problems we raise are avoided generally by resort to internally generated numbers of monetary units to quantify a vague notion of depreciation which disregards the economic and financial characteristics of durables.

the residual equity would be less than if some hypothetical figure were included. For this reason the equity-debt ratio would have a lower value, and the measure of the assets available to creditors as collateral security would be smaller, than if some hypothetical figure were assigned. At the same time, and as a consequence, the rate of return on the current cash equivalent of all assets, or on capital, would be greater. Further, there being no opportunity cost of these assets, the periodical offsets to gross revenue would be less, the periodical increment to residual equity would be greater, and the rate of return would, for this reason also, be higher. The rate of return would, thus, be higher both because of its smaller denominator (net assets or residual equity) and its higher numerator.

What effects would this have on the firm's capacity to secure support for new contributions from creditors or constituents? In the case of neither of these groups is the measure of the aggregate current cash equivalent of assets, or the rate of return on that sum or on capital, the sole basis for evaluating existing investments or further investments in the firm. The measure of the aggregate current cash equivalent of assets indicates the capacity of the firm to adapt itself to take advantage of changes in its markets. A firm which has little capacity for adaptation may be valued by external supporters at a smaller value than a similar firm with considerable capacity for adaptation; for inflexibility in a fluid environment detrimentally affects the expectations of security of capital and regularity of income. The rate of return on the aggregate current cash equivalent of assets gives the basis on which rates of return on alternatives may be appraised. If the denominator of the rate of return included some figure for nonvendible durable goods, it would not give the amount available for alternative investment, for to the extent of the figure for nonvendible goods no alternatives are available. The exclusion of such hypothetical figures, thus, corresponds to the choices actually open to the firm.

It is conceivable, therefore, that two firms, one having a high measure of assets and a modest rate of return, the other having a lower measure of assets (because some are nonvendible) and a higher rate of return, would be evaluated by constituents and creditors in terms which are not as divergent as the asset measures and the rates of return, taken severally, would suggest. The higher rate of return of the second firm would be moderated by its lower degree of flexibility. Given a treatment of nonvendible durables such as that suggested, it may be supposed that firms would not too readily regard assets as having no market price; they would be under some pressure, for the sake of the appearance of flexibility, to obtain market prices wherever possible. It is also conceivable that trade associations or some independent service agency may act as a clearing house for market prices for a wide range of industrial goods. The difficulties of obtaining current cash equivalents may not be great if an aggregate plant is considered as a collection of vendible items, each of which could be sold (and, therefore, could be priced in the market) even if there is no intention to sell them.

In respect of nonvendible goods, there seem to be two possible solutions to the problem of representing their acquisition and holding in the accounting system. The first is to set off the initial outlay against the residual equity directly on acquisition, and to record the possession of these goods by memorandum only in the statement of financial position. This may appear to be a severe treatment, but it is probably no more severe than writing off developmental costs as they are incurred, whether in industrial or mining operations. By definition, the amount of the outlay is sunk in a series of expectations. Alternatively or additionally, a memorandum account may be appended to the usual financial position statement, setting out the amount of the outlay and an equivalent part of the residual equity.

INDEXED CALCULATIONS

If, however, the general system outlined is modified, a third possibility will become available. It will be recalled that in dealing with short-term inventories the initial outlays on goods and services were corrected to obtain contemporary measures by the application of newly discovered prices of those goods and services. In effect this meant the representation of the current cash equivalent by the amount of cash the firm would have to hold, if it had no inventory, in order to be in a position immediately to acquire the inventories it did then hold. Can the same notion be applied to durables?

A firm does not know the goods and services which entered into the production of purchased durable goods. It does know the market price paid at the time of purchase. If it could be assumed that a firm holds a collection of durables, movements in the specific prices of which could be represented by a specific price index, it would be possible to obtain the current cash equivalent *of the purchase price* of the collection at any time by the application of such an index to purchase prices. But the problem of obtaining an objective measure of depreciation is not solved. If market prices or objectively based approximations to them are not available, only hypothetical and, therefore, subjective estimates of the magnitude of depreciation can be obtained.

Table E sets out a series of transactions and events the same in kind as Table C, but in a manner appropriate to the data we assume to be available in the present section. That is to say, the prices of X and Y are not available, but there is an index of the prices of the class of goods into which X and Y fall; the index is given by the symbol d_n, d_1 being the durable goods index at time t_1. A hypothetical rate of depreciation is to be selected; for the purpose of the example, a life of five intervals is assumed.

The opening inventory is repriced in accordance with the index d in each interval, so that the depreciation calculation may be based on magnitudes pertinent at new price levels; the index is applied equally to X and Y. The new "prices" stand in lieu of ascertained market prices. Because depreciation is based on hypothetical calculations and not on actual prices as in the earlier formulation, a surplus over book value arises in respect of the sale of Y in the interval ended t_1; this is due to the failure of indexed calculations to represent actual changes in the market.

The method of calculating the magnitude representing depreciation may be illustrated for X. Assume that, at t_0, X has five periods of life yet to run. The opening measure of X is "repriced" by the application

TABLE E
Transactions in Durables Inventories—Period (t_0, t_3)
Indexed Calculations with Depreciation Rates Assuming
a Five-Period Life

Price Data		Net Monetary Assets Money Units	Durables		Residual Equity Money Units
			X	Y	
			Money Units		
$p_0 = 100$ $d_0 = 100$	Position t_0	1,500	900	1,200	3,600
$p_1 = 110$ $d_1 = 105$	Inventory "repriced"		45	60	105
		1,500	945	1,260	3,605
	Depreciation		⟨189⟩	⟨252⟩	⟨441⟩
	Sold Y	1,100		⟨1,003⟩	92
	Revenue	1,000			1,000
	Position t_1	3,600	756	—	4,356
$p_2 = 115$ $d_2 = 112$	Inventory "repriced"		50		50
		3,600	806	—	4,406
	Depreciation		⟨202⟩		⟨202⟩
	Purchased New Y, t_2	⟨1,600⟩		1,600	
	Revenue	500			500
	Position t_2	2,500	604	1,600	4,704
$p_3 = 120$ $d_3 = 122$	Inventory "repriced"		54	143	197
		2,500	658	1,743	4,901
	Depreciation		⟨219⟩	⟨349⟩	⟨568⟩
	Revenue	1,500			1,500
	Position t_3	4,000	439	1,394	5,833

of d, which for the first period is $(d_1 - d_0)/d_0 = .05$. One-fifth of the resulting figure (945 units) is regarded as the measure of depreciation and the remainder is carried forward. This amount (756 units) is subject to the next change in the specific index; multiplying it by $(d_2 - d_1)/d_1$ gives 50 units and a "price" at t_2, therefore, of 806 units. Three-fourths of this amount is carried forward, and so on. Note that the balance at t_3 is two-fifths of the original measure converted, as a result of changes in the specific index from 100 at t_0 to 122 at t_3:

$$900 (122 - 100) /100 \times 2/5 = 439$$

If no changes in the price indexes occur in the following two intervals, the amount would be written off by two equal instalments and the whole process would have disposed of the representation of the asset over five intervals as required.

Table F is analogous to Table D. Items (i) to (iii) are identical; items (iv) to (vi) are obtained in a similar manner, but they differ in amount due to the use of price indexes, instead of actual prices, and the hypothetical depreciation rate.

(vii), $V(x)$, is obtained in the manner previously indicated, except that calculated prices are used instead of actual prices. Thus, for X in the period ended t_1, the opening price is 900 units; converted to the scale of t_1 by application of p_1/p_0 ($= 110/100$), this becomes 990 units.

TABLE F
Changes in Residual Equity—Period (t_0, t_3)
Index Calculations with Depreciation Rates Assuming
a Five-period Life
Based on Table E

Period Ended		t_1	t_2	t_3
(i)	Opening Equity R	3,600	3,960	4,140
(ii)	Rp	360	180	180
(iii)	$R(1 + p)$	3,960	4,140	4,320
(iv)	Opening Retained Income, S	—	396	564
(v)	Sp	—	18	24
(vi)	$S(1 + p)$	—	414	588
(vii)	$V(x)$, relative price variation, X	⟨45⟩	16	28
(viii)	$V(y)$, relative price variation, Y	⟨60⟩		73
(ix)	⟨(Mp)⟩	⟨150⟩	⟨164⟩	⟨108⟩
(x)	⟨$W(x)$⟩, depreciation, X	⟨189⟩	⟨202⟩	⟨219⟩
(xi)	⟨$W(y)$⟩, depreciation, Y	⟨252⟩		⟨345⟩
(xii)	Realized surpluses	1,092	500	1,500
(xiii)	Income, S	396	150	925
(xiv)	Closing Equity (iii) + (vi) + (xiii)	4,356	4,704	5,833

The closing price of the good in opening condition is obtained by applying d_1/d_0 ($= 105/100$) to the opening price, giving 945 units. If from this is subtracted the opening price expressed in the scale of t_1, $V(x)$ for the period will be found to be $<45>$ units. The opening price for the period ended t_2 is 756 units (see Table E) and the same process is applied. In the same manner (viii), $V(y)$, is obtained.

(ix), $<(Mp)>$, is the same as in Table D, for the holdings of net monetary assets are the same in both cases.

(x), $<W(x)>$, is obtained in the manner indicated in the description of Table E; as also is (xi), $<W(y)>$.

(xii), Realized surpluses, includes the surplus on the sale of Y in period ended t_1.

For the same data other than inventory price data, this process gives measures of periodical income different from those given by Table D. This is due to the fact that indexed "prices" of Table E do not correspond with actual prices of Table C; and for this reason, too, the relative price variation and depreciation calculations of the two tables differ. No importance should be attached to the relative magnitudes of the differences between the two Tables D and F; some are large, some small, due simply to the data adopted for the illustrations. The important thing is that there are differences and that they can be large or small depending on the adequacy with which a specific index reflects the actual prices of the goods in an inventory and on the adequacy with which the hypothetical depreciation charge reflects the change in cash equivalent through holding and use. It is inevitable that under the method of indexed calculations, there will be corrections such as the surplus on the sale of Y; these corrections arise from inadequacies in the methods adopted for representing changes as they occur; their amounts are no less income or charges against income simply because they occur in lump sums at isolated points of time.[16] If contemporary financial position is to be indicated, it is desirable that approximations to current resale prices be obtained whenever possible, in lieu of, or in correction of, indexed or other hypothetical representations; and that depreciation charges, even though hypothetical, be modified in the light of new conditions as they arise.

It has been found necessary, in the light of postulated difficulties, to depart from the originally stipulated ideal of obtaining financial position and increments to residual equity on the basis of current resale prices. But the latter is maintained as a matter of principle; the departures are a matter of expedience, or of necessity, in the face of ignorance of the more pertinent price data.

---

16 Such surpluses or deficiencies are sometimes described as realized capital gains or losses. Inasmuch as they are nothing more than recognitions of past inadequacies in the information available or the process employed, they deserve no such description.

If there were markets for all durables in all conditions, there would be no need to resort to other modes of approximation. But when we have to resort to approximations, they will of necessity be approximations to the prices which would be generated in the market if there were such a market. It may seem that we have abandoned the position taken earlier on the deficiencies of specific index numbers. But the deficiencies stand. We are obliged to accept the aid of specific indexes in lieu of the actual prices only because of the thinness of the market. For the purpose of calculating a surrogate "price" where an actual price is not obtainable, a specific index is used, not a general purchasing power index. The result of the calculation is required to have the same function as an actual price, inasmuch as changes in prices relative to the prices of other specific goods are the signals which give rise to changes in consumption, investment, and production patterns. The use of a general price index is confined to corrections of measurements made in units of different dimension than the units used at the point of time of measurement and summarization.

REPLACEMENT PRICE CALCULATIONS

We have contended that replacement prices are irrelevant on the grounds that replacement may not be in contemplation at any time and may in the event not occur, and that they do not indicate the measure of means available for adaptation. We have, however, resorted to replacement prices as means of getting an approximation to current cash equivalents on the ideal basis, both when dealing with short-term inventories and when suggesting methods of obtaining evidence of current resale prices of durables. To be consistent with these departures, we cannot, therefore, disallow the use of replacement costs, as an aid or as an approximation, in accounting for durable goods inventories.

As in all other methods of approaching the problem, there are difficulties. It may not be possible to obtain the price of identical goods in new condition. It may not be possible to obtain the price of identical goods in equally used condition. Indeed the replacement price problem may, in many cases, only be resolved by the application of specific indexes of prices in the manner already illustrated. In all cases, replacement price does not, however, represent the capacity for adaptation. It represents the sacrifice which would have to be made if the decision to replace were taken. In all uses of replacement cost, therefore, it is likely that the prices used to ascertain financial position and the increment to residual equity will differ from market resale prices, and to that extent, the financial position would be overstated or understated by comparison with the ideal measure of current cash equivalents.

If, then, we accept replacement price as a basis for measuring financial position and changes in residual equity, it is because replacement price is a convenient and available approximation to current cash equivalent, not because it implies replacement.

Given replacement prices, it would not be difficult matter to set up their effects in terms of the general formula which has been used in previous examples. No illustration is, therefore, offered of the method of treatment.

ASSIGNMENTS OF COSTS TO PERIODS

The measurement of short-term inventories at a point of time was dealt with summarily in an earlier section, where it was suggested that the basis of measurement should be the goods and services sacrificed in their production, priced at the closing prices of those goods and services. The question arises, what goods and services are to be considered as sacrificed in the production of commodities?

For all firms, whatever the range of products sold, there are some sacrifices made which are strictly costs of being in business. They may be necessarily incurred whether the firm actually employs its resources at a high or low proportion of their technical capacity. Only in the case of a single product firm may they be considered as related in any way to particular finished goods; but even in this case, the mere fact that costs have been incurred gives no ground for supposing that they will be recovered in the price of the product. All such expenses will be regarded as falling on the income of the period in which they are incurred, subject only to the proviso that time-costs (those which run for defined intervals and are charged to or paid by the firm on a time basis) for periods which straddle balancing dates shall be apportioned on a time basis. On the going concern principle as it has been applied to short-term inventories, amounts prepaid may be carried forward as monetary assets (and, therefore, not charged against revenues of the past period), and amounts accrued but unpaid may be carried forward as liabilities (and, therefore, charged against revenues of the past period).

A less clear-cut group of sacrifices are those which vary in some way with the scale of production or trade but are not clearly identifiable with any particular product or products. These are joint costs. There are many conceivable ways, based on technical properties of products or processes, of distributing joint costs over products jointly made, but they all rest on hypotheses unrelated to market resale price and unrelated to any other objective criterion. The only thing objectively discoverable about joint costs is that they have been incurred. This seems to be ample reason for treating them as falling on the income of the period in which they were incurred, and carrying forward no part of them as short-term inventory.

The remaining sacrifices are those clearly identifiable with goods produced or in the course of production. These we may describe as direct or identifiable costs; they include principally the costs of labor and materials used in production. But if labor and materials have been used wastefully, the aggregate cost of inventory will carry forward, as a charge against the following period's income, the elements of waste. To ensure that this does not occur, inventory will be priced at the quantities of labor and materials necessarily sacrificed, multiplied by the unit prices ruling at the closing date. The quantities necessarily sacrificed are obtainable on technical grounds independent of the accounting process.

The position taken here in respect of these classes of sacrifices is in a sense arbitrary, as indeed is every decision as to the sacrifices which shall be considered as potential charges against future income. The proposals above, however, give effect to two general notions, (a) that internal apportionments do not rank as objectively determinable facts for a firm in the same way as do market prices; and (b) that the greater certainty attaching to an actual payment than attaches to expectations of future recoveries of costs warrants the recognition of payments not identifiable with goods produced as costs of the periods in which they are made rather than as costs of succeeding periods. There is also an ancillary reason for treating common costs as period costs and not inventory costs. As the cash equivalent of inventory items requires to be recalculated when the price of any component changes during their holding, the smaller the number of component items the smaller the number of recalculations necessary to maintain the record in terms of current cash equivalents. Not only that; every change in the composition of production will have a bearing on the distribution of common costs; the inclusion of these costs on any *pro rata* basis would complicate inordinately the calculation of the cash equivalents of inventory items, irrespective of the effects of changes in prices. The basic question is not whether some method of apportioning costs can be conceived; nor is it whether *physical* goods or capacities remain at the end of a period. It is whether there is a residual quantum of resources having an *economic* property represented by an actual price in the market or a putative market price at the close of a period.

"THE BLACK BOX"

The illustrations given and the discussion of them will have indicated the complexity of the impact of transactions and price changes on the state of affairs of business firms. The transactions of even modest firms would be a thousandfold greater, and those of large firms may run to many million times greater in a year. Whether or not the consequences which have been depicted are traced, or are traceable at a given stage of the technique of accounting, they are, nevertheless, occurring. Raw materials prices, wage rates, interest rates, charges for local government and other services, finished product prices—every kind of price changes or is liable to change within the space of a year; including the price of money in terms of goods, the general purchasing power of money. The only way of coping with this extreme variety and complexity is by resort to the notion of "the black box."[17]

Consider the economic system in which, by fine specialization and differentiation of functions, goods and services become available to consumers from their origins as basic raw materials produced in the rural and extractive industries. It is almost, if not completely, impossible to visualize the whole of the processes which contribute to the production of one's helping of breakfast cereal, to mention only one commodity used in a day. Ordinarily, we do not think of the variety of skills—of farmers, grain brokers, shippers, engineers, chemists, carton-makers, advertisers, financiers, stockholders, salesmen, and so on—employed in the process; or of the materials required in the process or emerging as by-products from the process and, thus, making the process a technical and economic possibility. In its practical complexity the whole process is indefinable, because no individual has the means of knowing in their entirety the repercussions of a past decision to make a breakfast cereal. For greater reasons the whole economic system is indefinable. When economists seek to analyze the system or any part of it, they resort to models which ideally will reflect what is going on in the system but in much simpler and, therefore, more tractable form. The many particular inputs, for example, are reduced to a smaller number by the use of such concepts as skilled labor, unskilled labor, raw materials, ancillary services, products, and so on. The system is, thus, definable in principle, even though the complexity of it defies attempts at definition in practice. Such a system is described as a black box. A single firm is likewise a black box. Acting man is a black box to an observer. Both the economic system and the single firm, however, require to be managed or regulated. If certain goods (outputs) are to emerge, certain other goods or services (inputs) must be introduced to the system.

Similarly, if certain financial outputs are to emerge, certain inputs measured in financial terms must be introduced to the system. The

17 See, for example, W. Ross Ashby, *An Introduction to Cybernetics* (London: Chapman & Hall, Ltd., 1956), Chap. 6; and Beer, *Cybernetics and Management*, Chap. VI.

homeostasis or stability of the firm, we have argued, depends on a financial information system which is isomorphic with changes in the financial state of the firm. But in an exceedingly complex case, we are forced to adopt a model which gives effect to those changes from time to time even though it does not trace them all—another black box. However, we already have the knowledge of what is going on "in there" in principle. We can design a model which will produce the output required and can specify the appropriate selection of inputs.

We specify that every transaction of the firm shall enter the record system at its price, and be represented by a double-entry. The many transactions of the firm are, thus, reduced to one form, but are recorded in two places. We specify that every nontransaction event (change in specific prices) which affects the financial state of the firm shall enter the system, when it occurs, in respect of the items held whose prices are affected. All equivalent goods will then appear at equal unit prices at any time; and all sacrifices of equivalent goods will then be designated by the same cash equivalents. The inventory account will be augmented by these changes and the income account will be augmented correspondingly. The costs of goods sold on removal from the inventory account will be their current cash equivalents; and the balance remaining in the account at any time will be the current cash equivalent of inventory on hand.

But during any period in which the general level of prices is changing, knowledge of the change is not readily accessible at all times. The above-mentioned transfers to the income account will, therefore, represent gross changes in prices of goods held, whereas the income component of these changes is the gross change less the effect of the change in the dimension of the monetary unit. Consequently, the sum of the costs of goods sold will not be a sum of measures in units of the same dimension. Further, the outlays which are common costs of all operations or of broad classes of operations are not identifiable with particular goods sold and do not enter into calculations of the cash equivalents of inventory items; nor during a period are the outlays measures in units of the same dimension. Nevertheless, we specify that the sum of the costs of goods sold be aggregated and that the aggregate be transferred to the debit of the income account; and that the sum of all outlays for the period which do not enter into inventory be also transferred to the debit of the income account. Similarly, the sales revenues obtained through the period are not measures in units of the same dimension. Nevertheless, we specify that their sum, the money amounts of the total bargains, be transferred to the credit of the income account.

To eliminate the defects just mentioned, we resort to a stratagem arising from the characteristic of double-entry accounts and the definition of income. Income has been defined as a substantive increment in capital, an increase in purchasing power. Capital is equivalent in magnitude to residual equity at any time; and income is calculated on the basis of the maintenance of capital. The opening balance of residual equity (or capital) is, therefore, transformed into units of the dimension prevailing at the close of the period by application of an index of the general level of prices. The numerical magnitude of the difference is debited (credited) to the income account if the general level of prices has risen (fallen), with a corresponding credit (debit) to the residual equity account. The balance of the income account will then be the income for the period; it will be transferred to the credit of the residual equity account.

Although this process does not trace the particular effects of all the specific changes in the period, it necessarily gives their aggregate effect. The non-monetary asset account balances have been continually brought up to their current cash equivalents. The monetary asset account balances and the liability account balances are in cash or current cash equivalents. The amount by which the measure of net assets has changed has been modified by the change in the dimension of the monetary unit. The inputs of the black box have been designed so that the outputs give income and financial position as they have been defined.

SCHEMATIC SET OF RULES

There follows a set of rules which indicate the mode of derivation, through a double-entry system, of an income account and balance sheet in accordance with the conclusions we have reached. The treatment is schematic only, but it is sufficient to accommodate all variants of the events and transactions represented. For simplicity, it is assumed that all transactions in durables and outlays not inventoried pass directly through the cash account, and all purchases and sales of goods (and services) of the nature of short-term inventories pass through the payables and receivables accounts. The double-entry counterpart of the narration is given in the right-hand column.

Cash Account

A1	Dr	actual cash balance at t_0	Cr	F1
A2	Dr	cash received from debtors or on durables sales	Cr	B3, D4
A3	Cr	cash paid to creditors, for durables and for outlays not inventoried	Dr	D2, E3, G6
A4	Dr	actual cash balance at t_1	See	F4

Receivables Account

B1	Dr	actual claims at t_0 (excluding bad debts)	Cr	F1

B2	Dr	charges to debtors at invoiced amounts	Cr	G1
B3	Cr	cash received from debtors	Dr	A2
B4	Cr	debts discovered in period to be irrecoverable	Dr	G6
B5	Dr	balance is cash equivalent of receivables at t_1	See	F4

Short-term Inventory

C1	Dr	actual inventory priced at cash equivalent at t_0	Cr	F1
C2	Dr	purchases at purchase prices	Cr	E2
C3	Dr	if positive (Cr if negative) all changes in the current cash equivalent of inventories as changes in prices occur	Cr	G2
C4	Cr	at time of sale all goods sold at their current cash equivalents immediately prior to sale, that is, current cost of goods sold	Dr	G4
C5	Dr	balance is the current cash equivalent of inventory at t_1 if there have been no losses. The amount is verified directly by counting and pricing	See	F4
C6	Dr	unexplained surpluses (Cr unrecorded losses) if on direct verification there are differences between "book" and actual figures for C5	Cr	G3

Durables Inventories

D1	Dr	current cash equivalent at t_0 of inventory at t_0	Cr	F1
D2	Dr	purchases at purchase prices	Cr	A3
D3	Dr	if positive (Cr if negative) all changes in the current cash equivalent of durables as changes in prices occur, including changes due to change in the condition of durables due to depreciation	Cr or Dr	G5
D4	Cr	selling prices of all durables sold at the time of sale	Dr	A2
D5	Dr	balance is the current cash equivalent of durables inventory at t_1 subject to provisos of C5, C6 above	See	F4

Payables Account

E1	Cr	actual payables at t_0	Dr	F1
E2	Cr	charges by creditors at monetary amounts	Dr	C2
E3	Dr	all payments to creditors	Cr	A3
E4	Cr	balance is current cash equivalent of payables at t_1	See	F4

Residual Equity

F1	Cr	balance at t_0 is equal in amount to $(A1 + B1 + C1 + D1 - E1)$		
F2	Cr	at t_1 amount of the capital maintenance adjustment	Dr	G7
F3	Cr	at t_1 income of the period	Dr	G8

F4   Cr   balance at t_1 is equal in amount to
            $(A4 + B5 + C5 + D5 - E4)$

Income Account

G1	Cr	sales of short-term inventory	Dr	B2
G2	Cr	price variations on short-term inventory	Dr	C3
G3	Cr	discovered surpluses on check at t_1	Dr	C6
G4	Dr	current cash equivalents at time of sale of short-term inventory	Cr	C4
G5	Cr	price variations on durables including depreciation charges on durables (generally Dr)	Dr or Cr	D3
G6	Dr	at prices paid all costs not assigned to inventory	Cr	A3, B4
G7	Dr	the result of applying to F1 the relative change in the general price index between t_0 and t_1; designate as capital maintenance adjustment	Cr	F2
G8	Cr	balance is income of the period. Dr to close the account and transfer to residual equity	Cr	F3

INCOME ACCOUNT

The form of the income account yielded by the above rules may be indicated.

Revenues:	from sales of short-term inventory	
	from sales of durables	——
	Total revenues	——
Costs:	(i) current cash equivalent, at time of sale, of short-term inventories and durables	
	(ii) price adjustments to short-term inventories and durables (Cr. if prices have risen)	
	(iii) depreciation and obsolescence	
	(iv) purchase prices of services not assigned to short-term inventory	
	(v) capital maintenance adjustment	——
	Total costs	——
Business Income:	Total Revenues minus Total Costs	
Windfalls:		——
Total Income:	Business Income plus Windfalls	==== 18

[18] In case the validity of the addition and subtraction is questioned, on the ground that only magnitudes measured in the same scale may be added or subtracted, it is pointed out that the items other than actual prices are corrections of actual prices of the same kind as the correction 1.54 added to the number one to obtain the length of one inch in centimeters.

The term *revenues* has been introduced to represent receipts of money or claims to money. Revenues are contributory to income, but their amounts are not unequivocally income. The purchasing power of the monetary amounts received may rise or fall after receipt, depending on how the cash proceeds are deployed, and on whether, if cash is held, the general level of prices rises or falls. The purchase prices paid—cost items (i) and (iv)—are instances of the class, *expenditures*, which includes also prices paid on the acquisition of durables. Revenues and expenditures are recognized by entry in accounts at the point of time at which legal rights, measurable in money, are established by or against a firm by performance, on the one part at least, of any bargain. All executory contracts are excluded from recognition. The significance of this point of time is that it is the point at which the risks of holding money and the risks of holding goods are exchanged. This is said, in respect of revenues, to be the point of realization.

Although five classes of item are shown as costs, it may not be supposed that, individually, they are significant or interpretable by reference to an income account of another period. The aggregate of the price adjustments, cost item (ii), for example, is not a measure of the shifts in prices relative to anything but the last previously recorded prices. Nor may the difference between this aggregate (which would have a negative value among the costs if individual prices were to rise) and the amount of the capital maintenance adjustment (which would have a positive value if prices generally were to rise) be a necessarily adequate indication of the net effect of changes in the general price level and changes in specific prices.

As we observed in Chapter 5, there is no good reason for supposing that any purchase of goods is predicated only on the prospect of gains from seller's margins. On the contrary, it is reasonable to suppose that goods are purchased also in anticipation of, and to take advantage of, expected shifts in relative prices and expected shifts in the general level of prices. All forward contracts are expressions of such an intention and all purchases of durable goods are, in a sense, hedges against future rises in the costs of the services they yield.

No valid distinction may, therefore, be drawn between changes due to buying and selling transactions and changes due to relative or general price variations. Only the aggregate effect, business income, may be employed in assessing the performance of a firm or its managers. However, if the effects of both transactions and external events are not brought into account in the period in which they occur, no valid comparisons of successive periods may be made; for gains and losses may be diffused through contiguous periods, confusing the effects of economic events and actions taken in those periods severally.

An objection may be raised on the ground that until a gain is realized by the occurrence of a transaction, there is no reasonable expectation that the corresponding increase in assets will be available for division among constituents or for other purposes; hence, it may be argued, business income should not include the effect of relative price variations unless and until sale of the relevant assets occurs. But this rests on a naive notion of the process of managing assets. The increase in assets corresponding to realized gains is not retained as cash and accumulated for the purpose of making cash divisions among constituents. Cash balances are not income-producing assets. They will be accumulated only in the amount and about the time that cash distributions are expected to be made. The possibility of making distributions, thus, does not rest on the amount of realized gains, but upon decisions as to the appropriate uses of cash balances through time. There is, consequently, no reason why the whole amount of income as derived above should not be considered as potentially divisible among constituents.[19]

RESIDUAL EQUITY ACCOUNT

The opening balance of the residual equity account will be augmented at the close of the period by two amounts. The first will be the amount necessary to restate the opening measure in terms of the closing scale. We repeat that this process is only permissible if the amount of the residual equity is obtained at each point of time by reference to contemporary cash equivalents of assets and liabilities based on ruling market prices or the best approximations thereto. The amount of this adjustment is, in no sense, income and it has been excluded above in the determination of total income. The designation *capital maintenance adjustment* seems appropriate, for, in one sense, that is its function.

But if, after the first period of operation, there are retained profits, these, too, must be subjected to the same correction in each period so that periodical income is not misstated. The amount of this adjustment is not income of the period, but it is part of the retained income expressed in contemporary terms. On the principle of maintaining the purchasing power of constituents' *original* contributions, it is part of the surplus representing assets available for division among constituents. Its separate identification is unnecessary except as an explanation of differences when comparative figures are presented for successive periods. In the worked illustrations of

---

19 Though we have taken no cognizance of taxation on incomes, note may be taken of the possibility that "realization" is accepted as a defining characteristic of income for taxation purposes. But taxation rules and decisions are adopted for the purpose of ascertaining taxpayers' obligations. The fact that certain rules, of convenience for administrative purposes, entail the use of procedures which conflict with the measurements necessary in the market place, does not make the forces of the market of no effect. It is with adaptation to and exertion of these forces that our analysis is concerned. See also Chapter 13.

this chapter, the corrections to constituents' original contributions and to retained income have been shown separately.

The second amount by which the residual equity is augmented is the total income of the period just closed.

BALANCE SHEET AND FINANCIAL POSITION

The above processes will yield a balance sheet of the following form:

Balance Sheet As At End of Period

(All amounts are approximations to cash equivalents at this date)

Assets

Cash: by count.

Receivables: by count, after excluding those having no current cash equivalent, (that is, excluding actually bad debts).

Marketable securities: by reference to market resale prices.

Short-term inventories: by reference to physical stocks at current prices of components, with an upper limit of market resale price.

Durables inventories: by reference to market resale prices or deliberate approximations thereto—see text.

Equities

Short-term payables: by count.

Long-term payables: future payments discounted to present at contractual interest rate (generally equal to face value).

Residual equity: Constituents' contributions: original contributions adjusted for changes in dimension of the monetary unit.
Retained income: accumulated retentions adjusted for changes in dimension of the monetary unit.
Total Income of the period just elapsed.

The processes described manifestly link the opening financial position with the closing financial position, and both positions are corroborable by reference to objective reality as at the times for which they are determined. Without the constant reference to market prices, the rich interconnections between the environment of the accounting system and the accounting system itself, the system becomes a mere formality, and its results are incapable of significant analysis and interpretation.[20]

---

[20] Beer, writing of regulatory systems generally, designates this as the principle of "completion from without." Beer, *Cybernetics and Management,* Chap. IX.

IGNORANCE AND INACCURACY

The problems created by the lack of information on contemporary prices can only be resolved by expedients which are accepted deliberately as devices for obtaining approximations to measures otherwise unobtainable. If the expedient becomes the rule, there is no test as to what a system of calculation should produce to serve the function it is intended or expected to serve. If an expedient or convenient approximation is not replaced by its objectively determinable measure when the latter is available, expediency will have triumphed over principle.

This raises the question: what significance can be attached to a statement of financial position in which liabilities and monetary assets are assigned numbers of money units representing their current cash equivalents in the ideal sense, short-term inventories are assigned numbers of money units based on current acquisition cost notions, and durables inventories are assigned numbers of money units based on, say, indexed calculations with hypothetical depreciation rates? Only one kind of significance. It is the best available approximation in the existing state of knowledge, given that the discovery of the magnitudes in question is pursued scientifically and without regard for the magnitudes which the managers or constituents of firms might prefer from their separate points of view.[21] It will, of course, only remain the best available approximation if the discovery of the pertinent magnitudes is regarded as a process of discovery and not of mere habit. There is no virtue in persisting with one method of approximation if another and better method becomes available. Consistency in objective is to be preferred to consistency in method. The consistent application of a method will not yield consistently relevant information unless the method has been deliberately designed with the objective of relevant information in view.

The problems of inaccuracy and approximation have customarily been met by overt or covert devices. Among these devices the most obvious and most readily justifiable is to regard as income available for division among constituents, a smaller sum than the income computed, by whatever process income is computed.

The amounts by which divisions of income fall short of income in any

21 "von Neumann . . . distinguishes submaximal knowledge from maximal knowledge and calls the incompletely determined state to which the former refers a *mixture;* the state characterized by a single surely known state function is then often called a *pure case* . . . usually the state of a single system, which is a pure case to begin with, is converted by measurement into a mixture . . . Measurement destroys the state as a pure case." Margenau, *The Nature of Physical Reality*, pp. 381–3. See also pp. 150–1 above.

year have two functions. One is to enable firms to grow by the retention
and use of part of the increase in assets through income-earning operations.
The other is to provide against the inaccuracies of measurements made due
to deficiencies in the supply of information and against the contingency
that assets may subsequently fall in price. If the present cash equivalents of
assets and obligations are determined with the degree of care and detachment here proposed, there would be no need to set off specific deductions
against the measures of assets, such as provision for doubtful accounts.
All such provisions are interferences with the capacity of accounting
statements to reflect what has happened period by period; they introduce looseness to the system and the possibility of abuse because such
provisions are anticipatory and, therefore, not corroborable. It is sufficient
to regard the balance of undivided income as of itself a buffer against the
possibility of errors in measurement and against possible adversities that
have not yet arisen.

But the problems of ignorance and inaccuracy are not to be confused
with the problem of irregularity in performance. It is of the nature of
some enterprises that their revenues, and hence their incomes, are subject
to fluctuation, from a modest to a marked degree. In particular, if the
processes outlined in this chapter are followed, it may be urged that
they will produce fluctuations in the statements of financial position and
periodical income which are not representative of the average or long-run
effects of operations.

In the first place, if the function of accounting is regarded as measurement or discovery, the only criterion of choice of a method is whether one
method represents the facts more closely than another. If fluctuations
occur, their occurrence is a matter to be taken into account by those who
use the produced information. If fluctuations occur but the system does
not reveal them (or conceals them), the facts are not made available to
actors, whether managers or constituents. Censorship is not, however, one
of the functions of the accountant. If his system conceals, it fails in its
function. In the second place, no one should presume to foretell that a
shift in one direction will be remedied in due course by a shift in the other
direction. We cannot foresee what the long-run or average effects of operations will be; there can thus be no basis on which manipulative elimination
of the effects of fluctuations can be justified. The matter will be raised
again in the following chapter. In the third place, if all incremental
changes are brought into account as they occur, it is not improbable that
the fluctuations in financial position and periodical income will be less
severe than if some of those changes are brought into account only when
they have accumulated over a succession of periods to unusually large
amounts.

REVIEW

This chapter brings to completion the development of a system of double-entry accounting which takes account of the full range of factors which impinge on the financial position of a firm from time to time. In principle, the double-entry system takes simultaneous cognizance of the changes in the monetary measures of resources at the disposal of a firm and the legal or equitable interests in those resources. The tracing of these changes is a complex process, and the market is in any case an imperfect generator of the requisite information. But the discovery of the magnitudes of the monetary equivalents or measures of assets and equities, even if those magnitudes are subject to errors of estimation, is of practical moment in a market environment where prices of goods and money are observably variable. Any system which fails to take account of these characteristics of the environment of business fails to represent the financial properties of a firm and of the consequences of its operations; and fails, therefore, as a signalling system to those who make financial decisions in respect of the firm.

The treatment has been limited and schematic. But a sufficient variety of the problems which may be encountered has been introduced to enable other classes of transactions and assets to be dealt with in accordance with the same principles. The determination of income and its constituent parts by reference to the best available approximations to the ideal of objectively determined financial positions is the key to the production of contemporarily relevant information. On this basis, the resulting financial statements will yield mathematically valid and presently useful test ratios which are comparable with ratios derived at other points of time, notwithstanding changes of prices and changes in the dimension of the monetary unit, and comparable with ratios derived at the same time on the same principles in respect of other entities.

Argument

10.11   Under static conditions (there being no change in the price level or in specific prices and excluding new contributions and withdrawals by constituents) income of a period (t_0, t_1) is the difference between the measures of capital at t_1 and t_0, inventories of non-monetary items being priced at contemporary cash equivalents at t_0 and t_1.

(3.53, 3.83, 5.33)

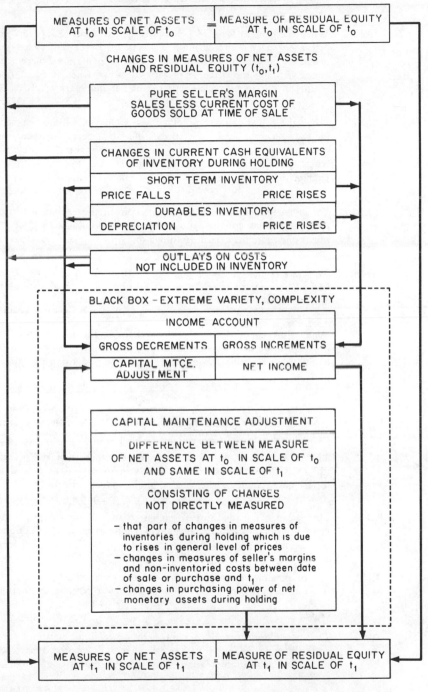

MEASURES OF NET ASSETS AT t_0 IN SCALE OF t_0	MEASURE OF RESIDUAL EQUITY AT t_0 IN SCALE OF t_0

CHANGES IN MEASURES OF NET ASSETS
AND RESIDUAL EQUITY (t_0, t_1)

PURE SELLER'S MARGIN
SALES LESS CURRENT COST OF
GOODS SOLD AT TIME OF SALE

CHANGES IN CURRENT CASH EQUIVALENTS
OF INVENTORY DURING HOLDING

SHORT TERM INVENTORY	
PRICE FALLS	PRICE RISES

DURABLES INVENTORY	
DEPRECIATION	PRICE RISES

OUTLAYS ON COSTS
NOT INCLUDED IN INVENTORY

BLACK BOX – EXTREME VARIETY, COMPLEXITY

INCOME ACCOUNT

GROSS DECREMENTS	GROSS INCREMENTS
CAPITAL MTCE. ADJUSTMENT	NET INCOME

CAPITAL MAINTENANCE ADJUSTMENT

DIFFERENCE BETWEEN MEASURE
OF NET ASSETS AT t_0 IN SCALE OF t_0
AND SAME IN SCALE OF t_1

CONSISTING OF CHANGES
NOT DIRECTLY MEASURED

– that part of changes in measures of
  inventories during holding which is due
  to rises in general level of prices
– changes in measures of seller's margins
  and non-inventoried costs between date
  of sale or purchase and t_1
– changes in purchasing power of net
  monetary assets during holding

MEASURES OF NET ASSETS AT t_1 IN SCALE OF t_1	MEASURE OF RESIDUAL EQUITY AT t_1 IN SCALE OF t_1

Figure 10
OUTLINE OF CHAPTER 10: ACCOUNTING FOR
TRADING VENTURES.

10.12   When the general level of prices changes, without changes in the prices of specific non-monetary assets held, the difference between the measures of capital at t_1 and t_0 includes an increment (positive when the price level falls, negative when it rises) due to the change in purchasing power of net monetary assets.

(3.83, *4.35*, 4.39, *5.41*, *9.32*)

10.13   When the prices of non-monetary assets change, without changes in the general level of prices, the difference between the measures of capital at t_1 and t_0 includes an increment (positive when specific prices rise, negative when they fall) due to the change in specific prices of non-monetary assets.

(3.53, *4.35*, 4.39, *5.41*, *9.33*)

10.14   For given total resources, every decision on the exchange of net monetary assets for non-monetary assets simultaneously determines the amounts of the holdings of both.

(3.66, *9.32*, *9.33*)

10.15   To separate the effects of changes in the general level of prices and of changes in specific prices on the measure of capital is unnecessary.

(2.33, 3.74, 9.16, 10.14)

10.21   When the general level of prices changes, the maintenance of the capital at t_0 is represented by transforming the measure of capital at t_0 to its equivalent in units of the dimension prevailing at t_1.

(3.83, 4.39, *5.34*)

10.22   *The absolute difference in the numbers of units representing a given capital at t_1 and t_0 is designated "capital maintenance adjustment."*

10.23   The income of a period (t_0, t_1) under other than static conditions is the difference in the measures of capital at t_1 and t_0 minus the amount of the capital maintenance adjustment.

(5.25, *5.41*, 5.52, *10.22*)

10.24   Money being the medium of exchange and all production being geared to consumption, a consumers' goods index is acceptable as a transformation rule for changes in the general level of prices.

(2.621, *3.61*, *4.35*, 4.38, 10.21)

10.31   Where possible, changes in the current cash equivalents of all non-monetary assets shall be obtained by reference to market prices.

(4.16, *9.33*)

10.32   The possible degree of accuracy in determining current cash equivalents is no greater than the accuracy of the means of measurement available (that is, the adequacy of the information provided by the market).

(*3.64*, 10.31)

10.33   Approximations to current cash equivalents are permissible where the market itself does not provide adequate information directly.

(4.23, 9.45, 9.46, 10.32)

10.34   As the risk of holding goods is not vacated until the point of sale, an approximation to the current cash equivalent of the short term inventory of a going concern is the current price of the goods and services necessarily sacrificed in acquiring such inventory.

(3.75, 4.24, 4.26, 10.33)

10.35   Approximations to the current cash equivalents of durables may be obtained by transformations of prices at t_0, using a price index of specific classes of goods, or by using replacement prices.

(4.24, 4.26, 10.33)

10.36   The measure of depreciation and obsolescence of any durable through any period is the difference between its current cash equivalent at t_0 (however approximated) transformed to units of the prevailing dimension at t_1, and its current cash equivalent at t_1.

(9.58, 10.35)

10.37   The use of approximations gives rise to differences between estimated ("book") residues and market resale prices when durables are put out of use. These are corrections of prior errors of estimation and, as increments, do not differ from other increments (positive or negative) to capital.

(10.31, 10.33)

10.41   The numerosity of events and transactions limits the possibility of continuous and detailed tracing of the effects of general and specific price changes.

(*1.18*, *6.11*, 6.21, 7.31)

10.42   The dual effects of exchanges shall enter the accounting system as they occur and at their then monetary amounts.

(6.22, *6.42*)

10.43   The dual effects of specific price changes shall enter the system as they occur.

(6.22, *6.42*, 10.13)

10.44   The dual effects of changes in the general level of prices shall enter the system whenever the income of a past period is to be discovered.

(6.22, 10.12, 10.41)

10.45   An income account and balance sheet based on the operations 10.42, 10.43, 10.44 will be articulated; the balance sheet indicating financial position at t_1 in units of the dimension then prevailing, and the income account indicating the aggregate substantive change in residual equity in the same units, subject to errors of estimation.

(6.73, 7.41, 10.41, 10.42, 10.43, 10.44)

10.51   If approximations to current cash equivalents are continually sought, systematic error due to difficulties of measurement will be minimized and from time to time corrected.

(7.35, 7.55, 10.32, 10.45)

Corporate Business

11 Business corporations constitute a significant segment of the trading ventures in most modern industrial societies. Their characteristics and modes of operation warrant special consideration, for many of the propositions to which importance has been attached find their best exemplification in the case of corporate business. Not only that; corporations execute or affect such a large proportion of the business of private and governmental sectors that it is a matter of social importance that their practices be based on principles appropriate to their functions.

FEATURES OF BUSINESS CORPORATIONS

The corporation or company is a creation of the laws of sovereign states, having, under the statutes permitting incorporation, many of the common powers of individuals, a number of powers superior to those of individuals, and some obligations not imposed on individuals and unincorporated firms. Generally, they have power to buy and sell all kinds of goods, services, and titles to property. They are able to engage in legal actions in their corporate names. Subject to limitations in some communities, they are able to invite the general public to subscribe for their shares or stock, bonds, notes, and other securities; and where they have such powers, they are generally required to make publicly available financial information as to their results and positions from time to time.[1]

The power to invite the public to subscribe to security issues could scarcely be effective without two particular provisions. The first is the limitation of the liability of shareholders for the debts of the corporation. If there were no such limitation, the risk of having to meet obligations incurred by agents of shareholders or of the corporation would effectively limit the extent of corporate business and the growth of individual corporations. The second provision is the transferability of fully paid shares. In the absence of such a provision, no shareholder would be able to liquidate his investment in the event of personal necessity. Being a creature of the law, a corporation has a potentially indefinite life. No individual would then wish to divest himself of resources for the term of his less indefinite life. These provisions are supported by the freedom of corporations to issue securities in the denominations of their choice; where it is desired to create a wide market, the denominations may be quite low. Further, corporations may issue securities having widely divergent characteristics in the pursuit of financial support. They range from shares, in respect of which subscribers may expect high returns to be paid out of the income of the corporation in recompense for the risks they bear, to secured bonds and debentures, in respect of which subscribers may expect regular but fixed interest receipts with relatively less risk and greater safety of their investment. The multiplicity of variants within this range enables corporations to meet the diverse combinations of income and safety considerations which prospective subscribers may entertain. The general effect of these provisions and powers has been to create a widespread public holding of, and extensive dealings in, company securities.

THE SECURITIES MARKET

The market in company securities is a part of the market for all instruments of credit. Stockholders, bondholders, trade creditors,

---

[1] Only features essential to our argument are mentioned in the text. More generally and for discussions of the alternative ways of regarding corporations see, for example, C. A. Cooke, *Corporation, Trust and Company* (Manchester: Manchester University Press, 1950), Chap. I; John P. Davis, *Corporations* (New York: Capricorn Books, 1961), Chap. I; Dewing, *The Financial Policy of Corporations*, 1953 ed., Chap. 1.

bank depositors, and holders of governmental securities are all operators in this market. The issuers of securities are their counterparts in this market. But for any individual person holding money, the market for instruments of credit is also part of the market for all goods, services, and claims. His choice of assets—money, securities, or consumers' goods—depends on his evaluation of the satisfactions obtainable, directly or indirectly from the alternatives open to him; his choice within the class, securities, is similarly dependent. Issuers of securities have, therefore, to consider the characteristics which will make any given issue acceptable in the market at the time of issue. The supply of securities is, therefore, differentiated in a number of ways. For example, as to maturity, common stocks are interminable, loan securities may run for long or short terms, bank deposits on current account are terminable on demand. As to risk, common stocks bear the risks of enterprise; government bonds are relatively free of such risks, interest and repayment being guaranteed by the fiscal powers of government.

As is the case with differentiated goods, the heterogeneous characteristics of securities entail differential prices or costs to the issuers and differential incomes to the classes of subscribers. Like other prices, the prices paid for credit by corporations are not unilaterally determined. They are determined by the actions, in the market, of all buyers and sellers of the present use of money. For any individual issuer of securities the prices being currently paid by other issuers provide information on the terms and conditions under which he must compete.

COMMON STOCK FINANCING

The trading operations of companies differ little if at all from those of non-corporate ventures. But in respect of their financing and management they differ materially. The independent legal existence of corporations and the limited liability principle under which they operate give to their directors or managers a degree of independence not available to the agents of the constituents of unincorporated firms. The degree of independence will vary as we shall presently point out. Nevertheless, it is necessary to take it into account when considering the financing and financial decisions of companies.

Suppose a company begins by issuing common stock: in exchange for money contributions, or other contributions expressed in terms of money prices, it issues certificates of title equivalent in face value to the contributions received. Stockholders thus acquire proportionate interests in the assets and the product of the assets of the corporation. The face value of the stock certificates issued is generally described as the capital of the company. This usage of "capital" is conventionally accepted. It is inconsistent with our usage of the term to denote the measure of the assets equivalent to residual equity, and inconsistent with any usage of "capital" which has reference to a stock of assets. We will continue to use "residual equity" of the interest of stockholders in the assets of the company, and the terms "common stock" and "bonds" to indicate the securities to which residual and specific equities attach.

At this first stage in the life of the company suppose its financial position to be represented by:

Assets		Residual Equity	
	Money Units		*Money Units*
		Common stock, 100 units	
Cash	10,000	at 100 money units each	10,000

Its cash will be exchanged, in whole or in part, for trading assets of the kind appropriate to its chosen field of business. Suppose at the end of a year's trading its position is given by:

Assets		Residual Equity	
	Money Units		*Money Units*
Cash	3,000	Common stock	10,000
Short-term inventories	9,000	Income	2,000
	12,000		12,000

For simplicity, we assume no change in the general level of prices.

The company's directors (in some cases, the shareholders in general meeting on the recommendation of the directors) may then decide to pay a dividend to stockholders. The income expectations of stockholders will have been formed in part by the stated expectations of the promoters at the outset, in part by assessments of the trade in which the company operates, and in part by comparisons with the dividends being paid currently on investments in the stock of other companies of similar risk. Suppose the expected rate of dividend on the sum invested by stockholders is 10 percent and such a dividend is paid. The position will then be:

Assets		Residual Equity	
	Money Units		*Money Units*
Cash	2,000	Common Stock	10,000
Short-term inventories	9,000	Retained income	1,000
	11,000		11,000

At the beginning of the next period, the expectations of stockholders will be different. The income generating capacity of the company itself is known to exceed the rate represented by earlier expectations; and the resources available to the company for the next period exceed those available in the first period by the amount of retained income. For both reasons the valuation of the stock, and, hence, the market price of the stock, will tend to rise. For even greater reasons, if a higher rate of dividend is paid than the initially expected rate, the market price will tend to rise, for investors will expect a continuation of short-term cash returns of the same order.

Necessary Information

It will be clear that, although a company may begin with shares of stock having a fixed monetary denomination, at no time thereafter need the market price be related to the initial issue price. Considerable literature has developed around the problem of share price formation.[2] What is of interest here is the general kinds of information assumed to be or required to be available to the share market.

Of these the most common is the actual dividend or dividends paid in the past, as an indication of expected dividends in the future. The amounts of past dividends are obtainable independently of any understanding of other financial information, which may be one reason for the use of dividend yield (current dividend divided by current price) as an index of the attractiveness of a share. But dividend yield is a relatively poor guide if future dividends may vary. A second piece of information commonly required is the amount of periodical income. This is a derivative of the accounting process, and its magnitude depends on the processing principles adopted. It is not unreasonable to suppose that, notwithstanding defects in principle, reported income is interpreted in the same way as men ordinarily understand personal income, that is as a gain in command over resources available to be alienated or reinvested. Clearly, if the results of the accounting process are to serve as a guide, the principle of isomorphism may not be disregarded in the derivation of income. Nor may fluctuations in income be concealed without concealing one of the risk elements in any given case. The price to earnings ratio (current share price to corporate income per share) is a superior guide to the dividend yield, for it recognizes earning capacity as the source of dividends which may vary as income varies.

---

[2] As a sample, see Myron J. Gordon, *The Investment Financing and Valuation of the Corporation* (Homewood, Ill.: Richard D. Irwin, Inc., 1962); Benjamin Graham and David L. Dodd, *Security Analysis* (New York: McGraw-Hill Book Company, Third edition, 1951); A. J. Merrett and Allen Sykes, *The Finance and Analysis of Capital Projects* (London: Longmans Green & Co., Ltd., 1963). These are sufficient to sustain the following discussion of necessary information; any similar selection would serve our purpose equally well.

Strictly, the ratios should refer to expected dividends and expected income; current dividends and income are accepted as working approximations.[3]

Given income and dividends, the amount of retained income is given. This increment in residual equity represents both a sum out of which dividends may be paid in future and an increment in the assets employed which may be expected to produce its own contribution to future income of the company. The "payout ratio" (dividends to income) is also given by the magnitudes of income and dividends. If a given payout ratio may be assumed, the expected dividend is derivable from the expected income by use of the payout ratio; but there is no strong ground for supposing that there is stability in payout ratios through time except in limited types of industry.[4]

The debt to equity ratio is recognized as having a bearing on financing though its relationship to share prices is disputed.[5] But at least in marginal circumstances, it is limiting. It is derived from financial statement magnitudes. Clearly any process which understates or overstates past incomes, and, hence, retained income, will distort the ratio, interfering with the prospect of raising additional debt finance on the equity, and interfering with the right of potential and actual lenders to be informed.

As the risk to which the future income is subject varies inversely with the adaptability of a company, an indication of the liquidity of the assets and the maturities of obligations is required. The attention which has been paid to calculations of past and prospective cash flows also evidences concern with liquidity; the rate of cash flows has a direct bearing on capacity for adaptation and capacity to pay cash dividends.[6]

This brief statement, based on the literature of share price formation,

[3] " . . . the facts of the existing situation enter, in a sense disproportionately, into the formation of our long-term expectations; our usual practice being to take the existing situation and to project it into the future, modified only to the extent that we have more or less definite reasons for expecting a change." Keynes, *General Theory*, p. 148.

[4] Molodovsky gives payout rates over a thirty year period for the Dow-Jones Industrial group. They show some degree of stability in recent years. But although "companies with the stablest earnings show the smallest year-to-year changes . . . all around such islands of *terra firma* swirls the greatest variety of percentages of payouts." Nicholas Molodovsky, "Valuation of Common Stocks," *Readings in Financial Analysis and Investment Management,* Eugene M. Lerner, ed. (Homewood, Ill.: Richard D. Irwin, Inc., 1963), pp. 265–6.

[5] For example, F. Modigliani and M. H. Miller, "The Cost of Capital, Corporation Finance, and the Theory of Investment;" David Durand, "The Cost of Capital in an Imperfect Market: A Reply to Modigliani and Miller;" and Modigliani and Miller, "Reply," *American Economic Review,* June 1958, Sept., 1959. And Ezra Solomon, *The Theory of Financial Management* (New York and London: Columbia University Press, 1963), Chaps. VIII and IX.

[6] See Perry Mason, *"Cash Flow" Analysis and The Funds Statement* (Accounting Research Study No. 3, American Institute of Certified Public Accountants, 1961) and references there cited.

and supported by reference to reported practices of security analysts and the financial press, indicates the dependence of the market on information derived by accounting processes. The literature seldom broaches the question of responses to changes, or appraisals of prospective changes, in levels of prices. But the taking into account of the information suggested above implies that the information shall be contemporaneously pertinent and, therefore, of the kind which previous chapters have been directed towards developing. If the financial information is not of this quality, it is believed that it will be treated, generally, as if it were, for a communication believed to have some bearing on future events will be interpreted in the context of its receipt. If the belief that the information is presently pertinent is misplaced, there can be no dependable foundations for the valuations based upon it; prices will be based on fictions.

DEBT FINANCING

The freedom of corporations to issue securities conferring different rights, in terms of income from the proceeds of business and equities in the assets, may result in there being two or more classes of financial supporters. For illustration, we consider a company having two classes, common stockholders and bondholders.

Provided the fixed interest rate payable on bonds does not exceed the expected rate of return on the projects to be financed out of new money, the making of a bond issue will be in the interest of stockholders. The amount of the difference between the two rates accrues to the residual equity, and the corresponding assets are available for dividend payment or retention and reinvestment. It would, therefore, seem that the larger the debt to equity ratio (the greater the leverage), the greater will be the advantage of stockholders. If bond issues are supported by charges over specific assets or over assets in general as collateral security, however, the larger the debt to equity ratio the smaller will be the margin of safety for secured and unsecured creditors alike. There will thus be a point beyond which bond issues may not be made at all, or if made they will be made only at higher interest rates. Furthermore, the higher the debt to equity ratio, the higher will be the fixed interest proportion of the periodical proceeds, that is, corporate income plus fixed interest payments. If the periodical proceeds are subject to fluctuation while the interest on debt is fixed, the amplitude of fluctuations in periodical income will be greater than that of fluctuations in periodical proceeds. Dividends will tend to vary more widely and, in the extreme, there may be no dividends at all in some years. The increased riskiness of income prospects will force down stock prices or force up dividend expectations, making it difficult for such a company to raise new money either by stock or bond issues. The margin of safety is further threatened by the possibility that any creditor, though small and unsecured, in seeking to enforce his remedies, may compel the forced liquidation of some assets, and even the whole enterprise.[7]

It will be clear then that stockholders' and bondholders' interests may be regarded as complementary as long as an adequate level of income is maintained; but that in marginal situations they come into conflict. Bondholders commonly limit the powers of corporations to run into debt by provisions in bond indentures designed to secure the maintenance of liquidity and asset backing. The essence of the management of multiple-strata financing is, thus, the balancing of the conflicting interests of the classes of securityholders on which a company depends.

Necessary Information

Superficially it may seem that, as the rate of interest on any given issue of loan securities is contractually fixed and as the obligation of an issuing company is backed by legally enforceable charges over some or all of the company's assets, bondholders require no information about the operations and positions of companies. But it may readily be shown that the information said to be necessary to stockholders is equally necessary to bondholders.

As to dividends, failure to pay dividends on common stock of an order consistent with the market's expectations is interpretable as incapacity to pay the market price for money at risk. It is one of the signs which may provoke a tightening of contractual controls to the point of enforcing the remedial provisions of security indentures or trust deeds. As to corporate income, its magnitude and its relationship to stockholders' dividend expectations are indications of the capacity to pay interest in spite of business fluctuations and to maintain the basis of the charge over assets given in favor of lenders. If, by reason of low corporate income, stockholders lose confidence, the confidence of bondholders will also suffer and the impulse to cut their losses by realization of the security will be stronger.

Manifestly, the debt to equity ratio has a bearing on bondholders' valuations on grounds already discussed. And where there are debts of differing seniorities and maturities, it is patent that each class of creditor

---

7 "On April Fool's Day, 1932, a Mrs. Helen Samuels—who held a mere $2,000 of stock in Insull Utility Investments—quietly applied for the appointment of a receiver. Within a few short weeks . . . thousands of American investors had been ruined in the greatest financial failure in the history of the world." Aylmer Vallance, *Very Private Enterprise* (London: Thames and Hudson, 1955), p. 167.

requires to know his ranking in relation to others. The liquidity of assets has also an obvious relevance; it may affect the regularity of future interest payments and the regularity and magnitude of dividend payments with consequent detrimental effects on bondholders' evaluations. Bond indentures seek to provide against default by stipulations relating to future borrowing, dividend payments, sinking funds, and the relationship between short-term assets and short-term obligations.

OWNERSHIP AND CONTROL

In earlier chapters, we have considered the firm as an entity managed by an agent acting in the interests of its constituents, the owners of the residual equity. In the present chapter, we have suggested that the interests of stockholders and bondholders are in potential conflict, but we have proceeded as though the holders of residual equities have indirect though effective control over the operations of firms. This latter presumption is only true of corporations the common stocks of which are closely held. Stockholders of corporations have indirect control over operations by virtue of their power to appoint directors to manage corporate affairs, their power to vote at general meetings, their right to be informed, and their power to take remedial action in critical conditions. In the ordinary course of events, however, management is left very much in the hands of directors and officers appointed by them. The necessary remoteness of individual stockholders and stockholders as a class from the operations of complex corporations has created the independence of management to which passing reference has been made. The management group is a participating group in the same sense as every other participating group in the cooperative system which is a corporation. It is, therefore, possible for its particular system of subjective values to impinge on the interests of others by way of its demands for compensation in money, power, or prestige, and less obviously by way of a desire to be free of the constraints which interfere with these.

The divorce of ownership and management has been said to have destroyed the effectiveness of the control which stockholders have a formal, legal right to exercise.[8] In particular, directors have considerable powers in respect of the dividends paid out of periodical income; the amounts divided may differ materially from corporate periodical incomes. It is, therefore, argued that managements are able to free themselves of the

---

[8] Adolf A. Berle, Jr. and Gardiner C. Means, *The Modern Corporation and Private Property* (New York: The Macmillan Company, 1932). The separation of ownership and control is not a modern phenomenon. It dates back to remote antiquity.

constraints of the pricing system of the securities market.[9] This may perhaps be true, but within limits.[10]

Latent control may become effective control when major prospective changes in corporate policy are announced or when past operations have proved to have been unsatisfactory. On the one hand, incumbent directors may be unseated. On the other hand, unless dividends are consistent with the expectations of stockholders, in the light of contemporary conditions and available alternatives, stockholders are able to cast a vote of no confidence by selling their stock and running down the market price to a level consistent with their new dividend expectations. Or, other corporations may buy up the stock of the delinquent corporation, forcing out the management of the latter. Or stockholders may take steps to liquidate the corporation. There is ample evidence of the effectiveness of these remedies; the possibility that any one of them may occur, to the personal detriment of the management group, is a check on disregard of the market.

But the impact of the market is not limited to the potential actions of stockholders. Bondholders also, as we have noted, may react unfavorably if their interests are threatened, and even unsecured creditors may bring about the collapse of flimsy corporations.

ACCESSIBILITY OF INFORMATION

All these responses are expressions of valuations; and they all depend on the accessibility of information. We have to consider two classes of information, that which is independently ascertainable by investors and that which is supplied by corporations themselves.

9 "... removal of the market place as ultimate arbiter of capital application...." Adolf A. Berle, Jr., *The 20th Century Capitalist Revolution* (New York: Harcourt, Brace & World, Inc., 1954), p. 41. To consider the securities market as the ultimate arbiter of capital application seems to involve divorcing the securities market from the whole complex of markets of which it is only a sub-system. Rivalry within firms and between technologists in different firms, technological advances, shifts in interest rates, and many other factors, exert some kinds of pressure on management affecting the application of capital. There seems to be considerable evidence that, though the managements and directorates of corporations are not directly under the overt scrutiny of stockholders as a body in many respects they behave as if they were, largely because of the richness of the interrelationships in the market places of an interdependent society. See, for example, R. A. Gordon, *Business Leadership in the Large Corporation* (Washington, D.C.: The Brookings Institution, 1945) and various papers in Edward S. Mason, ed., *The Corporation in Modern Society* (Cambridge, Mass.: Harvard University Press, 1961).

10 "... the manager and the capital owner are each active in his own distinct sphere, but their spheres of action are interrelated by virtue of mutual orientation ... the specifying and modifying decisions of the manager presuppose and are consequent upon the decisions of the capitalist. If we like, we may say that the latter's decisions are of a 'higher order.'" Lachmann, *Capital and Its Structure*, pp. 98–9.

At a general level, investors have or can have knowledge of the growth or decline of particular trades and industries: as these trends affect the interests of other persons such as employees and the actions of governmental authorities, they are matters of public comment. They have or can have knowledge of political, social, and economic events which may influence particular trades or industries; these, too, are public knowledge. They have or can have knowledge of movements in commodity prices. But investors do not invest in trades or industries; they invest in the securities of selected firms in trades or industries. To choose between the firms in a given trade, they will want to know something of the probability that one will perform more satisfactorily than others. At the more specific level, and of the nature of public knowledge, investors have or can have knowledge of the dividends paid by, and the ruling market prices of the securities of, corporations. But as we have shown, all these data are insufficient for the making of informed valuations and choices.

Investors, to choose in an informed manner, will want to know the relative capacities for adaptation of firms individually, of their capacities to expand if the trade generally is expected to expand, or to switch to other operations if the trade generally is expected to contract. And they will want to know of the prospective dividend flows and other gains from investments in different firms. These specific indications can only be obtained from the financial statements of firms. In general, information of these specific kinds is vouchsafed to investors as a matter of public policy in the case of corporations which may seek public financial support.

The directions from which the requirements of financial publicity may be established are three. In the first place, the right to invite the public to support financially a business venture is a right not freely granted to individual persons; and its effectiveness is secured by the additional right to grant to shareholders the immunity associated with limited liability. For these particular advantages, granted by the legislature on behalf of the community, it is reasonable to expect a *quid pro quo*: and the form it takes is the publication of financial information of prescribed quality. In the second place, it is a matter of social importance that the securities market be an effective market. Buyers of tangible goods have the opportunity of examining the goods and remedies against vendors of faulty goods. In the nature of things, an investor in company securities can not examine physically the firm he invests in, and it is difficult to assign any precise meaning to what is, or may be demonstrated to be, faulty. The only convenient representation of a firm as a whole which is relevant to the purely financial interest of an investor is its set of financial statements.

But further, the functions of the securities market are (a) to secure that available investable funds find their way into companies which, according to the tests of the market in their products and the securities market itself, are the most efficient; and (b) to provide a means of liquidating investments when investors require or consider it desirable to do so. Only if the market has the means of discovering which firms are relatively more efficient will the supply of investable funds be directed towards firms which, on the tests mentioned, are likely to contribute the more effectively to supplying the wants of the community. And only if the information available to the market is contemporary and reliable will buyers and sellers of securities be able to buy and sell in the knowledge that their judgments are not being defeated by defects in the information provided.[11]

Statutes which regulate the formation and conduct of such companies require that they shall publish prospectuses for new issues; that they shall publish periodical financial statements, and that they shall register in a publicly accessible registry these documents and other statements relating to their affairs. These provisions may have stemmed originally from a desire to protect creditors in their dealings with corporations where stockholders have limited liability.[12] But with the growth of investments and trading in equities, the information has become an essential element of informed action in all sectors of the securities market.

This information is of the class supplied by corporations themselves. Now, as the self-interest of directors and management must be granted some right to expression in a cooperative system, as they have a measure of independence, and as the financial information may be used either in judgments as to their performance or in valuations which constrain their actions as corporation officials, it is conceivable that they may regulate the flow of information to the market. To avoid this, statutes and regulations have sought to provide that financial statements shall be authenticated by independent auditors appointed for the purpose. The avowed object of prescribing the contents of these statements and of independent auditing is to secure "full and fair disclosure of the character of securities sold . . . in the public interest and for the protection of investors" or "a true and fair view" of the results and states of affairs of companies from time to time.[13]

[11] It is generally believed that "corporate organizations are no longer [that is, since the Securities Exchange Act of 1934] permitted to deceive their stockholders by use of unrevealed accounting tricks." Charles Amos Dice and Wilford John Eiteman, *The Stock Market* (New York: McGraw-Hill Book Company, 1952), p. 328. But if the argument of this book is accepted, existing methods, exclusive of "tricks," do not perform their task as well as they could.

[12] Bishop Carleton Hunt, *The Development of the Business Corporation in England, 1800–1867* (Cambridge, Mass.: Harvard University Press, 1936), pp. 128 ff. On a more general scale the mercantile agencies thrived on the need of creditors and potential creditors to be informed of the financial positions of debtors; Roy A. Foulke, *Practical Financial Statement Analysis* (New York: McGraw-Hill Book Company, 1945), Chap. I.

[13] The quoted verbal formulations are from the U.S. Securities Act of 1933 and from Companies Acts of countries following the English tradition. They are substantially equivalent in intention.

These institutional arrangements, designed to secure a fair market in securities, provide additional support for some propositions already established on less extensive grounds. In Chapter 7, the case for uniformity of information processing rules for all entities of a given class was stated. In the present chapter the class of interest is the whole class of business corporations in the securities of which the public may invest. To impose uniform accounting rules upon all such corporations may seem, in view of the diversity of corporations, to force them into one Procrustean bed. Business firms are not the same; the operations and the markets of retailers, wholesalers, and manufacturers differ; a steel manufacturer is vastly different from a manufacturer of plastic toys. But from the viewpoint of the securities market, what is produced by firms in all these fields is money; dividends, or interest payments, or gains on the sale of securities. Investors do not prefer an investment in a steel corporation to an investment in a plastic toys corporation on the ground that the one produces better steel than the other does plastic toys, on the ground that steel making is more "important" than making plastic toys or on any other non-financial ground. Each investor may take into account the different characteristics of the classes of business in which he may invest, but only for the purpose of discovering that class or corporation which is expected to serve best his preference for money in certain quantities and at certain times of his own choosing. To the investor all money is money, whether it comes from electronic engineering or popcorn vending. Therein lies his interest in financial information.

No given investor, furthermore, can be considered to be committed to stock or to loan securities. In view of the conflict of interest between residual equity holders and debt holders, it may at any time turn out that a holding of bonds is preferable to a holding of stocks; and although, in general, it may be possible to think of bondholders as holders for long terms, the same is not necessarily true of any bondholder or of the bondholders of any company. Even if the reasons given earlier for the usefulness of information of the same quality to stockholders and bondholders alike were not readily admitted, the ground for uniformity of information to both groups is consolidated by the feasibility of switching holdings from one class of security to another in the same company.

On similar grounds the principle of isomorphism is strengthened. If the principle is applied equally by all companies, it will, subject to the approximations found to be necessary, produce financial statements which are in similar and contemporary terms. Investors or prospective investors in all companies may then make valid comparisons between companies engaged in quite different pursuits. And only then could it be said that the disclosures were fair to all investors and to all companies and in respect of all classes of security. A consequence may be that the operations and incomes of some companies will be shown to fluctuate more widely than those of others. But, if this is one of the characteristics of some companies, it bears on the evaluation of risk, and, for the protection of investors, it must be known. To conceal it by resort to other principles is neither fair to investors nor fair to other companies. The disclosure of such fluctuations is not inconsistent with the equalization of dividend payments which is effected simply enough by retaining some part of periodical income when immediate dividend expectations fall short of actual income.

Although, in trading ventures, we have recognized that the constituents or stockholders occupy a pivotal position, in no respect has the system we have developed been influenced by an investor's viewpoint. The emphasis has been on the objectivity of the statements of the system, the requirements that they shall be corroborable by all people of equal competence and that they shall be commonly interpretable, whatever may happen to be the viewpoint of the interpreter. Viewpoints may well affect valuations, but not interpretations. That the system shall possess this quality of objectivity is supported by the requirements of full and fair disclosure and authentication, since only objective statements can be equally fair to different interested parties, and only objective statements can be authenticated. But further support may be gained from consideration of the characteristics of corporations as voluntaristic cooperative systems.

CORPORATIONS AS VOLUNTARISTIC COOPERATIVE SYSTEMS

We consider as voluntaristic cooperative systems, systems of persons pursuing their own interest by actions temporarily oriented to one instrument of satisfaction. By temporary orientation, we mean that the persons are free to pursue their interests through association with one such system or another at their option, and will choose between such systems on the basis of the expected outputs of each, towards their ends, per unit of input on their part. The stockholders, bondholders, directors, managers, workers, customers, suppliers, and so on, of companies are distinctive classes of participant in systems of this kind. A cooperative system in which there is a sharing of contributions and rewards will retain the support of its participants only as long as the expected rewards are valued more highly than the expected rewards from an alternative system.[14] But withdrawal in

14 Much of the literature of the theory of organizations plays down, if it does not disregard, the existence of external alternatives and the relativity of evaluations, assuming that individual participants are concerned only with inducements and contributions *within* a given organizational system. See, for example, Elton Mayo, *The Social Problems of an Industrial Civilization* (London: Routledge & Kegan Paul, Ltd., 1949). Others refer to organizations adapting to the external environment without explicitly indicating that the necessity arises from the comparative valuations

favor of another system is not the only possible means of increasing one's rewards. Given that there are favorable alternatives available to any class of participant, members of that class may seek to raise their rewards relative to those of other participants in the *same* system, that is at the expense of those other participants. Such moves depend, as all moves do, on knowledge of alternative systems; but they also depend on knowledge of the distribution of rewards within the same system.

In view of the strategic positions of stockholders and bondholders (including also other types of financiers), some indication of respective rewards will be required, even apart from the statutory publicity requirements of corporations. But what kind of indication?

Suppose that the principles of isomorphism and objectivity are not followed, and suppose that there are alternative sets of rules which may be adopted and abandoned at the option of management. It will then be possible at some times to influence favorably the valuations of stockholders, actual and potential, and at other times to influence favorably the valuations of bondholders, actual and potential. To influence stockholders, for example, management may choose those rules which show a higher periodical income, and thus permit a higher dividend payment than other rules based on other principles. The attractiveness of the company's stock will be maintained or improved. But a higher dividend payment means a greater reduction in liquid resources and in total assets; subsequently, the margin of income safety for bondholders and the equity to debt ratio will be lower, adversely affecting the valuations of bondholders. The effect on existing bondholders' valuations may not be serious in the short run unless they are able to renegotiate their contract; but the prospects of raising new money by bond issues on equally favorable terms will be affected. In other words, the attempt to favor one group at the expense of the other will set in train responses in the same system which interfere with adaptation—for management may well find occasion and wish to raise new loan money on equally favorable terms at any time—and, therefore, militate against the very interests of those favored.

Or, again, suppose that "in the long-run interests" of stockholders, rules are adopted which by comparison with rules under our principles, understate periodical income, and, therefore, understate periodical repre-

---

(From Page 280)

of individuals who are free to move as well as free to be "integrated"; for example, Chris Argyris, "The Integration of the Individual and the Organization," *Social Science Approaches to Business Behavior* (Homewood, Ill.: The Dorsey Press, Inc. and Richard D. Irwin, Inc., 1962); John M. Pfiffner and Frank P. Sherwood, *Administrative Organization* (Englewood Cliffs, N.J.: Prentice-Hall, Inc., 1960). Graham and Dodd note a different type of one-sidedness which characterizes some of the literature, namely disregard of the role of stockholders; Graham and Dodd, *Security Analysis,* p. 610.

sentations of assets and residual equity. This so-called conservatism has a depressing influence on security valuations. It gives a lower apparent basis on which debt may be secured and a lower apparent equity to debt ratio. The one may reduce the willingness of potential bondholders, the other the willingness of potential stockholders, to take up new issues. Insofar as favorable terms of issue are in the interests of stockholders, short-run under-statement may have opposite effects to those on which they are said to be justified. What is in the long-run interests of any investor or class of investor, indeed, is not known or knowable to directors or managers. It is a matter of evaluation, of comparison with other shorter-run and longer-run advan-tages, which individual investors alone can make. But they cannot make these comparisons without a firm foundation of knowledge of the present state of a corporation.

The assumption that management is in the best position to know what is in the best interests of investors disregards the consequence of the independent position of the management of corporations, namely that the management group has an interest of its own to promote and protect. Prestige, power, and perquisites are not wanted by corporations. They are wanted by the persons who manage them. The management group is no less a competing group within a system of cooperative groups than is any other. The concealment or distortion of information may be viewed as one expression of this. The assumption indeed disregards the abundant evidence of the ineptitude of individual managers and boards of directors which has culminated in company failures.[15]

Furthermore, the connection between successive financial statements, through the continuous recording process, entails that any distortion of income in one period will necessarily involve distortion in the opposite direction in a subsequent period or periods. By maintaining the use of fictitious data and disregarding market prices in the short run, the restora-tion of statements to coincidence with the market may be deferred or staggered. It may, however, fall, adventitiously but of necessity because it can no longer be concealed, at a time when the company wishes to make new issues or otherwise to modify the relative rewards of stockholders and bondholders. The consequences of distortion may, thus, bring into play retributive and potentially inconvenient forces. In any case, distortion

---

15 "It is of course always possible that people will draw wrong conclusions from facts correctly stated, but this is no reason for withholding information from them. The justification offered for hiding profits is often that shareholders, if they knew the true profits, would make irresponsible claims and thus jeopardize future earnings. This may be so, but the other half of the argument rests on an assumption of managerial infallibility and omniscience not often borne out by the facts." Lachmann, *Capital and Its Structure*, p. 93. "It was Insull, not Capone, who wrecked the financial structure of Chicago." Thurman W. Arnold, *The Folklore of Capitalism* (New Haven: Yale University Press, 1937), p. 276.

clearly discriminates in favor of one or the other class of short-run or long-run stockholders, for there can be no presumption that all investors are long-term investors.

We may extend the argument to embrace other classes of participants, for, as we observed in Chapter 3, the rationale of associations, of which the corporation is one kind, lies in the ends of the participants.[16] The worker group shares in the financial distributions in terms of wages for labor contributed. The customer group shares in terms of goods for financial contributions. The supplier group shares in terms of financial distributions for goods and services contributed. As, in the case of corporations, financial statements are publicly available, each such group may evaluate the relative contributions and rewards of other groups with reference to its own; and, if any sense of grievance arises, pressures for higher wages, lower prices of goods sold, or higher prices of goods purchased, may be generated. Only if the financial statements are objective and contemporarily relevant can any fair judgment be exercised by these groups; and only thus can the effect of redistribution of rewards be assessed, acknowledged, or rebutted. And, on the score of uniformity of the quality of information in the face of these different interests, any person may become a stockholder, though he may be at the same time a bondholder, an employee, a customer, and even a supplier (for example, through being a stockholder in other companies). It would clearly be impolitic to supply information of different quality to stockholders and others in these circumstances.

In general, ignorance of the future stands in the way of comprehension of the consequences of understatement or overstatement, whether the consequences are considered from the viewpoint of stockholders, management, or the corporation as such. The only justifiable practices, therefore, are those which yield objective and presently relevant information, so that all participants, present and prospective, may make their own judgments on the basis of the facts. Only thus may management avoid unwarranted pressures from specific participating groups, and only thus will each such group be able to assess the consequences of any pressure by other groups to improve their relative rewards within the system.

The above argument has depended on one or both of the assumptions that (a) the mobility of participants as between firms is effective, and (b) the capacity of one group to bring pressure to bear on management is effective within firms. It may be thought that these are rather weak assumptions, for institutional forces and inertia interfere with both. But

[16] "All economic activity in a market economy is undertaken and carried through by individuals to make provision for their own ideal or material interests. This is naturally just as true when economic activity is oriented to the patterns of order of corporate groups ... Even if an economic system were organized on a socialistic basis, there would be no fundamental difference in this respect." Weber, *The Theory of Social and Economic Organization*, p. 292.

institutional forces (stock exchange committees, labor organizations, consumers' associations, trade associations) also contribute to the effectiveness of the corrective mechanisms.[17] In particular, it may be suggested that the securities market is a less effective control on managerial and directorial discretion that we have supposed. Certainly, if the supply of investable funds continues through time to exceed the demand, management will be able to maintain support at a lower price, that is to retain large proportions of periodical income. But credit conditions do become less easy from time to time forcing even large but unadaptable firms to the wall. It is a mistake on the part of the management of a corporation and on the part of any participating group to imagine that the possibility of failure does not exist for the corporation.[18]

ACCOUNTING AND ACCOUNTABILITY

Some clarification of the relationship between accounting and accountability seems necessary at this point. Both terms have a common root and there may be some presumption that they have other properties in common.

We have argued that accounting is concerned with giving an account. Giving an account may seem necessarily to entail a recipient, not simply a generalized recipient but a particular recipient or class of recipients. If a particular recipient is contemplated, there is at least the possibility that, unselfconsciously if not explicitly, a report may be influenced by the attitude of the giver to the receiver in contemplation. But it is possible to give an account which does not contemplate a recipient of a particular class; the reporting of events generally in the public press is of this kind. That is the view we adopt of accounting; its function being to give an account *about* particular events, not to give an account *to* a particular class of persons. Its relative freedom from subjectivity and its serviceability as a form of interpersonal or social communication follow from the adoption of this view.

Accountability, on the other hand, is a characteristic of the relationships between particular persons and other particular persons or classes. A person

---

17 This is the substance of Galbraith's concept of countervailing power. John Kenneth Galbraith, *American Capitalism, The Concept of Countervailing Power* (London: Hamish Hamilton, 1957, rev. ed.)

18 " ... company directors who ignore the signals of the market do so at their peril ... in the long run a market economy substitutes entrepreneurs who can read the signs of the times for those who cannot." Lachmann, *Capital and Its Structure,* p. 71. The "process of Creative Destruction is the essential fact about capitalism. It is what capitalism consists in and what every capitalist concern has got to live in." Joseph A. Schumpeter, *Capitalism, Socialism and Democracy* (London: George Allen & Unwin, 1947), p. 83, and Chap. VII generally.

is accountable if he is liable to be judged or to be called upon by others to give an account. Accountability cannot be generalized; it always involves particular persons or classes of person and takes a particular form. In various ways consumers, employees, financiers, and so on are liable to judge or to call to account the actions of corporation managers. Likewise, the stockholders of companies, reinforced by stock exchange listing rules and audit provisions, hold management accountable. That one part of the account given by management takes a form derived from "accounts" in the technical sense is in a way incidental. The terms of issue of securities and the amounts paid in dividends are actions for which management is accountable, and they are ascertainable by others independently of accounting statements. And it has already been suggested that financial positions are discoverable, and, therefore, changes in position are discoverable without recourse to accounting methods and records.[19]

If, however, the aid of these methods and records is invoked, the financial aspects of the performance of managers may only be fairly judged on the basis of accounts *about* that performance. Recognizing that they are accountable, managers may seek to explain, excuse, or justify; to caution or to show caution; and they may succeed in tempering the judgments of those to whom they are accountable. But these are emotive communications, not informative communications. Accountability is nullified if, by virtue of the methods of accounting employed or of modification of the resulting statements at the direction of management, the occasion for criticism on the one hand and explanation or justification on the other is not apparent.

This argument in no way forbids the elimination of detail and the rearrangement of details in the preparation of financial statements for publication. In the interest of comprehensibility, it is legitimate to reduce the detailed statements required for administrative purposes to more compact form, consistently with the principle that critically different items shall not be merged. But whatever the reduction in quantity of items shown in published financial statements, the quality of the information may not be allowed to suffer by the use of principles, alternative to those relevant in administration, which tend to the comfort either of the accountable group or of the group to which the account is given.

SOME SPECIAL PROBLEMS OF CORPORATIONS

Some special features of corporations have been selected for amplification. The general principles to be followed are implicit in

19 This has long been the practice of credit grantors and mercantile agencies. See Foulke, *Practical Financial Statement Analysis,* Chap. I; and Sprague, *The Philosophy of Accounts,* p. 27, cited p. 136 above.

the methods already discussed. These observations are illustrative and tentative rather than exhaustive. It is believed that other problems and more complex instances of those here mentioned may be resolved on the same general grounds.

Share and Stock Issue Prices

There are different practices on the issue of shares by corporations. Some corporation statutes require shares or units of stock to have a par or face value, and initial issues are usually made at a price equivalent to this face value. Other statutes permit the issue of shares having no par value, and initial issues are then made at a stated price. In either case, once the shares have been issued and the issue price has been fully paid in, the issue price has no necessary bearing on future transactions in shares. They will be bought and sold in the light of expectations of the company's prospects and the prospects of alternative investments. Their prices will vary from the issue price. The issue price is nothing more than a fact of past history. It has no necessary bearing on the prices of subsequent issues by the company of shares of the same class; these may be issued at higher prices or lower prices (subject to some constraints in par value jurisdictions) than the price of the initial issue. It is common to speak of such shares being issued at a premium or at a discount, generally with reference to the par or face value. But the issue price is simply a price and it does not seem that any special importance can be attached to a premium or discount as such on share issues.

We may regard all constituents' contributions in respect of fully paid shares as of one kind, in which each constituent has an interest proportionate to the number of shares or units of stock he holds. No distinction need be drawn between the nominal value of shares and premiums or discounts, for the nominal value is without substantive significance.[20] It is simply a historical price. As information, nominal values or initial issue prices of fully paid shares, like other historical prices, are more likely to be misleading than informative. To avoid this possibility is desirable. As one possibility we envisage a rule, relating to statements of financial position, to the effect that the stockholders' equity would be shown at any time as one sum, inclusive of paid in contributions and accumulated income, expressed in units of contemporary dimension; that the number

[20] Par or nominal value appears to have had significance in the early stages of the development of the limited liability principle in some countries, when the liability of shareholders for the debts of companies incorporated under specific statutes was fixed at an amount equal to or based on the nominal value but in addition to the amount initially paid in. At present, the liability of shareholders is generally limited to the issue price; the nominal value has no function now in this connection.

of shares or units of stock outstanding would be shown; and that the amount paid in, transformed to units of contemporary dimension, would be shown parenthetically. Under statutes of incorporation and regulations relating to dividends in some countries, it is provided that the capital of a company may not be reduced by the payment of dividends, where capital is defined as the money amount paid in or deemed to be paid in on shares or stock. This appears to be a consequence of a conception of corporate capital as a fixed fund on the existence of which creditors are entitled to rely. But as a business corporation is not a trust, and as the capital of a company in the above sense may be reduced by trading losses, and as, in any case the dimension of the monetary unit changes through time, this conception does not seem to be a useful one. On the other hand, any device which breaks down the habit of referring to shares by their initial price, would seem to lead to more critical examination by investors of the positions and results of corporations.

It will be observed that no cognizance is taken in the accounts of a company of the market's valuation or pricing of its shares. These prices represent expectations of others than the company itself, as the securities represent assets of others than the company itself. Insofar as a company is deemed to have a superior income earning capacity than other companies, the price of its shares will include a goodwill element. But the magnitude of this element will fluctuate as investors' relative valuations fluctuate, and it is unrelated to issue prices. It is one of the functions of the securities market to indicate by differential prices which companies are accorded goodwill elements by comparison with others.

Investments in Subsidiary Companies

The possibility of corporations investing in other corporations gives rise to special problems in information processing. As we have already indicated, any single firm may undertake many different kinds of enterprise in its own right. By diversification of activities, there are the possibilities of the reduction of risks and the more economical combination or utilization of resources. Both tend to promote the interests of constituents.

A firm may, for any of a variety of reasons, choose to conduct different parts of its operations under the names of separate subsidiary companies, each having its own accounting and other systems. Each will be treated as a separate entity and for each the principles and rules we have developed will be applied as if it were an independent firm.

But if the residual equities in subsidiary companies are wholly owned by a (holding) company, it is of some importance that the whole collection of enterprises be treated as one for some purposes. It is of no consequence that they may be engaged in quite different operations, for the residual equity in the subsidiary companies runs to the residual equity-holders of the holding company and we have contended that this group is concerned simply with money returns. The use of paper titles, stock of subsidiary companies, and debts owed by or to the holding company, makes it possible that the assets and equities of a holding company may be increased by decisions of the management of the holding company without any change in the relationship of the group to its environment. Such decisions may be made of convenience or of necessity. Knowledge of the existence of intercompany claims and obligations is necessary to those who enter into financial relationships either with holding or subsidiary companies, for internal obligations within a group may be made on much less security than would be required in the case of claims and obligations beyond the group.

To provide for the elimination of any such internal effects, it is appropriate to consider the group as one entity, notwithstanding that each company is in law a separate entity having its own rights and powers. This calls for a consolidation of the financial positions and results of all companies in a group. In the process, the investment in the subsidiary companies, by way of shares and net advances shown as such in the holding company's balance sheet, will be replaced in the consolidated balance sheet by the assets and external liabilities of the subsidiaries. This substitution may be made without remainder if the principles already developed for balance sheets generally are applied.[21]

It is observable that some companies which are components of groups engage in transactions at other than market prices. For reasons which will be developed in the following chapter the practice is of doubtful propriety. But when it does occur, the gains or losses arising from such internal prices will be eliminated by reference to the market, for all measurements of assets and liability balances.

The process is rather more involved if the holding company holds sufficient shares in subsidiary companies to control their operations (for example by being able to appoint a majority of the directors) but does not own the whole of the residual equity. In this case a proportionate division of the residual equities and the periodical incomes of subsidiary companies may be made and designated "minority interest" in the consolidated accounts.

By reason of the necessity of adding only measurements made in the

21 There being no place for goodwill (see above, pp. 209 ff.), there is no place in the present system for the so-called "goodwill on consolidation," the difference between what was paid for a going concern and the current cash equivalent of its net assets.

same scale, and, therefore, generally at the same time, consolidation of accounts is logically valid only if the intervals and terminal dates of the separate accounts of companies in a group are the same.

Acquisition of Subsidiaries by Purchase or Exchange of Stock

Subsidiary companies may arise not only by splitting off operations but also by purchasing the residual interests of the stockholders in independent companies which then become subsidiaries. An acquisition of this kind is a market transaction like any other. The representatives of the buyer and seller groups may be supposed to act in their own best interests. They will, therefore, take account of the contemporary prices of the assets and liabilities to be acquired or sold, as the case may be. The buyers may, in the event and as the result of negotiations, pay more or less than the contemporary measure of net assets, on account of future benefits expected to be gained by one of the represented parties or the other. If the amount paid exceeds the current cash equivalent of the net assets, the measure of the residual equity of the constituents of the buying company will, to that extent, be reduced. The amount of the premium differs no whit from premiums of other kinds paid to acquire future benefits. If the amount paid falls short of the current cash equivalent of the net assets, the measure of the residual equity of the constituents of the buying company will be augmented. The magnitudes of these differences may necessitate that they be shown separately (as windfalls, for example) in the accounts of the holding company. But the acquired company, being a new company by virtue of its new ownership and its new general relationship to the environment beyond the group, will have no cause to take cognizance in its accounts of the premium or discount on the transaction. Only in this way will the accounting of the acquired company conform with the prerequisite that it represent the affairs of an identified entity in relation to the market environment.

Suppose, on the other hand, that one company acquires another by exchanging its shares for the shares of that other. Specifically, suppose there are two companies for which the following are the data at a point of time:

	A Company	B Company
Number of shares outstanding	50,000	10,000
Residual equity, in money units	75,000	21,000
Price per share, in money units	2	1.7

And suppose that after negotiation A acquires B on the basis of a one-for-one share exchange, A issuing new shares for the purpose. A thus acquires net assets having an aggregate current cash equivalent of 21,000 money units, and that is the effective issue price of the 10,000 shares issued to the shareholders of B. The market prices of the two companies' shares before the event have no bearing on the matter otherwise than as representing factors considered at the time of negotiation.[22]

Bonds and Other Securities

We have held to the principle that financial position is represented by the current cash equivalents of assets and obligations as determined in contemporary markets. If a company issues bonds which are publicly traded, there will be a market which will yield present prices of the issue from time to time. The question arises whether these prices should be used in the measurement of indebtedness.

We incline to the view that the contractual amount of the bonds outstanding at any time is the amount of the debt then to be shown. The same degrees of freedom may not be postulated in respect of debts as for assets. If, of course, there arises a sufficient margin between current price and the discounted payouts to redemption, and if the company is in a sufficiently liquid state, it may buy in its bonds to its advantage. But, until it does so, the market price may be regarded only as indicating a possibility of gain. Generally, it may be supposed that until a company actually buys in its bonds before their due date, the valuation of the gain from employing the corresponding resources in the business exceeds the valuation of freedom from the debt.

Marketable bonds and other securities of other companies held as an investment will, following the general rules for asset measurement, be priced at market prices.

CONCLUSION

The consideration of corporate business reveals at first glance so many diverse interests, temporarily cooperating but potentially in conflict, that the possibility of informing them by means of one uniform set of statements seems remote. The ends of holders of the residual equity and of senior equities, the ends of managers individually, the ends of workers and other groups of participants are diverse at any time and

22 The notion of a "pooling of interests" is a fiction based on other grounds than effective administration. It would not occur given the system here proposed provided fiscal rules were logical consequences of this system.

variant through time. The subdivision of corporate organizations into holding and subsidiary entities and the absorption of some companies by others give rise to difficulties in resolving the financial consequences of intragroup activities.

The diversity, however, lies in ends, not in the facts which shape those ends. The corporate system, however complex, does work as a whole through the processes of the market; and the measurements emerging from the interactions of the market place are alone relevant to the choices of any participant in corporate business and to the existence of any given corporate unit. Statements which embody those measurements are independent of the ends of particular participants. The actions of none will be informed if the statements are biased in favor of the viewpoint of any one class. Any such bias distorts the view even of the favored class, for it misrepresents the relationships of that class with all other classes.

The qualities of objectivity, relevance, neutrality, and uniformity, therefore, apply with great force to the financial statements of corporations. Equity as between the varied groups having interests in corporate business may only be expected, and the securities market will only be a fair market, if the information published has these qualities.

Argument

11.01   *Corporations are legal persons having potentially indefinite lives, independent of the lives of their incumbents or constituents from time to time.*

11.02   *The limited liability company is a business corporation, the constituents of which by law have no liability for corporate debts beyond a stipulated sum.*

11.03   *Discussion is limited to companies which may invite the public to subscribe funds for their purposes.*

11.04   *Securities are paper titles representing equities in assets. Discussion is limited to common stock or shares, holders of which assume directly the risks of a corporate business, and loan instruments conferring rights in assets senior to those of stockholders.*

11.05   Limited liability and the transferability of securities are conditions precedent to a public market in corporate securities.
                                   (*2.43,* 3.24, 9.21, *11.01, 11.02, 11.04*)

11.06   The public market in securities is part of the wider market in all goods and services for investment, production, and consumption.
                                   (*3.64,* 11.05)

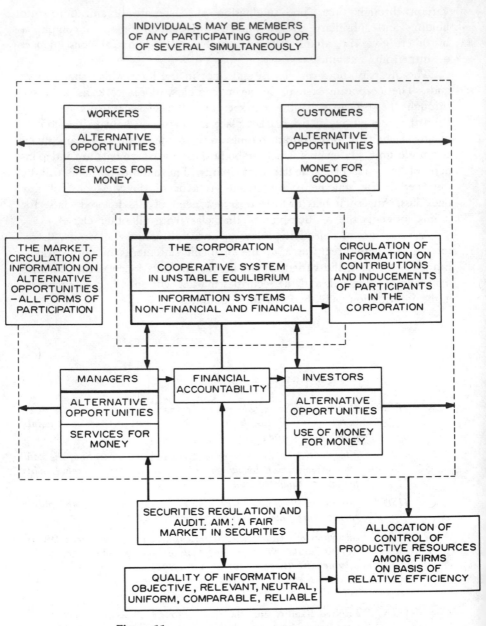

Figure 11
OUTLINE OF CHAPTER 11: CORPORATE BUSINESS.

11.07   The role of the public market in securities is to provide a means for the informed liquidation of security investments and a means of rationing the available investable funds among users according to the success (as measured in monetary terms) with which firms meet the needs of the commodities market.

(3.24, 9.14, 9.43, 11.06)

11.11   The securities market is informed generally by non-price information—production, trade, labor statistics, public comment on economic and political conditions and policies.

(3.65, 3.74, 7.11, 11.07)

11.12   The securities market is informed generally by price information —goods prices, security prices, interest, and dividend payment rates.

(3.64, 3.74, 7.11, 11.07)

11.13   The securities market is informed differentially as to specific firms by statements of financial position and periodical income.

(3.12, 4.14, 4.22, 9.15, 9.21, 11.07)

11.14   Statutes and regulations secure the rights of investors, potential investors, their advisers, their agents, and the public generally, to authenticated financial information with the object of creating a fair and informed market in securities.

(3.41, 4.22, 7.41, 9.15, 11.07)

11.21   Investors of all kinds choose between securities having regard for their subjective preferences for size and regularity of income and for safety of their investments.

(2.30, 2.73, 3.12, 3.24, 11.04)

11.22   Holders and prospective holders of shares and loan securities alike base their evaluations of particular securities at least in part on processed information believed to be indicative of past performance (periodical income, retained income) and present capacity (liquidity of assets, total cash equivalent of assets and respective equities in assets).

(2.28, 11.11, 11.12, 11.13)

11.23   An investor may hold stock and, or, bonds, and may switch from one to the other as his expectations of particular companies or securities shift, under singular or general influences.

(2.30, 11.03, 11.21, 11.22)

11.24   Informed choice as between the different securities of any company may be exercised only if the financial information supplied is equally relevant to the choice of any such security, and neutral with respect to the ends of individual investors.

(7.25, 7.26, 11.14, 11.23)

11.25   Informed choice, as between the securities of all corporations traded in the securities market, may be exercised only if the financial information supplied by all companies (a) is derived by uniform rules, (b) is derived by systems which are isomorphic with actual events and (c) is objective and therefore generally interpretable.

(6.21, 7.27, 7.41, 11.14, 11.21)

11.31   Any person assuming any given role in relation to a company may also assume another role or other roles concurrently.

(3.33, *3.41*, *9.13*, *11.02*)

11.32   The rewards or inducements offered for the contributions of all groups of participants are publicly discoverable—the prices paid for labor service, inventory supplies, the use of money (interest and dividends), and the prices and qualities of the product sold.

(3.24, *3.52*, 11.11, 11.12, 11.13)

11.33   Not only may participants choose between the continuation and the termination of participation on the basis of alternative inducement-contribution schemes of other firms; they may also choose to contest the relative rewards of other classes of participant in the same firm.

(3.24, 3.25, 11.31, 11.32)

11.34   Reasoned responses by participants to any given inducement-contribution scheme will occur only if the financial information is objective and, therefore, generally interpretable.

(1.68, *7.11*, 7.22, 11.33)

11.35   Financial information which is not objective will not enable management to anticipate the possibility of intergroup inequity, internal contests, and external competitive responses.

(1.68, 3.25, 11.34)

11.36   Financial information which is not objective will not forestall such contests, for its inconsistency with other information is discoverable and it may, therefore, be deemed to impugn the good faith and competence of management.

(*1.42*, 7.56, 11.14, 11.32, 11.33)

Financial Communication within Organizations

12 The greater the size of an entity, in spatial dimensions or in variety of functions, the greater the advantages to be gained by specialization, and, generally, the greater is the number of agents or servants it will employ. Both factors tend to increase the possibility of internal strain. If the entity is to serve its several functions in respect of all participants, it is necessary that it shall be so designed and managed that these strains do not interfere with its functioning, nor with its capacity to withstand the impact of the environment. As long as its continuation is in prospect, it will thus require to have the characteristics of a homeostatic system. We will be concerned here with the internal functioning of complex entities or organizations; but will not, thereby, be freed from recognition of the mutual interactions of organization and environment.[1] Generally, we will be concerned with organizations which are trading firms or corporations.

[1] To conceive the firm as a "price-and-output decision maker' *on the one hand* and as an "administrative organization" *on the other,* as does Penrose, seems to involve unnecessary abstraction. See Edith Tilton Penrose, *The Theory of the Growth of the Firm* (Oxford: Basil Blackwell, 1959), pp. 13—15. We view the firm as "an administrative organization making price and output decisions." See also Andreas G. Papandreou, "Some Basic Problems in the Theory of the Firm," *Survey of Contemporary Economics,* Vol. II, B. F. Haley, ed. (Homewood, Ill.: Richard D. Irwin, Inc., 1952), pp. 187–8.

INTERNAL SPECIALIZATION OF FUNCTIONS

The sensory and effector mechanisms of an organization are analogous to those of a person. The means of sensing stimuli and acting in response to them are embodied in servants and agents as extensions of the organization. But servants and agents are independent volitional entities in their own right. They are not organic parts of organizations. They may come and go. They may believe their functions within an organization to be of greater importance than other functions, in a manner not open to, say, the hand and the brain of a single person. They may believe their judgments to be superior to those of their fellow servants or agents. Being, in the last resort, autonomous, their employment does not automatically entail that effector-agents shall respond in a manner appropriate to the organization in a given state of strain. As specialization is a device by which the span of attention is limited, any stimulus may give rise to a response which, though appropriate in a limited technical context, is inappropriate to the context of the entity as a whole—its internal condition and its external relationships. From the employment of specialist agents, it does not even follow that sensory or receptor agents will interpret all pertinent events as organizational stimuli, due to the selectivity of perceptions.

COORDINATION

Responses appropriate to the present condition and the ends of an organization will occur only if the actions of agents are coordinated. Coordination is an emergent property of a system. It is not a function of any component person or persons within the system.[2] Insofar as the knowledge and the responses of agents are brought to an order consistent with the attainment of specified ends, those responses are coordinated.[3] The definition of functions or classes of action and the assignment to persons of roles and the powers necessary to make the roles functional are antecedent conditions of coordination. So, also, is the establishment of interpersonal communications, for the sensory, deliberative, and affective processes of an organization are not naturally integrated as is the case with natural persons.[4]

Commonly, the rules under which powers are assigned provide for

[2] Neil W. Chamberlain, *The Union Challenge to Management Control* (New York: Harper & Row, Publishers, 1948), p. 27.

[3] Obeying what Follett refers to as "the law of the situation." Henry C. Metcalf and L. Urwick, eds., *Dynamic Administration, The Collected Papers of Mary Parker Follett* (Bath: Management Publications Trust, Ltd., 1941), p. 58.

[4] "... without communication there can be no organization..." Simon, *Administrative Behavior,* p. 154. "An organization might almost be defined as a structure of roles tied together with lines of communication." Boulding, *The Image,* p. 27.

an hierarchy of roles[5], to the incumbents of each of which there is some residual discretion. At the lower end of the hierarchy, discretion is very limited; at each higher level, there is increasing scope for discretion, the ultimate discretion residing in the top executive who is responsible for the assignment or delegation of powers. But at every level there is some element of discretion. Any act of one agent which has a discretionary element, which limits the actions of other agents, or requires other actions on the part of other agents, will only give rise to appropriate responses if those others are informed of it. The making of decisions otherwise than at the point of action and the responses of others to actions taken will only be consistent with one another if communications between them are adequate. In general, the greater the specialization of functions and the greater the discretionary element in assigned powers, the greater is the necessity of efficient means of coordination and communication.

TECHNICAL LANGUAGES

Consider the communications of any highly developed functional division of business. Between the members of any such technical division, there will be a language system which serves well the need to communicate among themselves. They will use words of the vernacular language with special connotations; they will use signs peculiar to their technical fields and even, in some cases, peculiar to their fields within particular organizations. If, however, any member of such a specialist group wishes to communicate with his counterparts in other organizations, a common language will be necessary. In most technical fields there is an accepted language which may be described as supra-organizational. They are the languages of mathematics, chemistry, physics, psychology, and so on.

Similarly, if any member of a specialist group wishes, or is obliged, to communicate with other members of the same organization but of different specialisms, he will have to translate from his technical language to the vernacular or teach other members of the organization his technical language. The latter alternative is by far the more difficult, for the meaning of technical signs becomes confused unless it is reinforced by continual use in a technical context. The simpler alternative commends itself; indeed it is some protection for the organization against the development of mystiques.

If, now, there is any specialist group which wishes, or is obliged, to communicate with all other specialist groups, or with the senior officers of all such groups, either repeated translation will be necessary or it will be regarded as a matter of plain economy that the language of the group shall be generally interpretable throughout the organization.

[5] Simon, *Administrative Behavior,* Chap. VII; Thompson, *Modern Organization,* Chap. 4.

We have shown that the tests of the securities market are financial tests. The management of a business organization will, therefore, of necessity, be directed towards meeting these tests (it will, of course, at the same time be meeting the tests of the commodities and labor markets). If the organization is to be coordinated so that it meets these tests, then each division and each divisional executive will be implicated insofar as his divisional operations make contributions to or demands on the pool of resources available to the organization as a whole. The ubiquitous concern with financial limitations and tests will necessitate that at least at a financial level some coordination shall be achieved: and this will depend on the performance of the financial information processing group, the accounting group.

Coordination does not mean reduction to an arbitrary order; it means reduction to an order consistent with the ends of the organization. If the accounting system is to generate statements which will evoke, in a variety of agents of diverse specialisms and skills, responses which the designata of these statements would themselves evoke, the accounting rules and the statements they produce will necessarily conform with the understanding, and the past and immediate experiences of all parties. If, furthermore, financial information is to serve as a coordinative device, the information generated will be such that each specialist shall be able to apprehend the situation as it exists at other points within the organization which affect or are affected by his own actions. We may say, categorically, that any financial test of internal performance and any financial information used in the coordinative process are of little consequence unless they embody information which is relevant beyond the firm, in the marketplace.

ACCOUNTING AS AN INTERNAL TECHNICAL LANGUAGE

Accounting is a technical language. Its messages require to be generally interpretable throughout an organization. It is not a language by which accountants communicate with one another. It is not solely a language by which accountants communicate with non-accountants, the circumstance with which Chapter 8 largely concerned itself. In large organizations, it is a language by which non-accountants communicate with one another through the mediation of accountants.[6] It is not the only

6 Internal intelligence agencies "may be useful in overcoming the barrier of language." Herbert A. Simon, Donald W. Smithburg, Victor A. Thompson, *Public Administration* (New York: Alfred A. Knopf, Inc., 1950), p. 258. This is one of their formal and ostensible functions. The opposite, informal tendency, wittingly or unwittingly to create barriers, is less readily observable, more subtle. For a treatment more general than our own, see the work cited, pp. 229 ff.

or even necessarily the most important means of communication between non-accountants, of course; but, for its purposes and within its scope, it is a necessary means. The arguments of Chapters 7 and 8, therefore, apply with much greater force in the case of large organizations than in the limited case there considered.

But so, also, do some of the cautions. Accounting is not only an internal language system. It is a supra-organizational system. Its methods and its products are used by all organizations having financial relationships with other organizations and persons. Like all such widely used devices, its technology provides a focus of interest for specialists from many organizations, leading to the formation of professional groups and the development of group sentiments. Professional groups are means by which experience is shared and knowledge of new and more efficient methods of performing technical tasks is disseminated among organizations. The very concern of their members with technical matters, however, tends to effect their intellectual separation, as experts, from others. Where the tasks within an organization of any class of experts are limited to a localized phase of operations involving close concern with physical objects and other persons, intellectual separation is conditioned by the necessity of coping with tangible circumstances.

It is otherwise in respect of the tasks of information collection and processing.[7] The concern of experts in these tasks is with symbols and ideas, a class of symbols and ideas representing events and tangible objects throughout an organization. Those events are not localized, and the comprehension of their variety may be so demanding that refuge may be taken in a purely technical conception of the information processing role, a conception justifiable enough within the professional group embracing persons from many organizations, but inconsistent with performance of the function required within each specific organization. Intellectual and experiential distance from the events recorded, and from the effects both of the events themselves and of the information yielded by the recording process, serves to isolate information processing groups unless the feedback is virtually as rich as the flow of information.[8]

Further, the tasks of information collection and processing are, like most other tasks, specially localized and assigned to a group much smaller than the whole organization. Spatial proximity of members of the group

---

[7] See also R. J. Chambers, "The Role of Information Systems in Decision Making", *Management Technology*, Vol. 4, No. 1 (June 1964).

[8] " . . . self-containment decreases and interdependencies increase the likelihood of developing an efficient communication code." James G. March and Herbert A. Simon, *Organizations*, (New York: John Wiley & Sons, Inc., 1958), p. 164. " . . . a decrease in the frequency of interaction between the members of a group and in the number of activities they participate in together entails a decline in the extent to which norms are common and clear." Homans, *The Human Group*, p. 362.

tends to strengthen their beliefs as against the diverse demands and beliefs of other functionaries. Small groups, generally, have much greater properties of cohesion and capacities for defense against criticism than larger and, therefore, more diffuse groups.[9] These factors also tend to isolation from other divisions of an organization and from the point of view of the organization as a whole system. There is also a form of defensive isolation emanating, on the other hand, from the fears of those who supply basic information to the information processing unit. Monitoring by an alien group, whether alien by focus of interest or by seniority in rank, is often countered by resistance designed to reduce the pressure of such a group on performance.[10]

Such isolation, it has been noted, is a condition of the operation of the law of entropy, and it would not be surprising if the language system were to break down and its contribution to the coordinative process were to diminish. Suppose the information processing division were to respond to specific demands for information for superficially distinct purposes, such, for example, as internal coordination and external reporting. If it is not perceived that the two are related, systems based on quite different and inconsistent concepts may be developed. Or, in pursuit of an abstract idea of technical comprehensiveness, much more information may be tendered than can possibly be used.[11] Thus, for example, it is strongly suggested in some quarters that statements both in terms of original prices and contemporary prices should be supplied.[12] Conflicting information and an oversupply of information tend, the one to the loss of significance of the terms employed in the system, and the other to confusion of the organization—both instances of increasing entropy. Only if precautions are taken against these possibilities will accounting serve as an internal and general technical language.

The argument is strengthened by consideration of accounting as part of the organizational memory.[13] An individual acting on his own behalf

[9] Homans, *The Human Group,* Chap. VI; March and Simon, *Organizations,* Chap. 3; Thompson, *Modern Organization,* Chap. 8.

[10] "The subordinate, dependent on his superior for advancement, may tell the latter only what he wants to hear and only so much as will protect the subordinate's position." Homans, *The Human Group,* p. 461. The same applies in respect of the relationship of the accountant to his management, and the relationship of the management to the constituents of a firm.

[11] Millikan notes some work of Bavelas and Perlmutter "which suggests that an individual's capacity for making sound judgment about a complex situation may be seriously impaired by supplying him with a lot of information which he believes should be relevant but whose influence on the situation is not clear to him." Max F. Millikan "Inquiry and Policy: The Relation of Knowledge to Action," p. 164. The same applies to the beliefs of the suppliers of information.

[12] Notably the literature on supplementary information, both as footnotes and as completely parallel representations, in published financial statements.

[13] Simon, *Administrative Behavior,* pp. 166–7.

will, if his affairs are complicated, supplement his own memory with formal records. A large organization has even greater difficulties in drawing on its past experiences. Its agents have other roles which may confuse their personal recollections. They may be assigned different roles from time to time within the organization, so that they are not available continuously to supply recollections in respect of a given organizational function. And they may terminate their associations with a given organization under a variety of circumstances. There is, therefore, no effective substitute for written records as a means of communicating with the past experience of organizations. If contemporary communications and records are to serve in the future as memory, inconsistent systems, or systems in which the prime terms may have different referents through time, cannot be tolerated.

ECONOMIC AND TECHNICAL DECISIONS

For the purpose of internal administration, divisional specialists are not all concerned with the full range of accounting information representing financial position and results. They are not concerned, for example, with legal, financial relationships. They are concerned with inputs and outputs, with costs and prices. They are concerned with these in rather greater detail than is sufficient for the determination of aggregative change. Further, it is questionable, as we pass from higher to lower levels in the hierarchy of powers within an organization, whether financial tests and financial consequences continue to have meaning. To suppose that operative personnel, junior supervisors, and even senior supervisors may be expected to see the organization in its full economic setting would be fatuous. There is at least the probability, and not uncommonly it amounts to a certainty, that the understanding of the repercussions on the whole organization of inefficiency is limited to a vague feeling among those at middle and lower levels of the hierarchy. There would, therefore, seem to be some limits to the usefulness of financial information, which by its nature is primarily oriented towards effects beyond the organization. That the coordination of operations at a financial level is necessary should not lead to the neglect of other means of coordination and other tests of performance. A functional distinction should be drawn between economic and technical decisions.

The decisions of the prior order are economic decisions. To attract resources or the means of acquiring resources, a firm must first find a class of activity which is expected to pay the price of risk bearing and waiting. The bases of decisions to exploit any such opportunity are the known techniques of operation (the equipment and classes of skill complementary to it) and the expected costs and expected proceeds of operation. Suppose that some such decision is taken and that the requisite plant, shops, labor force, and services are available. The only decisions remaining, in the short run, are technical decisions, namely, how to secure the maximum effective output per unit of physical input whatever level of utilization of the plant is chosen.

Given the skill of divisional supervisors or managers, such questions may be resolved in terms of engineering efficiency: the number of useful products per unit of material consumed, or per hour of labor, or per hour of machine time, and so on. Or if we view the problem of divisional managers as seeking increasingly efficient operation, the questions may be restated in the form, "How may the number of useful products per unit of material, labor or machine input be increased?" A competent supervisor would, by definition, be one who is able to judge changes in efficiency by reference to technical data and direct inspection; and it is undeniable that physical norms can be established over wide ranges of operation on the basis of product specifications.

If, however, it transpires that the prior economic expectations are not satisfied or that the expected level of efficiency is not attained, new economic decisions are required. These specify a new set of required resources, given which the technical problems may be tackled as before. Even though the two types of problem may not be identifiable with specific levels in the hierarchy of powers, they are, as we have said, distinguishable functionally. We may posit that at the lower levels in an hierarchy the concern with technical questions preponderates over the concern with economic questions; skilled factory personnel are primarily concerned with quantities, as are sales personnel, for example. But at each successively higher level attention shifts increasingly to economic questions. Note, however, that we do not assume that there is any level which is concerned solely with one type of question or the other.

Where technical problems preponderate, communications will be largely of a technical character, and goals and tests of performance will be specified largely in nonfinancial terms. As a motivational factor, goals which are specified in terms of the known or expected competences of those for whom they are set are superior to goals specified in terms only vaguely comprehended.[14] Technical personnel may vaguely understand that efficiency has some financially favorable consequences for the firm; but there can be little doubt that the significance of technical efficiency is immediately apparent. If the highest degree of technical efficiency, at the level of operations decided by senior personnel on economic grounds,

---

14 "... the greater the clarity of goals associated with an activity, the greater the propensity to engage in it." March and Simon, *Organizations*, p. 185.

is continually being sought, each technical division is making its best contribution to the results of the whole organization.

We should, therefore, be wary of attempts to push too far the use of monetary representations of technical events, either as a motivational device or as a means of assessing performance. Monetary representation and calculation we have argued to be apposite only in respect of transactions in market places; monetary terms represent only one property of objects and events. At technical levels, such other information systems as will indicate numerical, physical, and qualitative properties of objects and events will be valued and used in their own right, and no monetary representations will be effective substitutes for them.

At the same time it may be supposed that supervisors of technical departments will be subject to some financial constraints in respect of expenditures made for the service of their departments. If departmental demands for cash outlays in a given future period are to be coordinated, there will be some allocation to each department for this purpose and each supervisor may be held accountable for the sum allocated. But it may not be supposed that supervisors may be held accountable for all such expenditures—in particular, expenditures on the acquisition of plant. If departmental demands for plant are coordinated at a higher level in the hierarchy, decisions as to the plant actually acquired will be made at that level; they are economic decisions. Further, the degree of utilization of a given plant in a period is also an economic decision made at a higher level than the operating level. Supervisors may not, therefore, be held accountable for the consequences of any such decisions. Again, on the foundation we have already laid regarding the nature of depreciation and obsolescence, the periodical measure of these factors is beyond the control of supervisors; and the inclusion of any part of the periodical measure in product costs, for the purpose of making intertemporal comparisons of costs as a guide to efficiency, is clearly of questionable validity.

As a matter of *informing* supervisors of the investment under their control or of the costs and proceeds of departmental operations, departmental statements in monetary terms may be made available. If this is done, it is necessary that every singular statement in any summary statement shall be in contemporary terms, for two reasons. As the firm confronts the market in terms of contemporary prices, the measures relevant to every supervisor at every level in the organization will necessarily be contemporary measures or prices, or the best possible approximations thereto; otherwise conscious coordination with the market in view would be impossible. Secondly, it is the common experience of all persons that the significance of a money sum in terms of goods varies from time to time. As we have already argued, they will presume that money amounts appearing in any contemporarily dated document will be in units of the same, and contemporary, dimension; that being the only dimension of which they have contemporary experience, either in their roles as participants in the firm or as individuals beyond those roles. If these conditions are not satisfied, supervisors will not even be informed; having themselves access to contemporary information, they will be disposed to distrust what they are given, and the possibility of conscious coordination is likely to be replaced by internal conflict.[15] [16] Further, if in lieu of reducing monetary statements to the same and contemporary terms, the statements are expressed in other, but dated, terms, on the assumption that each party given access will be able to make his own interpretations, coordination will fail, except by accident; for the recollections, and, therefore, the interpretations, of all persons differ.

The informative function of all such communications is by no means insignificant; for, wherever there is a discretionary element in action, internal communications are the means by which the discretion is informed. But if we consider other functions of the same or similar information, as tests of past performance or guides to decisions having greater economic components and consequences, the above argument holds for greater reasons.

It may appear to some that the internal operations of an organization may be insulated from the external environment; that it may be possible to draw a line of demarcation so that those responsible for external effects (economic decisions) are given contemporary information, while those responsible principally for technical effects are given internally devised financial signals, even though they do not reflect contemporary prices.

But a double standard can only result in an equivocal language system, giving rise to, rather than resolving, problems of coordination. Every executive in a linked hierarchy faces two directions: he is concerned with the performance of divisions lower in the hierarchy than he and he is responsible to officers higher in the hierarchy. Or in terms of our division of technical and economic questions, he is concerned more with technical effects looking downwards but more with economic consequences looking upwards. On any such executive faced with a double standard—internally

---

[15] " ... only a single system of communication and authority may be tolerated. If duplicating systems are permitted, the least result to be expected is that one will threaten the reliability and acceptance of the other ... all phases of the company's operations must be serviced by connected channels. There must be no blind alleys or dead ends preventing the flow of information or the passing of orders to any segment of the business *from* any segment." Chamberlain, *The Union Challenge to Management Control,* p. 225.

[16] Anyone familiar with the relationships commonly found to exist between production or sales departments and accounting or cost accounting departments will have ample knowledge of the existence of these conflicts. The principles proposed would, we believe, mitigate such conflicts.

devised signals and external market prices—there is imposed an intolerable burden of translation from one to the other, if coordination (internal consistency with external conditions) is to be attained. Further, as any person moves from junior supervisory to senior supervisory roles, economic questions become of increasing importance. Where there is a double standard, the transition from one role to another will be accompanied by considerable uneasiness (and, therefore, inefficiency); and indeed so strong is the force of habit that he may carry with him a regard for internal norms rather than the regard for external conditions which is appropriate to his new role.

There is, of course, no question that any set of rules whatever may be imposed on an organization or any part of it by its senior officers. And, after a fashion, any such set may be made to work, for the follies of arbitrary rules may be countered by *ad hoc* rules which restore action to consistency with reality. However, we are concerned here with the deliberate design of information systems conducive to coordination, not with the wasteful corrections necessary when such systems are poorly designed.

COST CALCULATION GENERALLY

We turn to consider some of the kinds of cost calculation which are conceivably useful to persons concerned as supervisors or managers with economic efficiency.

At the inception of any venture all calculations are hypothetical. The outlays necessary to acquire buildings, equipment, materials inventories, labor services, and so on are estimated, generally on the basis of prices discoverable at the time. The proceeds of the sale of the product expected to be produced by it, over the expected life of the special durable goods employed at least, are estimated. These estimates may take account of expected changes in individual prices of goods bought or sold; but in the belief that, generally, the purchase prices and sales prices of goods and services interact, tending to move in the same direction, these calculations may be made in terms of prices at the time of calculation. Once these calculations have issued in a course of action, on the ground that the venture is economically feasible, a new situation arises. Adaptation of the venture begins. It is no longer as free to choose its future courses because of investments in specific durables; but neither is it entirely constrained to follow out its anticipated program.

From the literature of economic analysis at the microeconomic level, it appears to matter little for our purposes whether a firm operates from a monopolistic position, a position of perfect competition, or a position of monopolistic competition. If any firm seeks to maximize its income, whether maximization is or is not considered subject to explicit constraints, it is concerned with the margins between its costs and its selling prices. Expositors of the theory of price, cost, and output all deal with costs as a premise of action. In every circumstance, a knowledge of costs of actual operation may then be supposed to improve the choosing between existing and alternative courses of action. In few cases will costs determine product prices, but neither is cost irrelevant to price, except under perfect competition. Generally, costs determine whether alternative courses of action (new inputs, new products, or new methods in lieu of old) should be considered in the light of new information on purchase and selling prices. Thus, like the discovery of financial position, the discovery of costs is directed towards future actions. The choice between continuing a past course of action and an alternative turns on comparison of the expected costs and outcomes of both. Insofar as the calculation of the cost of a new action is based on contemporary costs, the present cost of the present or past course of action requires to be known; otherwise discovery of the differential advantage of one over the other in the same scale is not possible. No less than for the discovery of financial position is the discovery of present costs dependent on transformations of initial prices to contemporary terms.

SPECIFIC AND COMMON COSTS

As goods are sold at unit prices, one would like to have knowledge of unit costs. The determination of unit costs *ex post* from time to time may appear to be a simple matter. But it is not simple, even in the case of a single product firm. Given that a firm has an established plant, the discovery of the costs of operating entails measurement of the material and labor inputs of all kinds. The material required and the labor required for directly working up the material are both capable of physical estimation *ex ante* and physical measurement *ex post*. Multiplication by the unit cost of those services in contemporary terms and division of the result by the number of units produced will give unit cost for these components. The costs of supervision and ancillary services through to administration are also discoverable and assignable to units of product in the single product firm.

The cost of the use of equipment, however, is less readily discoverable; *ex ante,* because at least the rate of physical deterioration and of technical and economic obsolescence cannot be known; and *ex post,* because of the common difficulty of discovering contemporary market prices. Conventional formulas may be employed in the absence of this knowledge; but, as we have already shown, conventional formulas have deficiencies as approximations to the facts. Variations from time to time in the output quantity also create difficulties. If the demand for a product is high, it is clear that economic obsolescence of the equipment required to produce it is relatively low, unless technical developments lead to its supercession. If the output is high, wear and tear on the equipment will be high. And if the output is high, the unit proportion of any given total amount estimated to cover wear, tear, and obsolescence will be small. It is patently difficult to catch the net effect of these influences in a conventional formula. The only possible response to these difficulties is to adopt a conservative view of the potential life and output of a plant when contemplating its acquisition;[17] and, thereafter, to consider the price of its output to consist of (a) the short-run costs of operation, material, labor, and other costs identifiable with products, and (b) a general margin out of which a lump sum, determined by conventional formulas or by other means already suggested, may be regarded as depreciation cost, and the balance may be regarded as profit.

This suggestion may appear to lack precision; but the lack is due to the complexity of the gross facts. The above view is supported, moreover, by the circumstance that once the decision to invest in a durable good has been made, and affirmed for any production period, the cost of using that good for the period is fixed; adaptation in the period is limited to short-run costs. Further, long-run adaptation, by the disposal or the replacement of a durable good, is not based on past recoveries of depreciation charges, but on the future expected outputs and depreciation and equipment servicing costs of alternative equipments.

But, even for the single product firm, it is questionable whether any calculation of total unit cost is necessary or informative once the decision to produce is made effective. The income for the firm related to the current cash equivalent of its net assets will give the rate of return for comparison with other opportunities. The ways open to the firm for improvement of the rate all lie in the direction of reducing specific costs or increasing the efficiency of specific technical operations. To reduce all specific costs to costs per unit adds nothing to the information already given in the income account.

The problem of discovering unit costs increases greatly in complexity as the number of products and processes increases. Not only may a variety of products be produced by the same equipment, but there are many other common costs of operation. Supervisory, managerial, and clerical costs are all common costs of operation. Considerable ingenuity may be directed towards devising ways of allocating these common costs to divisions of a firm and to its products. But all such exercises are productive

17 See Lutz and Lutz, *The Theory of Investment of the Firm*, p. 192.

of monetary calculations which are not prices. The greater the manipulation of actual prices by subdivision, allocation, and reaggregation of fractions of prices, the less reliable will be the outcome as indicative of any price; for every such process entails the use of a hypothetical distribution base which has no foundation in a market process, that is, which is entirely subjective for the firm.[18] The problems of the multiproduct firm reinforce the earlier conclusion that all-inclusive unit costs (of the *ex post* variety) are of little significance in relation to adaptive behavior. For short-run adaptation, one is concerned with the direct costs of services entering directly into the process of producing particular goods; and with the short-run costs of providing the essential ancillary services.[19] The former can be linked with units of output. The latter may only be linked directly with the quantum of essential ancillary services; some other test must be employed than a cost per unit of product where common ancillary services are employed, if the efficiency with which those services are provided is to be scrutinized.

Suppose, for example, that a firm is organized as follows. There are three manufacturing departments producing, in common, five products. There is a service department providing common services to the three manufacturing departments. There is a sales department and a general administrative department which includes the general management of the whole firm. The general administrative costs are common costs of all departments and products; some of these costs are costs of being in business whatever the number of departments and products. The sales department costs are common costs of all products. It is conceivable that unit product costs could be computed as follows:

(i)   Distribute some hypothetical part of the general administrative costs to all five other departments on some hypothetical basis;

(ii)   Discover the specific departmental costs of each department;

(iii)   Distribute the costs of the manufacturing service department to each of the three manufacturing departments on some hypothetical basis;

18 " . . . rational money accounting presupposes the existence of effective prices and not merely of fictitious prices conventionally employed for technical accounting." Weber, *Theory of Social and Economic Organization,* p. 179. How much of the results of the intricate cost calculations proposed by some and produced by others are of this "fictitious" character is a matter for serious speculation.

19 "If we shift attention to decisions, then we must shift from making arbitrary allocations, since the allocations will not be the basis of decisions." Harold Bierman, Jr., *Topics in Cost Accounting and Decisions* (New York: McGraw-Hill Book Company, 1963), p. 63.

(iv)   Discover the specific, identifiable costs of each product;

(v)   Distribute the sum of part of (i), part of (iii) and the whole of (ii), for each manufacturing department over the products processed in each, on some hypothetical basis;

(vi)   Distribute the sum of part of (i) and the whole of (ii) for the sales department over the products sold, on some hypothetical basis.

(vii)   Distribute the residue of (i) over the products sold on some hypothetical basis;

(viii) The sum, per product unit, of (iv), (v), (vi), and (vii) will give the unit cost.

The operations of the firm are clearly complex and interrelated. And so, consequently, is the calculation of unit product costs. But note particularly that although such a method of cost calculation is conceivable, its execution depends on a whole series of hypotheses, hypothetical bases for distributing common costs. Plausible grounds may be advanced for many methods of distributing common costs at every point in the process; but the outcome is none the less a fabrication of hypotheticals.[20] If it were a fact that the management of such a complex business required the calculation of unit costs, these defects would have to be accepted. But we deny that such calculations of total unit costs are necessary. They may well be misleading. The relationship between total unit cost and selling price may suggest the abandonment of any given product, notwithstanding the fact that its price contributes in some way to meeting the common costs of the firm. The folly of such a course would be apparent to any person of experience. But then, why produce information which has no

[20] A variety of methods, all yielding different unit "costs," may be found in any book on cost accounting. And as every method has a number of subvarieties, the potential number of methods of finding total unit cost is enormous. Under these circumstances total unit cost can have no meaning. Kreps gives a sobering example of methods used in electrolytic caustic soda and chlorine plants. "The joint costs of the process up to the point of the split-off of the chlorine from the caustic were found to be distributed between the bundle of products derived from the caustic and that derived from the chlorine in several different rations: 50–50, 40–60; 60–40, 39.008–35.46 (atomic weights of sodium hydroxide and chlorine), and 56.73 to 43.27. The pseudo-mathematical precision of the last ratio had its origin in a criterion no more scientific than that of distributing the joint costs so that both the caustic and the chlorine would earn an equal book profit. The plant in question had formerly used a 50–50 basis, which resulted in the chlorine department showing a loss. The absentee bankers who controlled the enterprise gave orders to discharge the chlorine foreman, but the superintendent at the works managed to retain an efficient subordinate by establishing the new ratio." T. J. Kreps, "Joint Costs in The Chemical Industry," *The Quarterly Journal of Economics*, Vol. XLIV, No. 3, May 1930, p. 426. See also R.H. Coase, "Business Organization and the Accountant," *The Accountant*, 1938, reproduced in *Studies in Costing*, David Solomons, ed. (London: Sweet & Maxwell, Ltd., 1952), pp. 105–158.

potential for selecting responses; or which in the hands of the inexperienced will lead to erroneous responses?

DIRECT COSTING

The type of cost calculation envisaged, therefore, is as follows. Unit costs of material and labor directly used in the production of each product will be ascertained in terms of contemporary prices; these may be called the direct costs.[21] Divisional, short-run service costs, specific to particular facilitative operations, will be ascertained. All costs which are fixed regardless of the level of operations of the period in contemplation will be ascertained. Both the latter classes will be considered as costs to be met out of the general margin between selling price and direct costs. Direct costs, then, will be significant present knowledge as indicating the avoidable costs in the event of abandonment of any particular product or for comparison with the avoidable costs of alternative products, given that the same ancillary services will be employed. Divisional short-run service costs will be significant as indicating the costs of facilitative services, and the avoidable costs of those services in the event of contemplating alternative ways of providing them or of substituting for them. Fixed costs will be significant as indicating the avoidable costs in the event of the consideration of long-run adaptations of processes or scale.

These separate types of decision are in some ways linked, but they are, nevertheless, separable in any specific case. Suppose that it is believed, on the basis of aggregate net income for a period or on the basis of market prices, that some way of securing a higher net income, or of preventing the level of net income from falling, is to be discovered. At any such point of time the firm has a given product range, a given processing apparatus, a given organization of facilitative functions, and, as an outcome, a given net income. It is not free to abandon all features of its existing operations, that is, to change them all at once. If it were to calculate all-inclusive unit product costs, it would be necessary to recalculate these costs for every possible alternative course of action; for as these costs involve proportionate allocations on the basis of the existent scale and organization, any change in one respect would affect the unit product cost of every line of product. The objective of the exercise, however, is not to select that range of products and that set of facilitative operations which in a given nonexistent circumstance is the set for which,

21 The type of "direct costing" here proposed differs, of course, from systems elsewhere proposed under a similar rubric. To be presently interpretable and relevant, we require that cost elements be expressed in contemporary terms. Generally, other systems, both of the absorption costing and direct costing variety, relate to the manipulation of money magnitudes identical with actual purchase prices.

individually, product costs are at a minimum.[22] It is to select a way of maintaining or increasing net income. The solution to this problem is obtained directly, simply by estimating, for each possible alternative course of action, the increment to costs and, or revenues which would flow from its adoption, by comparison with the already existing set of products, processes, and other services. Actions and the consequences of actions are always and inevitably incremental. A system producing total unit costs confuses the distinction between the avoidable or alternative costs in the short run, the medium-long run, and the long run.

ANTICIPATORY AND RETROSPECTIVE CALCULATIONS

The preceding discussion has identified two classes of calculation both of which yield premises of action. Discovered cost is an informational premise; anticipated cost is an expectational premise. The distinctive characters of the two types of calculation has already been established in Chapter 4. It is on the basis of this distinction that it may legitimately be said that different costs may be calculated for different purposes.[23] Within each of the two classes it is also legitimate to obtain different aggregations of cost elements depending on the narrowness or the extensiveness of the problem being considered. But within each of the two classes, the elements of cost will ideally be represented by unequivocal magnitudes; and as the aggregation of elements of cost is always potentially in contemplation these magnitudes will be of such quality that they may legitimately be added and related. The notion that different costs may be calculated for different purposes may not be used in defense of alternative concepts of cost within each of the two classes. There

22 "It is impossible, from the data describing a single rational act with a single clearly defined immediate end and a specific situation with given conditions and means, to say whether or in what degree it is economically rational. The question is meaningless, for the economic category involves by definition the relation of scarce means to a plurality of different ends. Economic rationality is thus an emergent property of action which can be observed only when a plurality of unit acts is treated together as constituting an integrated system of action. To carry unit analysis to the point of the conceptual isolation of the unit act is to break up the system and destroy this emergent property. So long as analysis is confined to the unit act, in talking of the rationality of action, it is impossible to mean anything but the technological aspect of the property of rationality . . . unit analysis is limited by the relevance of the unit formulated to the frame of reference being employed." Talcott Parsons, *The Structure of Social Action* (New York: Free Press of Glencoe, Inc., 1949), pp. 739–40. The frame of reference is, in the present context, the whole firm.

23 For example, J. Maurice Clark, *Studies in the Economics of Overhead Costs* (Chicago: The University of Chicago Press, 1923), Ch. IX.

cannot be a concept of cost which is appropriate for inventory pricing and a different concept which is appropriate for the assessment of operating efficiency within the class of retrospective costs, for example.

The consideration of alternative courses of action is a matter of comparing anticipatory calculations. In this context, the notions of incremental and marginal costs and revenues are employed in economic analysis. The calculations thus made are *ad hoc* and specific to the perceived alternatives; they refer to incremental or marginal changes to a given scale of operations.[24]

Retrospective calculations of cost are of a more continuous kind, if, as we suppose, they are to be the means of securing coordination and adaptation. The elements of cost they yield will always be based on contemporary prices, following the conclusions of Chapter 10 and the distinction drawn between initial purchase price and cost at time of use. They may be employed in anticipatory calculations, but only subject to correction in the light of expectations. They are pertinent in the adaptive process insofar as they indicate unexpected tendencies of the immediate past and suggest the directions in which alternatives should be sought. But they neither provide conclusive evidence of the impropriety of unexpected tendencies nor suggest what alternatives may be chosen. They are signals to be interpreted. It seems impossible to conceive that the marginal cost of a past operation can be ascertained; for the very undertaking of the operation will have changed the relationships between all other operations and between their costs. Scrambled eggs may not be unscrambled. The distinctive roles of marginal cost and discovered cost must be recognized and the methods of each must be appropriate to those roles.

24 It has been suggested that businessmen are unfamiliar with and do not use the notion of marginal costs and revenues. But "the basic 'feel' of marginal analysis may be much commoner than it would appear on the surface." George Leland Bach, *Economics, An Introduction to Analysis and Policy* (Englewood Cliffs, N.J.: Prentice-Hall, Inc., 1962), p. 469. To deduce from the calculations of cost accountants that marginal analysis is not employed is to disregard the flows of information from other sources and their evaluation by businessmen. Stigler, dealing with the individual seller, opines: "To insist on recovering historical costs is irrational, and people who obstinately insist on doing so must be phenomenally lucky to avoid the bankruptcy courts." Stigler, *The Theory of Price*, p. 149. It is not unlikely that businessmen regard the retrospective cost information supplied on particular operations as indicative of marginal cost, as their choices relate to limited (marginal) changes in operations. But the avoidance of the bankruptcy courts by many of them may be explained in terms of their recognition of retrospective data as only part of the data available, rather than in terms of the propriety or relevance of the retrospective data provided. The tendency to the use of "direct costing" may be considered as a long term conceptual feedback. On the tendency see *Direct Costing* (National Association of Cost Accountants, Research Series No. 23, April 1953) and James S. Earley, "Recent Developments in Cost Accounting and the 'Marginal Analysis,'" *The Journal of Political Economy*, Vol. LXIII, No. 3, June 1955. The whole situation seems to support the significance of the distinction between retrospective and anticipatory calculation drawn in the text.

REVIEW AND APPRAISAL OF PERFORMANCE

We admit that past experience is one of the foundations of future action. It would seem, therefore, that a careful analysis of past performance would throw some light on the validity or effectiveness of past decisions, in particular those past decisions which have been embodied in operating plans or budgets.

But consider the sequence of actions and events which follow the adoption of a specific plan, even a flexible plan. A plan or a budget may be regarded as nothing more than a method of proceeding to a stipulated position or result. Although general trends may be presumed, there can be no certainty that these trends will eventuate, either at the time or in the magnitude assumed. For greater reason, there can be no certainty that any specific event or events implied in a general trend will occur. If events or trends turn out to vary from those expected, an adaptive trading organization will not simply maintain its planned volume of business (for example, by cutting prices) when demand declines or refuse to take more orders when demand rises. It may do either of these things, of course; but it may also react in other ways. In any period there may be numerous unplanned adjustments to circumstances.

What then can be said of the achieved aggregate result at the end of the period? The result is simply a reflection of the general capacity for adaptation of the organization. It cannot be said, even if the stipulated result is obtained exactly, that the decisions embodied in the plan were well taken; we may even be inclined to suppose, rather, that the stated result was "manufactured," so accustomed are we to the vagaries of circumstances. If planned results are the yardstick by which actual results are assessed, whether expressed in absolute magnitudes or rates of return, an entirely subjective basis is employed. For as we have said, anticipations and expectations are subjective, and judging ourselves by our own anticipations is also subjective. The only effective tests of performance are the aggregate results of others operating through an interval under similar environmental conditions.

That an achieved aggregate result is simply a reflection of adaptive capacity does not rob it of importance. Capacity for adaptation to the environment is a much greater guarantee of survival than the capacity to meet a prescribed goal. Preoccupation with the fixing of specific aggregate results may well result in the targets being set at levels deemed in advance to be attainable, a procedure which distracts attention from the competitive character of the environment. Internally manufactured goals are no effective surrogate, in terms of survival value, for the continuous appraisal of the new opportunities and constraints continually made apparent in the market.

These observations hold, generally to a less serious extent, in respect of technical operations and technical measures of performance. Changes in technology may make necessary the abandonment of old specifications and measures of efficiency. Of these changes technical people will be aware, ideally, by virtue of the wide dissemination of new technical information or knowledge. But the durability of existent producers' goods and the limits to economic choices imposed by existing investments entail that there is some stability, often over extended intervals, in the technical conditions of any firm. Measurements of efficiency in technical terms and direct comparisons of those measurements through time, thus, provide readier means of appraising efficiency than monetary measures of the same events. The essential variability of prices and of the dimension of the monetary unit severely limit the usefulness of intertemporal comparisons in monetary terms.

STANDARD COSTS—A SOLUTION?

A suggestion already raised and rebutted on other grounds may be reconsidered in the light of this discussion of cost calculations. It may be supposed that the vagaries of external prices and of the dimension of the monetary unit may be eliminated from internal calculations in monetary terms and monetary measures of efficiency by the adoption of standard costs which would be analogous to standard production and product specifications. We have seen that the complexity of organizations and the difficulties of coordination through time are met by the development of internal, conventional sign-systems. Perhaps such a standard sign-system may be developed for cost calculation and the internal communication of cost information.

The conventional basic units of time, length, weight, volume, and so on are invariant units within the limits of ordinary experience. It is this property which makes possible the use of these units in standard specifications. The idea that, by conversion of measures in such different scales to a common monetary measure, a single measure of cost and a single basis for judging efficiency can be derived is attractive; for it would relieve the strain on the attention at any time, and make unnecessary the statement of expected performance from time to time. But such a hope is demonstrably unfounded.

A "standard cost" of a product or process would be based on a number of assumptions, all of which are untenable. A standard cost computed at a certain time would bear all the marks peculiar to that time. The calculation would be based on standard unit prices of the labor or material inputs; these may be actual prices at the time or some hypothetical prices based on the actual prices. But the variability of prices is notorious, and, as we have argued, even actual prices paid are not necessarily, thereafter, adequate representations of cost. The calculation would be based on a certain combination of products. But as we have shown the combination of products, in variety and quantity, is subject to short-run variations as variations in prices of products relatively to one another occur; and also as variations in the prices of the necessary factors of production relative to one another occur. The calculation would be based on a standard level of activity of the firm as a whole. But the level of activity will vary from time to time as market demand for the product and market supply of the factors vary; and the level of activity will vary with the adaptability of the firm on the occurrence of these changes. The calculation would be based on a given standard of technology. But technology is also subject to change. And to more changes than the ostensible technical variety. If a state of technology is assumed, represented by so many man-hours of labor per unit of equipment (however measured), the mere process of learning, a continuous process, may enable the same product to be produced more expeditiously and, therefore, more economically through time.[25] In total effect, a standard cost would be a product of applying to stated physical standards a set of weights, all relevant at one time and on the basis of knowledge at that time alone.

Now the advantage of a standard lies in its usefulness under varying conditions through time.[26] Only if it is invariant under varying conditions through time is the cost of setting up a standard worthwhile. Manifestly, a standard cost calculated in the above manner has no such property. Every change in the conditions which specify it would require that the "standard" be recalculated, otherwise the gearing of actions to internal standards will fail to secure the firm's adaptation to its environment.[27] The parameters are so susceptible to variation that "standard" can have no useful meaning. Attention has already been drawn to the costs of having a double language system; these costs of reinterpretation are in the present case augmented by the costs of setting up the "standard."

Any cost designated a standard cost will tend to create the belief that the standard cost is significant for calculation and action, particularly among technical people who are accustomed to the invariant property of physical standards. A standard cost system, which by definition lacks the

25 See Frank J. Andress, "The Learning Curve as a Production Tool," *Harvard Business Review*, Vol. XXXII, No. 1, 1954.
26 On standardization of measurements, generally as well as monetary measurements, see Churchman, *Prediction and Optimal Decision*, p. 118ff.
27 That norms change more slowly than actual behaviors is well known. The judgment of actual behaviors by reference to long standing norms can only be misleading. See Galbraith, *The Affluent Society*, Ch. 2; Homans, *The Human Group*, Ch. XIV, XV.

property of isomorphism, will not produce responses which are appropriate to a homeostatic system.

The appropriate basis for judgments of actual costs at any time is the cost, in terms of current cash equivalents at that time, of the standard specifications of labor-time and materials expressed in physical units. Only such a comparison will be a comparison of measures in monetary units of the same dimension, and only such a comparison will be indicative of the level of operating efficiency at that time. As a motivational device, standards in physical terms are more effective at technical levels and freer of doubtful assumptions which disregard the uncertainty and unpredictability of future events and responses to them.

CONCLUSION

The type of retrospective cost calculation which emerges has the same qualities as the financial information suggested in previous chapters. Its freedom from hypothetical allocations and apportionments, and its character as a further form of analysis of the information yielded by the general accounting process indicated, secure both its objectivity and its relevance, as feedback, to the process of adaptation. No examination has been undertaken of the general behavior through time of particular cost elements. But whether the product of the further analyses of cost accounting is used for one purpose or another, the adaptive process will be poorly served if the system is not isomorphic with changes internally which are represented by externally significant magnitudes. The function of the internal circulation of financial information is to secure coordination within consistent with conditions beyond an organization. The survival of an organization will be threatened if the signals of the environment are intercepted as they enter the organization; the threat may only be survived by the input of additional energy in the form of costly *ad hoc* retranslations from and to monetary magnitudes relevant in the market place.

Argument

12.11   *An organization is a homeostatic system consisting of a collection of agents of the constituents of an association, all having assigned roles, and having itself a role defined by the constituents.*
         (3.21, 3.31, 3.32, 3.41, 4.11, 4.12)

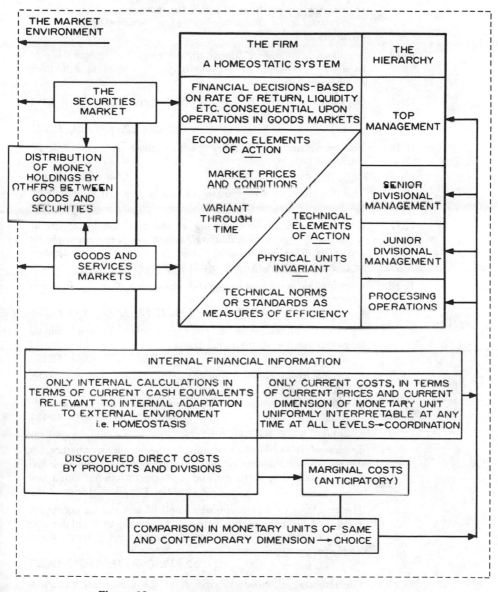

Figure 12
OUTLINE OF CHAPTER 12: FINANCIAL COMMUNICATION
WITHIN ORGANIZATIONS.

12.12   *In complex organizations, roles are so assigned as to constitute an hierarchy of positions in which the incumbent of any position is accountable to the incumbent of a position senior in the hierarchy.*

12.13   *A collection of agents having similar roles and accountable to an agent next senior in the hierarchy will constitute a division of an organization.*

12.14   Organizations having similar roles have agents (and tend to have divisions) having similar roles.

(3.23, *12.11, 12.12, 12.13*)

12.15   To the incumbent of every position there is some residual discretion.

(2.26, 3.24, *12.12*)

12.16   The incumbent of any position may change from time to time.

(3.24, *12.12*)

12.17   *Coordination is the consequence of the selection by agents of responses to organizational stimuli which are consistent with the actions of other individual agents or divisions of an organization and consistent with the role of the organization.*

12.18   Coordination is secured by the communication of instructions and information.

(*3.22*, 3.25, *12.11, 12.12, 12.13*, 12.15 *12.17*)

12.21   Divisional differentiation of tasks gives rise to intradivisional languages specific to divisional tasks.

(*3.21*, 8.37, *12.13*, 12.18)

12.22   Interdependence between the hierarchical or operational roles assigned in a given organization entails that there shall be an interdivisional language.

(*3.26*, 8.37, 12.18)

12.23   Interdependence between an organization (or any agent or division of it) and other persons or organizations, whether for the purpose of learning or for the purpose of substantive interaction, entails that there shall be supra-organizational languages.

(1.15, 1.63, *3.26*, 8.37, 12.14 12.18)

12.24   The responses to organizational stimuli of any person occupying a series of positions successively will be consistent with the role of the organization if the intradivisional and interdivisional languages are consistent.

(*12.12*, 12.16, 12.18, 12.21, 12.22)

12.25   The language of monetary signs is at the same time intradivisional (to accounting and financial divisions), interdivisional (all means employed and all outputs having monetary properties) and supraorganizational (in respect of all organizations having financial relationships with other entities).

(*3.64*, 8.24, 12.21, 12.22, 12.23)

12.26   Only monetary signs which are consistent in all such uses will secure coordination of the actions of agents of the organization and homeostasis of the entity in its environment.

(*12.11*, 12.18, 12.24, 12.25)

12.27   Financial communications within an organization shall be consistent with the financial communications beyond the organization and both shall be isomorphic with the monetary properties of the entity at any time and from time to time.

(*1.32*, 1.68, *3.11*, 3.14, 6.21, 12.26)

12.28   Divergence between intraorganizational and extraorganizational information leads to entropy of the sign system and to failure of coordination; the information loss may be countered only at the cost of repeated retranslation.

(8.35, 8.36, 12.26)

12.31   In complex organizations, the relationships between consecutive events are complex, confusing the identification of cause and effect as aggregative effects have many causes in common.

(*1.32*, 1.75, 3.25, *12.12*)

12.32   The formation of expectations on the basis of past experience is facilitated by the identification, at the point of input to the record system, of the point of input of resources to the action system.

(2.25, 6.21, 12.31)

12.33   *Measurements in physical scales are invariant through time.*

12.34   Intertemporal measurements of performance in physical scales are comparable, enabling judgments of relative efficiency to be based on technical norms.

(9.21, *12.33*)

12.35   Intertemporal measurements of performance in the monetary scale are comparable only if made or transformed to units of the same dimension and only if all common causes are constant.

(4.39, 12.31)

12.36   The variability of common causes (usage of capacity, combinations of processes and of products, factor prices) invalidates the establishment of norms in the monetary scale.

(4.36, 12.31)

12.41   The complexity of an action system requires that it be regarded as a "black box," marginal inputs being chosen on the basis of expected marginal outputs of the system.

(2.52, 12.31)

12.42   *The direct cost of any operation at any time is the sacrifice identifiable with the operation, measured in contemporary terms.*

12.43   All costs of operation may be classified as direct costs of some product, process or division, or as wastes.

(2.23, 2.24, *12.42*)

12.44   The direct cost (*ex post*) of any product, process or division at any time is the closest approximation to the marginal cost (*ex ante*) at that time; its use in deriving marginal cost is subject to the fewest hypotheses as to common causes and effects.

(1.76, 12.32, 12.43)

12.45　　The relative marginal costs and marginal revenues of alternative products, processes or divisions, are the bases of decisions to continue with or to diverge from a present course of action.

(9.17, 9.42, 9.55, 12.41)

Service and Governmental
Organizations

13 In Chapter 9, trading ventures were described as entities engaged in the purchase and conversion of goods and services and the sale of the same goods or their product, all operations being subject to the market process. Commonly, buying and selling are done at a price per unit. Sale at a price per unit enables customers to "cast their vote," as it is picturesquely described, for one good or class of goods as against another or others. Similarly, the sale of securities in small parcels at unit prices enables investors to cast votes for some firms as against others, on the basis of past performance and investors' expectations of the future performance of firms in the goods and services markets. The actual and expected profitabilities of ventures in commodities determine both the goods which shall be produced and the firms which shall produce them. We regarded the firm as an instrument by which its constituents seek to increase their satisfactions. Under interdependence, what is sought is increase in the generalized means of obtaining satisfactions, not merely greater command over monetary tokens as such.

We turn now to some classes of organization which do not conform with the above pattern. Their observable forms and functions are numerous.

SERVICE AND SOCIAL ORGANIZATIONS

The most elementary organization of this kind is the social, cultural, or political association which for its purposes needs no moneyed funds and acquires no rights in property. There may well be transactions between constituents as individuals and the association of constituents; but these will not be market transactions. The operations of the association may be regarded as coterminous joint production and joint consumption: and both are judged or valued directly, without reference to the monetary calculus or the market process. Such organizations lack the one feature which is central to our study. Organizations of the same kind which acquire and dispose of funds and property rights do fall within our interest. But market operations and the capacity to engage in them are ancillary. The dominant objective of association is not quantifiable in monetary terms. Therefore, although constituents are willing to contribute some part of their means for the pursuit of a joint objective or satisfaction, the comparison of expected costs with expected accomplishments is a direct comparison of values, not mediated by a common scale.

This type of relationship between expected costs and expected consequences is common to all activities except those of indirect exchange. Charitable associations, parent-teacher associations, hospital auxiliaries, and a host of similar organizations found in every community attest to the variety of circumstances in which direct evaluations must be made by constituents: comparisons of funds contributed with nonfinancial achievements expected, not only for a single association, but as well for alternative existent associations. After reaching a certain minimal size and for certain functions these associations develop identifiable interest groups: commonly a class of financial contributors, a class of administrators and a class of beneficiaries, generally mutually exclusive in membership.

As we have shown, in a market economy, financial contributors are the class without which no project can effectively be launched, whether the project is charitable or mercantile. However, there is no common substratum of support for nontrading associations such as market demand provides for trading enterprises. Financial contributors are linked to these organizations by nothing stronger than their goodwill, their temporary intellectual, emotional, or other nonpecuniary involvements. Such persistence or long-run stability as these organizations may have depends on the continued engagement of the sympathy of financial supporters, rather than on the canons of financial administration customarily adopted in relation to the maintenance of a residual equity. Residual equity, in fact, has no role analogous to the role it has in trading enterprises.

At the other extreme, the beneficiaries have no means of securing continued service. They offer nothing except the opportunity for others to manifest their goodwill. But commonly, the values attached to charitable and similar functions by the society at large are such that continued service may be provided as long as the administrative class is active. But to the administrative class, there are other ends besides the mere performance of charitable and similar functions. The organization provides the administrative class, often with income and security, frequently with prestige, and sometimes with power.[1] The administrative class of participants provides the continuity of functioning which secures the continuity of the organization, even if it performs its functions in modes other than the ideal with which it was launched. It is not surprising, therefore, that in many circumstances—charities, professional and trade associations, some educational institutions—when one thinks of the organization, one tends to think principally of its administration. And in view of the difficulty of relating costs to services performed, the problems of holding such administrations accountable are not simple of solution.

These institutions are, of course, confronted with an economic problem. We may suppose the constituents to expect that the funds employed are employed in the most efficient manner. If the tasks which comprise the activities of an institution are uniform in character, it is possible perhaps to discover the total disbursements (substantive and administrative) per task and to judge whether the disbursement per task is acceptable on the basis of comparisons with the same ratio for other periods or for other institutions. Where the tasks are diverse and more or less unique, each must be judged on its merits. The decision is at the discretion of the administration and the style of the organization may be described as bureaucratic.[2] Some index of performance may, however, be devised in respect of administrative costs; for example, the administrative cost per thousand monetary units of substantive disbursements. Even such indications as these are not entirely reliable; but, in the absence of better indications, they may serve to keep administrations aware of supervision, aware of the fact that they are accountable.

It would seem to be a reasonable rule in the administration of eleemosy-

---

[1] Peter B. Clark and James Q. Wilson distinguish three kinds of incentives; material, solidary and purposive. "Incentive Systems: A Theory of Organizations," *Administrative Science Quarterly,* September 1961. Solidary incentives, which include status, prestige, and power, play a significant, if not a predominant, part in the class of organizations here considered.

[2] In the taxonomical sense, not the emotional, denigratory sense. "Bureaucratic management . . . is the method applied in the conduct of administrative affairs, the result of which has no cash value on the market." von Mises, *Human Action,* p. 305.

nary and personal service entities that operations should be limited by the quantum of funds actually under the control of the administration from time to time. Pledges and membership dues, for example, do not constitute legally enforceable obligations, either by their nature or because litigation to enforce them is unpalatable. Well established entities may, on the security of durable assets and in some measure on the expectation of future receipts, be able to augment the funds available at any time by borrowing. But the tests applied by lenders are not purely financial tests; they are in part tests of the commitment of the community or some section of it to service operations of a specific kind. It is true that the tests applied to business ventures also include tests of a similar kind, but in their cases the consequences of past action are ascertainable as a monetary residue and inure to the benefit of financial supporters themselves. The diverse interests of contributors, administration, and beneficiaries, and the inadequacy of direct linkage of information on contributions with information on benefits, usually gives rise to public regulation of the terms defining the account-ability of the administrations of entities having rights to invite public financial support.

PUBLIC UTILITIES

Consider, now, a type of organization intermediate between the trading venture and the consumer-type organization of the previous section. This type includes all public utilities—highway, railroad, and other transportation systems, water supply, electricity supply systems; and similar enterprises. These undertakings may be conducted by privately owned corporations which raise funds on the security of their assets and incomes, and which pay interest or dividends to their securityholders. Because of the heavy outlays necessary to establish utilities deemed to be in the public interest, franchises to do so are given sparingly by legislatures. A monopoly or quasi-monopoly is thereby created, and with it the possi-bility that the quantity, quality, and price of the service given may be fixed without regard for the public interest. To avert the latter consequence, the prices of the services provided by utility companies, and the dividends and interest they may pay on their stocks, are commonly regulated by judicial or inquisitorial authorities. Thus, at least two classes of prices are governed to some extent by extra-market (political) considerations; explicitly, by whatever is for the time encompassed by "the public interest." The same applies in the case of public utilities conducted by public corpora-tions. In all these cases, the produced goods or services are sold at a unit price, but the price is not the outcome solely of the interplay between market forces.

Privately owned utility corporations depend on the contributions of stockholders in the same way as business corporations generally. The regulated monopolies are attractive to investors who prefer regularity of income to prospects of market price gains. Publicly owned utilities, on the other hand, do not depend on a residual equity to provide the fundamental security on which loans may be raised; and indeed, though some may raise loan funds to finance expenditures on their durable plant and equipment, others may acquire such funds by appropriations from the public revenues or other public funds, without direct recourse to the market in securities. Thus, the price mechanism of the market is not the sole allocative device depended upon either for funds or other resources. If it were, many of the existent publicly and privately owned utility undertakings would long since have ceased to attract investors. Their preservation, because they are deemed to be in the public interest, is due to the power of government to endow them with special privileges (for example, monopolies or preferences in respect of the land, sea, and air carriage of the mails) or with direct or indirect bounties or exemptions.

Although utility corporations are to some extent governed by political considerations, their economic aspects may not be confused with policy without loss of the information which informs policy. Consider a utility which is expected to provide a service into a distant future. It will require to set up a plant and the services necessary to its operation over an interval in which it has the expectation of continuation of its franchise even if its operations are subject to new forms of competition. The questions arise, both for its administration and for the regulatory authority which supervises it: shall its prices be fixed (a) on the understanding that periodical deficits will be met out of general revenues of government in the form of subsidies? (b) on the understanding that only the initial cash outlays shall be recoverable in the price, the question of replacement thereby being deferred? or (c) on the understanding that contemporary costs of the embodied services shall be recoverable in the price?

Fixing prices on the understanding that periodical deficits will be subsidized entails a principle of discrimination in favor of the user of the service as against the nonuser.[3] Insofar as the general revenues of government are pledged for this purpose, it is a matter of public interest that the extent of the indirect subsidization of one class of the community be known. And it can be known only if the context of the term "deficit" is known, that is, if it is known on what principles the accounting process is carried out. This leads directly to the second and third questions posed above.

Fixing prices on the understanding that only the initial cash outlays shall be recoverable in the price entails a principle of discrimination in favor of immediate users as against future users if prices of equipment rise, and in the opposite direction if prices of equipment fall. Although the

---

[3] An illustration of the administrative influence on the allocation of economic power; see Kuhn, *The Study of Society,* pp. 621ff.

prices of short-term inventories and services enter into costs in their higher amounts as prices rise, the equipment costs (depreciation) do not. To price on this basis means that present consumers are paying less than the contemporary cost of the whole service inputs. This may be done for reasons of economic policy (such as keeping down the level of prices) or of political strategy. But unless the accounting for the operation is carried out in contemporary terms, there can be no indication of the extent to which discrimination is being exercised, or of the cost of the policy adopted, or of the cost to the community of supplying the service, should the question of alternative means of supplying it, or of alternatives to the service itself, arise. There is no reason, in principle, why a pricing policy of the kind referred to should not be adopted; for policy is an expression of values, and values are various and variable. As suggested, however, there is reason for adhering to a form of accounting which represents the consequences of any policy, a form which is neutral as between policies. If the form of accounting is permitted to change with changes in policy, any attempt to scrutinize and to evaluate specific policies will be thwarted.

Fixing prices on the basis of recovering full contemporary costs of the embodied services is nondiscriminatory as between present and future users. Of necessity, such a policy requires a form of accounting substantially similar to that indicated for business firms generally. Although this form is apposite in the case of all utilities, the price policy here referred to is more likely to give rise to its adoption than other price policies.

In general, the type of accounting which has been shown to be appropriate to business firms will indicate for utilities the relevant costs of operation and the extent of subsidization or discrimination inherent in any regulatory decision or administrative policy.[4] Rival regional or trade groups may claim differential advantages in the form either of expenditures from public moneys on regional development, contributions from public moneys in the form of bounties, or exemptions and concessions from contributions to the public funds. The existence of pressure groups entails that many decisions will be the resultant of the forces of group self-interest and of the judgments of professional administrators.[5]

[4] An extended treatment of the issues in public utility investment and pricing is given in James R. Nelson, ed., *Marginal Cost Pricing in Practice* (Englewood Cliffs, N.J.: Prentice-Hall, Inc., 1964), a series of papers on the electrical industry in France.

[5] Contrast the following observations: "The salaried professional in the service organization is free of this pressure [of economic necessity], and the organization supported by community or philanthropic funds is not dependent on fees from clients either. These conditions would seem to be more conducive to promoting disinterested service." Peter M. Blau and W. Richard Scott, *Formal Organizations, A Comparative Approach* (London: Routledge & Kegan Paul, Ltd., 1963), p. 62. "Regulatory commissions often seem to work more in the interests of the regulated than of those they are supposed to protect, for the simple reason that they are in so much closer contact with the former." Kuhn, *The Study of Society,* p. 681.

GOVERNMENTAL SERVICE ORGANIZATIONS

This brings us to the most general of the types of organization which are not profit-oriented. These are represented by the central or local governmental authorities which supply goods or services to whole communities or to sections of communities without tribute in the form of a unit price. Examples range from public libraries, parks, and gardens, to public law enforcement, national health, and defense. In these cases, the recovery of the cost of providing the service through some form of pricing is deemed to be either inappropriate, because it is not intended to ration the service provided among members of the community; or impossible, because the service is consumed collectively and not individually. Services of these kinds are, therefore, financed out of the proceeds of taxes, power to levy which vests in the respective governmental authorities; or they are financed out of loans secured upon or guaranteed by the ultimate power to tax.

We have here a class of operations materially different from those of privately owned, profit-oriented firms.

In the private sector, the market indicates to actual firms and promoters of firms the kinds of services for which a demand exists, and at what prices. The market communicates this information by its unwillingness to pay the same price per unit as the supply overtakes demand, or by bidding up the price when demand exceeds supply (other things remaining constant). But in the public sector, for services consumed collectively, there is only one entity in respect of which marginal value means anything; and that entity is the society as a whole. Any of its constituents or any group of constituents may voice approval or disapproval of expenditures on additional supplies of collectively consumed services. Insofar as choices must be made as between the quantities of different services provided, they must be made without benefit of the atomistic "polling" of the market place which is available to the private business sector. We defer, for the moment, the question of the accountability of those who make such decisions, and turn to the consideration of financial position which was our primary concern when dealing with private persons and firms.

FINANCIAL CRITERIA

Financial position and periodical income, as we defined them in earlier chapters, are almost entirely irrelevant to the entities now considered. The residual equity which was the basis of borrowing "on the equity," may provide such a basis also in the case of privately conducted nontrading entities; it has no such role at all in the case of, say, the administrative functions of government. As we have said, the power to levy taxes on part or the whole of the community is a far greater guarantee of the security of loans to government and of the regularity of the interest income from these loans.

The composition of assets and obligations we regarded as indicating the liquidity of assets, the solvency of the firm, and its adaptability. These qualities are not simply to be disregarded in the case of nontrading entities. To nontrading entities in the private sector, they are quite important; though, in emergencies, such organizations may depend for extrication on the goodwill and sympathy with their purposes of the community they serve. To nontrading entities in the public sector liquidity of assets, solvency of the entity, and adaptability of its operations are secured generally by the same powers, to tax or to expropriate in the public interest, to which reference has been made. There are occasions when the stability of the government of some political unit is in doubt; investments in the securities of such governments are then manifestly speculative. But generally, there can be little question about the solvency of governments of the kind which one may entertain about the solvency of business firms. If there were any such doubt, no informative light would be thrown on the matter by a document of the style of the business balance sheet.

Again, we regarded the financial position, represented in the balance sheet, as indicating the resources available and the potential scale of operations in the immediately following interval. The same does not apply to public nontrading entities. The scale of operations in any future interval is determined by, and itself determines, the funds which the entity is able (in the case of voluntarily supported entities) or decides (in the case of governmental authorities) to raise.

In the same connection may be mentioned the rate of return on funds employed which, in the business sector, provides a means of choosing between alternative courses of action. The "returns" from the operations of social, cultural, or eleemosynary organizations are not measurable in the monetary calculus—unless the money outlays on their procurement may be said to measure them (this indeed is how they are treated in social accounting). For any given entity, the ends it seeks to promote from time to time may, and do, vary; intertemporally, they are incommensurable. And the "returns," as we have noted, are generally consumed in the course of their production. Thus there cannot be any sense in which a rate of return on funds employed has meaning in the case of the organizations mentioned above.

The same applies to the affairs of government. Public officials are concerned with economizing no less than private managers. They have control over limited means which will serve only some of the diverse public wants. But, in exercising choice, they are unable to set the rate of return from sanitation against the rate of return from public expenditure on education. Ends open for selection are incommensurable even if the prospective benefits of particular policies are calculable; and many such benefits, because they may arise indirectly and over long intervals are not even calculable.[6] In such circumstances, financial criteria of efficiency are not obviously relevant, if they are relevant at all.[7] Again, in modern societies, governments are not merely passive in their relationships with the private sector of the community. Courses of action may be chosen with the intention of influencing the behavior of the community at large. What applies to lesser entities does not provide criteria of choice for the more influential or distinctive actions of government.

Patently, the public functions of governmental authorities, while they are performed through, and influence actions in, the market, entail concepts relating to their financial affairs which differ significantly from those which are appropriate to private business investment and operation. It does not follow, however, that all the principles we have enunciated are inapplicable. We have to discover which are and which are not.

Governments engage in market transactions. They buy goods and services. They withdraw purchasing power from the private sector for the purpose; and they withdraw purchasing power from one segment of the private sector and make it available to other segments. They engage in cash and credit transactions. A form of accounting yielding a record of the creation and discharge of obligations of and to others from time to time is necessary.

The question arises whether the accounting system should be isomorphic with respect to cash movements or isomorphic with respect to changes in obligations. A system which is isomorphic with respect to changes in obligations (that is, an accrual system) will serve to indicate the income and expenditure of an accounting period more precisely. It would prevent the possibility of the deferment of the collection of revenues and the settlement of obligations, without making these decisions a matter of public record, to suit administrative or political convenience. It would indicate the income arising from the tax measures of a given fiscal period and the expense arising from the decisions made during the same period. The variety and extent of governmental activities give rise to difficulties of assessment and it is not always easy to determine the revenues and obligations outstanding.

[6] For some of the difficulties of relating costs and benefits even in the case of utilities, see Arthur Smithies, *The Budgetary Process in the United States* (New York: McGraw-Hill Book Company, 1955), Chap. XIII.

[7] "Success or failure of a police department's activities cannot be ascertained according to the arithmetical procedures of profit-seeking business. No accountant can establish whether or not a police department or one of its subdivisions has succeeded." von Mises, *Human Action,* p. 305.

If it be supposed that the characteristic feature of the operations of bureaucratic organizations is behavior according to rules, the possibility of establishing rules for the purpose must be admitted.

As the agencies and officials of government are numerous and geographically widespread, an internal communication system by which cash receipts and expenditures are coordinated and supervised in accordance with the mandate of the administration is necessary. As, in democratic societies, the administration is accountable to the constituents, who through taxes and loans are the financial supporters of public activities, some form of periodical accounting is necessary. As any given administration may persist over a number of years, recurrently requiring revenues to meet planned expenditures, review more frequently than the constitutional life span of an administration is necessary, if opposition and constituents are to be able to exercise their powers of review.

There emerges a double-entry accounting system, serving as organizational memory and one type of organizational communication, isomorphic in respect at least of cash movements, periodically yielding summaries of transactions and monetary balances. But what of the non-monetary resources under the control of the administration and the equities in them at any point of time—matters which are significant features of the accounting of business firms?

There is the same need of a record of holdings of non-monetary resources; it stems from the same possibility of unwitting loss or deliberate misappropriation of property. The geographical dispersion of public property gives rise to extensive rules designed to secure its protection. The aim of protection is served by a continuous physical inventory of holdings of resources. The question is whether any administrative function is served by an inventory in monetary terms.

Governmental activities are generally not subject to short-run shifts in the demands of constituents for public services. They are likewise free of shifts in the general supply conditions of the services they render or of alternatives to them; for, in respect of these services government is the sole supplier. Short-run adaptation is not an imperative of the same order as it is in the case of business. A public building may not be sold if it seems that a bridge should be built; nor is it necessary to raise loans on the security of charges over specific items of public property. Short-run adaptation takes the form rather of changing the priorities of expenditures planned but not yet executed, or of discovering additional ways of raising revenues or loans. Initial acquisition prices, as such, we have shown, generally, to have no relevance to subsequent decisions; neither in the present context, for the reasons just given, have contemporary prices of durable goods any meaning in relation to short-run administrative decisions. A continuous monetary record based on contemporary prices appears to have little justification.

As for the equities, the loan indebtedness of governm
constituency as a whole) will be a matter of record, as ᵢ
obligations to, or claims of, domestic and foreign persons and ᵤ
individually. But no meaning can be assigned to the notion "residual ᵥ
in the case of governmental accounts.

Consider the problems of the financial administration of government. Its demand for revenues and its plans for disposing of revenues are in a sense mutually determined. Uncertainty as to the outcome of these proposals will entail that there will, *ex post,* be surpluses or deficiencies, even if the planned revenues match the planned expenditures. And to procure particular economic consequences, surpluses or deficits may be planned. But, generally, legislatures do not give the executive freedom to raise sums beyond those required for approved purposes, nor if such sums are, in fact, raised may they be spent without approval of the legislature. Approvals of expenditures are made from year to year. There is an element of substantive discontinuity in financial operations which calls for some variation from the style of accounting found appropriate to continuing business activity.

FUND ACCOUNTING AND BUDGETING

One object of all administrations, private and public, is to secure in each financial period that relationship between financial inflows and outflows which is appropriate to the nature of the organizations they manage. In the case of organizations which are oriented to profit making, the whole of the resources available may be regarded as a single pool, for the test of the use of the whole is the periodical surplus. In the case of organizations or parts of organizations not so oriented, neither the contributions to them nor their performance are determined by market forces; and the distribution of available means between competing ends is not determined on the basis of their contribution to a single measure of the effectiveness of the use of the resources as a whole.[8] The functions to be performed are segregated and to each such function there is appro-

---

[8] Observing the difficulties which others have found in defining income and the subjective elements in individual interpretations of income, Vatter has proposed that the concept be left undefined and that the accounts of profit-oriented business ventures be designed around the notion of funds. The effect is to assimilate the accounting methods of business and non-business organizations. William J. Vatter, *The Fund Theory of Accounting and Its Implications for Financial Reports* (Chicago: The University of Chicago Press, 1947). But to do so disregards the integrating function of periodical income in the operations of business ventures. The distinctive orientations and tests of performance of business and non-business organizations make it inevitable that there shall be distinctive forms of accounting for them. See Weber, *The Theory of Social and Economic Organization,* p. 176.

priated a fund; a sum of money usually, in keeping with the vernacular usage of "fund." The executive responsible for each such function is then held accountable in terms of the fund.

The entity, about which the accounting for such a fund centers, is not, of course, the fund.[9] It is the role or function or collection of actions for which the fund is set aside. The amount of the fund, determined by legislative decision, sets one of the bounds to executive discretion. A given administration may, of course, be accountable for two or more funds. Thus, an educational foundation may have an educational fund and a working fund, the one to cope with its substantive operations, the other to provide for its administration in a given financial period. Its administration may then be appraised independently on two bases, the final judgment of its efficiency emerging from the weights given to substantive performance and administrative efficiency.

Many types of fund are identifiable in the administration of organizations not oriented to profit making.[10] A single general fund may suffice for small organizations. Specialization and subdivision with growth necessitate the creation of subdivisions of a general fund. Special levies or taxes raised for specific purposes give rise to special funds. Operations as an agent or trustee necessitate trust funds in respect of assets held in trust.

Where the resources coming under the control of a single administrative unit are to be disbursed through a number of subunits, the instrument of coordination is the budget. The budget reduces the proposals originating in spending divisions to consistency with the means expected to be available and to some extent with the diverse ends of the legislative authority. It establishes the amounts of funds available to divisions; it may specify the types of expenditure and the particular amounts which may be spent to acquire services of a given type or for given tasks. Notwithstanding that some services to be used in a given period arise out of expenditure in the past and some current expenditures are for future sevices, the budget is usually framed in terms of cash receipts and payments. Reference has already been made to the significance of the specificity of goals and, by

9 Note the definition of fund as "a sum of money or other resources segregated for carrying on specific activities or attaining certain objectives in accordance with special regulations, restrictions or limitations and constituting an independent fiscal and accounting entity." National Committee on Governmental Accounting, *Municipal Accounting and Auditing* (Chicago: 1951), p. 234. This use of "entity" conflicts with our usage; a fund is no more an entity in the case of governmental accounting than the residual equity is in the case of accounting for other organizations. The amount of a fund constitutes one of the "limitations" of the "entity" in our terminology. The notion of an entity as a person or persons acting a specified role is particularly apt to such circumstances.

10 R.M. Mikesell and Leon E. Hay, *Governmental Accounting* (Homewood, Ill.: Richard D. Irwin, Inc., 1961), Chap. 1.

inference, the specificity of constraints. Both as an indication of limits and of convergence on those limits as a period progresses, a budget based on cash movements is more effective in the pure service organization than one including accrued and deferred elements. Under budgetary management, the function of accounting is to record the disbursements against particular appropriations of funds so that the contraints embodied in the budget are made effective.[11]

Fund accounting does not, therefore, have the same significance throughout an organization as does business accounting, for it does not provide a measure which is effective in the market supplying funds. However, the information it produces may, under certain conditions, be used as indicative of performance other than the mere matter of working within budgetary constraints. If, as a matter of principle, the funds appropriated periodically are allocated as between working costs (or recurrent costs) and new investment (or nonrecurrent costs), it is at least possible to compare recurrent costs with those of previous periods. As the service given by any division may vary from year to year (for example, the service given to the total population, for a general administrative function; to the pensionable population for a social services administration), actual working costs would be reducible to comparable terms by expressing them in relation to a conventional common unit base (per thousand of the relevant population). And as the level of prices generally and of specific prices may vary, some correction for the change in the dimension of the monetary unit may be necessary if intertemporal comparisons are to be made.

As for nonrecurrent expenditures and existing long-term investments, these are matters for only occasional review, and, when they become necessary, *ad hoc* calculations on the basis of contemporary prices may be made. There seems to be no good reason why a continuous record in contemporary terms should be maintained simply for this nonrecurrent purpose. Nor does it seem necessary in the costing of services for the purpose of appraising performance to include the costs of long-term durables. First, the decisions to make such long-term investments are made at higher levels than that of the service unit itself. And, second, insofar as the initial cost of many such durables is met out of current revenues, those durables are virtually free goods thereafter. Thus, three types of consideration lead to the conclusion that accounting on a cash basis is appropriate to pure service organizations: (a) the general comprehensibility of a statement in cash terms renders it a practical basis for approving budgets and for holding an administration accountable; (b) the specificity of statements in cash terms makes them a ready means of motivation and

11 The term "budgetary management" has a connotation similar to von Mises' "bureaucratic management" referred to previously.

supervision within the administrative organization; and (c) the service organization is not subject to the rules relating to the financing of business projects and enterprises.

Periodical accounting statements on a cash basis require to be supplemented by schedules of obligations to and by other entities for the purpose of reviewing the full consequences of the policies adopted. They require to distinguish running expenditures from nonrecurrent expenditures. So that attention is not confined, on review, to monetary magnitudes without regard for the effects obtained, periodical financial statements should be supplemented with key statistics of performance in non-monetary terms, preferably in and as part of the financial statements. Occasional reconsideration of long-term investments will be based on contemporary prices which may be obtained directly when necessary.

A NOTE ON TAXATION

It will have been noticed that throughout this study no particular reference has been made to the effects of taxation laws and principles on the concepts employed and the methods suggested. The omission is justifiable on several grounds.

The taxation codes of public authorities differ from place to place and the rules of most authorities have differed from time to time. There is, therefore, nothing of a general kind about them such as there is about the general ways of doing business in industrially developed countries. There is no other uniform principle in respect of taxation than that taxes must be paid.

From the point of view of the tax paying entity, the obligation to pay taxes differs little from the obligation to pay other debts. There is, of course, the difference that other debts are incurred under specific contracts at stated prices, and their amounts are not often disputable, whereas a tax liability is not readily identifiable with services received and taxpayers may seek to arrange their affairs to avoid attracting taxation imposts. It is proper to regard the function of accounting as including the discovery of the liability. Given the tax rules, this is the same function as is performed by accounting for all other equities and assets, revenues and costs.

By disregarding the effects of taxation rules, the analysis was able to be quite general; being related to economic action its conclusions are apposite whatever the rules of the taxing authorities. But we do not wish to leave the matter without some comment on the interference with accounting concepts and methods which has been provoked by tax rules.[12] We will

---

[12] See Arthur M. Cannon, "Tax Pressures on Accounting Principles and Accountants' Independence," *The Accounting Review*, Vol. XXVII, No. 4, October 1952; George E. Lent, "Accounting Principles and Taxable Income," *The Accounting Review*, Vol. XXXVII, No. 3, July 1962.

refer particularly to "income" taxation. What is income for taxation purposes and what are allowable charges against income for taxation purposes have become more significant questions to business firms, as tax rates have risen, than what is income in an objective sense.

The use of income as a basis of taxation is justifiable on the ground that periodical income presumably implies that there is an increment to an initial stock or capital which can be taxed without impairing the original income generating capacity. It was perhaps inevitable that, in seeking the magnitude of income, recourse would be had to the sum so designated in accounting statements, even if some modification of this sum were to be adopted as the tax base. But most modern income taxation codes were introduced before adequate attention had been given to the definition and quantification of income. At the time the rates of taxation were of such a modest order that definition may have mattered little. However, as rates have risen the question has become of increasing consequence. The reaction has been to introduce new modifications and to graft them on to the original base, rather than to reexamine the base. For example, the last-in, first-out principle for pricing short-term inventories owes its popularity to a taxation rule; capital gains and losses have been distinguished principally because of taxation rules; and supplementary depreciation and investment allowances have been incorporated in taxation rules to alleviate some of the burdens of adhering to the old base.[13]

From the viewpoint of the administrators of a tax system, the tax rules promulgated at any time are simply the rules which will yield a planned revenue. There is no implication that these rules should become the rules upon which business enterprises keep their accounts for managerial and other purposes. It is common to complain of the rigidities of bureaucratic administration, though rigidities have an understandable rationale in that they increase predictability. It would be surprising if business organizations, which we hold to be essentially flexible and adaptable, should assume the straitjacket of tax rules for purposes unrelated to taxation liabilities. Yet this has occurred extensively. The allowance by the taxation authorities of *ad hoc* concessions to basic data have led to *ad hoc* changes in general accounting.

This has tended at least to terminological confusion. The legislature, by its mandate, is empowered to determine the basis of taxation. If this basis does not coincide with an established accounting concept or magnitude, it is in the interest of clarity that it should have a specific designation. The income tax is a tax on and out of income; but not the income which the taxpayer would otherwise consider as income. Confusion would be eliminated by use of a term such as "tax base" in lieu of taxable income. The term income or business income would thus be freed from the

[13] None of these terms is mentioned as a point of principle in the preceding chapters. See also Chap. 14.

administrative rules adopted for taxation purposes; it could be considered independently and its magnitude could be determined independently of the tax base. The function of the magnitude of income cannot be held to be well served if its measurement is confused by definitions external to the firm and irrelevant to the firm's operational purposes.

The acceptance of tax rules as accounting precedents has also tended to the acceptance and endorsement of highly questionable taxation rules. We refer to one which is at the heart of our analysis. The style of accounting prevalent at the time of the establishment of modern tax codes paid no regard to shifts in prices of durable goods used by taxpayers or to shifts in the dimension of the monetary unit. Accordingly, the tax rules based on that accounting disregarded the matter. In most countries, except in emergency or other special conditions, the maximum aggregate sum allowable for the services of durable goods in computing tax liability has been the initial price. This practice violates the principle of the maintenance of capital in computing income under nonstatic conditions. What, therefore, purports to be a tax on income is, during a period of rising prices, potentially a levy on capital as to part of the tax liability.

Insofar as the remainder after taxation is not wholly withdrawn, capital may be maintained notwithstanding the tax. But adherence to the practice used in computing tax liability for calculating income may well lead to the withdrawal of more than will leave intact the initial capital of a period. Objection may also be raised on the score of the accountability of the taxing authority. We do not protest the power or the right of an administration to raise in taxes any sum it determines. But in a period of rising prices a given tax rate on an income which is calculated without regard for changes in the dimension of the monetary unit may entail a higher tax rate on an income which is calculated with regard for such changes. To know what the rate actually is on the latter basis seems to be a matter of critical interest to the constituency, whereas under most tax codes this information is just not produced.

On the one hand, therefore, public authorities might be expected to devise tax rules which are consistent with the maintenance of capital if they intend to tax income, whether or not business firms use the same rules. This is in keeping with the principles of concern with the public interest and of concern with the level of productivity and income generated in the private sector. On the other hand, business firms might be expected to keep their own accounts on the basis of the maintenance of capital, whether or not taxing authorities use the same rules. Otherwise they cannot arrange their affairs in an informed manner, nor can they know the effective rate of tax on business income if taxing authorities use other rules. Ideally both would use the same rules, rules based on the maintenance of capital in computing income. The same applies to the rules of regulatory authorities in regulated industries.

The realism and relevance of accounting would be far more effectively preserved by the independent pursuit of definitions and measurements adequate for the purpose of business administration and communication than by following rules definitive of a tax base. The past success of proposals for *ad hoc* concessions suggests that adequately supported demonstrations of the propriety of changing the tax base to accord with a concept of income grounded in business reality would not be disregarded.[14]

A further consequence is worth noting. Governments are under frequent pressure to relieve the tax burden on one sector of the community or another, for the protection of local industries, for the promotion of infant industries, and similar reasons. If this burden is relieved by granting particular dispensations in methods of computing the tax base, the existence and amounts of such relief or assistance is disguised. Instead of recording the total liability to tax and offsetting explicitly the effects of concessions, the taxing authority is accountable only for the net amount of tax arising from the modified rules. Comparison of alternative systems and judgment both on the policies of government and on the merits of firms or industries receiving assistance are confused if they are not suppressed altogether.

Finally, a word on the treatment of taxation in the accounts of business firms or corporations. Amounts assessed and amounts paid may both vary from year to year (a) due to fluctuations in the amount of the tax base, (b) due to changes in the allowances and in the rates of tax, (c) due to the time of determination of matters in dispute, and (d) due to provisions for relieving tax burdens in the event of losses. In keeping with the general position that hypotheticals should be kept to a minimum, the income of any year should be charged with an estimate of the tax payable on the tax base of that year. No part of the amount estimated to be payable in respect of any year will then be spread over other years. At any balancing date, one does not know whether there will be a future income over which any such apportionment may be spread. And in any case, given that the estimate turns out to be the amount of the assessment, that amount is the amount by which the financial position is thereupon affected. To carry from one period to another some so-called advantage, notwithstanding that the whole of the assessed tax is payable or paid, is to give precedence to a fiction over a fact. Variations in the amount of tax payable through

14 For the official view on one phase of the matter, note:" ... Treasury Department officials have made clear that they will not endorse any price-level allowance for tax purposes unless it is coupled with appropriate recognition in the accounts." Paul Grady, "Economic Depreciation in Income Taxation and in Accounting," *The Journal of Accountancy,* April 1959, p. 60.

time suggest that, in the analysis of results, the ratio of business income before taxation to capital employed is the better measure through time of the operational performance of firms, though the ratio of business income after taxation to capital employed gives the effective rate of return.

CONCLUSION

No more than a brief survey of the financial features of service and governmental organizations has been attempted. However, it has served to indicate some material differences betweeen these organizations and firms which include profit making among their objectives. Accounting for public utilities differs in no material particular from accounting for trading firms of other kinds, even though their financing and price policies may be regulated. Accounting on a cash basis for service organizations is justifiable on grounds previously established, namely the discontinuity of operations resulting from short-term budgeting and the ready interpretability of cash transactions for motivational and coordinative purposes. Finally, it is argued that accounting in the private sector, if done according to the principles outlined in previous chapters would lead to a clearer understandng of tax burdens; that it may lead to more realistic taxation codes; and that the amounts and justifications of governmental subsidies and bounties would require then to be made explicit, and would not be disguised by *ad hoc* adjustments to taxation rules.

Argument

13.11   *Public utilities are entities engaged in buying and selling goods and services at a price per unit under publicly granted franchises, their operations being financed by the issue of securities in the securities markets or by the community through its government.*

13.12   Where franchises confer monopolistic powers or public privileges, and where the security of investments in utilities is guaranteed by government (both reducing risk), interest or dividend rates on securities and unit prices of the product are regulated by government "in the public interest."

(3.25, 3.42, 3.65, 3.75, *13.11*)

13.13   The object of regulation is to secure the supply of publicly valued services at minimum unit prices and, generally, at cost.

(2.30, 3.23, 13.12)

13.14   The reduction of risk and the regulation of prices entail extra-market (bureaucratic) discrimination as between classes of participant (all members of a community being deemed to be participants in public utilities).

(3.24, 11.07, *13.11*, 13.12, 13.13)

13.15 The degree of discrimination (by limiting interest rates payable, by subsidization out of public revenues, or by the appropriation to the public revenues of surpluses) is a matter of public interest.

(3.24, 3.25, 13.13, 13.14)

13.16 The degree of discrimination from time to time is objectively ascertainable only if costs are computed in contemporary terms, revenues (that is, costs to users) being expressed in units of contemporary dimension.

(4.39, 11.31, 13.13, 13.15)

13.17 Rate of return on capital is irrelevant as a criterion of performance of public utilities.

(9.16, 13.12, 13.13, 13.14)

13.18 Interfirm comparisons being unavailable as criteria of performance, the use of intertemporal comparisons of current cost per unit of service (expressed in monetary units of the same dimension) is consistent with the minimum cost principle.

(4.39, 9.21, 13.12, 13.13)

13.21 *Private service organizations are entities which acquire resources by gift or subscription for defined purposes and deploy those resources on the basis of extra-market criteria.*

13.22 *The participants in private service organizations are financial contributors, administrators, and beneficiaries.*

13.23 The possibility of conflict is mitigated by laws and regulations defining roles of participants.

(3.25, *3.41*, *13.22*)

13.24 The incentive to contribute financially to private service organizations is non-pecuniary.

(2.25, *13.22*)

13.25 *A fund is a sum of money appropriated or to be appropriated for the performance of a specific function or group of functions of a service organization.*

13.26 The resources of a service organization may be appropriated to one or more funds.

(*13.21*, *13.25*)

13.27 Administrators of service organizations are accountable for funds appropriated to specific functions in terms of money receipts and payments.

(9.42, *13.21*)

13.28 Administrators of service organizations are accountable for the performance of specific functions in terms of comparisons of monetary contributions or disbursements with non-pecuniary consequences.

(*1.41*, 9.42, *13.21*, 13.24)

13.31   *Public service organizations are entities which acquire resources by taxes levied on the constituents of a society, and deploy those resources (on the basis of extra-market criteria) in the provision of services in common to all constituents.*

13.32   The power to tax and to provide services in common is vested in the executive government by the constituents.

(*3.41*, *13.31*)

13.33   The levying of taxes and the provision of services being based on extra-market criteria, may be discriminatory as between constituents in the public interest.

(13.14, *13.31*, 13.32)

13.34   For the exercise of these powers the executive is accountable to the legislature and through the legislature to the constituents.

(*3.31*, *12.12*, 13.15, 13.32)

13.35   Funds are appropriated and performance of the executive is reviewed periodically, the financial operations of the executive being, therefore, discontinuous.

(2.14, 2.15, 13.34)

13.36   The coordination of the financial aspects of the diverse and widespread operations of government is effected in terms of money receipts and payments to and from specific funds.

(4.15, *12.17*, 12.22, *13.25*, 13.35)

13.37   The executive is accountable for funds appropriated to specific functions in terms of money receipts and payments.

(9.42, 13.35)

13.38   The executive is accountable for the performance of specific functions in terms of comparisons of monetary levies with non-pecuniary consequences.

(*1.41*, 9.42, *13.31*, 13.33, 13.34)

13.39   The accounting systems of service organizations shall be isomorphic with changes in balances of monetary items.

(13.27, 13.36, 13.37)

13.41   The financial operations of public service organizations being supported by the power to tax, balance sheets indicative of financial position in the commercial sense are irrelevant.

(*4.22*, 13.32)

13.42   For the purpose of making decisions beyond the regular and recurrent decisions of public service organizations, *ad hoc* calculations in terms of expected costs and current costs are sufficient.

(12.44, 12.45, 13.35)

A Theory of the Development
of Accounting Practices

14 The conclusions reached in the preceding chapters of this
book diverge from many of the contemporary views on
and practices of accounting. We have defined accounting
in a way that relates it to deliberate and informed action.
We have envisaged its function as a measurement function productive of
contemporary knowledge which is the only common basis on which reasoned action may be taken. We have established some rules and principles by
which this function may be performed, for the arrangement of the affairs
of an entity both within and beyond itself. We have demonstrated that
monetary calculation in an uncertain and changing environment will necessarily take account of these changes if it is to be serviceable; and that the
general practice of accounting, like the general practice of any art, shall
be based on similar general principles and uniform rules.

By contrast, the accounting function has not hitherto been adequately
defined or related to the adaptive problems of entities. Consequently, there
has been some confusion as to the nature of its products and as to the

concepts which its exponents seek to quantify. On this basis, an extensive array of alternative rules and principles has developed and been accepted, the consequences of which have been major, unsuspected, and sometimes catastrophic disclosures of the differences between recorded magnitudes and magnitudes which are effective in the market place. There have been extended arguments over such questions as the priority of the income account and the propriety of maintaining the linkage between financial accounts and cost accounts. From our analysis, it appears that many of these disputed questions are pseudoquestions which arise only because of the anomalous character of the information actually produced.

Readers with some knowledge of existing accounting methods may be surprised that no discussion has been offered of the various methods of pricing short-term assets at a point of time (average cost, first-in first-out, last-in first-out, and others), or of the methods of determining depreciation costs of durables (the fixed instalment method, the reducing instalment method, and others). The reason for their neglect is that they do not conform with a unifying notion of the kind we have employed, namely that accounting information shall be relevant to adaptive behavior under uncertainty and environmental variability. There being no unifying concept, there can be no test upon which the superiority of one of these methods over another can be judged. Under the conditions we have taken into account and given the quality of information we have demonstrated to be necessary, all these methods may be judged to be unsystematic responses to vaguely felt uneasiness. Their inconsistent effects on balance sheets and income statements were only tolerable by dismissing the significance of one of them. As it happened, it was the balance sheet that suffered, notwithstanding that financial positions at successive points are the primary data from which income is but an inference.

We could at this stage let the matter rest. But our theory would then leave unexplained the existence of the practices which are, in fact, followed. It seems preferable to extend the argument, so that the theory not only indicates what, on reasoned grounds, the principles and practices of accounting may be expected to be, but also to demonstrate why they are not what they may be expected to be. Only a broad sketch will be offered here, for explanation of the extensive variety of specific views held and practices followed would involve us in equally extensive excursions into the history and literature of accounting. The foundations of much of what follows have been laid in preceding chapters.

ACCOUNTING AS A PRACTICAL ART

Accounting has generally been regarded by its practitioners as a practical art, molded by the exigencies of practical affairs. In this it differs from no other practical art. But merely to describe it in this way explains nothing. The forms it has taken and the rules of its practitioners require to be explained in terms of the choices of its practitioners.

Accounting has its roots in the forms and skills of bookkeeping. It is not without significance that most of the early treatises on bookkeeping were directed to the keeping of books of account *by merchants* and other persons themselves, not by a separate class of persons serving merchants as experts in bookkeeping.[1] As keeper of the record and manager of his own affairs, it was competent for the merchant to keep the record as he thought fit. His diligence in this respect was his own affair; if he failed to exercise due care the consequences fell directly on himself.

When and where in the following three centuries bookkeepers came to to be employed is immaterial. But there can be little doubt that merchants retained the right to determine their own methods of bookkeeping. The double-entry form persisted as an ideal and increased in use; but it is a form in which nonsensical as well as realistic entries may be cast. The possibility of divergent bases for determining the amounts entered was ever present. The right of business men to devise their own rules for their own information was admitted in the English courts[2], has generally been admitted by practitioners, and is not uncommonly supported by expositors of the accounting process.

But it appears to have been lost to sight that serious problems of communication, retention, and interpretation arise (a) when the merchant himself no longer can have direct access to the facts as a check on their written representations, because of the sheer numerosity of the facts; (b) when the bookkeeper is, himself, limited in perception, limited in acquaintance with the merchant's intentions, and personally autonomous in many respects; (c) when a "merchant" is no longer a single person but in many cases a corporation to and from which servants may come and go; and (d) when the financial information relating to firms can no longer be held to be private, but must be communicated to others in the course of business.

[1] Addressing himself to the "real merchant," Pacioli observed: "The second thing looked for in business is to be a good accountant and sharp bookkeeper..." Lucas Pacioli, *Double-Entry Book-keeping*, trans. Pietro Crivelli (London: The Institute of Bookkeepers, Ltd., 1939), p. 2. There is abundant evidence of the point made in the text in the writings of Pacioli's copiers and successors. The long titles of the treatises (original or translations) of Jan Ympyn Christoffels (1543), John Weddington (1567), John Mellis (1588), Simon Stevin (1605), Richard Dafforne (1632), to name a few, all suggest that the prince or the merchant is the addressee. It is not until the middle of the eighteenth century that the titles suggest that the texts are written for intermediary persons; for example, William Weston, *The Complete Merchant's Clerk* (1754): Richard Roose, *An Essay to Make a Compleat Accomptant* (1760); John Cooke, *The Compting House Assistant* (1764). See H.J. Eldridge, *The Evolution of the Science of Bookkeeping*, second ed., rev. by Leonard Frankland (London: Gee & Company (Publishers) Limited, 1954).

[2] See, for example, the judgment of Fletcher Moulton, L.J., *in re The Spanish Prospecting Co. Ltd.*, (1911) 1 Ch. 92; *The Accountant L.R.*, Vol. XLIII.

Each of these facts of contemporary business requires a modification of the formerly justifiable view that businessmen know what they want and are entitled to have it. When so many individual persons become involved with the accounting process, as producers or as users of financial information, it becomes necessary to discover rules which shall do no violence to the informative function. But who was to do the discovering?

Not the merchants or managers themselves. Being practical men, accustomed to the uncertainties of mercantile affairs, "the slings and arrows of outrageous fortune," they were and apparently still are unconcerned with the nuances of words and symbols. In very many respects they were able to do without formal information, for the constant influx of new information,—on prices, products, processes, territories,—was, and still is, the most common stimulus to action. That being the case, it was of relatively little consequence that accounting statements might diverge from representations of contemporary facts. Further, in their financial dealings with others they were quite prepared to accept that financial statements were mere products of bookkeeping, to be disregarded under pressure of circumstance. Revaluations of assets upwards and downwards, for example, appear to have been treated as *ad hoc* tactical moves, made to be realistic only under severe pressure, but otherwise made to be attractive or distractive. Again, if, in fact, conventional processes failed to reveal pertinent and contemporary facts, on the ground of their own self-interest merchants and managers would be content to leave them alone; for financial statements which are not indeed representative of the facts, particularly "conservative" statements, will serve to shield them from the criticisms of others. All of these possibilities are perfectly good reasons why merchants and managers would not concern themselves with the propriety of accounting rules and methods. To assert that accounting as it is done is as it should be done, because the rules and methods have been developed out of practical use and necessity, is to concede that the above reasons are valid for all users of the results. They are good practical reasons, for managers. They would certainly not be conceded to be good reasons by other users of the resulting information.

As a consequence, or in anticipation, of these opportunistic uses of accounting, legislative and regulatory bodies have intervened. These bodies have been more concerned with prescribing rules than with discovering pertinent rules. True, they have often made inquiries before proceeding to prescribe. But such inquiries are of a political nature, designed to ensure that some consideration is given to the views of those whose interests are affected. In much the same way as we suggested in the preceding paragraph, submissions to committees of inquiry are affected both explicitly and implicitly by the interests of the parties represented. This is admittedly legitimate under democratic principles, or where the effectiveness of the rules eventually prescribed depends on the goodwill and cooperation of parties of interest. But the capacity of deliberative bodies to devise rules which are equitable to all parties depends on the submission of evidence on behalf of all parties, and the cogency of the arguments of those submitting their views. Now it cannot be known in advance whether the interests of others than those obviously concerned will be affected; and the manner of application of chosen rules may adversely influence some who would in advance endorse the principles prescribed. It is quite possible that, although certain principles and rules are laid down, they or their subsequent application may work unexpectedly to the detriment of some parties of interest. In substance, the function of rule making or prescription is to reduce a potentially chaotic set of practices to some degree of manageable uniformity. But we have not yet found who was to discover, rather than to prescribe, rules which would do no violence to the informative function of accounting.

It may be supposed that the task really lay in the hands of accountants. But at the very time when it became necessary to prescribe rules, the practice of accounting was, itself, in a relatively rudimentary condition by present standards.[3] It was, as we have suggested, dominated by ownership or managerial direction. Accountants had then had no experience of the conditions which would come to make it necessary to escape from this direction, namely widespread public investment in corporation securities and highly complex business structures. Therefore, although accountants in public practice may have observed widely divergent practices used by different firms, the closeness of ownership and control would have justified the presumption that these practices nevertheless yielded comprehensible information. Finally, as the skills of the bookkeeper and accountant were then acquired by practice, and as entrants to the profession did not commonly undertake educational programs at a high tertiary level, there was no opportunity for constructive comparison of the art of accounting with other arts and sciences. It would have been surprising indeed, therefore, if even a small number of accountants had envisaged their function as social, not entirely private; as concerned with the more efficient conduct of business and other enterprises under conditions of interdependence by the production of information which is at the same time both privately and socially useful and necessary.

The following conclusions emerge. The development of accounting

[3] The grant of the right of incorporation with limited liability was intended to be accompanied by adequate financial publicity. This may be regarded as the "trading" of a public privilege for a public obligation. Such a legal-political notion was not likely to be appreciated; if appreciated, it appears not to have been respected, once the enabling legislation was passed. The time to which we refer is 1830–1860. See Hunt, *The Development of the Business Corporation in England 1800–1867*, Chaps. IV and VI.

practice, the adoption and abandonment of principles or rules, merely on the basis of what was useful or justifiable at some time results in private usefulness (for concealment or other tactical effects) being accepted as equally good grounds with general informativeness. Communicative and uncommunicative practices alike may thus be justified. And where both may be justified both will be used, to the confusion of people dependent on the result. Second, the passing on of practices as traditions disregards the shifts in the context of practice, in the community at large, which require that traditional modes be reconsidered and indeed changed. A practical art may, thus, come to be practically artless, though ancillary functions may secure its persistence. Third, practices which are found in use side by side will, as a consequence of the above tendencies, be self-contradictory or inconsistent and will yield statements which are inconsistent with the factual relationship of an entity to its environment. Any regular observer of accounting practice and business events will be aware of abundant evidence of each of the consequences mentioned.

ACCOUNTING UNDER CRITICISM AND COMPARISON

Accounting has not been without its critics within and its observers from without. It is of interest to inquire into the effects of their observations on the practice of accounting. We select only a few examples.

A number of scholars have linked the development of business over the past few centuries with the availability of the methods of double-entry bookkeeping.[4] But what may once have been necessary, useful and relevant may well now be otherwise. What then of more recent critics and observers?

During the 1920's, it was manifest to some that the financial affairs of corporations were far less adequately disclosed than their quasi-public nature warranted. Abundant evidence was adduced to the effect that many companies had no consistent policy in respect of depreciation costs; that some varied such charges deliberately for the purpose of smoothing out fluctuations in income; that there were cases in which goodwill and other assets were represented by a single aggregate money amount, when goodwill was by far the larger part of the total, and when indeed goodwill should not appear as an asset at all; that there were long delays in making financial information available; that holding companies were able to withhold information on group debts by reason of the inadequacy of their own balance sheets to reflect the debts of subsidiaries; that balance sheets and income accounts tended, by deliberate intention or by indifference, to

---

4 See, for example, Fred L. Nussbaum, *A History of the Economic Institutions of Modern Europe* (New York: Appleton-Century-Crofts, Inc., 1933), pp. 158ff.; Schumpeter, *Capitalism, Socialism and Democracy*, pp. 122–4.

mislead or to obfuscate readers, in virtue of their highly condensed nature or of the use of technical terms incomprehensible to lay readers, or even to professional readers.[5] The relatively new form of property, the company share, had gripped the imagination of a people unaccustomed to high finance. The concentration of industrial power combined with the fragmentation of ownership demanded "disclosure of all pertinent data [to keep] the spirit of speculation ... in strict confinement."[6]

About the same time the defects and inconsistencies of accounting practices, the naivete of its theory, and the omissions of its expositors were being examined. It was contended that accountants had no complete system of thought about income, and it was pointed out that financial position, or financial condition, was not defined in the literature. In view of the dominant position of these two concepts, these were serious omissions. It was contended that accountants had no theory of value or valuation, and that, hence, balance sheets and income accounts were confused mixtures of measurements made under diverse and conflicting rules.[7] It was alleged that accounting was incomplete and that its processes were mathematically unsound.[8] By recourse to the literature it was shown that "the significance of periodic accounting profit is ... the algebraic sum of the separate significances of the various conventions, doctrines, rules and practices which at any particular time constitute the common law of accounting"; in short, that the accounting concept of profit has no discoverable meaning.[9] It was shown that accounting concepts were inconsistent, self-contradictory; and it was alleged that the financial information which emerged from the use of the rules they entailed was deceptive.[10]

The critics within the profession do not appear as critics for the sake of criticism. They held out visions of a more comprehensive and realistic service than accounting by its nature was then able to yield.[11] Their pleas

[5] See, for example, William Z. Ripley, *Main Street and Wall Street* (Boston: Little, Brown & Company, 1927).

[6] Ripley, *Main Street and Wall Street*, p. 207.

[7] Canning, *The Economics of Accountancy*, pp. 160, 179, 319.

[8] Sweeney, *Stabilized Accounting*, Chap. I.

[9] Stephen Gilman, *Accounting Concepts of Profit* (New York: The Ronald Press Company, 1939), p. 605.

[10] MacNeal, *Truth in Accounting*, Chaps. II and III; Gilman, *Accounting Concepts of Profit*, Chap. 15. Henry Rand Hatfield, "What is the Matter with Accounting?," *The Journal of Accountancy*, Vol. XLIV, No. 4, October 1927.

[11] For example, Thomas H. Sanders, *Company Annual Reports* (Boston: Division of Research, Graduate School of Business Administration, Harvard University, 1949), p. 56. MacNeal's concluding sentences are particularly urgent: "Accounting is at the crossroads. It can yield to inertia, refuse to recognize its own opportunity, ignore the public need, and continue slowly to dig its own grave. Or it can grasp its opportunity, adopt a progressive, scientific attitude with reference to its methods, and thereby serve both the public and itself to an extent scarcely imagined today." MacNeal, *Truth in Accounting*, pp. 323–4.

for a greater regard for truth and the facts of commercial life, and for a "progressive scientific attitude," might have been supposed to command some sympathy.

But none of these criticisms and pleas has had any noticeable influence on the bases of the practice of accounting. Why?

First, the time which has elapsed since serious criticism was offered has been very short as historians reckon time. In all human affairs, it is notorious that beliefs and practices become institutionalized. They become part of the fabric of society. They become matters for acceptance and reverence as articles of faith, rather than as experiments for the learning of better practices. This process itself takes time; accounting has assumed its present form and place over at least four hundred years of commercial use. But to upset any established belief also takes time. The belief in the sanctity of the human body for twelve centuries (from Galen to Vesalius) stood in the way of advances in the study of human anatomy. The belief in a geocentric universe persisted a similar interval, from Ptolemy to Copernicus. Sentiment, habit, fear, and jealousy stood in the way of the acceptance of the views of Harvey on the circulation of the blood, of Jenner on inoculation against smallpox, of Semmelweiss on the prevention of puerperal fever. They have been paraded in opposition to such widely divergent things as steam locomotion, business incorporation, female suffrage, non-Euclidean geometries, deficit budgeting in public finance and automation.[12]

It would be folly, therefore, to suppose that accountants have been remiss in not responding to criticism in the short interval to which we have referred. The institutionalization of accounting has come about through the acceptance of its procedures by businessmen, legislators, lawyers, brokers, and the community at large; it has not been entirely at the hands of accountants.[13] In other fields, general acceptance of new ideas has often had to await the more general development of theoretical and practical knowledge, the assimilation of isolated insights into a comprehensive view. The lack of a comprehensive notion of the function of accounting has militated against the assimilation of the ideas of the critical.

12 For some illustrations of the personal elements in the opposition to new ideas see, for example, Henry E. Sigerist, *The Great Doctors* (Garden City, N.Y.: Doubleday & Company, Inc., 1958); Jürgen Thorwald, *The Century of the Surgeon* (London: Pan Books Ltd., 1961); Jane Muir, *Of Men and Numbers* (New York: Dell Publishing Co., Inc., 1962).

13 See also R.J. Chambers, "Financial Information and the Securities Market," (*Abacus*, Vol. I, No. 1, 1965.) Note also: "The failure of accounts to adapt themselves to the changing needs of management was not due to a reactionary attitude on the part of accountants. Fundamentally, it was due to the fact that accounts have grown into the institutional framework of Society." DR Scott, "The Influence of Statistics Upon Accounting Theory and Technique," *The Accounting Review*, Vol. XXIV, No. 1, January 1949, p. 83.

Indeed it seems highly likely that the pace of events has made difficult the development of any such comprehensive notion. The second decade of the century saw the widespread development of income taxation, which imposed immediate tasks and conceptual problems on accountants when accounting thought was in its infancy. Most taxation laws appear to have taken, as their foundation, the practices of accounting as they then existed. And as rules of law are demonstrably slow to change, accounting practice tended to be constrained by the rigidities of the law. The tendency persists and is one of the stoutest impediments to change. The process of submitting to the findings of the Courts had, of course, begun much earlier. Whether from humility, expedience, or excusable incapacity at an early stage to formulate concepts appropriate to accounting, accountants have relied for definitions and distinctions very heavily on statutes and judicial dicta. It is the function of law to prevent, and the function of the judiciary to resolve, disputes; whereas we have contended that it is the function of accounting to discover facts. The definitions and distinctions of the one may be quite inappropriate to the other. Nevertheless, the strong association with legal and administrative rules may well be considered to have impeded the reexamination of accounting practices, in spite of incisive domestic criticism.

The rate of growth of corporate business, the development of internal accounting, the necessity of elaborate accounting for wartime contracts— to mention only some of the broader types of coercive circumstances—all thrust heavily upon the profession. Under the influence of these developments, it seems understandable that opportunities for reflection on criticisms from within would be limited. Some action, expedient or experimental, was more in demand than reflection.

ACCOUNTING AND ECONOMICS

As accounting and economics are generally concerned with different aspects of the same thing, economic behavior, it may have been supposed that accountants and economists would have benefited mutually from their respective literatures. This appears to have occurred only to a very slight extent, and even to a misleading extent. Much of the economic theory of the firm was built first on the assumption of perfectly competitive markets, one of the assumptions of which is perfect knowledge of the market by operators in it and, presumably, perfect responses to that knowledge.

In particular, entrepreneurs were supposed to base their actions on knowledge of present prices and beliefs about the behavior of costs and prices in the future; they were and are supposed to make their anticipatory calculations on these foundations. Generally, no questions were raised about the use of knowledge acquired in the course of past experiences; for as decisions are always about a future process or state, it is sufficient to consider the future in the light of the present, it being presumed that the present state is discoverable. If the present state is discoverable and the characteristics of future transactions can be estimated, hypothetical revenue and cost curves and schedules may be derived. But if the present state is discovered as a product of a series of events up to any present time, and if the conventions relating to the recording of that series of events may influence the entrepreneur's appreciation of the position of his firm, some theory of the link between recorded experiences and anticipatory calculations is necessary as a foundation for a theory of entrepreneurial behavior. If present position imposes constraints on action, some theory of the discovery of present position is necessary.

To such questions the attitudes of economists have varied widely. Some have ignored the matter, supposing that the market will resolve the problems of choice notwithstanding that there may be other sources of information beside the market and inconsistent with it. Others have ignored the matter, supposing that other sources of information will necessarily be consistent with the market. Some economists have directed critical attention to the flaw implicit in disregard of the variable dimension of the monetary unit and the variability of prices generally.[14] Others have noted that adherence to the purchase price basis in accounting for non-monetary assets has produced the variety of rules in current use, the consequence of which is that there is no determinate solution to the problem of income measurement.[15]

The interest of some economists in the product of accounting processes has increased with increasing attention to the derivation of macroeconomic magnitudes, to social accounting. Those who have wanted to discover *ex post* the aggregate consequences of economic activities of whole communities or sections of them have had to make corrections for known defects, in relation to their purposes, in conventional business calculations. Inventory prices, depreciation allowances, and measurements made for intervals through which specific prices and the general level of prices have changed, have been adjusted. But these adjustments have been regarded, alike by economists and accountants, as necessary only for the peculiar purpose of social accounting, and not, therefore, to be considered of the essence of accounting for other purposes.[16]

---

14 von Mises, *The Theory of Money and Credit*, p. 204.

15 Lutz and Lutz, *The Theory of Investment of the Firm*, Chaps. XVIII, XIX.

16 See, for example, Richard Ruggles, *An Introduction to National Income and Income Analysis* (New York: McGraw-Hill Book Company, 1949); John P. Powelson, *Economic Accounting* (New York: McGraw-Hill Book Company, 1955).

Again, some general economics texts have appended to their chapters on income or similar topics a brief treatment of conventional accounting, but without any attempt to question the difference in connotation of income as it is used in the text and the concept of income implied in the accounting treatment.[17] Other writers have briefly referred to balance sheets, but only to conclude that except for short-term assets and obligations, the methods of assigning money magnitudes to items in balance sheets produce irrelevancies.[18] One writer indeed has proffered the disarming view that "accounts are bound to be untruths . . . but accounting is not lies" and that its products should be used as "evidence rather than as definitive information."[19] One wonders what an untruth is evidence of, except of untruthfulness; and what use readers can possibly make of "untrue evidence," surely a contradiction in terms. None of the above treatments does much to bridge the gap between economists and accountants in their ways of looking at things.

On the other hand accountants have generally been untrained in economics and many have professed unconcern with the questions posed by economists and the methods employed by them. And it seems that some who have attempted to rationalize the views held by accountants and economists on matters of common interest have sometimes confused the anticipatory viewpoint of economics with the retrospective viewpoint of accounting. Marginal cost in economics, for example, is not what is yielded by direct costing.[20] The role of replacement cost in economics is not the same as the role of assignments of monetary magnitudes to balance sheet items. The valuation of which economists speak is not the assignment of measured magnitudes to variables which we have contended is the function of accounting. Marginal cost, replacement cost, and valuation are all anticipatory. Any attempt to employ these terms or to discover their magnitudes in the course of or as the result of a process of retrospective calculation, confuses the distinctive difference between the past and the future. Awareness of the necessity of preparing accounting statements which shall be relevant to the future is not lacking. But the end is not achieved by simply borrowing economic concepts which have an inde-

[17] For example, Paul A. Samuelson, *Economics, An Introductory Analysis* (New York: McGraw-Hill Book Company, 1948), Chap. 6; Bach, *Economics, An Introduction to Analysis and Policy*, Chap. 17.

[18] For example, P.W.S. Andrews, *Manufacturing Business* (London: Macmillan & Co., Ltd., 1949), p. 67; Richardson, *Information and Investment*, pp. 166ff.

[19] K.E. Boulding, "Economics and Accounting: The Uncongenial Twins," *Studies in Accounting Theory*, W.T. Baxter and S. Davidson, eds. (London: Sweet & Maxwell Ltd., 1962), p. 55.

[20] As expounded, for example, by F.C. Lawrence and E.A. Humphreys, *Marginal Costing* (London: Macdonald & Evans, 1947); N.A.C.A. Research Series No. 23, *Direct Costing*.

pendent function in the making of choices different from and complementary to the results of a well designed accounting system.

For the intellectual distance between accountants and economists we hold neither to account. But its existence we may suppose to be in some measure responsible for the failure of accountants to pursue the more rigorous procedures of related disciplines.

ACCOUNTING UNDER SOCIAL AND ECONOMIC STRESS

The kind of criticism to which we have referred is in a sense highly localized; it is criticism by persons, isolated in time and, generally, isolated in intellectual milieu. But there have also been some publicly observable events which have focused attention on deficiencies of accounting practices. Again, we may distinguish external and internal sources of stress.

There have been many occasions during the present century when commercial and financial misdemeanors of considerable news value have cast doubt upon the adequacy of accounting to inform those who need information to protect their interests. No industrial community has been free of them—to name just a few, there have been the Royal Mail affair in Britain, the Kreuger collapse, and the McKesson and Robbins case. Each of these had some effects, through changes in the specific rules or principles sanctioned by legislative and regulatory bodies. Had there been any framework within which these rules could have been integrated with other rules and principles, their effects may have been general rather than specific. But, in the event, the new rules displaced no old rules; they became simply additional rules, additional alternatives. However, there have been other more general stimuli as well.

Severe post war inflation in Europe after 1918 provided exemplary conditions for the demonstration of the inadequacy of an accounting which disregarded monetary instability. The speculative fever during the 1920's, particularly in the United States, was accompanied by upward revaluations of assets on a large scale. The stock market crash of 1929 was followed by much soul searching by the New York Stock Exchange and the American accounting profession. One of the consequences was the sacrifice of the notion of a dynamic accounting which would keep pace with shifts in economic affairs, perhaps in revulsion from the excesses of the preceding years. The cost doctrine was elevated to the status of an article of faith and embodied in regulations under the New Deal legislation creating the Securities and Exchange Commission.

We do not protest the value of regulation to secure uniformity of practices in a field of wide public interest. We do question the formulation of rules before adequate analysis of the matters in respect of which they are made. The cost doctrine, in fact, disregards one of the most important features of an adaptive society and condemns an accounting based on it to being a sterile half-history.

An incident in the process of establishing the cost doctrine may be instructive. With reference to the general import of the accounting operation, it was observed, "In an earlier age, when capital assets were inconsiderable and business units in general smaller and less complex than they are today, it was possible to value assets with comparative ease and accuracy and to measure the progress made from year to year by annual valuations. With the growing mechanization of industry, and with corporate organizations becoming constantly larger, more completely integrated and more complex, this has become increasingly impracticable."[21] It seems permissible to consider the statement as asserting both an ideal, and the impracticability of pursuing the ideal, of measuring progress from year to year by an attempt to put a present price upon assets from time to time. But when business firms become more complex, their administration requires an instrument no less efficient as an indicator of progress than is available to less complex firms. Indeed the instrumentation must be more complete and more efficient for much more is at stake. Jet airplanes carrying scores of passengers would have been impossible, if, on looking at the meager instrumentation of the earliest airplanes, the discovery of any more comprehensive instrumentation was deemed to be impracticable. The growing complexity of business required a form of communication no less pertinent than before, even if the process of its derivation were to be much more sophisticated. The assertion that this was becoming increasingly impracticable amounts to capitulation in the face of complexity. The adoption of the cost doctrine was evidence of a tendency, already noted, of systems to seek a function they can perform when the performance of an original function imposes stresses beyond their capacity.[22] Ideally, one would suppose that technical advancement would brook no impediment. But to give direction to advances, a clear statement of the functions and limitations of the expertise is prerequisite. The general literature of the time suggests that the prerequisite was lacking.

Had there been any solid core of accounting principles, other than

[21] Letter of the Chairman, Special Committee on Cooperation with Stock Exchanges of the American Institute of Accountants to The Committee on Stock List, New York Stock Exchange, Sept. 22, 1932. Reproduced in Bishop Carleton Hunt, ed., *Twenty-Five Years of Accounting Responsibility 1911–1936, Essays and Discussions of George Oliver May* (New York: American Institute Publishing Co., Inc., 1936), p. 113.

[22] See p. 143 *supra*.

mere rules of practice, it is possible that a less extreme remedy would have been sought. Other countries were not at the time so strongly committed to the discovery of a remedy for what in the United States was seen as an abuse. But through time, the cost doctrine came to be accepted elsewhere, though with less dogmatism in practice due to the absence of anything as specific as the Securities and Exchange Commission regulations on financial publicity. The potential consequence is even greater divergence in practices than in the United States; but, at least, the possibility remains open that, through the forces of the market, some companies at least are obliged to disclose more up-to-date information from time to time than is yielded by rigid adherence to the cost doctrine.

Attempts have been made to rationalize the propriety of the cost doctrine on a variety of grounds since its apparent adoption. We say "apparent adoption," for there does not seem to be any ground for supposing that such a doctrine has been followed generally, either in the past or at present. The balance date pricing of short-term inventory at the lower of cost and market prices has a long history and it is still very widely used.[23][24] The last-in, first-out principle can only be argued to be a cost based method, if the date for which a cost is stated is deemed to be immaterial; we have strongly contested this position. Revaluations of durable assets have been and continue to be made in places where the cost doctrine is said to be fundamental.

Perhaps the most universal justification for holding this doctrine is the so-called stewardship notion, the import of which is that business managers are accountable for the money tokens that come into their hands. No doubt they are, but a cash account is all that would be required to serve this function. The superstructure of accounting processes and financial statements generally would have no justification if this were the primary function of accounting.

There can be little doubt that the pressures brought to bear to introduce LIFO, methods of accelerated depreciation, and initial investment allowances, from time to time and place to place, have all stemmed from the basic deficiencies of the cost doctrine. In a sense, they all support the position argued in preceding chapters; they are superimpositions on initial purchase prices chosen so that the results approximate current costs. That this was their general effect has not been clear because accounting has been supposed to be committed to quite a different principle. If it had

---

[23] A.C. Littleton, "A Genealogy for 'Cost or Market,'" *The Accounting Review*, Vol. XVI, No. 2, June 1941; Lawrence L. Vance, "The Authority of History in Inventory Valuation," *The Accounting Review*, Vol. XVIII, No. 3, July 1943.

[24] See the periodical publications, American Institute of Certified Public Accountants, *Accounting Trends and Techniques;* Canadian Institute of Chartered Accountants, *Financial Reporting in Canada;* and for comment, Chambers, "Financial Information and the Securities Market," *Abacus,* Vol. I, No. 1, 1965.

been clear, that is to say, if there had been any attempt to find the general proposition under which all these *ad hoc* devices may be subsumed, there would have been less tolerance for the contradictory elements of the cost doctrine and its appendages.

The resurgence of inflation beginning in the mid-forties reawakened debate on the merits of static accounting, bound to original cost of acquisition. In Europe, South America, and Japan, the severity of the problem brought forth official sanctions for variations of the initial cost doctrine. In England and the United States professional associations were moved to inquire into the possibility of preferable alternatives. But, under the pressure of immediate circumstance, it is notoriously difficult to investigate and to report dispassionately on practices which have become habitual and to the justification of which so much effort has recently been devoted. One inquiry into the vexed question of income determination produced a majority report and a host of reservations and dissents.[25] Perhaps for the latter reason, no substantive change occurred in theory or practice.[26]

However the matter did not rest there. Professional associations have felt an increasing commitment to the specification of rules of practice. In England and in the United States, extensive statements on particular procedures which were deemed to be allowable or acceptable have been promulgated. But in neither case has such a series of pronouncements been preceded by a clear statement of the function of accounting which would serve as a test for the admission of new rules in place of old rules. The consequence has been a vast proliferation of alternative possible rules, having demonstrably contradictory effects on the determination of income and financial position.[27] These rules all have some common sense, practical justification. But as they are not regarded as the occasion or reason for

[25] Study Group on Business Income, *Changing Concepts of Business Income* (New York: The Macmillan Company, 1952).

[26] Some conclusions of Thurman Arnold seem apposite: "The confusion accompanying most liberal reform movements is due to the fact that they are generally attempts to make the institution practice what it preaches in a situation where, if the ideal were followed, the function of the institution could not be performed ... A social need which runs counter to an abstract ideal will always be incompetently met until it gets a philosophy of its own. The process of building up new abstractions to justify filling new needs is always troublesome in any society, and may be violent." Arnold, *The Folklore of Capitalism*, pp. 375, 378. The import of which, for our purposes, is that, without a new or newly accepted philosophy of the function of accounting, piecemeal proposals for amelioration are unlikely to be generally received.

[27] For the evidence of diversity see *Accounting Trends and Techniques*, published annually by the American Institute of Certified Public Accountants. A comparison of Australian, Canadian, and United States practices is given in Chambers, "Financial Information and the Securities Market." For a recent demonstration of the divergent effects of different practices, see Leonard M. Savoie, "Accounting Improvement: How fast, How far?," *Harvard Business Review*, July-August 1963, p. 148.

jettisoning less acceptable rules, the whole body of rules lacks the disciplined and orderly quality which characterizes systematic development.[28]

More recently, however, there are signs that, at least in the United States, professional associations sense a commitment not merely to pronouncement but to more rigorous inquiry.[29] Whether, as previously, this will issue in debate without impact on practice remains to be seen.[30] But the very existence of an inquisitive attitude, it may be supposed, will tend to spread an appreciation of the fact that practices are debatable at a deeper level than their surface effects, and will condition attitudes towards the acceptance of a more comprehensive and consistent system of thought.

PROFESSIONALISM

We consider one other factor which appears to have some bearing on the development of accounting practice. There are some grounds for believing that bookkeepers were long regarded as a specially skilled class; the skills of writing and arithmetic have not long been the skills of the common man. More particularly, the special forms and processes of bookkeeping have nurtured the notion that special skill is requisite; and it seems clear that when laws began to be written on the keeping of corporate accounts, the legislative elite believed that some degree of special skill was, in fact, possessed by those who were to keep proper books of account.

In fact, accountants in England labored diligently to acquire the exclusive public recognition which is commonly the mark of the social acknowledgment of a profession.[31] Associations of accountants assumed powers of disciplinary action over their members and control over admission to their associations by prescribing experience and examinations. These are the externally observable features of almost all professional associations. They

28 " ... in creative thought common sense is a bad master. Its sole criterion for judgment is that the new ideas shall look like the old ones. In other words it can only act by suppressing originality." A.N. Whitehead, *An Introduction to Mathematics* (New York: Oxford University Press, Inc., 1948), p. 116.

29 See "Report to Council [of the American Institute of Certified Public Accountants] of the Special Committee on Research Program," *The Journal of Accountancy*, December 1958. Examples of the tendency towards more rigorous analysis are the studies which have emerged from the program: particularly, Maurice Moonitz, *The Basic Postulates of Accounting* (1961), and Robert T. Sprouse and Maurice Moonitz, *A Tentative Set of Broad Accounting Principles for Business Enterprises* (1962), Accounting Research Studies Nos. 1 and 3.

30 Against a much wider setting Arnold observed: "Public debate is necessarily only a method of giving unity and morale to organizations. It is ceremonial and designed to create enthusiasm, to increase faith and quiet doubt. It can have nothing to do with the actual practical analysis of facts." Arnold, *The Folklore of Capitalism*, p. 379.

31 See Nicholas H. Stacey, *English Accountancy, 1800 to 1954* (London: Gee and Company (Publishers) Limited, 1954), Part I.

are valued by the society and by the members of associations as giving some warrant of skill and capacity for expert service in a limited field, and as giving some nucleus of solidarity against sectional interests which would, in relation to that field, impair the capacity for giving expert, disinterested service. But these features, valuable as they are, are not of themselves sufficient.

In the first place, the notion of self-discipline is not to be regarded solely as agreement not to engage in activities, outside the field of expertise, which may be inimical to the association. The heart of the notion of professional self-discipline is self-discipline *within* the field of expertise. This entails that there shall be a body of specialized knowledge which satisfies the criteria of objectivity; knowledge *about* the field of expertise, of the matters to which one's skill is to be applied, rather than knowledge of skills only. While ever there is doubt about the function served by the exercise of a skill, the existence and the extent of this necessary body of knowledge remains in doubt. It is then quite competent for the practitioner to exercise his skill towards any number of conflicting functions, for his subjective judgment is the sole test of admissible functions. A practitioner will necessarily apply his judgment to the particular case before him; what professional self-discipline will forbid is his right to determine for himself his role in general. Functions, and therefore roles, may change through time. But it seems evident that lack of a definition of function in the course of the growth of accounting practice was contributory to the development of diverse rules on an *ad hoc* basis, a development quite inconsistent with professional self-discipline.

Professional self-discipline entails that the practitioner shall be subject to the exercise of sanctions by his professional equals, but again with respect to his professional behavior. In the absence of a body of specialized knowledge and an avowed function, such sanctions cannot be exercised, for, on the one hand, a potentially deviant practitioner will not know from what he deviates, and, on the other, his peers will not know the criteria by which deviant behavior is to be identified. If sanctions are exercised in such a case they can be exercised only on conventions as to what constitutes *non*professional behavior, not on what constitutes *un*professional behavior. The codes of ethics of professional associations tend to indicate what their members may not do, rather than give a positive indication of what constitutes professional behavior.[32]

---

[32] Of seventeen points representing the rules of professional conduct listed by Carey only one is positive in the sense to which we allude: "accountants must conform with generally accepted accounting and auditing standards." John L. Carey, "Practical Applications of Professional Ethics," Chap. 5 in *C.P.A. Handbook* (New York: American Institute of Accountants, 1957 printing). Even in respect of this proposition, the question "what are these generally accepted standards?" has not been settled. For some observations on professionalism generally see, for example, Blau and Scott, *Formal Organizations*, pp. 60 ff.

One of the bulwarks of professional integrity is the principle that the practitioner shall not become involved, otherwise than in respect of his professional field, with his client in the practice of his profession. The principle does not restrain involvement outside of the practitioner-client relationship with persons who may at the same time be clients. In the practice of medicine and teaching, the principle is commonly phrased in terms of emotional involvement, for emotional involvement prejudices the exercise of independent judgment. It may not be so obvious, though it seems unquestionably to be the case, that if in the exercise of his profession an accountant accepts the judgment, the opinion, or the tactical point of view of managers or other officers on matters of professional concern without independent corroboration, he commits himself to involvement of a substantially similar kind. To contend that managers shall have what they demand, where what they demand may prejudice the preservation of the interests of others or the exercise of judgment by others, is to forgo professional independence; to admit that intellectual or emotional involvement or self-interest dominate. Such a situation is the antithesis of professionalism; it is evidence of intellectual serfdom.

It seems not unlikely that this implication of submission to direction and influence was not apprehended in the course of the development of accounting as a professional practice from bookkeeping as a skill. Indeed, there are grounds for supposing that it has not been apprehended in more recent times. There has been much discussion of the role of the accountant in the managerial process, and of anticipatory "accounting." The implication of much of it is that accountants should concern themselves with futures, with valuations, with possible specific courses of action, and indeed with decision-making of the substantive kind. Now there is no reason why accountants, as persons, may not engage in any of these kinds of speculation. As persons, they may assume positions of executive responsibility, becoming executants instead of accountants. But it does not follow that anything an accountant does or becomes is for that reason to be deemed to be accounting. Which brings us to a further facet of professionalism.

The professional is an expert in a strictly bounded field. His role in society is acknowledged only because he professes in a bounded field. He is not expected to be expert in other fields. As evidence, we may note that if an expert presumes to pronounce in other fields, even his prestige in his own becomes questioned if not tarnished. A professional man is not expected to be wise in a general sense; to profess general wisdom is everyman's prerogative. The sage, the seer, and the soothsayer are not regarded as experts in a society where there is respect for skill based on specialized knowledge. It would not be surprising that if accountants concerned themselves with the discovery of the objective facts of the past and present and also with the subjective beliefs and possibilities of the future, their expertise in both areas would suffer and the recognition of that expertise by social acknowledgment of professional status would also suffer. There is ample evidence in the official utterances of officers of associations of accountants and by rank and file members that they, themselves, do not believe their associations to be accorded the social recognition given to other professions. If there are grounds for this belief, we may suppose them to lie in the lack of specificity of function to which we have already referred.

Accountants may not consider themselves as part of the management team, to use a current phrase, without acknowledging the notion of a team. A team does not consist of one may playing many roles; it consists of a number of men each performing his assigned role. It is our contention that the role of the accountant is the discovery of certain kinds of facts. We may suppose that inadequate apprehension of the limitations necessary for expertness and inadequate appreciation of the importance of present knowledge as a basis for all choice and action has had not a little bearing on the profusion of alternative accounting methods.

CONCLUSION

The observations of this chapter are principally of a sociological kind. We have sought to answer such question as: how does it happen that accounting practices do not coincide with the reasoned conclusions of the preceding chapters? how does it happen that, whereas in other disciplines there is a tendency towards unification of ideas and uniformity of practices, in accounting the tendency has been towards diffuseness of ideas and diversity of practices? Evidence from different directions appears to converge towards several conclusions.

As accounting has been regarded as a purely technical operation, and as in its early development there were no avowed principles other than the formal principles of bookkeeping, its concepts and practices arose in part from the demands, pressures, and constraints of businessmen and interpreters of the law, and in part from the inertia of the community generally. The diffuse nature of the interests of members of society at large is ineffective against the immediate coercion of circumstance; and whereas accountants, internal and external to firms, may have assumed a professional role, the immediate pressure of ownership and management groups has tended to make the accounting process subservient to those groups and subservient in an inconsistent manner as the temporary exigencies of those groups have changed from time to time.

In these circumstances, the generation of professional solidarity is thwarted, for if there is no uniform principle by reference to which professional competence may be judged, there is no foundation on which a stand may be taken against incompetence or wilful deviation. The process of development appears to have been circular and self-defeating. In the absence of a uniform guiding principle, businessmen were obliged to decide what practices should be adopted. In the absence of any means of focusing their dissatisfaction, because they knew not who was responsible, the investing public was obliged to accept what information they were given. In the absence of any feedback of a substantial kind, from the public or from the management group itself, the accounting processes became habitual but open to accretion. No particular group may be held responsible for this state of affairs; but every group suffers from its consequences.[33] The consequences are the difference between the practices which emerge from analysis of the relationships between information, evaluation, and action which have concerned us in previous chapters, and the wealth of contemporary practices which cloud the vision and obfuscate the judgment of accountants and users of accounting information alike.

It may seem that, as between the general system of ideas put forward in preceding chapters and the system of ideas underlying extant practices, there are material differences which imply outright rejection of many contemporary practices. And it may be contended that existing practices cannot be as radically defective as our argument implies, otherwise business firms, investors, and financial intermediaries could scarcely have survived and profited. But such an argument ignores three factors at least. The first is the resilience of men and of societies of men. Human societies did not disintegrate under the despotic monarchies and oligarchies of the past; we may now consider such forms of government archaic, even barbaric, but men have survived them. Mankind did not perish for want of knowledge of anatomy, of the circulatory systems, or of immunology. Men are able to communicate with other men to a limited extent, even though their verbal languages have nothing in common.[34] The second factor ignored by the hypothetical argument is the enormous richness of the

---

33 The growth of such a state of affairs is not to be considered as due to lack of intelligence on the part of any person or any class of persons. One may persist in acting in a stereotyped fashion, in relation to a given system, "because his thinking about each aspect of that system is isolated from [his thinking about other aspects] and he cannot see the interrelationships and the necessary overall changes that must be made; and . . . because of the rigidity of his concepts induced by his emotional thinking about 'the system.'" Krech and Crutchfield, *Theory and Problems of Social Psychology*, p. 141.

34 " . . . we must not deny the probability that societies can tolerate, even without disintegration, much more disorganization and even ruin than many people recognize." David Riesman with Nathan Glazer and Reuel Denney, *The Lonely Crowd*, (Garden City, N.Y.: Doubleday & Company, Inc.; abridged; original publ. Yale University Press, 1950), p. 45.

circulation of information other than information yielded by the accounting process. A society like a natural organism can survive in spite of the loss of some of its cognitive apparatus. The third factor ignored is that many firms have not survived and many investors have suffered heavily through defects, not of judgment, but of the information produced by the accounting systems on which they have relied.

But the general system proposed does not, in any case, entail rejection of the system of ideas underlying extant practices. Rather, it entails the consistent adoption of many of the reasons for existing practices, whereas existing practice (as distinct from specific practices) accepts the admission and rejection of its own principles simultaneously.[35] Consider some examples. Periodical summarization and reporting is an accepted principle; but devices which carry forward and defer the recognition in accounting of events occurring in a given period are also accepted. The matching of costs and revenues in contemporary terms is accepted if the last-in, first-out method of short-term inventory pricing is accepted; but at the same time other principles of pricing are permitted. The desirability of consistency of financial statements, within themselves, is admitted, and is entailed in the double-entry principle; but the application of such methods as the last-in, first-out method gives inconsistent balance sheets and income accounts; for while income accounts are an approximation to matching in contemporary terms, balance sheets become increasingly less representative of financial position in contemporary terms. The variability of prices is admitted, at least by the recognition of the effects of depreciation, the pricing of marketable securities, and the lower of cost and market rule for pricing short-term inventories; but in many other respects its consequences are disregarded. Examples could be multiplied.

Periodical summarization, matching, and consistency (and many other such principles) are constituent parts of the conceptual scheme presented; and for the same reasons as they are parts of the traditional scheme. The difference between the two, therefore, lies not in basic rationale, but in the consistency with which the consequences of reasons, already acceptable and accepted, are themselves accepted. We have been concerned not with the mere survival of business, nor with the generation of information which may, under the same style and form, differ in quality from time to time as choices between opposing accounting principles are exercised. Rather we have been concerned with the design of information systems which will enable cooperative systems to advance their affairs as knowledgeably as ingenuity and reason can secure and as human limitations will permit.

[35] See also R.J. Chambers, *The Resolution of Some Paradoxes in Accounting* (Vancouver: Faculty of Commerce and Business Administration, University of British Columbia, 1963).

Argument

14.11   The totality of the circumstances and components of every problem situation, every action and every experience are unique and uniquely interrelated.
(*1.32*, 1.34, 1.37, 2.24, 2.28, *3.11*, *3.12*, 3.14)

14.12   The solution of unique problems is the characteristic feature of all practical activity.
(2.24, 2.25, 14.11)

14.13   The time available for reflection and action being limited, analysis of the components of similar problem situations with the object of deriving general solutions is limited.
(*1.18*, *1.23*, *1.52*, *1.72*, 1.76, 14.12)

14.14   The greater the complexity of any problem situation or any class of such situations, the smaller is the possibility of testing beliefs employed in their resolution.
(1.75, 14.11, 14.13)

14.15   The greater the variety of problem situations occurring in the experience of any person, the less probable is the derivation of general solutions.
(*1.16*, *1.17*, *1.18*, 14.13)

14.16   The greater the complexity of any problem situation the greater is the tendency to rely on precedent and transmitted precept.
(*1.23*, 1.45, *1.61*)

14.17   Every precedent is unique; the interpretation or weight given to any component of a precedent is subjective.
(1.67, 14.11, 14.16)

14.18   The greater the dependence on precedent of any class of actors, the greater the diversity of rules which will prevail among that class of actors as a whole.
(*1.41*, *3.12*, 14.17)

14.19   The greater the diversity of rules generally prevailing in respect of the derivation and communication of information, the greater the entropy of the system.
(*7.51*, 8.35, 8.36, 14.18)

14.21   The greater the complexity of any class of actions, the greater is the number of causes assignable to any specific event.
(*1.41*, 1.75, 14.11)

14.22   The greater the number of causes assignable, the greater the probability that causes will be assigned subjectively, that is in accordance with the bias of the assignor.
(*1.21*, *1.22*, 14.21)

14.23   Increasing entropy of an information system is a potential cause of financial failure and loss.
(1.68, 8.36, 14.19)

14.24   The greater the subjectivity in assigning causes, the greater the tendency to disregard as a cause the increasing entropy of the system.

(14.22, 14.23)

14.31   The greater the isolation of any part of a system from its related parts, the greater the tendency for entropy to increase in that part.

(7.52, *12.11*, *12.17*, 12.28)

14.32   The theory of the role or function of accounting is related to the theory of economic behavior in organized systems; the practice of accounting is related to actual economic behavior in organized systems.

(*4.41*, *4.42*)

14.33   *The theory and practice of accounting have been isolated from related disciplines and practices.*

14.34   Isolation has impeded the feedback which would operate against the tendency for entropy to increase.

(*7.53*, 7.54, 14.31, 14.32, *14.33*)

14.41   The less specific the definition of any named role or function, the greater is the probability that it will include or come to include diverse functions.

(*3.31*, 8.35)

14.42   The less specific the definition of any function, the greater is the difficulty of discovering and restraining deviant behaviors.

(14.17, 14.41)

14.43   The wider the range of activities undertaken by any person, the less expert is that person in respect of any given activity.

(*1.13*, 1.15, *1.17*)

14.44   The wider the range of activities undertaken by any class of persons, the less is the possibility of self-discipline within that class, and the less expert is the class as a whole.

(*3.12*, 14.42, 14.43)

14.45   Any tendency to widen the range of activities undertaken by any class of persons is a tendency towards increasing entropy which may only be reversed by further differentiation of functions.

(1.15, *1.17*, *3.21*, 14.44)

14.51   An observable tendency towards the reduction to systematic form of the propositions of accounting may be expected to reverse the tendency for entropy to increase.

(8.35, 14.19 14.34)

Epilogue

We have not come to the end of the road. In a very real sense, much of the journey lies ahead. Only the broadest questions have been broached, and perhaps not all of those. To the minutiae of everyday transactions and their treatment in accounting, little attention has been given. But having examined the common and general problems which have given rise to the greatest amount of contention, and having found what seem to be practicable and consistent solutions to these, it seems improbable that lesser problems would strain the conclusions. The history of the development of knowledge cautions us against overrating the extent of our knowledge at any time, and against too strong a commitment to it. Nevertheless, we believe that progress has been made in some directions, the nature of which may be briefly sketched.

A RESUMÉ

At the outset the general and specific features of contemporary practice were disregarded so that the "brute facts" with which accounting practices must cope could be examined without confusion. The analysis proceeded on the basis of the present characteristics of industrial societies, their basic laws, customs, and institutions. As these are relatively slow to change, the conclusions may be expected to be pertinent under conditions which have prevailed at least for some time past; the evidence adduced in support of many propositions would otherwise not be regarded as evidence at all. The conclusions may also be expected to be pertinent for some time to come.

The foundation of the inquiry lies in the postulated limitations of the capacities of men, the goal-oriented nature of rational behavior, and the features of behavior under conditions of interdependence of persons, scarcity of means in relation to ends, and uncertainty as to the future. Scarcity of means entails individual concern about more or less. The role of money as a medium of exchange reduces this concern, in part but a significant part, to more or less general command over scarce means; the necessary function of monetary calculation emerges for all persons and institutions which buy or sell goods and services for whatever purpose.

It was found to be possible to separate and distinguish an aspect of monetary calculation, the unique function of which is to provide knowledge of a classified but aggregative kind not otherwise available to actors. This knowledge of financial position and of periodical changes in financial position is antecedent to and an essential foundation of all evaluations and choices. Financial position was held to be independent of future expectations, expectations being formed on the basis of the facts represented by a statement of financial position. The facts, thus discovered and represented, limit the expectations which may be entertained and the actions which may be undertaken. Only if the facts are discovered and represented as clearly and as well as the instruments of discovery permit will they serve to temper the ebullience or to foster the venturesomeness of actors. The uniqueness and universality of this aspect of monetary calculation were the bases on which a specialized set of processes, accounting processes, could be justified. The domain of accounting was defined accordingly.

That ends are served by the possession and use of means, and that all means are the subject of legal rights in favor of particular persons or other entities, enabled us to deduce the double-entry principle. It is the great merit of the double-entry principle that it brings simultaneously within one framework measures of the *economic properties* of resources and of the *legal or equitable rights* of others in those resources. A set of rules giving effect to this principle was developed, within the framework of which the financial aspects of events, transactions, and the relationships of a given entity with the rest of the society can be represented. That a knowledge of aggregate magnitudes and relationships between subaggregates is necessary entails that this system shall have the properties of a measurement system, that the specific magnitudes of the system shall be the products of a measurement process. Measurements of the effects of events and transactions on financial position are made by reference to market prices, for prices are the indicators of what must be done to shift one's position to one's preferred position in a market economy. The ideal measurement is the contemporary monetary equivalent (or current cash equivalent) of assets and obligations, costs, and revenues.

In the case of continuing entities, a continuous record of changes in financial position is necessary if financial position or any feature of it is to be discovered with ease whenever necessary. This record will be isomorphic with the events and transactions it represents. The events referred to include changes in prices during the holding of goods and changes in the purchasing power of money, both of which are ineluctable elements of the environment. They impose difficulties on the measurement of changes through time and of positions at points of time where markets are thin or imperfect, for we rely on markets to generate current cash equivalents or market resale prices of goods. Some ways of approximating the ideal were explored. Adopting the view, common in other fields, that methods are always open to improvement and measurements are always open to refinement, a continuous attempt to improve the quality of the information yielded by approximation methods was recommended. In practice, the possibility of there being errors of estimation and approximation was seen to be met by margins of safety in the disposition of income, by reserves.

The particular function of accounting, the discovery of the facts which at any time predict the limits of action, is thus strictly a scientific function; a continuous research function, inasmuch as the facts are continually changing. Its processes will necessarily be carried out with the same detachment from the facts, and the same pertinacity in seeking the facts, as any other form of scientific inquiry.

In the typical situation, the function of accounting is divorced from the functions of evaluating and acting. The consequential problems of determining what information is relevant to action and under what conditions that information is communicated to actors of different kinds were explored. It emerged that financial communications are essentially social communications—social in a wider or a narrower sense, as the case may be. The messages expressed in the technical language or sign-system of accounting are not, therefore, a matter of private meaning only, private to the originator or to any specific receiver. Their function in the adaptive process entails that they will be widely interpretable, and that the methods of their derivation shall be substantially uniform. The statements generated shall also have the properties of contemporaneity, only thus being relevant to contemporary action situations; and objectivity, only thus being relevant to the wide range of potential respondents and only thus being capable of independent authentication or corroboration. Both financial statements expressing relationships of an entity with the rest of the society, and financial statements (cost accounts) expressing relationships and events domestic to an entity, will necessarily be of the same substantive quality; otherwise, effective adaptation within the entity with the object of meeting the environment beyond it will be impossible.

The greater part of the argument concerned itself with business enterprises, but some consideration was given to non-business entities, those oriented to ends which do not include profit making. It appeared in the latter case that the financial or economic aspects of operations are subject to quite different constraints and entail a form of accounting different in material respects from that appropriate to business-type entities.

The type of accounting which emerged from the analysis differs from the contemporary practices of accounting. Some observations on the conditions under which the literature and practice of accounting have developed provided a tentative explanation of the divergence. The tendency for new influences to assert themselves gave rise to the presumption that the future elimination or reduction of those divergences may be expected.

In all, then, the inquiry has yielded both a theory indicative of an ideal system of accounting within the framework of the postulates adopted, and an explanatory theory of contemporary practice. The explanatory theory comprises the whole work, embracing the derivation of what might be expected under the circumstances represented by the postulates (which are believed to correspond with the observable environment of accounting) and the examination of the conditions under which what is indeed found differs from what might be expected.

THE METHOD EMPLOYED

We have attempted to employ the methods of other forms of rigorous, empirical inquiry. We have tried to discover the elements of the environment and to represent them in terms and basic propositions which might command general assent. To this end, we have sought to be explicit at all points. That certain terms in common use are commonly understood has been assumed; it is, nevertheless, possible that some such terms are not as commonly understood as we have supposed. But an effort has been made to define all terms of a technical nature, for the system of ideas and conclusions can be no better than its definitions. These definitions differ in some respects from the definitions of others; their formulation has been influenced by the necessity that the resulting system shall have adequate linkages with observable events and things and shall yield comprehensible results. Where propositions necessary to the argument have been postulated, their postulation has been made explicit; where postulates are conclusions of other fields of study we have tried to indicate their acceptability by reference to the views of scholars in those fields. An attempt has been made to show that the conclusions follow from the definitions and postulates and that they will yield practicable methods of accounting. The system of ideas developed is not simply indicative of a model, a design for an accounting system which could be made operational if only the world were of a certain hypothetical, but presently unobservable, kind. It is a theory anchored in the observable features of economic action under conditions of interdependence and uncertainty.

The exercise has not been extended to the point of axiomatization of the system.[1] It is quite possible that many of the concepts and propositions employed are reducible to more elementary concepts; we have found not a little difficulty as it is in indicating the relationships between the propositions we have adopted as postulates and the conclusions drawn from them. It would be presumptuous to suppose that the field of accounting has, as yet, been sufficiently explored and developed to warrant the belief that any comprehensive body of theoretical propositions may be readily accepted. Notwithstanding the attempt repeatedly to resort to the elements of the observable environment, the practical world, there is little doubt that some of the conclusions reached in this study will not command immediate assent, for they differ significantly from contrary propositions now widely held. At the same time, we see no strong grounds, in reason, for withholding assent. As was suggested in the last chapter, exactly the same reasons are advanced in support of many extant practices as we have arranged systematically in the course of the argument. If the conclusions appear to be strange, it will only be because these reasons have not been regarded hitherto as constituting a system of reasons.

Nor, in any case, are we unmindful of Gödel's conclusion that "the axiomatic method has certain inherent limitations, which rule out the possibility that even the ordinary arithmetic of the integers can ever be fully axiomatized."[2] If in such a well developed field as mathematics no

[1] "A theory is said to be axiomatized when it possesses a set of primitive or undefined concepts with the help of which all its remaining concepts can be defined, and a set of primitive statements or postulates from which all the remaining statements can be derived as consequences." J.H.Woodger, "The Technique of Theory Construction," *International Encyclopedia of Unified Science,* Vol. II, No. 5 (Chicago: The University of Chicago Press, 1939), p. 66. See also, Rudolf Carnap, *The Logical Syntax of Language* (London: Kegan Paul, Trench, Trubner & Co. Ltd., 1937) pp. 271 ff.

[2] Ernest Nagel and James R. Newman, *Gödel's Proof* (London: Routledge and Kegan Paul Ltd., 1959), p. 6.

assurance can be had that its conclusions are free of inconsistency, it would be foolish to suppose that such an assurance can be had in fields whose theories are only in the process of developing.[3] The defect has not, however, stood in the way of the usefulness of mathematics and the theory here presented, one may presume, will be appraised on the ground of its usefulness. Empirical sciences by their nature may not attain to the same elegance as purely logical demonstrations; they may, nevertheless, strive towards the elimination of inconsistency and towards increasing degrees of comprehensiveness.

Quite apart from questions of the validity of our inferences and the consistency of the system is the possibility that alternative postulates to those used could have been used. Our postulates are a selection from an extensive range, if not an infinite range, of possible statements about the environment of action and of accounting which could have been selected. It is therefore possible that an alternative theory indicative of a different type of accounting may be established by the selection of other statements as postulates. Nevertheless, there is abundant evidence in the practices adopted in the world of commerce and administration to support the belief that our conclusions are not materially in error, notwithstanding their disagreement with long-standing practices. Major unexpected reversals of form by companies, major restatements of the "values" of assets, catastrophic losses by investors in companies, *ad hoc* devices grafted on to otherwise avowed rules, and the multiplicity of inconsistent rules presently accepted as available alternatives—these are not explicable solely in terms of errors of judgment or of newly changed circumstances. These are themselves adaptive responses to, or cataclysmic consequences of, the inadequacy of many formal and habitual rules to secure the regular flow of relevant information. The anomalies, as well as the positive features of economic behavior, have influenced the foundations we have chosen.

It has long been asserted that accounting, being a practical art, is conditioned by the demands of practical circumstance. In a sense this is true. But the conditioning has been piecemeal; at any time partial; and through time staggered. Under these conditions of growth, reflection on and analysis of the *total* demands of practical circumstance have been limited, and it is not surprising that they have left a legacy of unordered and conflicting rules. We presume that the preceding chapters will have demonstrated that the processes of observation, analysis, and inference may be depended upon to yield a coherent system of ideas, and to suggest a clear and consistent set of rules, no less in the field of accounting than in other fields of practical expertise.

No longer may it be said that accounting is not in the least theoretical

3 Irving M. Copi, "Artificial Languages," *Language, Thought and Culture,* Paul Henle, ed. (Ann Arbor: The University of Michigan Press, 1958), p. 115.

and that its rules are simply practical expedients.[4] Indeed, it never was realistic to assert that the rules chosen lacked a theoretical base.[5] The vast range of alternative practices, in respect of short-term and durables inventories for example, testifies to the fertility of the imagination of accountants; for every one of them implies a particular theory or way of looking at the circumstances which stimulated its invention. The actual state of accounting is not that it has no theories, but that it has an almost inexhaustible quantity of implicit, partial, and contradictory theories. Ockham's razor has not been near the stubble. What it has lacked is a coherent theory by reference to which established practices and newly proposed practices may be appraised.

The laws of human behavior in a society in which a significant part of interpersonal intercourse is mediated by money and in which such behavior is informed by monetary calculation are no less adequate and compelling bases for deriving means of coping with human problems than are the laws of motion. Their explicit recognition and the explicit development of their consequences are protection against the uncontrolled proliferation of *ad hoc* theories and practices.

THE CONSEQUENCES

We may state some of the principal consequences which flow from the conclusions reached.

1. We have conceived accounting as having a specific and definite function in socio-economic affairs. The function is no less significant for being limited to the continual discovery of the existent financial relationships of entities with their environments, for every specialism is significant simply because it is limited. The proposed conception distinguishes between fact and value, between the foundation of judgments and judgments or evaluations themselves. Confusion of the two can only lead to wishful thinking about present constraints and opportunities, whereas separation of the two provides an unequivocal orientation to the discovery of the facts, however palatable they may be.

The significance of the process of discovery may not be disparaged without at the same time disparaging the significance of the fruits of scientific inquiry, the significance of the news gathering agencies of the world, and the significance of all elementary education. The best expressions

---

[4] Arthur H. Woolf, *A Short History of Accountants and Accountancy* (London: Gee & Co., 1912), pp. xxix, xxx; and more recently, for example, C.A. Smith and J.G. Ashburne, *Financial and Administrative Accounting* (New York: McGraw-Hill Book Company, 1955), p. 2.

[5] "Action without thinking, practice without theory are unimaginable." von Mises, *Human Action,* p. 177.

of all these endeavors pay no regard to the particular uses to which the discoveries of men will subsequently be put. They serve a wide range of "consumers" with diverse and competing ends. To some of these the discovered facts will mean nothing; others will use the discovered facts for purposes which are individually or socially of great importance. But unless the discovery of the facts is pursued with detachment and a sense of the significance of pure discovery, the specialists in discovery will fail in the function which society has entrusted to them.

2.   Given this conception, the terms necessary for the development of a method of performing the function have been defined and developed. Definition without prior specification of the function is a sterile exercise. Lacking the foundation of a specified function, debate over definitions may be interminable. Given the foundation, the examination and refinement of definitions may proceed, for redefinition and explication are constrained by the necessity of correspondence with the function and with the facts of the environment in which the function is performed.

3.   Though the accounting function provides a necessary part of the premises of choice, it does not provide the whole. The factual premises of choice are provided by many streams of information; many of these streams provide information of generically different kinds, and, in their cases, the possibility of the conflict of evidence does not arise. This is not so in the case of accounting information and the information relating to prices or monetary equivalents flowing directly from market places. In an action framework, these two streams are generically of the same kind. If the one is not based on the other, accounting data on the contemporary market, conflicts of evidence are unavoidable, as is the consequential distrust of the process. Given an action framework, there can be no legitimate debate over the use of alternative sources of data or rules for manipulating data which have not ostensible connections with a contemporary market environment. Alternative ways of discovering a magnitude there may be, as there are various ways of finding the volume of a regular solid. But in any specified context there may not be alternative, equally apposite concepts, or different, equally apposite measurements. Much of the debate on alternative asset measurement bases and "supplementary" financial statements may be considered as debate over pseudoproblems which have arisen out of inadequate specification of the function which is peculiar to accounting.

4.   Disregard for the effects of changes occurring in the passing of time, both within and beyond an entity, entails disregard for contemporary information as a premise of action. There can be no legitimate debate about the propriety of incorporating price changes of every kind, each in its appropriate way, in an accounting system, given an action framework. Nor can there be any argument about the possibility of having independent and qualitatively different accounting methods for internal and external pur-

poses. A homeostatic system by definition requires that internal responses shall correspond with external stimuli; in a system of autonomous individuals designed to be a homeostatic system, confusion between the perceptions of internal and external states will be avoided only by securing the provision at all points of qualitatively similar information.

5.   Contemporary data are the link between past and future actions. Knowledge of the present state being a premise of future action, and knowledge of the rate of change of state being also a premise of choice, as between possible actions given the present state, there can be no legitimate argument about the logical or axiological superiority of information yielded by balance sheets and income accounts. Information of both kinds is necessary to informed action; and as the magnitudes yielded by both types of statement may be related for analytical purposes, both statements will of necessity contain qualitatively similar information.

6.   The principles underlying the discovery of a present state in no way cut across those underlying the construction of hypothetical systems for proceeding towards another state. Budgeting and anticipatory cost calculation are based on hypotheticals and on the evaluation of alternative hypotheticals. The realm of discovery and the realm of planning are characteristically and logically different, even though what is discovered and what is done interact through time. Insofar as we have been concerned with designing a discovery system, we have been concerned with the general goals and the general constraints of actions. No specific device for the selection of specific courses of action is contemplated and no comment is offered on any such device. But whether one employs statistical decision-selecting devices or less sophisticated ways of choosing, no such choice can be exercised with reasonable expectation of success unless it proceeds from a discovered present state. Nor can any extrapolation of or inference from the past be instructive if expectations of the future have been allowed to obtrude into representations of the past.

A COPERNICAN REVOLUTION?

The development of accounting thought seems to have distinct parallels with the development of pre-Copernican astronomy.

The Hellenistic notions of the perfectness of the circle among plane figures and of the sphere among three-dimensional figures were the foundations of the conceptual schemes of the Greek astronomers and their successors. The stars were believed to be fixed in a great rotating sphere of which a spherical and fixed earth was the center. The irregular behavior of the sun and planets—"the wandering stars"—was explained in terms of complex circular motions defined by systems of deferents, epicycles, eccentrics, and equants. These additional concepts were necessary if observable motions were to be reconciled with the basic assumption of circular motion. But the result was not a single system of ideas; there were many such systems in the Ptolemaic tradition. Generally, their results coincided satisfactorily enough with observable motions of the heavenly bodies; but with the passage of centuries (for example, from Ptolemy of the second century A.D. to Copernicus of the fifteenth and sixteenth centuries) and with the accumulation of observations, it was observed that discrepancies occurred, indicating that those systems were deficient in some respects.

The system of Copernicus retained many of the features of its Ptolemaic precursors. But its principal departures were in regarding the sun as the center of the "sphere of the stars" and the earth, not as fixed but, as having motions of its own, including rotation about the sun in the same way as the stars and planets. Though it eliminated some of the elements of the earlier systems it was no less complex and it yielded no better predictions than those systems. Its principal effect was to give a different focus of attention to the study of astronomy and a different way of looking at the earth and its relationship to the universe around it. It paved the way for Kepler's rejection of many of the remaining elements of the older astronomy and, eventually, to the vastly simpler gravitational hypothesis of the Newtonian system. In the course of this simplification, the theory gained greatly in explanatory and predictive powers by comparison with its antecedents.

More important still, however, was the change in man's appraisal of his own position in the universe. A geocentric universe went hand in hand with an anthropocentric philosophy. Once the earth came to be accepted as only one of a number of bodies having similar properties, belief in the uniqueness of the earth and of man's position on it was overthrown. The revolution was not merely scientific, it was cultural in the widest sense.[6]

The conceptual schemes in which accounting has been set are likewise many, and they have changed as new observations have suggested deficiencies. Early forms of accounting seem to have been in contemplation of their usefulness to owner-managers of business enterprises and to wealthy householders; one of its vestiges is the belief that in management subsists the right to determine accounting practices and the knowledge to choose practices which are relevant to the function of management. Perhaps earlier than, but certainly during, the nineteenth century, accounting appears to have been strongly influenced by the objective of protecting creditors; one of its vestiges is the notion of conservative accounting. During the late nineteenth century and particularly during the twentieth, accounting has been influenced by the growth to prominence of investment in private

[6] See Thomas S. Kuhn, *The Copernican Revolution* (Cambridge, Mass.: Harvard University Press, 1957).

securities, and the notion that the role of managers of corporations is a fiduciary one; one of its vestiges is the view that financial statements are simply reports on the monetary stewardship of management. And finally, in the twentieth century, accounting has been strongly influenced by what has been thought to be necessary for managerial decision-making; one of its vestiges is the belief that financial statements based on different premises are necessary for different kinds of decision.

These and other vestiges of the specific orientations mentioned have remained in the corpus of accounting doctrine. A whole series of antithetical propositions is required to explain the diverse and divergent practices currently used; and this series is inadequate to predict the kind of accounting which will be found in any given and defined situation. This is not surprising if, as it seems, there have at different times been different fixed viewpoints (like the earth before Copernicus) from which the rules of accounting have emerged.

The effect of the arguments of this book is to shift the focus of attention from the parties of interest (creditors, investors, managers) to the entity under consideration; to regard the entity as the subject of inquiry; and to regard all participants in its activity as so many interrelated forces bearing on one another as they change position and direction voluntarily or under the influence of forces beyond the entity. The shift does not ignore the participants; it recognizes them all. But there is also a shift of another kind, a shift in the way in which accounting is to be regarded. It is not an isolate, having peculiar characteristics which mark it off from other forms of inquiry; this view is analogous to the pre-Copernican geocentric and anthropocentric view of the universe. Rather, it is one of the many forms of inquiry all of which have their specific motions, but all of which conform with the common laws of rigorous observation and reasoned discourse.

In the system which emerges, many of what have appeared in the past to be *ad hoc* and *post hoc* rationalizations cease to have this questionable character. They become incorporated as legitimate parts of the general foundation of accounting. In the transmutation, they undergo some modification, the rules based on those reasons more so than the reasons themselves. In substance, the same common sense reasons which have justified their original admission as grounds for adopting specific practices, justify the general principles which emerge from the integrated view we present of the entity in its relationships with other persons and entities.

In some ways the body of general principles enunciated is more complex than its antecedents. If the possibility of entropy is disregarded; if it is assumed that feedback actually occurs and does indeed ensure rectification of an information generating system; if it is supposed that an entity or any part of it may be considered independently of its environment; then, of course, a simple system will be accepted as satisfactory. A system which does not make so many simplifying assumptions will necessarily be more complex, in respect of things that matter. At the same time it will have much greater explanatory and predictive power.

On the other hand, the body of principles enunciated is materially less complex in other respects. In stipulating that specific ends are beyond inquiry it removes from the arena of debate many questions not soluble within its own framework. In dealing with all judgments as relative, it removes the difficulty of quantifying absolutes, for it removes absolutes from the discussion. In specifying the underlying characteristics of behavior and in defining the information relevant to action, it removes the multiplicity of rules which have hindered clearer perception of the function of accounting and which have made difficult its practice. In place of a series of unrelated conceptions, it substitutes a body of propositions, based on observable phenomena, systematically related and interdependent, contributing to an integrated view of the function of accounting in the world of affairs.

As was observed at the outset, evaluation and action are everyman's business. To provide the corroborable and corroborated financial statements which will serve as foundations for everyman's evaluations and actions is the business of the kind of accounting here envisaged.

Indexes

INDEX OF NAMES

378

SUBJECT INDEX

379

Balance sheet *(Cont.)*
  financial position given, 136, 140, 259-60, 265
  interpretation, 174-5, 192
  (See also Financial position)
Balancing date, 135
Beliefs, 25-8, 38-9
  corroboration of, 25, 30-1, 38
  of groups, 299-300
  persistence of, 5, 27, 33, 348, 360
Black box, 251-3
  accounting system as, 253-4
  action system as, 252, 319
Bonds (debentures):
  of corporations, 268-9, 273-5, 279, 290
  of government, 269, 328
Budgetary management, 332-3
Budgeting, 373
  of firms, 313
  of government, 332-3

Calculation, monetary:
  accounting as, 99, 102
  anticipatory, 83, 97, 101
    budgeting, 313, 332-3, 373
    hypothetical, 83-4, 101, 210, 314-5, 350
    regularity assumed, 236, 314-5
  contemporary, 81, 84, 91, 101-2, 195
  ratio scale used, 91, 95, 101, 195
  relates to prices, 80, 91, 101
  retrospective, 82, 84, 96, 101-2, 312, 316
Capital:
  of corporations, 269-70, 287
  definition, 114, 122
  measurement of, 114, 122, 254, 264
  (See also Maintenance of capital; Rate of return)
Capital gains and losses, 248n, 335
Capital maintenance adjustment, 256, 258-9, 264
Cash equivalent: *(See* Current cash equivalent)
Cash flow, 187-9, 258, 272, 279
Causal inference, 25, 30, 101, 128, 362
Choice:
  elimination of alternatives, 54, 58
  expectational premises, 83-4, 101, 199, 204-5, 311
  (See also Calculation, anticipatory; Expectations; Optimal adaptation)
  hierarchy of, 301-2
  influence of role, 62, 76
  informational premises, 15, 81-2, 112, 129, 156, 271-80, 311, 366, 372-3, 375
    (See also Adaptive behavior; Calculation, monetary; Cost; Financial position; Prices)
  revocability of, 68, 114-5, 200-201, 218, 220
  valuational premises: *(See* Evaluation; Maximization; Valuation)
Classification, 10-11, 29, 38, 84-7, 176
  of accounts, 133

Common denominator:
  monetary unit as, 93-4, 108
Common stock, 269-73
Communication:
  conventions, 181-2
  coordination and, 296-301, 318
  definition, 166-7, 184
  efficiency of, 168, 171, 173, 184-5
  feedback, role of, 161, 165, 178, 184, 360
  interference, 167, 169, 182
  intra-organizational, 295-320
  pragmatics, 177-8
  receiver, doubt of, 182, 185
  redundancy, 174, 185
  semantics, 169-72, 177, 184
  syntactics, 172-7, 184-5
  technical, 170, 179-80, 297-301
  varieties of, 178-9
  (See also Interpretation; Language)
Comparison:
  in choosing, 44, 61, 65-6, 129, 153, 187-8
  inter-firm, 194, 217, 262, 277, 313
  intertemporal, 95, 192-4, 217, 303, 314, 319, 333
  in perception, 24, 153
  in reasoning, 28
  uniformity necessary, 153
  in valuation, 44
  (See also Interpretation)
Conception(s), 29, 34, 38, 144
Conflict:
  in cooperative systems, 61, 75, 280-5, 294
  laws mitigate, 61, 76
Consensus, 146, 152, 169-72
Conservatism, 154, 282, 344
Consistency:
  of method, 260
  of statements, 32, 301, 304-5, 318-9, 372
  of statements and observables, 157, 294
Consolidated financial statements, 288-9
Constituents:
  of associations, 105
  of firms, 187-90, 215-17
  of service organizations, 323
Consumers' goods, 50, 57, 66-7, 75
  price index, 229, 264
Consumption, 51-4, 57-8, 110-2
  joint or collective, 327
Contemporaneity:
  of cost calculations, 306, 312, 316, 319
  of financial information, 174-5, 262, 273, 278, 283, 303, 367-8
Continuity, of firms, 94, 138, 220-1
Continuous record, 125, 127, 138
  adaptation aided, 84, 126, 165, 367
  modification, 136, 148, 150-1, 165
  (See also Isomorphism)
Control and ownership, 63, 275-6
Conventions, in language, 181
Cooperative system, 60-2, 75
  conflict in, 61, 75, 280-5, 294
  corporation as, 275, 278, 280-4, 294
Coordination, 298, 318
  budget as aid, 332-3

Coordination (*Cont.*)
  communication necessary, 296-301, 318
  in government, 332-3
  impediments, 304-5, 318-9
Copernican theory, 5, 373-5
Corporations, 105, 267-94
  capital of, 269-70, 287
  characteristics, 267-8, 275, 278, 280-4, 294
  common stock, 269-73
  financial publicity, 268, 277-8, 345, 354
  financing, 269-75
  interests of participants, 280-1, 283, 290-1
  investment in subsidiaries, 287-90
  limited liability, 268-9, 277, 291, 345
  ownership and control, 275-6
  roles of participants, 280-5, 294
  share (stock) holders, (constituents),
    275-85
Correspondence:
  objects and beliefs, 30, 39, 126
  objects and signs, 23, 34, 167, 184
  quality of information, 82, 99, 142, 156,
    164-5
Corroboration:
  of beliefs, 30-4, 39
  of monetary measurements, 243
  of statements, 84, 148-9, 164, 375
Cost:
  accrued and deferred, 135
  of acquisition, 64, 77, 200-201, 205-6
  of action, 41-4, 56
  apportionment subjective, 251, 307-9
  assignment to periods, 250-1
  calculation:
    anticipatory, 305, 311
    contemporary, 306, 312, 316, 319
    retrospective, 306-7, 311-2, 316, 351
  defined as sacrifice, 53, 56, 64, 77, 171,
    250
  of goods sold, 253, 256
  premises of action, 306, 311
  standard, 314-5
  types:
    direct, 251, 310, 319, 351
    discretionary, 118-9, 122
    fixed, 307, 310
    joint or common, 250, 307-9
    marginal or incremental, 312, 319-20,
      351
    opportunity, 201-3, 207, 218
    replacement, 201-2, 249, 351
    time, 250
    unit, 306
  time dimension, 77, 206, 319
  of use, 53, 77, 205-9, 218, 307
  volume and, 307
Cost accounts:
  and financial accounts, 303-4, 319, 342,
    368
Cost doctrine, 352-5
Costing:
  absorption, 306-10
  direct, 310-11
  standard, 314-16

Credit, 71-2, 77
Creditors, 72, 106-7
  protection of interests, 274-5, 278, 287
    (*See also* Bonds)
Current cash equivalent, 92
  approximation, 243, 250, 265
  of assets, 104, 115, 120, 188, 207, 217-8,
    238-50, 253-4, 264-5
  of depreciation, 207
  of equities, 106, 107, 120, 262
  financial position, 107, 254, 259
  of goods sold, 253, 256
  of liabilities, 106-7, 120, 254
  opportunity cost, 201-4, 218
  realizable price, 92, 218, 232-3, 238-9,
    243, 264
  relevance, 92, 217, 306-7, 366
Current ratio, 191, 193

Debt-equity ratio, 191, 272-4
Deduction (logical), 7, 31, 35, 39
Definition, 16, 29, 85, 169-70, 179-82
Depreciation, 208-9
  accelerated, 354
  definition, 208, 218, 242
  measurement, 207-8, 218, 239-49, 306-7
    dynamic conditions, 239-49, 265
    static conditions, 223
  methods of estimating, 342
  supplementary allowances, 335, 354
Differentiation of functions: (*See* Speciali-
    zation)
Disclosure, financial, 268, 278-81, 345, 347,
    354
Discounting, 107, 187, 196, 199-200, 218
Discretion:
  in organizations, 297, 304, 318
Discrimination, 22, 28, 37, 143 (*See also*
    Classification; Ranking)
Dividends:
  cash flows and, 258, 272
  equalization of, 280
  income and, 258, 260
  security prices and, 271
  variability of, 273
Dividend payout ratio, 272
Dividend yield, 271
Double entry principle: (*See* Accounting
    rules)
Doubt, 5, 8-9, 26, 28
  information reduces, 145, 157, 162, 182,
    185

Economics:
  accounting and, 11, 14, 349-52
  choice in, 48n, 312
Efficiency:
  financial, 188-90, 215
  relativity of, 188, 215, 313-4
  technical, 49-50, 53, 302-3, 314
Ends, 41-58
  of participants in firms, 187, 280-2, 321
  cooperative pursuit of, 60-2, 75, 322, 327

383

Income (*Cont.*)
  realization, 257-8
  seller's margin, 118-9, 257
  undivided (retained), 260-1, 272, 284, 293
  windfall, 117-9, 122, 256
Income account (statement), 113, 118, 122, 135, 140, 256-8
  capital maintenance adjustment, 256, 258-9, 264
  priority of, 342
Independence:
  in information processing, 147-8, 164, 184
  of professional experts, 358
Index numbers, 227-9, 231, 245
Individual differences, 59, 75, 159
Induction, 29-30, 35, 39
Inference, 13, 25, 30, 39, 101, 138, 362
Information:
  aggregative, 142, 149-50, 164
  consistency, 160, 294, 300-301, 304-5, 361, 372
  cost of, 45, 127, 132, 213, 219
  distortion, 154, 159-60, 282-3
  doubt and, 145, 157, 162, 182, 185
  losses, 150, 167, 169
  neutrality, 147, 156, 164, 280, 291, 294, 326
  objectivity, 98, 147-9, 156, 164, 280-1, 283, 291, 294, 368
  oversupply, 300
  regulated flow, 278, 281-3
  relevance, 149-51, 154-6, 164, 260, 283, 291, 294
  reliability, 142-4, 156-7, 161-2, 165
  uniformity, 152-4, 279, 283, 291, 368
  (*See also* Isomorphism; Knowledge)
Information content:
  of measurements, 89
  response selection potential, 145-6, 162, 238
Information, nonfinancial, 227, 293, 303, 344, 360-1
Information processing:
  accounting as, 141-2, 164
  (*See* Entropy)
  functional specialization, 141-2, 162
  systems design, 143, 154, 305, 361
  uniformity of rules, 152-4, 165, 279-83
Information processor:
  constraints of, 144, 154-5, 185
  independence, 147-8, 164, 184
  isolation of, 159, 182, 300
  role of, 144, 148, 156-7, 162, 299
Interdependence:
  communication under, 152, 299, 318
  social organization as, 60, 67, 75, 366
Interpretation:
  context affects, 24, 37, 167-8, 172, 193
  experience affects, 24, 37, 143
  of financial information, 91, 101, 152, 174-6, 294, 303-4
  of financial ratios, 193-5

of governmental accounts, 333-4
of observations, 24, 37
of statements, 149-50, 172-7, 185
Interest:
  as price, 72, 77
  rates, 72, 273
Inventories:
  durable goods, 197-209, 238-51
  (*See also* Depreciation)
  short term, 191, 231-8
Inventories, short term, measurement rules:
  average cost, 342
  current cash equivalent, 223, 231-6, 250-1, 255-60, 265
  F.I.F.O., 342
  L.I.F.O., 335, 342, 354, 361
  lower of cost and market, 232, 354
  price adjustments, 255-8
Investment, 52, 58, 197-209, 217-8 (*See also* Investors, choice of; Revocability of choice; Risk)
Investors:
  access to information, 277, 293
  choice of, 188-90, 217, 277, 280-1, 293-4
  protection of, 278-9, 293
  strategic position, 275-6, 281
Isochronism, 128, 133, 139
Isomorphism:
  in accounting, 126-8, 138, 253
  in accrual accounting, 132, 242
  in cash accounting, 132, 330
  in corporate accounting, 271, 279, 281, 293
  in cost accounting, 316, 319
  in governmental accounting, 329-30, 340
  in instrumentation systems, 126-7

Journal, 132-3, 140

Knowledge, 1, 2, 10-16, 26-35
  of accounting, 180, 365
  private, 146, 367
  public, 146, 277
  (*See also* Accounting, functions, discovery; Accounting information; Adaptive behavior; Beliefs; Choice; Information)

Language:
  accounting as, 171, 299-301, 318-9, 367
  consistency, 304-5, 318-9
  entropy, 170, 185, 319
  metalanguage, 180, 185
  natural, 169-70, 179-80
  object language, 180-1, 185
  standardization, 170, 179-80, 185
  technical, 170, 174, 179, 297-301, 318-9
  (*See also* Communication; Signs)
Law:
  predictive character, 2n, 34, 147
  scientific, 2n, 13n, 14n, 34-5, 147
  legal rights and duties, 63, 76, 104-5, 267-8, 275, 277

384

Ratios, financial (*Cont.*)
inventory to cost of goods sold, 192-3
no-dimensional magnitudes, 193-4, 217
price to earnings, 271
profit to turnover, 94-5, 192-3
receivables to sales, 192-3
validity, 94-5, 191-4, 262
Ratio of exchange, 64-6, 76
Ratio scales, 87, 90, 94-5, 101, 195
Rationality, 45-6, 56
Records:
aids to memory, 125, 168, 300-301
continuous, 125, 127, 138
as stimuli, 125, 138
(*See also* Isomorphism)
Realization, 257-8
Reasoning, 7-8, 28-35, 38
Recollection, 23, 127, 167
capacity limited, 35, 125, 142
Redundancy, 174, 185
Relevance:
of contemporary prices, 91, 200-201
of current cash equivalent, 92, 217,
306-7, 366
definition, 149, 164
feedback and, 159-61, 165
of financial position, 81, 96, 108, 205,
217, 282, 293, 350, 366-7
of information, 149-51, 154-6, 164, 260,
283, 291, 294
of monetary measurements, 78-80, 94
of processed information, 156, 164
Reliability:
of instruments, 127
of information, 142-4, 156-7, 161 2, 165
Replacement of assets, 114, 202
Replacement price, 92
approximation to current cash equivalent, 243, 249
and opportunity cost, 202
Revaluation of assets, 344, 352, 354
Revenue, 256-7
Residual equity:
account, 255, 258-9
balance sheet representation, 259
constituents as holders of, 215
of corporations, 269-70, 286-7
defined, 105-6, 120
magnitude equal to capital, 114, 122
measurement of, 106, 122, 196, 237, 258
price level changes, 115-8, 223-7
relative price change, 116-9, 225-7
Response, 21-3, 43
habitual, 27, 176-7
to information, 145-6
Revocability of choice, 68, 114-5, 200-201,
218, 220
Risks:
of creditors, 71-2, 107, 274-5, 286-7
of firms, 106, 199-200
of holding goods, 50, 196, 257
of holding monetary assets, 71, 196, 257
interest rates and, 72, 273
of security investments, 268, 273-4

Role(s):
changes in, 301, 305
consumer and producer, 66
in corporations, 283, 294
defined, 61-2, 75
entities defined by, 80
of information processor, 144, 148, 156-
7, 162, 299
legal rules based on, 63, 76
in organizations, 296-7, 305, 316-8
specialization and, 141-3
Sacrifice:
actions involve, 41, 43-4, 56
costs, 53, 56, 64, 77, 171, 250
Satisfaction:
goal of action, 44, 48-9, 56, 60-1
of participants of firms, 187-9, 215
Satisficing, 190
Savings, 51-3, 58, 110-1, 119, 122
Scales of measurement, 85 91 (*See also*
Measurement)
Scarcity, of means, 41, 46, 47, 56, 366
Science:
methods of, 6-8, 12-14, 367-71
scientific laws, 2n, 13n, 14n, 34-5, 147
Securities:
of corporations, 268, 291
of government, 269, 327-8
(*See also* Bonds; Shares [Stock])
Securities market, 268-9, 291-4
allocative function, 276-8, 291-3, 321
evaluation of shares (stock), 271-3, 293
fair market, 278-9, 293
information available, 277-8, 293-4
information necessary, 271-3, 277-84
informative function, 268-9, 276-7, 287,
293-4, 321
price formation, 268-9, 271, 276
Semantical rules, 169-72, 177, 184
Sensation, 21-3, 35-7
Service organizations, 322-4, 339
Shares (stock):
evaluation of, 271-3, 287
issue prices, 271, 286 7
market prices, 269, 271, 273, 276, 286-7
par values, 286-7
transferability, 268, 291
Shareholders (stockholders):
interests of, 275, 281-2
rights of, 268, 275-6, 286
(*See also* Securities Market)
Signs:
form, 173-7, 185
mental processes involve, 23, 37
objects as, 23-4, 38, 167-9
words as, 23, 29, 38, 169-70
(*See also* Communication; Information;
Interpretation; Language; Market;
Prices)
Sign-system: (*See* Language)
Social science, 12-14
Society:
environment of action, 59-60

387